Beyond the Flesh

Alexander Blok, Zinaida Gippius,
and the Symbolist Sublimation of Sex

Jenifer Presto

THE UNIVERSITY OF WISCONSIN PRESS

Publication of this book was made possible with support from the College of Arts and Sciences at the University of Oregon.

The University of Wisconsin Press
1930 Monroe Street, 3rd Floor
Madison, Wisconsin 53711-2059

www.wisc.edu/wisconsinpress/

3 Henrietta Street
London WC2E 8LU, England

Copyright © 2008
The Board of Regents of the University of Wisconsin System
All rights reserved. No part of this publication may be reproduced, stored in a retrieval system, or transmitted, in any format or by any means, digital, electronic, mechanical, photocopying, recording, or otherwise, or conveyed via the Internet or a Web site without written permission of the University of Wisconsin Press, except in the case of brief quotations embedded in critical articles and reviews.

5   4   3   2   1

Library of Congress Cataloging-in-Publication Data
Presto, Jenifer.
   Beyond the flesh : Alexander Blok, Zinaida Gippius, and the Symbolist sublimation of sex / Jenifer Presto.
     p. cm.
   Includes bibliographical references and index.
   ISBN 978-0-299-22950-4 (cloth : alk. paper)
   1. Blok, Aleksandr Aleksandrovich, 1880–1921—Criticism and interpretation.
   2. Gippius, Z. N. (Zinaida Nikolaevna), 1869–1945—Criticism and interpretation.
   3. Symbolism (Literary movement)—Russia.   4. Sublimation (Psychology) in literature.
   5. Sex in literature.   I. Title.
PG3453.B6Z69575   2008
891.71'3—dc22   2008011968

For Ruth and Salvatore Presto

Yet even if he had loved her, could he have wished for a more perfect union with his beloved than in these deep and mysterious caresses, than in the creation of an immortal image—a new being which was conceived and born of them like a child is born of its father and mother as if he and she were one?

Nevertheless, he felt that even in this union, chaste as it was, there was danger—perhaps greater than in a union of ordinary carnal love. They both walked on the edge of a chasm, where nobody had walked before, mastering temptation and the attraction of the abyss.
—Dmitry Merezhkovsky, *The Resurrection of the Gods:*
Leonardo da Vinci (*Voskresshie bogi: Leonardo da-Vinchi*) (1901)

Contents

Illustrations	xi
Acknowledgments	xiii
A Note on Transliteration and Abbreviations	xviii

Introduction
Beyond the Flesh: Russian Symbolism and the Sublimation of Sex   3

I. Poetry against Progeny: Blok and the Problem of
Poetic Reproduction   19

1. Unbearable Burdens: Blok and the Modernist Resistance
   to Progeny   21

2. Recurring Nightmares: Blok, Freud, and the Specter of
   Die Ahnfrau   41

3. Reproductive Fantasies: Blok and the Creation of
   The Italian Verses   70

4. A Time of Troubles: Blok and the Disruption of
   Poetic Succession   106

II. Writing against the Body: Gippius and the Problem
of Lyric Embodiment   133

5. *Style "Femme"*: Gippius and the Resistance to Feminine Writing   135

6. The Dandy's Gaze: Gippius and Disdainful Desire for
   the Feminine   160

7. Eternal Feminine Problems: Gippius, Blok, and the Incarnation
   of the Ideal   190

8. Body Trouble: Gippius and the Staging of an Anatomy
   of Criticism   217

Afterword
The Return of the Repressed: Illegitimate Babies and an
Unwieldy Body   241

Notes   251

Index   317

Illustrations

Portrait of Alexander Blok by Konstantin Somov   61

Caricature of Zinaida Gippius by Mitrich (Dmitry Togolsky)   158

Portrait of Zinaida Gippius by Léon Bakst   162

Photograph of Zinaida Gippius taken at the Moscow studio of Otto Renar   198

Acknowledgments

This book on gender and Russian symbolism began as a doctoral dissertation on Zinaida Gippius, written under the direction of James Bailey and Clare Cavanagh at the University of Wisconsin–Madison. I am extremely grateful to my dissertation co-chairs, as well as to David Bethea, Judith Kornblatt, Gary Rosenshield, and Yuri Shcheglov, for the advice and encouragement I received on this project during my years at Wisconsin. At Wisconsin, this project also benefited from the generous support of a University of Wisconsin Dissertation Fellowship and a Social Science Research Council Dissertation Write-Up Fellowship.

Although three of the chapters in this book started as thesis chapters, this book would not exist in its present form had it not been for the support of a number of individuals and institutions. An NEH summer seminar on gender and identity in Russian literature, led by Stephanie Sandler at Amherst College, afforded me the opportunity to consider in a more formal way the implications of gender theory for Russian literature and culture through stimulating discussions with the other members of the seminar. An Andrew W. Mellon Postdoctoral Fellowship in the Slavic Department at the University of Southern California gave me the necessary time to begin reconceptualizing the dissertation, as well as the opportunity to offer a graduate seminar on Russian symbolism. My interactions with faculty and especially graduate students in Slavic and comparative literature at USC during that fellowship year and for several years to come were instrumental in shaping this project. And a Marilyn Simpson Research Grant in the Humanities at USC allowed me to make research trips to a number of libraries. But of all the institutional support I have received, I am most indebted to the Comparative Literature Program and the Russian and East European Studies Center at the University of Oregon. My colleagues Anindita Banerjee, Kenneth Calhoon, Lisa Freinkel, Julie Hessler, Katya Hokanson, Alan Kimball, Yelaina Kripkov, Leah Middlebrook, and James Rice were most welcoming when I decided to make the move to Oregon. Moreover, Kenneth Calhoon, then director of the Comparative Literature Program, kindly granted me a release from teaching my first term at Oregon that allowed me to complete the revisions to this book.

In addition to these individuals and institutions, there are a number of people who had a direct impact on this book. I am indebted to Steve Salemson, former associate director of the University of Wisconsin Press, for taking an interest in the project and to Gwen Walker, acquisitions editor at the press, for remaining committed to the project, as well as to the deans of the College of Arts and Sciences at Oregon for granting me the necessary research funds to help offset publication costs. I am extremely grateful to the press's external reviewers, Catherine Ciepiela, Sibelan Forrester, and an anonymous reader, for their insightful comments on the manuscript and for their suggestions as to how to improve it. I am also very thankful to Eliot Borenstein, Clare Cavanagh, and Stephanie Sandler for generously sharing with me their reactions to the manuscript as well as to Yelaina Kripkov for helping me to decipher a number of difficult Russian passages. Besides benefiting from the suggestions of a number of friends and colleagues, this book has been significantly improved by the expertise of several graduate students. Peter Huk, Elena Vassileva, and Elina Yuffa assisted me with research at the early stages of the project. Later, Thomas Dolack helped me to reformat the manuscript, and Alexander Kashirin checked the translations and the Cyrillic passages for accuracy. Lastly, I must express my gratitude to Adam Mehring for ushering this book through the production process, to M. J. Devaney for her meticulous editing, and to Blythe Woolston for compiling the index.

Several of the chapters in this book appeared in print in an earlier form: chapter 1 appeared as "Unbearable Burdens: Aleksandr Blok and the Modernist Resistance to Progeny and Domesticity" (*Slavic Review* 63, no. 1 [2004]: 6–25); chapter 5 as "The Fashioning of Zinaida Gippius" (*Slavic and East European Journal* 42, no. 1 [1998]: 58–75); chapter 6 as "The Androgynous Gaze of Zinaida Gippius" (*Russian Literature* 48, no. 1 [2000]: 87–115); and chapter 8 as "Reading Zinaida Gippius: Over Her Dead Body" (*Slavic and East European Journal* 43, no. 4 [1999]: 621–35). I thank the editors of *Slavic Review*, published by the American

Association for the Advancement of Slavic Studies, of *Slavic and East European Journal*, published by the American Association of Teachers of Slavic and East European Languages, and of *Russian Literature*, published by Elsevier Science, for granting me permission to reprint this material in revised form.

Finally, I would like to acknowledge those people who have been most instrumental in my decision to dedicate myself to Slavic studies. John Fletcher gave me my first introduction to the Russian language through the independent study course in Russian that he organized in the Enfield, Connecticut, school system in conjunction with professors in the Russian Department at Smith College. Joan Afferica, Maria Nemcová Banerjee, Alexander Woronzoff-Dashkov, and Igor Zelljadt, my professors in Russian studies at Smith College, nurtured my interest in the field and have continued to take an interest in my work. David Bethea, Eliot Borenstein, Clare Cavanagh, and Stephanie Sandler have been encouraging and supportive of my research, even if it has departed from their own notions of scholarship. Anindita Banerjee, Eliot Borenstein, Kathleen Dillon, Julie Hessler, Katya Hokanson, Hana Píchová, and Irina Voskresenskaia have provided me with much needed friendship, moral support, and intellectual conversation. And my parents, Ruth and Salvatore Presto, have helped me throughout the years in immeasurable ways. I owe them the greatest debt of gratitude not only for their unflagging love and support but also for fostering in me a sense of creativity. I dedicate this book to them.

A Note on Transliteration and Abbreviations

In order to make this book accessible to readers both outside and inside the Slavic field, I have employed the Library of Congress system of transliteration in the body of the text with some modifications, rendering the endings *-ii* and *-yi* as *-y* and omitting the Russian soft sign. In those instances where a close English equivalent exists for Russian first names, I have opted for the English variant. I also use the conventional spellings of well-known Russian authors' surnames. However, I have followed the standard Library of Congress system when transliterating information that would be essential for specialists: namely, Russian titles, quotations, and all bibliographic information in the notes, including authors' names.

All translations are mine unless otherwise indicated in the notes. For the sake of economy, I have included most references to the works of Blok and Gippius within the body of text rather than in the notes. Below is a list of abbreviations of the primary texts from which I cite:

BBB   *Aleksandr Blok-Andrej Belyj, Briefwechsel* (Munich: Wilhelm Fink, 1969)

Dnev   Zinaida Gippius, *Dnevniki*, ed. A. N. Nikoliukin, 2 vols. (Moscow: NPK Intelvak, 1999)

IIA   Temira Pachmuss, ed., *Intellect and Ideas in Action: Selected Correspondence of Zinaida Hippius* (Munich: Wilhelm Fink, 1972)

PABR M. A. Beketova and V. A. Desnitskii, eds., *Pis'ma Aleksandra Bloka k rodnym*, 2 vols. (Leningrad: Akademiia, 1927, 1932)

PBKh Zinaida Gippius, *Pis'ma k Berberovoi i Khodasevichu*, ed. Erika Freiberger Sheikholeslami (Ann Arbor, Mich.: Ardis, 1978)

SS Aleksandr Blok, *Sobranie sochinenii v vos'mi tomakh*, ed. V. N. Orlov, A. A. Surkov, and K. I. Chukovskii, 8 vols. (Moscow-Leningrad: Gos. izd-vo khudozhestvennoi lit-ry, 1960–63)

Soch Zinaida Gippius, *Sochineniia: Stikhotvoreniia, proza*, ed. K. M. Azadovskii and A. V. Lavrov (Leningrad: Khudozhestvennaia literatura, 1991)

Stikh Zinaida Gippius, *Stikhotvoreniia*, ed. A. V. Lavrov (St. Petersburg: Akademicheskii proekt, 1999)

ZK Aleksandr Blok, *Zapisnye knizhki, 1901–1920*, ed. V. N. Orlov (Moscow: Khudozhestvennaia literatura, 1965)

ZL Zinaida Gippius, *Zhivye litsa*, ed. A. N. Nikoliukin (Moscow: OLMA-PRESS, 2002)

Beyond the Flesh

Introduction
Beyond the Flesh: Russian Symbolism and the Sublimation of Sex

Ordinarily the meaning of sexual love is supposed to lie in the propagation of the species, for which it serves as a means. I consider this view incorrect—not merely on the basis of any theoretical considerations, but above all on the basis of facts of natural history. That propagation of living creatures may take place without sexual love is already clear from the fact that it does take place without division into sexes. A significant portion of organisms both of the vegetable and of the animal kingdom propagates in a non-sexual fashion: by segmentation, budding, spores and grafting. It is true that higher forms of both organic kingdoms propagate by the sexual method, but the organisms which propagate in this fashion, vegetable as well as animal in part, *may* likewise propagate in a non-sexual fashion (grafting in the vegetable world, parthenogenesis in the higher insects). Moreover, setting this aside, and recognizing as a general rule that the higher organisms propagate by means of sexual union, we are bound to conclude that this sexual factor is connected not with propagation in general (which may take place also apart from it), but with the propagation of *higher* organisms.
    Vladimir Soloviev, *The Meaning of Love (Smysl liubvi)* (1892-94)

Until recently, scholars have been resistant to acknowledge the importance of the role of gender and the body in Russian modernism.[1] To some extent, this reluctance to make the body part of the corpus of Slavic criticism can be attributed to the fact that many of the early Russian modernists, influenced by the antiprocreative theories of the nineteenth-century Russian religious philosopher and poet Vladimir

Soloviev, demonstrated an ambivalent attitude toward the body and sexuality that has reinforced the tendency among Slavists to privilege the metaphysical over the physical and the otherworldly over the bodily. So pervasive, in fact, was the skepticism about matters of the flesh among some of the Russian symbolists that it might be argued that they were preoccupied with the eradication of sex. For instance, in her essay "Amorousness" ("Vliublennost'") (1904), the symbolist poet Zinaida Gippius dedicates herself to an explication of what her husband Dmitry Merezhkovsky had identified as "'the transfiguration of sex into a new Christian amorousness'" (*Dnev*, 1:258). "In genuine amorousness, even of today, which has barely arisen in humanity and is still powerless," she contends, "the very question of sex already melts and dissolves; the contradiction between soul and body disappears, leaving no place for struggle, and sufferings ascend to that height where they must turn into happiness" (*Dnev*, 1:260). Gippius intimates here that the tensions between body and soul would necessarily wither away once the sublime state of amorousness was achieved.[2] Yet, in spite of the markedly utopian orientation of the Merezhkovskys' notion of sublimated eros, Gippius's own poetic practices would seem to reinforce the notion that the question of sex remained unresolved and that body and soul were destined to remain in constant conflict. She continually pitted the body against the soul, the ethereal against the material, not only in her artistic writings but also in her everyday life, and, in this regard, she was not unique.

Among the symbolist works, Merezhkovsky's historical novel *The Resurrection of the Gods: Leonardo da Vinci* (*Voskresshie bogi: Leonardo da-Vinchi*) (1901) may be the most influential artistic expression of sublimated eros. In this novel, which constitutes the second part of his trilogy *Christ and Antichrist* (*Khristos i antikhrist*) (1905), he presents a portrait of the Renaissance artist that was to have a profound effect on Sigmund Freud. In *Leonardo da Vinci and a Memory of His Childhood* (*Eine Kindheitserinnerung des Leonardo da Vinci*) (1910), Freud expounds on the idea, articulated nearly a decade earlier by the Russian symbolist, that Leonardo's prodigious accomplishments in the realm of art and science were made possible by his denial of ordinary carnal love.[3] "In reality," Freud observes, "Leonardo was not devoid of passion; he did not lack the divine spark which is directly or indirectly the driving force—*il primo motore*—behind all human activity. He had merely converted his passion into a thirst for knowledge; he then applied himself to investigation with the persistence, constancy and penetration which is derived from passion, and at the climax of intellectual labour, when knowledge had been won, he allowed the long restrained affect to break loose and to flow away freely, as a stream of water drawn from a river is allowed to flow when its work is done."[4]

Although in recent years Freud's psychoanalytic reading of da Vinci has clearly eclipsed Merezhkovsky's novelistic rendering, it is Merezhkovsky and his fellow Russian symbolists who can be credited with putting into practice a distinctly symbolist notion of sublimated eros. Similar, in some ways, to the writers, artists, and intellectuals associated with the Bloomsbury group in London, the Russian symbolists were involved in untraditional unions that privileged artistic creativity over procreation and were often tolerant of extramarital affairs, both heterosexual and homosexual in nature. This was the case not only for Gippius and Merezhkovsky, who were involved for many years in a mystical ménage-à-trois with Dmitry Filosofov, but also for other famous symbolist couples such as Alexander Blok and Liubov Mendeleeva and Viacheslav Ivanov and Lydia Zinovieva-Annibal. The writers' fascination with sublimated love influenced not just their unorthodox marriage practices and their views about childbearing but also the ways in which they envisioned the creative process.[5] Although symbolist writers such as Konstantin Balmont and Valery Briusov, who were more inclined toward the decadent mode, sought inspiration for their art in ecstatic moments or *migi*, many of the other writers found creative inspiration in the obverse, that is to say, the denial of procreation and the body.[6]

This book is devoted to an examination of the latter creative method, a method I am calling the symbolist sublimation of sex, drawing on Gippius and Merezhkovsky's notion of sublimated eros as well as on Freud's more or less contemporaneous psychoanalytic concept of artistic sublimation.[7] By employing this term to describe the symbolists' creative project, I do not mean to imply that Russian symbolism "was merely filling the same roles and performing the same sociocultural and psychological functions that psychoanalysis had come to fill in German- and English-speaking countries," as Alexander Etkind has recently suggested in his discussion of psychoanalysis and Russian modernism in *Eros of the Impossible: A History of Psychoanalysis in Russia* (*Eros nevozmozhnogo: Istoriia psikhoanaliza v Rossii*) (1993). Rather I want to point to the fact the Russian symbolists were engaged in a particular modernist enterprise that was concerned with transcending the problems of gender and sexuality.[8] This study maintains, however, that while the symbolists displayed a great deal of skepticism about procreation and the body, typical as Freud would argue of creative artists in general and as Edward Said would claim of modernists in particular, they were not content merely with thinking through the body in their essays and philosophical writings.[9] Instead, they actively sought to work through their problems with the body by forging a creative link between their erotic lives and their artistic works. In such a fashion, they created a modernist poetics that paradoxically ended up putting the figure of the body—if not the body itself—at the center of artistic practice.

But while the symbolists can be credited with putting the figure of the body at the center of artistic discourse, it would be overstating matters to claim that they were only engaged in the merging of art and life, body and text, or corpus and corps. Since the appearance of the poet Vladislav Khodasevich's important essay on Russian symbolism, "The End of Renata" ("Konets Renaty") (1928), which shows how the plot of Briusov's novel *The Fiery Angel* (*Ognennyi angel*) (1908) coalesced with the tragic love triangle involving Briusov, Andrei Bely, and the lesser-known decadent writer Nina Petrovskaia, it has become somewhat of a critical commonplace to assert that all the Russian symbolists were involved in the blurring of the boundaries between art and life known as *zhiznetvorchestvo*, or life creation. "The symbolists," Khodasevich claimed, "did not want to separate the writer from the person, the literary biography from the personal. Symbolism did not want to be just an artistic school or a literary movement. All of the time it attempted to be a life-creating method, and in this was perhaps its greatest unfulfilled truth, but its entire history, in essence, flowed toward this truth."[10] Although Khodasevich's model of life creation can explain certain aspects of symbolist aesthetic practice, such as the tendency among some writers to emplot their lives within their artistic narratives, it does not account for the full range of the symbolists' mythmaking methods. Many of the symbolists were just as concerned with pitting art against life and creativity against procreation as they were with conflating art and life, and oftentimes these two seemingly antithetical impulses could exist simultaneously and to varying degrees within any one artist. This antagonistic relationship between the symbolists and the events of real life is something that has sometimes been glossed over in contemporary criticism on Russian symbolism, but it was central to the movement and should be acknowledged as an important variation on Khodasevich's formulation of life creation. And one of the key ways in which this antagonism manifested itself was in the symbolists' quest to overcome the confines of the body and to move beyond the flesh.[11]

This study hopes to contribute to our understanding of symbolist mythmaking through an analysis of the poetry, plays, essays, letters, diaries, notebooks, and memoirs of two key figures, the canonical male poet Alexander Blok (1880–1921) and the more idiosyncratic female poet Zinaida Gippius (1869–1945), both of whom were the subject of scholarly monographs in English primarily in the '70s and '80s and thus are due for a revisionist reading.[12] Blok and Gippius provide particularly interesting subjects of analysis on several fronts: not only were they engaged in a discussion about the role that gender and sexuality should play in creativity and the creation of culture but they approached the problem of the sublimation of sex in contradictory, yet complementary, fashions that demonstrate the range of mythmaking practices in Russian modernism. Blok evinced an inclination throughout his poetic career to pit poetry against progeny, an inclination that in spite of his resistance to generational continuity manifested itself in his tendency to organize his artistic works into a linear, narrative framework that mimicked the linear structure of kinship relationships. Gippius, on the other hand, depicted an antagonistic relationship between herself and the earthly and the bodily in her writings that was mirrored in her proclivity for organizing her poetic writings not in a linear, narrative fashion but rather in a markedly nonlinear fashion that reflected her philosophical questioning of and skepticism about the body—a subject that does not lend itself to the same linear structure as a family chronicle. By analyzing Blok's and Gippius's poetic myths in tandem, this book sets out to demonstrate that there was a strong relationship between the type of symbolist mythmaking they practiced and the shape that their poetic oeuvres assumed—a relationship that would be less apparent in a scholarly overview of this phenomenon in the Russian symbolist context.

Since this study is concerned with elucidating these two poets' problematic relationship with matters of the flesh, and these issues have arguably gained the most extensive treatment in Western feminist-psychoanalytic theory, I draw on the theoretical writings of Anglo-American and French feminist critics as well as on Russian and Western theory of the lyric and poetic biography. And in my willingness to engage with Western theories of gender, I depart from the tradition, inherent within many of the existing studies on Russian symbolism, of reading the symbolists' gendered practices primarily through the lens of their own philosophical writings on gender and sexuality.[13] I should note that while I find the strategies of reading prevalent within feminism and psychoanalysis to be particularly useful for examining the creative mythologies of the Russian symbolists, perplexed as they were by issues of sex and gender, I do not attempt to fit Blok and Gippius within a rigid feminist-psychoanalytic framework; rather, in the course of my analysis, I seek to uncover the ways in which these two poets pose a challenge to existing theoretical models that were formed primarily in reaction to Western literary and cultural practices. As a case in point, while it has become a critical commonplace among some feminist scholars to claim that working out a harmonious relationship between creativity and procreation produced more anxiety in women writers than male writers, I demonstrate that among the Russian symbolists it was not Gippius but Blok who exhibited the most profound tendency to imagine poetry as antithetical to progeny.[14] He routinely envisioned poetic production as a substitute for human reproduction and went so far as to declare himself the young mother of a cycle of poems he completed exactly nine and a half months after the birth and death several days later of his wife's child. And if Blok clearly resisted the appropriation of a model of creativity that might be characterized as stereotypically "masculine," then Gippius refused to engage in the type of creativity that the French feminists have referred to as *écriture féminine*, or the writing of the female body, opting instead to employ the masculine voice in her verse and to identify femininity and the female body with the perverse.

The difficulties encountered in attempting to read Blok and Gippius within either a feminist or a traditional, binary-gendered framework, which presupposes an identity of gender and anatomy, derive not only from the peculiarities of their creative personalities (Blok's intense awe of feminine creative power and Gippius's identification with the figure of the male dandy and homosexual) but also from the specificity of the Russian cultural context. Though these two poets engaged in gendered practices that at times appeared to be highly idiosyncratic and even incited gossip among their contemporaries (Gippius, for example, was rumored to be a hermaphrodite), they were not operating in a vacuum but were responding to philosophical concepts such as the valorization of androgyny and the eternal feminine and the privileging of affiliation over filiation that were central to Russian symbolism and that would continue to shape the development of Russian modernism. Blok's proclivity for envisioning poetic creation as dependent not only on the suppression of human procreation but also on the death of a child anticipates the infanticidal model of poetic creativity of the futurist Vladimir Mayakovsky. Similarly, Gippius's problematic relationship with femininity and the female body, poignantly reflected in her poetry, would continue to be an issue for the next generation of female modernists. Blok and Gippius therefore were more than leading practitioners of the symbolist method of the sublimation of sex; they were progenitors of two important creative models in the Russian modernist tradition. Through an examination of Blok's and Gippius's struggles to overcome the confines of the body and sexual reproduction in their lives and art, this study hopes to shed light on an important aspect of Russian modernism.

Organized around a particular theoretical problem rather than exhaustive in scope, this book presents Blok and Gippius as exemplars of the phenomenon of the symbolist sublimation of sex and does not purport to elucidate all aspects of the life and art of these two poets or, for that matter, of their literary relationship.[15] Not only do I read Blok and Gippius selectively, opting to focus on those aspects of their lives and works that best exemplify the problem at hand, but for the most part I discuss these two writers separately, referring only when relevant to the ways in which they responded to each other's views on gender and the body. By treating these two poets individually, I am able to offer a more detailed analysis of their attempts to transcend sex, one that reveals the specific trajectories of their mythmaking practices. Because I am concerned with examining the nature or shape of their poetic myths rather than with providing a history of their relationship or of the symbolist movement, I take certain liberties with conventional literary chronology, treating the younger, first-generation Russian symbolist, Blok, before the older, second-generation Russian symbolist, Gippius. This order of presentation not only allows me to show how Gippius, who outlived Blok by more than two decades, responded to certain symbolist notions of gender and sexuality well after the demise of the movement but also to read the more iconoclastic woman poet against the canonical male poet. Yet, in my emphasis on the symbolists' quest to transcend the confines of the body, I hope to reveal that Blok was no less troubled than Gippius when it came to matters of the flesh—this in spite of his consecrated status within Russian modernism.

This study, in keeping with its revisionist nature, tries to avoid rehashing aspects of Blok's and Gippius's lives and art that have already received ample treatment in earlier scholarship and therefore would be familiar to most readers of this book. In a study on the symbolist sublimation of sex, one might expect a lengthy discussion of how the European courtly love tradition, which Blok inherited from his predecessor Vladimir Soloviev, influenced his relationship with his wife, Liubov Mendeleeva, and numerous other women including his first love, Ksenia Sadovskaia, the actress Natalia Volokhova, the singer Liubov Delmas, and the various prostitutes with whom he apparently had liaisons. Later in life, Blok himself remarked: "I have had not 100, 200, 300 women (or more?), but only two: one was Liuba; the other was everyone else, and they are different, and I am different" (U menia zhenshchin ne 100 — 200 — 300 [ili bol'she?], a vsego dve: odna — Liuba; drugaia — vse ostal'nye, i oni — raznye, i ia — raznyi) (ZK, 303).[16] Although the question of how Blok's tendency to oscillate between Liuba and the others — between an ideal woman and her demonic double — developed from his understanding of Soloviev's views of love and of the divine Sophia is an important one, it has already received extensive critical treatment elsewhere and, therefore, I have opted not to dwell on it here.[17] Instead, I focus on the related issue of how sublimated eros fueled his creativity, resulting in a type of mythmaking that set creativity against procreation and that, in turn, affected the way in which he perceived kinship relations in his own family and in Russia at large — something that is crucial in the revolutionary context. Similarly, in the case of Gippius, one might anticipate an extensive discussion of the way the poet's concept of sublimated love fed into her own myth of a sexless marriage and of the role it played in her multiple purportedly unconsummated love affairs with both men and women.[18] Although I do make ample reference to Gippius's unconventional views of love and marriage, I have chosen to emphasize a slightly different issue here: namely the way in which her poetry itself was motivated not so much by a retreat from procreation as from a desire to transcend the confines of the physical body. Thus, in this study, Blok and Gippius emerge not only as two exemplars of the symbolist sublimation of sex but also as somewhat different writers from those who appear in earlier scholarship.

The first part of the book is devoted to an examination of Blok and the antiprocreative impulse in Russian modernist poetry. Chapter 1 argues that Blok embraced an infanticidal model of poetic creation that can be seen as a direct inversion of Harold Bloom's Oedipal model of poetic history, which envisions literary history as an intense rivalry between fathers and sons, one in which parricidal urges predominate. Though Bloomian patricidal tendencies certainly made themselves known in Russian modernism, particularly in the works of the futurists, who openly acknowledged their desire to throw their literary ancestors "overboard from the Ship of Modernity," infanticidal urges were so prevalent among the Russian modernists that we might say that the modernist tradition was constructed, figuratively speaking, on the bodies of dead children. Such fantasies are to be found primarily within the dominant male poetic tradition and play little role in the poetry of Gippius or that of other female modernists, despite their strong resistance to the generative impulse. Blok's immediate successor, Mayakovsky, evinced few qualms about embracing the theme of infanticide. And while Blok was much less inclined to publicly identify himself with infanticide than was the futurist poet, filicidal impulses played an important, albeit largely unacknowledged, role in his creative mythology. Blok did not just admit to harboring infanticidal fantasies in several notebook entries he penned shortly before his wedding; he also became increasingly invested in the theme of child death in the period following his nuptials.

Chapter 2 shows that Blok turned repeatedly in his poetry to the figure of the slumbering or ethereal mother who awakens and inflicts violence on her children. So persistent, in fact, is this shade-like figure in Blok's poetry from this period that we can speak of his creation of a spectral myth, a distinctly feminine variation on the Pushkinian sculptural myth discussed by Roman Jakobson. He embraces this myth more intensely in the period of reaction following the revolution of 1905 with his translation in 1908 of Franz Grillparzer's Romantic drama *Die Ahnfrau*, a work that details the demise of an Austrian aristocratic family of Slavic origins at the hands of a vengeful and adulterous foremother who returns from the dead to murder her last remaining male scions. Though Freud referred to the Austrian play as "arbitrary," Blok readily embraced it since it gave expression to the violent family romance that had been central to his disruptive sense of generational history. And as was the case with Pushkin's sculptural myth, this spectral myth interfaced in uncanny ways with the plot of Blok's own life. In January of 1909, on the very same night that Blok's translation of *Die Ahnfrau* (*Pramater'*), opened on stage in Petersburg, his wife was brought into the maternity ward pregnant with a child she had conceived by another man and had considered aborting. The child died shortly after his birth, and it was at this point that Blok, overcome by the apparent realization of the myth of the filicidal *Ahnfrau* in his own life, attempted once and for all to distance himself from the theme of child death, most notably in the poem "On the Death of an Infant" ("Na smert' mladentsa") (February 1909).

Nonetheless, in spite of Blok's efforts to exorcise the theme of child death from his oeuvre, he continued to be intrigued by the creative potential of child death, if not by the theme itself. Just a month after the death of his wife's child, Blok credited Nikolai Gogol, the most unprocreative and infanticidally inclined of his predecessors, not only with giving birth to his works but also with giving birth to Russia. Chapter 3 explores how this Gogolian model of artistic reproduction provided Blok with a model of poetic creation in the period immediately following the death of his wife's child. Blok did not, however, immediately undertake the reproduction of Russia; rather he first attempted the reproduction of Russia's "other motherland," Italy. Just two months after he delivered his famous Gogol address, Blok and his wife traveled to Italy, immersing themselves in Italian art and architecture, much as Gogol had in the previous century. This journey provided him with the impetus for his *Italian Verses* (*Ital'ianskie stikhi*) (1909), the cycle of poems to which, as noted above, he declared himself mother. Though Blok's proclamation of literary maternity at such a symbolically charged time might seem to support the notion, fostered by several feminist critics, that male appropriation of the maternal metaphor is for the most part unproblematic even in the wake of a child's death, I show that this was anything but the case for the Russian poet. Blok had experienced intense anguish over the death of his wife's child and had also envisioned the child as a kind of alter ego of himself. And through a close reading of *The Italian Verses*, I demonstrate that his artistic enterprise of poetic reproduction is fraught with intense anxiety that heralds from his inability to differentiate between the fate of his wife's dead child and that of his creative self.

Chapter 4 argues that the tension between poetry and progeny, which was the source of so much of Blok's creativity, culminated in his intense preoccupation with the disruption of generational succession in the final twelve years of his life. In December 1909, Blok's somewhat estranged father died in Warsaw, making him the last remaining male scion of his particular family line. Blok responded to this family tragedy by turning intermittently throughout the remainder of his life to the composition of his semiautobiographical narrative poem, *Retribution* (*Vozmezdie*), in which he superimposes his own family drama onto the increasingly violent family romance of Russia. Though Blok apparently planned to have his poetic alter ego, the son, die, he hoped that the son's family line would live on through the child he would father with a simple Polish woman amidst political strife. He found himself unable, however, to extend his fictional family narrative into the future and to complete that section of the poem dealing with the birth of the child. I contend that this failure is symptomatic of Blok's overriding resistance to the generative impulse and is evident in the very design of the poem. *Retribution* is a highly intertextual poem that turns repeatedly to literary works dealing with the death of a child, including Alexander Pushkin's play *Boris Godunov* (1831). Although scholars have often ignored the connections to this drama that deals with the Time of Troubles, which erupted in medieval Russia after the death (or murder) of the Tsarevich Dmitry, I demonstrate that it is central to Blok's antagonistic model of generational history. Blok had initially intended to name his poetic alter ego Dmitry as a way, perhaps, of paying homage not only to the dead tsarevich who haunts the earlier dramatic work but also to his wife's deceased child. And while he ultimately refrained from calling his hero Dmitry, he did invoke the Time of Troubles in the poem's prologue, which he completed a year after the assassination of the tsar and the other members of the royal family. Thus, in spite of the poet's attempts in this poem to compensate for the lack of a legitimate heir of his own through the creation of a child, this poem, like so many of his earlier works, is informed by child death and the disruption of generational succession.

The second part of this study is devoted to an exploration of the very different way in which Gippius worked out her complicated relationship with the body and sexuality. While she exhibited a strong resistance to the procreative impulse and reacted quite negatively to Blok's marriage and brief fatherhood, she differed markedly from Blok in that she did not make the denial of filiation the focal point of her own poetic myth. This is not to imply that she was any more comfortable with matters of the flesh than her male contemporaries; in fact, it can be argued that, as a woman poet, she was forced to struggle against earthly ties of a more essential variety—that of the female body. Chapter 5 demonstrates that in contradistinction to the intensely popular turn-of-the-century poet Mirra Lokhvitskaia, Gippius resisted identification with the feminine and the female body in her poetry. Desiring to write, in her words, "like a *human being,* and not just like a woman," she frequently adopted the unmarked masculine voice in her poetry and preferred the unmarked signature, Z. Gippius, for her poetry rather than the feminine signature, Zinaida Gippius-Merezhkovskaia.[19] Yet, in spite of her suppression of the feminine in her writing and her denial of the very category of female art, she often appropriated an ultrafeminine posture in the salon and in her informal interchanges with her contemporaries. I argue that Gippius's assumption of this extremely feminine posture, which she parodically termed *style "femme,"* was symptomatic of her profound ambivalence about her own femininity and her own female body. Gippius does not valorize essential femininity through this ultrafeminine pose; rather she associates the feminine with abjection, perversion, and even beastliness. This negative figuration of the feminine, though most visible in her salon performances, informs much of her poetry as well. Her early poetry contains highly ambivalent images of female creativity such as exhausted seamstresses and fleshy spiders that weave their webs endlessly. While such works can be read as expressions of metaphysical angst, I read them as negative comments on the process of female self-creation. For Gippius, the feminine in its earthly manifestation is almost always negative, and her assumption of *style "femme"* represents just one of the ways in which she exhibited a vexed attitude toward the issue of female embodiment.

Chapter 6 shows that yet another way Gippius revealed her ambivalent feelings about the feminine was through her assumption of a dandified posture. Though her identification with the figure of the dandy has been commented on, I contend that her dandyism was much more complicated than has previously been acknowledged.[20] The dandy is, after all, a cultural figure that is virulently masculine despite his effeminacy. He simultaneously distances himself from and identifies with the feminine, and therefore he can be said to possess a fragmented gendered consciousness. Gippius, we could say, adds yet another split to the divided consciousness of the dandy, since she identifies with an inherently masculine cultural figure that simultaneously embraces and disdains the feminine. This complicated gendered identity manifests itself in her notorious diary of purportedly unconsummated love affairs, *Contes d'amour* (1893–1904), where she identifies with the figure of the male homosexual or aesthete and exhibits a dandified contempt for woman, and in some of her lyrics. Gippius wrote several poems in which we might say that she figuratively talks through her lorgnette, romancing another woman through the misogynistic lens of the male dandy. In these lyrics, she does not simply employ the mask of the dandy to write veiled lesbian love lyrics and to avoid the taboo of speaking of same-sex love; she also exhibits an ambivalent attitude toward femininity and more specifically the female self. And hence her portrayal of woman is more indebted to the sensibilities of the World of Art group than it is to the symbolist cult of the eternal feminine that was fostered by Blok and other male symbolist writers.

Chapter 7 explores the specific ways in which Gippius took issue with the representation of the feminine in Russian symbolism and in particular in the poetry of Blok. She entered into a dialogue with Blok against the practice, which he and several of the other male symbolists engaged in, of valorizing the figure of the eternal feminine and even attempting to incarnate her (Blok most specifically by marrying his real-life muse and prototype for the figure of the Beautiful Lady in his early verse). This is not to say that she did not have respect for the feminine in the abstract; rather her objection was to the idea that it could be embodied. This phenomenon manifests itself most poignantly in a series of poems that she composed in 1905 and later dedicated to Blok. While nearly all of the poems Gippius gave to Blok depict the feminine in a positive light as the Solovievian world soul, this does not tell the whole tale of Gippius's relationship with the feminine or with Blok's poetics of the eternal feminine. If in and of themselves these poems would appear to reinforce many of Blok's notions of the feminine, they take on entirely new meaning when we look at the larger context in which they appear in her collection of poems. Gippius repeatedly paired these ethereal, disembodied poems about the feminine with other poems that represent the feminine in highly embodied and perverse terms, and thus she called into question the viability of the obsession with incarnation of the eternal feminine. Though Gippius's poetic exchange with Blok came to the fore in the early part of the twentieth century, she remained consistent in her overriding skepticism about the possibility of female embodiment, dedicating numerous poems after her emigration from Russia in December 1919 and well after the demise of the Russian symbolist movement to a critique of the very notion of the incarnation of the eternal feminine. For her the feminine could only be positive in its ideal and essentially incorporeal state, and her resistance to female embodiment extended to the idiosyncratic ways in which she positioned herself as a gendered body both in her writings and in the salon.

Chapter 8 turns to an examination of how Gippius's difficulty with the issue of female embodiment posed severe interpretive problems for her early critics and contemporaries. Gippius self-consciously put contradictory images of her body and her self on display, employing the masculine voice in her poetry and vacillating between flaunting her femininity and cross-dressing in the salon. Perplexed by her idiosyncratic brand of self-creation, her critics and contemporaries implicitly assumed that there was a physiological basis to her contradictory gender identities and even suggested that she may have physically been a hermaphrodite. Though Gippius did admit to experiencing profound ambivalence about her body and sexuality, I contend that her contradictory gender identities should be read primarily as part of a larger gender performance rather than as symptoms of possible physical or psychological abnormalities. By refusing to project a unified self in her life and art, Gippius not only questioned the stability of the very notion of gender but also the very idea of the naturalness of the body. In this sense, her elaborate gendered performances form an integral part of her philosophical questioning of the concept of embodiment. Nowhere is her ambivalent stance toward the body more apparent than in her unfinished narrative poem, *The Last Circle (and the Modern Dante in Hell)* (*Poslednii krug [i novyi Dant v adu]*), where she, much like Blok in his late unfinished narrative poem, tries to summarize or "lay bare" the nature of her poetic self-fashioning. In this final work, which was published in its entirety only posthumously, Gippius stages a figurative "anatomy of criticism," depicting herself as one of three souls the Modern Dante, a descendant of Dante Alighieri, encounters during his journey to the underworld. In a variation on the initial interchange between Dante and Virgil in *The Inferno*, Gippius's Modern Dante cannot determine whether he should read her shade as body or soul or as feminine or masculine. By presenting her poetic alter ego in this work not just as disembodied but as essentially unsexed, she manages to keep the enigmatic nature of her identify intact as well as to affirm the notion that her poetic myth operates beyond the flesh.

The afterword is dedicated to an exploration of the legacy of the two poets' symbolist mythmaking. I demonstrate that in spite of the fact that Blok and Gippius organized much of their poetic careers around the denial of the flesh, they ended up creating a poetics that put the figure of the body at the center of artistic discourse, and this, in turn, had a profound effect on their posthumous poetic myths. Though Blok may have exhibited a strong resistance to procreation, after his death rumors began circulating that he had fathered at least two love children—a son named Alexander and a daughter named Alexandra—thereby creating the myth that Russia's last major aristocratic male poet had produced heirs. Similarly, while Gippius exhibited a strong resistance to her own femininity and her female body, her personal secretary, Vladimir Zlobin, fostered the notion in his notorious memoirs *A Difficult Soul* (*Tiazhelaia dusha*) (1970) that her death was spurred on by female vanity—by her insisting on getting, against doctor's orders, a permanent wave while ill.[21] The female body, then, resurfaces to haunt Gippius's poetic myth in much the same way that the illegitimate children do Blok's. The existence of these legends speaks not only to the literal ways in which subsequent generations understood the interface of life and art in Russian symbolism but also to the impossibility of the symbolists' artistic project of operating beyond the flesh.

I

Poetry against Progeny
Blok and the Problem of Poetic Reproduction

Ô la berceuse, avec ta fille et l'innocence
Des vos pieds froids, accueille une horrible naissance:
Et ta voix rappelant viole et clavecin,
Avec le doigt fané presseras-tu le sein
Par qui coule en blancheur sibylline la femme
Pour les lèvres que l'air du vierge azur affame?
[O mother cradling your infant daughter, / Welcome the birth of this untimely monster! / And with your voice like viol and harpsichord, O singer, / Will you press upon your breast a faded finger, / Through which in sibylline whiteness woman flows / For lips starved from the air the virginal azure blows?]
    Stéphane Mallarmé, "Gift of the Poem" ("Don du poème") (1883)

I went then into the backroom of the office and sitting at the table, thinking of the book I have written, the child which I have carried for years and years in the womb of the imagination as you carried in your womb the children you love, and of how I had fed it day after day out of my brain and my memory.
    James Joyce, letter to his wife, Nora Barnacle Joyce (21 August 1912)

After [1949] I found it no longer physically possible to combine scientific research with lectures, belles-lettres, and *Lolita* (for she was on her way—a painful birth, a difficult baby).
    Vladimir Nabokov, *Speak, Memory: An Autobiography Revisited* (1966)

1

Unbearable Burdens
Blok and the Modernist Resistance to Progeny

La chair est triste, hélas! et j'ai lu tous les livres.
Fuir! là-bas fuir! Je sens que des oiseaux sont ivres
D'être parmi l'écume inconnue et les cieux!
Rien, ni les vieux jardins reflétés par les yeux
Ne retiendra ce coeur qui dans la mer se trempe,
Ô nuits! ni la clarté déserte de ma lampe
Sur le vide papier que la blancheur défend
Et ni la jeune femme allaitant son enfant.
Je partirai! Steamer balancant ta mâture,
Lève l'ancre pour une exotique nature!
[The flesh is sad, alas, and there's nothing but words! / To take flight, far off! I sense that somewhere the birds / Are drunk to be amid strange spray and skies. / Nothing, not the old gardens reflected in the eyes, / Can now restrain this sea-drenched heart, O night, / Nor the lone splendor of my lamp on the white / Paper which the void leaves undefiled, / Nor the young mother suckling her child. / Steamer with gently swaying masts, depart! / Weigh anchor for a landscape of the heart!]
        Stéphane Mallarmé, "Sea Breeze" ("Brise marine") (1866)

Among the many definitions of modernism is Edward W. Said's idea of it as an "aesthetic and ideological phenomenon" that radically questioned traditional notions of generational and historical continuity.

"Modernism," Said claims, "was a response to the crisis of what could be called *filiation*—a linear, biologically grounded process, that which ties children to their parents—which produced the counter-crisis within modernism of affiliation, that is, those creeds, philosophies and visions re-assembling the world in new non-familial ways."[1] Though this crisis of filiation was experienced by virtually all of the Russian modernists, perhaps no single poet felt this crisis more acutely or responded to it more directly in his work than Alexander Blok.[2] Born in 1880 into an aristocratic household that was disrupted by his parents' separation and eventual divorce, Blok developed an ambivalence about family life that only increased with the growing social and political turmoil in Russia. Shortly after the revolution of 1905, he came to the conclusion that the only true artist was the one willing to abandon hearth and home. "The primary sign that a given writer is not an accidental and temporary greatness," he writes in 1909, "is a feeling for the road [chuvtsvo puti]. It is necessary to constantly recall this well-accepted truth, especially in our time" (*SS*, 5:369). Family ties not only inhibited the poet's ability to feel the spirit of the times but also his very ability to create. For Blok, this resistance to family life became intertwined with very real fears that poetic production and human reproduction were two mutually exclusive activities.

Although Blok assumed this antiprocreative position rather early on in his poetic career, nowhere does his commitment to this disruptive vision of poetic creation come into more dramatic relief than in his discussion, after the 1910 crisis in Russian symbolism, of the acmeists and futurists, two new poetic groups that had radically different ideas about the role that generational continuity should play in modern culture. Whereas the futurists declared it necessary to "throw Pushkin, Dostoevsky, Tolstoy, etc. overboard from the Ship of Modernity," the acmeists exhibited much more reverence for the past and for their literary predecessors.[3] In spite of the fact that the futurists took a much more violent stance vis-à-vis Blok and the symbolists than the acmeists did, calling for, among other things, the "liberation of Russian literature from the muck in which Andreev, Sologub, Blok etc. had placed her" (*SS*, 7:233), Blok felt a much closer kinship with the futurists than the acmeists. And his affinity for the former demonstrates the extent to which he remained committed to a disruptive vision of history. According to Blok's idiosyncratic understanding of acmeism, which was by no means as unified or homogeneous a literary movement as he suggests, it represented a return to a poetic culture of domesticity and traditional values that was untenable for the writer in modern Russia.

The manner in which Blok maps out his relationship to the acmeists in his diary and notebooks entries of 1913 — the year that signaled the changing of the guard, so to speak, in Russian modernist poetry — reveals just how dedicated he was to a disruptive vision of poetic and generational history.[4] In a diary entry dated 10 February 1913, Blok attempts to convince himself that he is younger and stronger than the burgeoning group of acmeist poets. "It is time to untie my hands," he writes. "I am no longer a schoolboy. No more symbolisms — I am alone. I answer for myself *alone* — and I can still be younger than the 'middle-aged' young poets, who are burdened by progeny and acmeism [obremenennye potomstvom i akmeizmom]" (*SS*, 7:216). In a variation on the classical Bloomian Oedipal model of poetic history, which focuses primarily on the creative anxiety experienced by young poets in the face of their strong poetic precursors, the aging Alexander Blok refrains from asserting his poetic prowess over the preceding generation of poets, his poetic fathers and grandfathers, as it were.[5] Instead, he proclaims his poetic power over the new generation of poets, his younger acmeist cousins, so to speak — a power that derives from his renunciation of affiliation with any one literary movement as well as of filiation or childbearing. By effectively divorcing himself from the traditional generational patterns that inform both poetic and human history, Blok, already at a midpoint in his poetic career, adopts the classical posture of the avant-garde poet, who is typically alone, typically young, and of course childless.[6] In such a fashion, he anticipates the youthful pronouncements of the futurist Vladimir Mayakovsky, who a few years later would boldly proclaim: "I don't have a single gray hair in my soul, and there's no old man's tenderness there! Having shaken the world with the might of my voice, I walk a handsome twenty-two year old" (U menia v dushe ni odnogo sedogo volosa, / i starcheskoi nezhnosti net v nei! / Mir ogrómiv moshch'iu golosa, / idu — krasivyi, / dvadtsatidvukhletnii). At the ripe old age of thirty-two, however, Blok asserts his lyric vitality only quietly and introspectively within the relatively private realm of his diary and not "at the top of his voice" like the younger and more rebellious futurist poet would do some time later.[7]

The fact that Blok strikes a youthful pose and accuses the acmeists of being encumbered with the bourgeois trappings of family and children would appear to have more to do with the early onset of his own poetic midlife crisis, now that the symbolist movement was clearly waning, than with the reality of a modernist baby boom. If anything the modernist movement in Russia was in danger of suffering from zero population growth, not a population explosion.[8] As Said aptly points out in his discussion of Western modernism, "childless couples, orphaned children, aborted childbirths, and unregenerately celibate men and women populate the world of high modernism with remarkable insistence, all of them suggesting the difficulties of filiation."[9] And like their Western counterparts, the acmeists demonstrated a certain resistance to the generative impulse. Most of the major figures associated with the movement never produced any children, and in this they followed the lead of the symbolists, who were for the most part childless. And those poets who did have families, such as the acmeist couple, Anna Akhmatova and Nikolai Gumilev, identified themselves with literary bohemianism by congregating in the Petersburg cabaret appropriately named the Stray Dog (Brodiachaia sobaka) and embracing the themes of love, travel, and café culture in much of their early poetry.

Yet for all of their avowed bohemianism, the acmeists did, at times, demonstrate a willingness to treat domestic problems in their poetry. And nowhere can this better be seen than in some of the early work of Akhmatova, the leading member of the acmeist movement from the distaff side. If in much of her early poetry Akhmatova dedicates herself to overtly erotic themes that were far removed from the poetics of domesticity, in at least one of her early lyrics she addresses the problem of reconciling marriage with the bohemian lifestyle of the avant-garde, perhaps not thinking so much of herself as a woman poet as of her poet-husband. In her famous poem, "He loved . . ." ("On liubil . . .") (1910), penned in the same year as her marriage to Gumilev, Akhmatova's poetic speaker chronicles the difficulties that her adventurous lover encountered when faced with the tedium of family life. Looking back on their unhappy life together, her speaker wistfully recalls:

> Он любил три вещи на свете:
> За вечерней пенье, белых павлинов
> И стертые карты Америки.
> Не любил, когда плачут дети,
> Не любил чая с малиной
> И женской истерики.
> . . . А я была его женой.[10]

[He loved three things on this earth: singing at vespers, white peacocks, and worn maps of America. He didn't like it when children cried, he didn't like tea with raspberry, or female hysteries . . . And I was his wife.]

Akhmatova opens this deceptively complicated little lyric by defining the preferences of her as yet undefined male muse as inclined toward the exotic. With the catalogue of singing at vespers, white peacocks, and worn maps of America, she not only conjures up an image of him as world traveler and explorer (an image that, it bears noting, was not too far afield from Gumilev's own self-fashioning as poet-conquistador) but also suggests that domesticity was alien to his very nature.[11] White peacocks are unlike their more colorful feathered friends in that they are unable to reproduce—a fact of life that Akhmatova perhaps implicitly associates with her beloved here. Birds of a feather flock together, or so the old English adage goes. And in the next three lines of the poem, Akhmatova reinforces the notion of her beloved as reluctant family man when she describes his dislike of sticky domestic scenarios composed of crying children, tea with raspberry, and female hysterics. However, in the final line of this poem, which itself verges heavily on prose with its reliance on lists and catalogues, Akhmatova disrupts the sharp delineation between his likes and dislikes, the exotic and the domestic, as well as the poetic and prosaic, which she has hitherto maintained in the poem, when she interjects the final line containing an eye rhyme: ". . . And I was his wife" (. . . A ia byla ego zhenoi). With the addition of this prosaic fact (and poetic line whose verbal, if not visual, rhyme scheme breaks down at the very moment when the final word *zhenoi* (wife) with its mis-stress on the last syllable is uttered aloud), Akhmatova's poetic speaker reveals the true identity of her beloved to have been that of husband. And she implies that the very domestic activities he eschewed— noisy children, tea with raspberry, and family quarrels—were, in fact, an integral part of his reality.

Akhmatova's poem, operating as it does on the principle of the return of the repressed family drama, would appear to embody the very essence of lyric "middle age" from which Blok attempts to distance himself in his diary entry of 1913. The unhappy husband and wife who inhabit this poem are more reminiscent of Lev Tolstoy's middle-aged Stiva and Dolly, with their marital problems and brood of crying children, than they are of the youthful Levin and Kitty enjoying their "family happiness." Whether Blok had the messy domestic scenario of this particular poem in mind or the birth of Akhmatova's and Gumilev's son, Lev, in 1912 when he accused the new generation of poets of being "'middle-aged' young poets burdened by progeny and acmeism" remains unclear. But what is clear is that, in a discursive sense at least, the acmeists were much more inclined than their symbolist precursors to tolerate the incursion of quotidian details and domestic concerns into what had been for the symbolists the sacrosanct realm of the avant-garde.[12] This implicit concern with family life is something that emerges less in the domestic practices of the acmeists than in the names that were bandied about for the new poetic movement, acmeism and Adamism. Although the more canonical term, acmeism (which derived, as Gumilev explained, from the Greek *akme* meaning "the highest degree of something, the flower, a flourishing time" and "the prime of all powers, spiritual and physical") did not evoke the poets' fascination with domesticity and the realm of the ordinary, the movement's alternate appellation, Adamism, did suggest that this was a movement that was intimately concerned with family relations and domestic life.[13] Adam was, after all, not just the first earthly son — the "primordial Adam" (pervobytnyi Adam) that sprouted up in several programmatic acmeist poems — but also the first earthly father from whom all future generations derived.[14] Consonant with the image of Adam as father and progenitor, one acmeist poet and theoretician tended to make "family values" a cornerstone of the movement, if not a part of acmeist praxis. In particular, in his important acmeist manifesto, "Morning of Acmeism" ("Utro akmeizma") (1919), Osip Mandelstam would admonish the symbolists for their inability to keep house, something that he considered to be a necessary prerequisite to acmeist church building. "The symbolists," he claims, "were poor stay-at homes [domosedy]; they loved to travel, yet they felt unwell, uncomfortable in the cage of their own organisms or in that universal cage which Kant constructed with the aid of his categories. Genuine piety before the three dimensions of space is the first condition of successful building: to regard the world neither as a burden nor as an unfortunate accident, but as a God-given palace."[15]

Almost all of the major Russian symbolists were afflicted by this travel bug — some for purely artistic reasons and others for highly political ones. Blok visited Belgium, Italy, France, and Germany; Zinaida Gippius and Dmitry Merezhkovsky shuttled between Petersburg and Paris; Andrei Bely spent extended periods of time in Germany and Switzerland; and Viacheslav Ivanov lived in Italy, to cite only a few examples. And for Blok, as for many of his contemporaries, this restlessness became a central facet of his poetic self-fashioning. As Blok scholar Vladimir Orlov has indicated, "throughout [Blok's] entire oeuvre there runs a persistent and resilient motif of homelessness, of loss of simple human happiness, and of atrophy of the feeling for the 'family hearth' ['domashnii ochag']."[16] One of the primary ways in which he gave expression to this sense of homelessness was by presenting his poetic persona as perpetually in motion. From *The Verses about the Beautiful Lady* (*Stikhi o Prekrasnoi Dame*) (1901–2) to *The Twelve* (*Dvenadtsat'*) (January 1918), as Dmitry Maksimov has shown, the theme of the road is a dominant topos of Blok's poetry.[17] And in taking up the road, Blok followed in the footsteps of his beloved Russian writer, Nikolai Gogol, and of a long line of avant-garde wanderers from Charles Baudelaire's dandified flaneur to Arthur Rimbaud's scruffy poet-vagabond.[18]

Perhaps because of the seductiveness of the road, Blok found it easier to identify with the futurists than with the acmeists. Though almost all of the acmeists were avid travelers, it was the futurists who were responsible for taking poetry to the streets. Not only did they valorize the urban themes initiated in Russian poetry by the likes of Blok and Valery Briusov but they made the street the site of artistic performance.[19] And while Blok admits that he did not fully comprehend the intricacies of "the futurists' scandal-ridden debates" (disputy futuristov, so skandalami) (*SS* 7:232), he considers them healthier and more in tune with their age because of their ability to resist the weight of tradition and the forces of gravity. He declares David Burliuk to "have a fist [kulak]" (*SS*, 7:232) and the phenomenon of futurism to be "more earthy and alive than acmeism" (bolee zemnoe i zhivoe, chem akmeizm) (*SS*, 7:232), which was overcome by what might be termed the "unbearable heaviness of being."[20] The acmeists were not only "burdened" (obremenennye) or "pregnant" with family ties (*obremenennye* suggests both translations because of its etymological relation to the word *beremennaia*) but also weighed down by their cultural ties to the Western European poetic tradition.[21] "The futurists, as a whole," Blok writes in 1913, "are apparently a much more significant phenomenon than acmeism. The latter are puny [khily]. Gumilev is weighed down [tiazhelit] with 'taste.' His luggage is heavy (with everything from Shakespeare to Théophile Gautier)" (*SS*, 7:232). While Mandelstam declares his poetic predecessors to be suffering from the typically symbolist desire "to distract [themselves] with a stroll through the 'forest of symbols'" (razvlekat' sebia progulkoi v "lesu simvolov"), Blok diagnoses the acmeists with an entirely different strain of literary influenza, the anxiety of influence, that incapacitates them by depriving them of movement.[22] By depicting Gumilev as a weakling struggling with the baggage of his poetic precursors, Blok anticipates by more than half a century Bloom's discussion of the "weak poet," who is so overcome by the presence of his dead poetic ancestors that he is unable to make the necessary "swerve" away from them that would allow him to forge his own unique poetic path or *tvorcheskii put'*. And by emphasizing the burdens of family and poetic tradition, he assumes a position that is only slightly more respectful of his elders than that of the French futurist Guillaume Apollinaire who in the very same year cautioned that "one cannot be forever carrying one's father's corpse. It must be abandoned with the other dead."[23]

Blok's scattered comments on the acmeists in his diary and notebook entries of 1913 might suggest that he was prepared to throw his own excess cultural and personal baggage from "the Ship of Modernity" and sail off into the future, but his actual relationship with the past and with his own family was by all accounts much more nuanced and complicated. In his important study on the poet, Blok's contemporary Kornei Chukovsky emphasizes that the poet's lyric posture of rootless wanderer stood in direct opposition to his biographical reality or, as Boris Tomashevsky might put it, there was a marked disparity between his self-created "biographical legend" and the actual facts of his "curriculum vitae."[24] According to Chukovsky, "Blok was fond of seeing himself as a homeless tramp, when, in fact, very few people had ever received the same comfort and affection from Russian life that he had. [. . .] Compared to Blok, the rest of us seemed like orphans without ancestors or creature comforts. We didn't have an estate near Moscow where jam was forever cooking under noble, century-old lime trees; nor did we have his curls, his fathers and forefathers, his pile of toys and stately white horse. We were rich in heirs, not ancestors, whereas Blok was totally preoccupied with his ancestry, both as a man and a poet. He was the last of the poet-gentlemen, the last of the Russian poets who could adorn his house with portraits of his fathers and forefathers."[25] Not surprisingly, Blok turned to the theme of his aristocratic lineage in his numerous autobiographical sketches and in his unfinished semiautobiographical narrative poem, *Retribution* (*Vozmezdie*), which he began to work on shortly after his father's death in December 1909. And in this work, Blok reinterprets his relationship with his family's past, as well as with Russia's literary and cultural past and in particular to the work of Alexander Pushkin, the father of Russian literature.[26] And in so doing, he evinces a preoccupation with both familial and poetic origins.[27]

Yet for all his creative investment in his ancestors both poetic and real, Blok was, in the words of his own mother, plagued by a "lack of family feeling," and this is where, I suggest, he shows himself to be quintessentially symbolist and at odds with the culture of domesticity he implicitly associates with the acmeists.[28] If acmeism or Adamism appeared to Blok, at least, to inaugurate a vision of human history that we might characterize as essentially postlapsarian and "middle aged" (this in spite of the movement's valorization of the "primordial Adam"), then Russian symbolism was indebted to a view of history that was deeply nostalgic and utopian in its desire to recuperate a childlike, prelapsarian state before procreation became either a necessity or possibility.[29] This particular aspect of Russian symbolism has not escaped the notice of recent scholars. In her groundbreaking essay, "The Symbolist Meaning of Love: Theory and Practice," Olga Matich convincingly demonstrates that there was a strong utopian orientation in Russian symbolism, which manifested itself primarily in a resistance to the traditional forms of marriage. "The Symbolists," she maintains, "offered a variety of erotic practices as alternatives to the traditional bourgeois family. Among them were Platonic love for a soul twin, Dionysian *eros*, new versions of the romantic triangle, homoerotic love, narcissism, and romantic love for an unattainable object."[30] In Blok's own marriage, which was not consummated until more than a year after the wedding and was marked by infidelities on both sides, we can find several of these erotic practices in operation at once—namely romantic love for an unattainable object and new versions of the romantic triangle.[31] And it would appear that these deviations from the bourgeois norm were at least to some extent conscious on Blok's part. According to Blok's wife, Liubov Mendeleeva, he had theorized that "we did not need physical closeness, that this was 'astartism,' 'darkness,' and God knows what else. When I would tell him that I loved this still undiscovered world, that I wanted it, he would theorize further: such relationships cannot be lasting, no matter what, he would eventually leave me for others. But what about me? 'You too would do the same.'"[32] And Blok's own writings confirm the notion that they were to enter into a sexless or "white marriage." In a notebook that he began keeping just a month prior to his wedding in the summer of 1903, he insists that "the state of prohibition [zapreshchennost'] should always remain even in marriage" (*ZK*, 48), thereby espousing a Victorianism that, Matich has shown, would be typical of so many of the symbolist marriages and distinctly at odds with the "family values" later to be celebrated by Mandelstam, if not actually practiced by him or any of his fellow acmeists.[33]

Blok's decision to avoid consummation of his marriage may have been influenced by a complex of social and cultural factors, including the lingering influence of the utopian marriages of the 1860s and the antiprocreative theories of the nineteenth-century Russian religious philosophers, Vladimir Soloviev and Nikolai Fedorov, as well as perhaps by underlying physical and psychological issues.[34] By this time, Blok had already had his fair share of romantic liaisons and may have feared that he would pass a disease on to his wife and sully the woman who had ostensibly served as the model for the Beautiful Lady. As we shall see in the next chapter, the decadent theme of syphilis would enter into his writings, suggesting that he either contracted or feared contracting the disease.[35] But whatever the specific reasons, one thing remains clear: his reluctance to engage in conjugal relations with this wife ultimately became interconnected with the belief that reproduction would somehow have a negative effect on his poetic production. Though the idea that poetry was incompatible with progeny gains particularly clear articulation in Blok's denunciation of the acmeists child-rearing practices in 1913, this notion first begins to take hold considerably earlier, in the months leading up to his marriage, and appears at least in part to have been influenced by the theories of his friends and mentors, Gippius and Merezhkovsky, who had helped to orchestrate his literary debut on the pages of their journal, *The New Path* (*Novyi put'*), several months earlier in March 1903.[36]

Gippius, who preached sublimated love to her contemporaries and indulged in many symbolic activities to undercut the sanctity of her own marriage, including sporting a single braid as a sign of her virginity after ten years of marriage and somewhat later a necklace of the wedding bands of her married admirers, was apparently disturbed by Blok's decision to marry the woman who had supposedly served as the prototype for the Beautiful Lady in his early poems.[37] Believing that there was a dissonance between the mystical Solovievian aspect of Blok's poetry and the idea of marriage, Gippius attempted to convince her young protégé to call off the wedding. After all, Dante did not marry Beatrice, nor Petrarch Laura. As the heir apparent to Vladimir Soloviev and the courtly love tradition he had introduced into Russian letters, it would not be in Blok's best interest to marry his real-life muse, or so the logic went.[38] Initially, however, Blok appears to have scoffed at the Merezhkovskys' theory that marriage and poems would necessarily make for strange bedfellows, noting in a letter to his father written in the early summer of 1903: "Z. N. Gippius [. . .] and all her associates do not sympathize with my wedding [ne sochuvstvuet moei svad'be] and find it in 'disharmony' with my poems. For me it is somewhat strange, because it is difficult to grasp the completely abstract theory that the

Merezhkovskys are staunchly bringing to life to the extent of denying the reality of two undeniable facts: marriage and poems (as if either one of them is not real!). The principle blame is passed on me because I apparently cannot 'foresee the end,' which will clearly result (in their opinion) from my worldly circumstances [zhiteiskie obstoiatel'stva]" (*PABR*, 1:86–87).[39]

Although one can hardly blame Blok for resenting the Merezhkovskys' meddling (they appear here to have overstepped the boundaries of literary mentors and assumed the role of marriage brokers or *svakhi*), their concern about the effects that the poet's "worldly circumstances" would have on his art was by no means unusual within the larger context of European modernism. In spite of Gustave Flaubert's famous edict to the effect that if one wants to be avant-garde in one's art one should lead a conventional life, there had been a strong tendency particularly among the French modernists to resist conventionality and especially bourgeois domesticity. And for those writers who did allow themselves to succumb to the comforts and confines of domesticity, family life was frequently seen as more of a burden than a solace. This was certainly true in the case of the French symbolist Stéphane Mallarmé, who saw his own status as family man and provincial schoolteacher as inherently incompatible with his poetic aspirations. Particularly in the early years of his poetic career, after he had just become a father, Mallarmé was plagued by his family ties.[40] In his famous poem, "Sea Breeze" ("Brise marine") (1866), which he composed shortly after the birth of his first child, Geneviève, in 1864, Mallarmé can be seen, in the opinion of Robert Greer Cohn, as acting upon this "desire to flee from bourgeois domesticity."[41] Much like his own strong poetic predecessor Baudelaire, Mallarmé longs in this poem to escape to an exotic realm, a realm Baudelaire had described earlier in "Exotic Perfume" ("Parfum exotique") (1857) as "One of those lazy, nature-gifted isles, / With luscious fruits, trees strange of leaf and limb, / Men vigorous of body, lithe and slim, / Women with artless glance that awes, beguiles" (Un île paresseuse où la nature donne / Des arbres singuliers et des fruits savoureux; / Des hommes dont le corps est mince et vigoureux, / Et des femmes dont l'oeil par sa franchise étonne).[42] But unlike Baudelaire, who remained faithful to the bohemian lifestyle and to a Gauguin-like aesthetic of exotic isles, Mallarmé was forced to confront the responsibilities of marriage and children—a fact that becomes abundantly clear in this poem. Although Mallarmé's poem is ostensibly about escapism, it is cluttered with reminders of domesticity—the garden, the study, the mother and child. Mallarmé, though, remains adamant throughout the poem's first stanza, presented here in the epigraph, that these vestiges of home life will not inhibit him from accepting Baudelaire's invitation to take a voyage. Ultimately, however, Mallarmé's attempts at escape are frustrated, as the poet is left with "no fertile isle, no spar on which to cling" (sans mâts, sans mâts, ni fertiles îlots), though, it should be noted that he is accorded one of the pleasures of Baudelaire's earlier voyager—the "sailors' barcarole" (le chant des matelots).[43] And, thus, by concluding in disaster, this poem can be read as staging, in the words of Henry Weinfield, "the shipwreck of the Ideal against the shoals of actuality."[44] Or if we were to gloss the poem in Mayakovskian terms, we would say that "the love boat has smashed against the daily grind" (liubovnaia lodka razbilas' o byt).[45]

While I do not want to suggest that the Merezhkovskys necessarily had the particular case of Mallarmé in mind, the tragic clash between art and family life that this poem reflects is exactly the type of catastrophe they were attempting to avert when the encouraged Blok to call off his wedding.[46] Family life was no more compatible with the poetics of the Russian symbolists than it was with French symbolism. Judging from the comments Blok made on his impending nuptials in his notebook entries from the summer of 1903, it would appear that he did eventually "foresee the end" that the Merezhkovskys were prophesying and that Mallarmé's poetic speaker had so tragically confronted in "Sea Breeze" and elsewhere.[47] Although Blok did not share the Merezhkovskys' view that it would be impossible for him to unite marriage and poetry, he did express the fear that having a family would have a deleterious effect on his ability to produce poetry, and he set out to ensure that his poetic path would not be inhibited by the presence of children. In a notebook entry written on 16 July 1903, just a month before his wedding, he goes so far as to make a list of members of the Blok family who "still intend[ed] to reproduce" (imeiut v vidu eshche rasplodit'sia) (ZK, 50), suggesting that "if I were to have a child, it would be worse than my poems. Exactly the same . . ." (Esli u menia budet rebenok, to khuzhe stikhov. Takoi zhe . . .) (ZK, 51). With these statements, Blok not only sets up a sibling rivalry, as it were, between his poetry and progeny but also a reproductive rivalry between himself and his future wife, Liubov Mendeleeva, a woman whose first name meant "love" and whom Blok and his contemporaries Andrei Bely and Sergei Soloviev conflated with the otherworldly and all-powerful figure of the Beautiful Lady in his *Verses about the Beautiful Lady*. Given the erotic power of his imagined rival, as well as his own feelings of inadequacy, it would appear that he was always already doomed to failure. Blok suggests here that his own resistance to reproducing stems from a decadent streak in his family line: "I degenerated from the Blok family. Tender. Romantic. But the same type of poseur" (Iz semi'i Blokov ia vyrodilsia. Nezhen. Romantik. No takoi-zhe krivliaka) (*ZK*, 51). And based on an entry he wrote on 8 August 1903, just over a week before his wedding, it would appear that this degenerative streak ultimately prevailed.[48] As if in response to his earlier indication that any child would be inferior to this poems, Blok writes: "Better let the child die" (Pust' umret luchshe rebenok) (*ZK*, 53). And thus he willingly entertains the death of his progeny, if only to preserve the sanctity of his poetry.[49] In so doing, he reveals a certain affinity with the Old Testament figure of Abraham who was willing to sacrifice his son, Isaac, to prove his faith—not in art—but in God.

Such fantasies of infanticide would, as a rule, be anathema to the acmeists. Though the acmeists were relatively restrained in the number of children they produced, Akhmatova and Gumilev being the only two major figures to actually fulfill their reproductive functions as the latter day Adam and Eve of the acmeist movement, they were no advocates of infanticide. The same cannot be said of their more rebellious futurist cousins, obsessed as they were with cutting their ties to the rest of humanity. The futurists were actively involved not only with symbolically throwing their literary ancestors overboard from the "Ship of Modernity" but also, it would seem, their children as well. Though Russian letters would have to wait for the publication of Fedor Gladkov's novel *Cement* (*Tsement*) (1925) to see such an antisocial activity actually realized in print (toward the end of the text a child that has literally been thrown overboard from one of the returning ships washes up to the shore, reinforcing the idea that the construction of the new Soviet state demands sacrifices), the futurists were certainly forthcoming about their own aversion to children.[50] Roman Jakobson has observed that Mayakovsky "never recognized his own myth of the future in any concrete child. These he regarded simply as offshoots of the hydra-headed enemy."[51] As Jakobson has pointed out, the futurists' aversion to children sometimes manifested itself in murderous wishes. For instance, Mayakovsky brazenly proclaims, "I love to watch children dying" (Ia liubliu smotret', kak umiraiut deti) in his programmatic poem "A Few Words about Myself" ("Neskol'ko slov obo mne samom") (1913).[52] By styling himself as a willing witness of child death, Mayakovsky suggests in his "song of myself" that the vocations of poet and parent are mutually exclusive. To paraphrase a popular Russian saying, "art demands sacrifices" (iskusstvo trebuet zhertv). And while Fedor Dostoevsky's Ivan Karamazov might have proclaimed that he would return his ticket to heaven if it meant that even one little child would have to suffer, this was not a view that was espoused by Mayakovsky or, for that matter, Alexander Blok. And this speaks to the antigenerative underpinnings of their respective symbolist and futurist myths.[53]

But while an antipathy to procreation may have predominated among many of the Russian modernists, not all poets took the extreme position of a Blok or Mayakovsky. Gippius, for example, may have gone to elaborate lengths to prevent Blok's marriage to Liubov Mendeleeva and even to convince her contemporaries to avoid having families, but she never went so far as to imagine infanticide or filicide as a necessary precondition for her own creativity.[54] In spite of her willingness to appropriate rather unconventional gendered identities in her life and art, she appears to have been genuinely conflicted about her own inability to mother, even if she had never had a desire to assume the traditionally feminine role of a mother.[55] In a letter written to the young émigré writer Nina Berberova while in exile in France, Gippius admits: "With all the different relationships I have had with different human beings—it is maternal feelings [materinstvo] that I have never had toward anyone. It is an enormous shortcoming; it should be, especially since at one time I had extremely strong filial feelings [docherinstvo] toward my own mother, who was not at all like me . . ." (*PBKh*, 19). Gippius's regret about her own inability to embrace maternal feelings would appear to confirm the idea, fostered by some feminist critics, that maternity occupies a very special place in modern culture.[56] As Julia Kristeva observes in her essay, "Stabat Mater," "we live in a civilization where the *consecrated* (religious or secular) representation of femininity is absorbed by motherhood."[57] And because of the way in which motherhood is inextricably linked with femininity in modern society, it is presumably more difficult for women (even those as untraditional as Gippius) to deny maternal feelings than it is for men to disavow paternal feelings.

This is particularly apparent in the different ways society has responded to male and female poets who have chosen to treat their poetry as a substitute for progeny. "While one could undoubtedly find counterexamples on both sides," Barbara Johnson contends, "it is not surprising that the substitution of art for children should not be inherently transgressive for the male poet. Men have in a sense always had no choice but to substitute something for the literal process of birth.

That, at least, is the belief that has long been encoded into male poetic conventions. It is as though male writing were by nature procreative, while female writing is somehow by nature infanticidal."[58] That within the context of Russian modernism the exchange of poems for progeny was much less problematic for male poets than for female poets is suggested not only by the readiness with which some male poets appropriated the child's corpse or *trup* as a trope or *trop* for the creative process but also by the severity of the critiques that have been levied against those female poets who adopted similar discursive strategies. David M. Bethea, for example, criticizes Marina Tsvetaeva quite harshly for what he perceives to be her willingness to imagine the sacrifice of her child (and of her femininity) to her male poetic genius in her poem, "On the Red Steed" ("Na krasnom kone") (1921), a poem he insists has "powerful links with the death, eleven months earlier, of Tsvetaeva's second child, Irina." He reads the act of child sacrifice in the poem as evidence that Tsvetaeva's poetic speaker has "become the ultimate monster and, as Lady Macbeth would say, [has unsexed] herself" rather than as a complicated psychic reaction to the death of a child.[59] Certainly, in this poem Tsvetaeva violates the powerful taboo for women poets against speaking about the death of a child as anything but pure loss. But, in her defense, it should be noted that one would be hard pressed to find in Tsvetaeva, or in any other female modernist, for that matter, the type of programmatic antichild statements that appear among the male modernists.[60] In fact, Stephanie Sandler has persuasively argued, based on a reading of two other Tsvetaeva poems from the early twenties, "The Sybil" ("Sivilla") (1922) and "Under the Shawl" ("Pod shal'iu") (1924), that she clearly "departs from the opposition between mothering and writing noted by scholars of Western women's writing [. . .] and shows no inclination [. . .] to reject women's role as the giver of life in order to take on the role of bearing words."[61]

Poetry against progeny, then, is not the female poet's but the male poet's mantra in Russian modernism. Filicidal fantasies are prevalent enough among the major male modernist poets that we could say that the male poetic canon is constructed, figuratively speaking, on the bones of dead children. The typical path of the Russian modernist poet begins not just, as Harold Bloom would argue, with the symbolic killing off of his poetic father but also with the symbolic murder of his imagined children—a poetic act that is not fully accounted for in Bloom's model of poetic history. In *The Anxiety of Influence,* Bloom glosses over (or represses) the infanticidal tendencies embedded within the Oedipal drama, privileging instead the parricidal urges. And his insistence on doing so may derive not only from the fact that he relies heavily on Freud's interpretation of the ancient tragedy but also from the fact that he bases his theory of poetry heavily, although not exclusively, on examples from the romantic canon.[62] Modernism and especially the more radical flank of modernism, the avant-garde, was much more patently antiprocreative than romanticism, and this is revealed not only in the modernists' resistance to reproduction but also in the very problematic ways they envisioned filiation in their poetry.[63] This is not to imply that romanticism was a stranger to infanticidal fantasies or problems in filiation, emerging as it did in the wake of revolution in Europe. In Alexander Pushkin's play *Boris Godunov* (1831), for example, the regent Godunov is presented as being either guilty of killing the young Dmitry, heir to the throne, or, as Caryl Emerson notes, "guilty of *wanting* it — and thus his story, like Ivan Karamazov's, raises the Christian question of crime in thought, of the desire as deed."[64] But while murderous impulses toward children play an important role in Pushkin's text, as well as in other romantic texts such as Gogol's "A Terrible Vengeance" ("Strashnaia mest'") (1832) and *Taras Bulba* (*Taras Bul'ba*) (1835), I would argue that it is not until the advent of modernism that filicide is both deprived of its immoral status as well as elevated to the level of creative necessity.[65] Not only would filicide inform the visions of Russian history, outlined by symbolists such as Merezhkovsky and Bely in their respective novels *The Antichrist: Peter and Alexis* (*Antikhrist: Petr i Aleksei*) (1905) and *Petersburg* (*Peterburg*) (1916), but it would influence the models of creativity employed by a number of male modernists, particularly in the period following the failed revolution of 1905. Child death would be adopted as a model of poetic creation by representative symbolists and futurists such as Blok and Mayakovsky and, quite tellingly, by a more moderate futurist such as Boris Pasternak.

In fact, of all the Russian modernists Pasternak was probably the figure who was to most closely connect filicide to the artistic process. In his early, unfinished Hoffmannesque work, "Suboctave Story" ("Istoriia odnoi kontroktavy") (1917), Pasternak recounts the tale of a German church organist named Knauer whose dedication to his art leads directly to the death of his son.[66] While playing the church organ, Knauer becomes so engrossed in his music that he allows himself to inadvertently crush his young child who had wandered into the mechanisms of the organ. This story, with its religious overtones, operates within the religious paradigm that art demands sacrifices on the part of the father-creator, an idea that is underscored in a particularly heartrending scene in which the distraught father visits his dead son and subconsciously begins to play octaves on his child's body, reenacting, as it were, the intimate connection between creativity and child death. "But how he started," the narrator reveals, "when, suddenly, through the dense darkness of oblivion, he noticed what his left hand was doing to the body of his child! He snatched his hand hastily away as though it were a viper, or as if he had burnt his fingers plucking a blazing log from the carpet and had to blow on them. That incorrigible hand of his had been caressing his son in octaves! It had been playing on his corpse in octaves!"[67] After this macabre scene, which has a distinctly nightmarish quality about it, the distraught musician abandons his family and village, only to mysteriously reappear at the end of the story when he attempts, unsuccessfully, to reinstate himself as the church organist. Thus, Pasternak wittingly or unwittingly endows Knauer, the organist, with many of the aspects of the modernist poet of the Blokian variety: he not only sacrifices his progeny for his art but he is fated to be a homeless wanderer. We can surmise that by presenting such a portrait of the artist, the young Pasternak may have himself entertained typically modernist fears that the vocations of poet and family man were inherently incompatible. As the son of an artist himself, Pasternak may have identified not just with the filicidal father but also with the dead child.[68]

But while such fantasies of infanticide may have loomed in the background of the creative myths of male modernists, particularly those associated with the symbolist and futurist movements, few of them actually went as far as Blok and made infanticide their own personal poetic credo or remained faithful to this model of poetic creativity. Pasternak, whose "Suboctave Story" may well be the most cogent articulation of the antiprocreative tendencies among Russian modernist poets, appears to have eventually outgrown whatever early fears he may have had that paternity and authorship were mutually exclusive categories. Not only did he become a father himself but in his most mature portrait of the artist, *Doctor Zhivago* (*Doktor Zhivago*) (1957), he presents procreation as anything but inimical to the creative process. Though Pasternak makes it clear that his hero is versed in the antiprocreative theories of earlier Russian writers and philosophers (early on in the novel Zhivago, Tonia, and Gordon read and discuss Soloviev's *Meaning of Love* [*Smysl liubvi*] [1892–94] as well as Tolstoy's diatribe against marriage and childbearing, *The Kreutzer Sonata* [*Kreitserova sonata*] [1889]), he departs from the tradition of sublimated eros that had informed so much of early modernist poetry. Not only does Zhivago manage to produce several children with three different women (a level of fecundity that is, to say the least, highly anomalous for the modernist poet) but he develops a vision of the creative process that is intimately connected to, not antithetical to, the natural, biological process of reproduction. While his wife Tonia is pregnant with their second child in the domestic idyll of Varykino, where they take refuge during the civil war, Zhivago notes in his diary: "'I should like to be of use as a doctor or a farmer and at the same time to be gestating [vynashivat'] something lasting, something fundamental, to be writing some scientific paper or a literary work.'"[69] Although there is no denying that Zhivago's desire to write is spurred on directly by his own wife's pregnancy and is, in this sense, a compensatory activity, it is not tainted with the reproductive anxiety or infanticidal streak of either the young Blok or, for that matter, of his earlier protagonist, Knauer. Children and art can coexist in Doctor Zhivago's life in a way they could not in Pasternak's juvenilia, and this speaks of an erotic economy that is distinctly "postmodernist" and even "middle aged" in its celebration of both the literal and figurative types of filiation.

This is not to imply that Pasternak does not pay homage to Blok in *Doctor Zhivago* or that Pasternak's hero actually lives up to a domestic, fatherly ideal.[70] In the end, Zhivago is either separated from or separates himself from all of the women with whom he was ever involved, as well as all of his children, suggesting that the poetic path he follows owes much to the neoromantic Blokian image of the poet as homeless vagabond, if only by virtue of the tumultuous political times in which he lives. But if there is any one figure who best exemplifies and extends Blok's model of the poet as youthful wanderer and reluctant family man, it is not Pasternak or Pasternak's fictitious poet but Mayakovsky, the poet that Pasternak compares to such figures as Ippolit, Raskolnikov, and the hero of Dostoevsky's *Raw Youth* (*Podrostok*) (1875) in *Doctor Zhivago*. Mayakovsky made manifest many of the characteristics that were only latent in Blok. Whereas Blok earnestly dedicated poem after poem to his mother, Mayakovsky cried out "mama" in his famous poem, "A Cloud in Trousers" ("Oblako v shtanakh") (1914–15).[71] While Blok quietly voiced his reservations about having children in his personal diaries, Mayakovsky proudly proclaimed his love of dead children in his verses for the entire world to hear. Yet, despite the fact that Mayakovsky may well be the most notorious poet-mama's boy and child hater in all of Russian modernism, he does not necessarily provide the most interesting case study for an examination of the ways in which the tensions between domesticity and creativity can fuel a creative mythology. Because he committed suicide at the age of thirty-six, on the very cusp of middle age, he would never have to deal with the main challenges to the avant-garde aesthetic—the onset of middle age or the raising of children. Though his death was a tragedy, it ensured that his avant-garde image of the poet as childless, youthful wanderer would forever stay intact.[72] One cannot imagine Mayakovsky married with children any more than one can envision Rimbaud or any other exemplars of the avant-garde in such a fashion.[73] Time is not on the side of the avant-garde poet. And perhaps the only viable way a poet can be assured of retaining the position of child within the family romance of modernist poetry is by dying young or by eschewing all traditional family ties.

These are things about which Blok was also implicitly aware. Though he did not possess Mayakovsky's poetic or personal maximalism, he, like Mayakovsky, reportedly considered suicide in his early years, and he was heavily invested in promoting a youthful image of the poet. In his 1914 poem "Oh, I want madly to live" ("O, ia khochu bezumno zhit'"), which privileges childishness and boundlessness over domesticity and harmony, Blok expresses the desire that he would be remembered as "a child of goodness and light" (ditia dobra i sveta) (*SS*, 3:85). As Blok biographer Avril Pyman puts it, "the image of the child always 'a child of goodness and light,' heir by right rather than redemption to the Kingdom of Heaven, innocent of pretension and scoffing at sophistry, is never far from Blok's thought. The spontaneous reaction of this child within himself is, for him, the touchstone of truth."[74] As a self-styled child poet, Blok was extremely sensitive to the appearance of the new generation of young modernist poets, as well as to the possible appearance of a new generation of children. Though he was much quieter and more introspective about his own aversion to childbearing than Mayakovsky (virtually all of Blok's blatantly antichild statements appear in his notebooks), filicidal impulses played a very important role in Blok's creative mythology, informing the way he viewed not only the creative process but also the unfolding of modern Russian history.

Jakobson has observed that in Mayakovsky's case "the theme of child-murder and self-murder are closely linked: they are simply two different ways of depriving the present of its immediate succession of 'tearing through decrepit time.'"[75] What Jakobson has to say about Mayakovsky is also relevant to Blok. But if for Mayakovsky the acts of child murder and self-murder are intricately intertwined in an inherently suicidal model of poetic self-creation, then for Blok the act of child murder is inextricably connected to an antagonistic model of history in which violence is directed outward toward a child. This is particularly evident in the essays, poetry, and drama Blok composed following the events of 1905. At this time, he experienced the devastating effects of the revolution of 1905, whose failure he repeatedly identified with the death of a child, and he was forced to deal with the death of a child in his own life. Because of the way in which this filicidal model of history and of creativity intersected with the actual death of a child close to him, he was forced to confront the complicated relationship between poetry and progeny in a much more direct way than Mayakovsky ever would, and thus with respect to Blok the problem deserves special attention.

The discussion of Blok that follows is dedicated to an analysis of the ways in which he worked out the tensions between poetry and progeny in his life and art in the period from the revolution of 1905 to the Russian revolution and civil war. The next chapter demonstrates that Blok was drawn in the wake of the revolution of 1905 to a vision of history characterized by antagonisms not just between fathers and sons but also between mothers and sons. By acknowledging the potential for enmity between mothers and sons, Blok was able to work out the relationship between creativity and procreation that had plagued him since before his marriage but in a way that by and large absolved him from complicity in child death. By projecting violence onto a powerful mother figure, he would be able to identify much more fully with the child-victim, rather than with father-victimizer, and to implicate the mother in the destruction of the child. This model of history would be consistent with his tendency throughout much of his works to present himself as victim of the inchoate feminine forces of history and also to simultaneously idealize and demonize the feminine. It would also intersect in uncanny ways with a real-life family tragedy involving the poet, his wife, and her child.

2

Recurring Nightmares
Blok, Freud, and the Specter of *Die Ahnfrau*

"What children?" said Anna, screwing up her eyes and not looking at Dolly.

"Annie, and those that will come..."

"He may be at ease about that: I shall not have any more children."

"How do you know you won't?"

"I shan't, because I don't want them."

Lev Tolstoy, Anna Karenina (1877)

На позлащенной колеснице
Она свергает столу с плеч
И над детьми, безумной жрицей,
Возносит изощренный меч.
[On the gilded chariot, she throws her stole from her shoulders, and above her children, like an insane priestess, she raises up the sharpened sword.]

Valery Briusov, "Medea" ("Medeia") (October 1903, 1904)

Светлый и упорный, луч упал бессменный—
И мгновенно женщина, ночных веселий дочь,
Бешено ударилась головой о стену,
С криком исступленья, уронив ребенка в ночь...
[A light and unyielding continuous ray fell, and instantaneously a woman, a daughter of night revelries, hit her head madly against the wall with a cry of frenzy, having dropped her baby into the night...]

Alexander Blok, "A Tale" ("Povest'") (January 1905)

Although Alexander Blok adopted a filicidal model of poetic creation rather early on in his poetic career, he demonstrated a certain amount of resistance to openly expressing infanticidal themes in his artistic works. In the period immediately following his poetic debut, he refrained from publicly articulating this strife-ridden vision of history and of poetic creativity, relegating it primarily to the realm of his notebooks rather than directly expressing it in his creative works. This is not to suggest that murderous impulses played a less important role in his poetic mythology than they would in that of the enfant terrible of Russian modernism, Vladimir Mayakovsky. For the most part, though, Blok managed keep such antisocial thoughts in check, that is until the revolution of 1905. At this point, he began to give expression to the idea that the crisis in Russian history could be configured as a violent family romance, characterized by enmity between fathers and sons, and in this respect, he was not unique. His coeval and friend Andrei Bely would represent history in similar terms in his famous novel *Petersburg (Peterburg)* (1916), which was influenced, in part, by Dmitry Merezhkovsky's portrayal of an actual incident of filicide involving Peter the Great and his son in *The Antichrist: Peter and Alexis (Antikhrist: Petr i Aleksei)* (1905). In *Petersburg*, Bely represents the events of 1905 as an Oedipal drama motivated as much by filicidal urges as by parricidal ones. Lurking behind nearly every action in the novel is the ominous statue of Peter that is about to come to life and wreak havoc on the inhabitants of Petersburg, much as the statue had done in Alexander Pushkin's long narrative poem *The Bronze Horseman (Mednyi vsadnik)* (1833).[1]

While Blok also demonstrated a tendency to associate the unfolding of Russian history with an ominous father figure symbolized by the stature of Peter the Great—something that is apparent in his 1904 city poem "Peter" ("Petr")—his vision of Russian history was not animated solely by Oedipal tensions, nor was it dominated only by the figure of the father-statue that comes to life in a variation on what Roman Jakobson has identified as Pushkin's "sculptural myth."[2] According to Blok's complicated view of human history, the mother as both giver and protector of young life also played a crucial role in this family drama, and in this regard he evinced yet another affinity with Bely, who also represented the mother as an ambivalent figure in many of his works.[3] Perhaps Blok's most infamous indictment of the mother figure would come in the final months of his life. Ailing, he proclaimed in a letter to Kornei Chukovsky, "foul darling Mother Russia, who speaks through her nose, has devoured me after all like a sow her piglet" (slopala-taki poganaia, gugnivaia rodimaia matushka Rossiia, kak chushka svoego porosenka) (*SS*, 8:537).[4] This image of the destructive mother can be read not just as the product of the dying poet's imagination in the hungry days following the Russian revolution but also as the result of his sustained creative thinking about the historical process dating from the revolution of 1905. From that time on, Blok was drawn repeatedly to nightmarish tales of mothers who neglect, abuse, or even kill their children, a fascination that suggests he was conflating the violence of the revolution with child abuse. More intense images of the bad mother appeared in his work in the period of reaction following the events of 1905, culminating in his translation of Franz Grillparzer's romantic tragedy about a filicidal ancestress, *Die Ahnfrau* (1817).

Shortly after 1905, Blok's writings began to reflect a general sense of disruption of traditional family life. In his important essay "Stagnation" ("Bezvremen'e") (October 1906), he observes: "There was once on the earth the most pristine and light-filled holiday. It was the memory of the golden age. The highest point of that feeling, which is currently on the wane, is the feeling for the family hearth [chuvstvo domashnego ochaga]" (*SS*, 5:66). Blok locates the decline of the golden age in the generation of his parents, offering as an example of it Fedor Dostoevsky's story, "The Boy at Christ's Christmas Party" ("Mal'chik u Khrista na elke") (January 1876) from his *Diary of a Writer (Dnevnik pisatelia)* (1873–81). Although the Dostoevsky story chronicles the death of a recently orphaned boy on the streets of St. Petersburg from exposure to the cold, Blok intimates that it sustains the illusion of the golden age, since "from the street through the large window-pane the child caught sight of a Christmas tree and a pretty little girl and heard music, [and] that was for him some kind of heavenly vision, as if in a mortal dream he foresaw a new and bright life" (*SS*, 5:66). Such is not the case in the next story Blok discusses here, Leonid Andreev's "Little Angel" ("Angelochek") (1899), which was to provide him with the raw material for his own poem, "The Sugary Angel" ("Susal'nyi angel") (25 November 1909). Unlike the nameless street urchin in Dostoevsky's story, Andreev's main character, who happens like Blok to be named Alexander, may be invited to his benefactors' Christmas party, but this does not guarantee his salvation. "Sashka took just one little angel from the heavenly Christmas tree," Blok observes, "so that his path would not be terrible but sweet, as is fated for all such Sashkas, and he went from heaven into the cold night, into the deserted alley, beyond the partition, to his drunken father . . . Sasha and his father fell into a blissful sleep, and the little angel melted in the vent of the stove" (*SS*, 5:70).

For Blok, this story about the shattering of the Christmas ideal becomes a powerful reminder of how the dream of the golden age has been replaced by a decadent nightmare, a world reminiscent of that occupied by Dostoevsky's most unsympathetic character, Svidrigailov. The once happy home has been transformed into a haunted space in which "a female spider [pauchikha] has grown and taken on fantastic proportions: comfortable interiors, which were once the object of affection of artists and of domestic cares and the flowerbed of good manners, have become like Dostoevsky's 'eternity,' 'a rural bathhouse with spiders in every corner.' In boudoirs, in studies, in the quiet of children's nurseries, glimmers an infectious voluptuousness. While the wind sang its subtle songs in the stovepipe, a fat female spider warmed the voluptuous icon-lamps by the peaceful hearth of simple and good people" (*SS*, 5:67). Blok suggests that the infiltration of the home by the voluptuous female spider is not limited to the capital of St. Petersburg but extends even to Russia's borderlands: to "the green meadow" [lug zelenyi] of Nikolai Gogol's "A Terrible Vengeance" ("Strashnaia mest'") (1832). While Blok focuses in his discussion of Gogol's tale on the figure of divine retribution, embodied in the horseman or *vsadnik*, rather than on the family drama at work in this tale, his readers could not have helped but recall that the work deals first and foremost with the destruction of a Cossack family. The tale opens with a wedding that is disrupted by the appearance of an evil sorcerer, who turns out to be the long-lost father of the heroine, Pani Katerina. The evil wizard begins to torture his daughter with incestuous advances while she sleeps, entreating her to leave her husband and to marry him. Although the sorcerer is eventually captured, he manages to trick his daughter into disobeying her husband and releasing him from his prison. At this point, the wizard sets out on a path of destruction, savagely killing his daughter's infant son while she is asleep and then her husband. Thus, this tale of vengeance and the destruction of the family becomes yet another example of the stagnation that has come to the fore in Russia in the modern era.

In his own poem "In the far away light-blue nursery" ("V goluboi dalekoi spalenke"), which he completed on 4 October 1905 while at work on "Stagnation," Blok gives expression to this new sense of paralysis ushered in by the failed revolution. As in many of the literary works he discusses at length in his essay, he envisions the end of time as synonymous with the death of a child and the end of the family line. But if in the Dostoevsky story the boy dies on the street as the result of his own mother's recent death and in the Gogol tale the child is cruelly killed by his own grandfather while his tortured mother sleeps, Blok's own poem raises the question of whether the mother is responsible for the child's death, and, thus, it occupies a central role in Blok's feminization of the family drama. Framed as an address to the child's mother, the poem reads more like a cruel fairy tale than a monody for a grieving mother:

> В голубой далекой спаленке
> Твой ребенок опочил.
> Тихо вылез карлик маленький
> И часы остановил.
>
> Всё, как было. Только странная
> Воцарилась тишина.
> И в окне твоем—туманная
> Только улица страшна.
>
> Словно что-то недосказано,
> Что всегда звучит, всегда . . .
> Нить какая-то развязана,
> Сочетавшая года.
>
> И прошла ты, сонно-белая,
> Вдоль по комнатам одна,
> Опустила, вся несмелая,
> Штору синего окна.
>
> И потом, едва заметная,
> Тонкий полог подняла.
> И, как время безрассветная,
> Шевелясь, поникла мгла.
>
> Стало тихо в дальней спаленке—
> Синий сумрак и покой,
> Оттого, что карлик маленький
> Держит маятник рукой.
>   (SS, 2:83)

[In the far away light-blue nursery, your child went to sleep. A little dwarf crept in quietly and stopped the clock. Everything is as it was. Only a strange quiet reigned. And in your window, only the foggy street is frightening. It's as if something left unsaid that rings perpetually . . . Some sort of thread that bound the years has been unwound. And you passed, sleepily white, along the rooms alone. You, all timid, let down the shade of the blue window. And then, barely noticeable, you lifted up the fine bed curtain, and, like time, stirring, dawnless darkness drooped. It became quiet in the distant nursery; there reigns dark-blue dusk and peace, because the little dwarf holds the pendulum in his hand.]

Upon reading this poem, we are faced with no small amount of hesitation about how to interpret it. Should we read this lyric as being about the death or the murder of a child? And if this is a poem about murder, who are we to conclude is responsible for this violence? Are we to assume, as the fairy tale-like logic of the poem might dictate, that an evil little dwarf stole into the baby's room, like the evil wizard in Gogol's "A Terrible Vengeance," and murdered the child while the mother slept? After all, Blok does make ample references to "A Terrible Vengeance" in "Stagnation," even though he never discusses the specific scene where the father-wizard kills his daughter's child in retribution for her warding off his incestuous advances while she sleeps.[5] Or are we to surmise that since evil little dwarfs do not exist in real life but only in the never land of the Grimms' fairy tales and Gogol's *Dikanka* tales there must be a more prosaic explanation?[6] Perhaps the sleeping mother awoke to the child's screams and killed the child in a murderous rage, and the evil dwarf is merely the physical embodiment of this violence. These are some of the possible interpretations of this strange poem, which reads more like a childhood anxiety dream than a realistic tale of child death. Thus, it is the perfect example of what Kornei Chukovsky identified as Blok's "poetry of dream consciousness," filled with "fragmentary visions, disjointed episodes, smoky and broken images resembling the phantoms of troubled sleep."[7]

Consonant with the vague, nightmarish quality of the work, Blok himself reportedly evinced a great deal of difficulty rendering an interpretation of the poem. This hesitancy, in turn, elicited a number of questions from his own community of readers. The actress Natalia Volokhova, who heard Blok recite this poem at one of Vera Kommissarzhevskaia's Saturday meetings held at the Latvian Club in St. Petersburg in the autumn of 1906, reports that Blok was extremely ambivalent about how to read it.[8] In her memoirs, she recalls that "in response to our question of whether the child died or fell asleep, he answered entirely candidly and somewhat perplexed, 'I don't know. Truthfully, I don't know.'"⁹ And when pressed by a group of actors and writers at this same meeting for a more definitive interpretation of the poem, he allegedly conceded that the mother killed her child. Valentina Verigina reports that she inquired: "'Did the child die?' and received the answer: 'His mother suffocated him.' I recall that I broke out with: 'It can't be. There's no murder there!' Alexander Alexandrovich smiled and said: 'Well, he simply died. You can read it that way.' Indubitably, in this instance, an event from the papers made its way into the world of Blok's poetry and was expressed in such a fashion."¹⁰

Blok's alleged preference for the interpretation that the mother suffocated her child may have derived from a need to absolve himself of guilt rather than from a desire to remain faithful, like Dostoevsky in many of his entries of *Diary of a Writer*, to an event that may have been reported in the newspapers at the time.¹¹ To insist on the more literal reading, that is, on the idea that the child was killed by the evil dwarf, a dwarf reminiscent of the sorcerer in Gogol's "A Terrible Vengeance," and not by his mother may have been a dangerous enterprise for Blok, since it would have more directly implicated him, as a male poet, in the same type of sorcery or *koldovstvo* he traces back to the demonic trinity of his literary precursors, Mikhail Lermontov, Gogol, and Dostoevsky, in the final section of his essay "Stagnation." Though he readily acknowledges in this essay that "contemporary literature learned from the sorcery of Lermontov and Gogol [and] from the falls of Dostoevsky" (*SS*, 5:82), citing his fellow symbolists, Zinaida Gippius and Fedor Sologub, as contemporary exemplars of this tradition, he appears to resist positioning himself as an heir to this tradition of literary sorcery. Instead, he prefers to identify with the child-victim by purportedly assigning responsibility for the death of the child to the poem's sleepy mother.¹²

While this haunting poem, with its vague, dreamlike structure, certainly did much to reinforce the cultural myth of Blok as the child-victim of his generation, thanks to the fact that it was subsequently set to music and became a standard part of Alexander Vertinsky's art-song repertoire in the revolutionary year of 1917, this is by no means the only place where Blok gives expression to the theme of child death or neglect during this period. Most notably, in his cycle *City* (*Gorod*) (1904–8), he includes several poems that chronicle the difficult fate of the child during this crisis period in Russian history. For instance, in "In October" ("V oktiabre") (October 1906), Blok's lyric speaker, who sees "a boy, having turned blue from the cold, shiver[ing] in the courtyard" (mal'chik, posinev ot kholoda, / Drozhit sredi dvora) (*SS*, 2:193), appears destined to a similar fate. In the final stanza, he imagines: "I am flying, flying to the tiny little boy, amidst the blizzard and the flame ... Everything, everything is like it used to be, only without me" (Lechu, lechu k mal'chishke malomu, / Sred' vikhria i ognia ... / Vsë, vsë po staromu, byvalomu, / Da tol'ko—bez menia!) (*SS*, 2:194) But if in this poem, the adult speaker is implicitly conflated with the shivering child who bears a striking resemblance to the suffering and abandoned children in so many of Dostoevsky's works ranging from his first novel, *Poor Folk* (*Bednye liudi*) (1846), to later stories such as "The Boy at Christ's Christmas Party," in other poems in this cycle children are portrayed as imperiled by their mothers' presence.[13] In "You walk by without a smile" ("Ty prokhodish' bez ulybki") (29 October 1905), Blok's poetic speaker condemns a mother for bringing her son into St. Petersburg, a city haunted by Peter's legacy: "I want instantly to come out and exclaim: 'Mother of God! Why have you brought the Infant into my black city?'" (Ia khochu vnezapno vyiti / I voskliknut': "Bogomater'! / Dlia chego v moi chernyi gorod / Ty Mladentsa privela?") (*SS*, 2:177). Though Blok attributes demonic qualities to his poetic speaker, he persists in damning the mother for her perceived mistreatment of her child—that is, for her inability to see the dangers lurking within the city. In this poem, as in many of Blok's lyrics from this period, the mother may be compared to the Mother of God, but she is not far from the infernal realm of shadows. Blok writes: "You walk by. And behind you, above the blessed tracks, dark blue darkness rests" (Ty prokhodish'. Za toboiu / Nad sviashchennymi sledami / Pochivaet sinii mrak) (*SS*, 2:177). Whereas in this poem Blok presents the mother figure as merely guilty of ignoring the dangers present in Petersburg, in another poem from this same city cycle, "A Tale" ("Povest'") (January 1905), he implicates the mother—this time an infernal woman—in outright abuse. Here an intoxicated prostitute drops her child in the street in an act of spite directed toward a woman in one of the windows in the apartments above, but fortunately "someone lifted the crying child into his arms, and, crossing himself, stealthily wiped his eyes..." (Kto-to podnial ná ruki krichashchego rebenka / I, krestias', ukradkoi utiral glaza...) (*SS*, 2:164).

Although the image of the neglectful, abusive, or even murderous mother, who awakens from sleep or emerges from the nocturnal shadows of St. Petersburg, makes only occasional, fleeting appearances in Blok's poems dating from 1905, this ominous feminine figure would exert a powerful hold over him, so much so, in fact, that we could claim that he created his own uniquely feminine poetic myth in addition to drawing on what Roman Jakobson has been identified as Pushkin's essentially masculine "sculptural myth." Jakobson argues that Pushkin can be credited with creating a poetic myth dominated by the figure of the male statue that comes to life and wreaks havoc on the hero in the period leading up to and following Pushkin's marriage to Natalia Goncharova, reflecting his precarious relationship with both father and tsar. And he suggests that Blok readily appropriated the Pushkinian myth "in the poems of the cycle *The City* [where] he evokes the eternal life of a metallic Peter who vibrates between arrested sleep and dreadful activity" and in "The Steps of the Commander" ("Shagi Komandora") (September 1910-16 February 1912).[14] More recently, Adrian Wanner has convincingly argued that Blok's reliance on Pushkin's sculptural myth was much more extensive than Jakobson acknowledges, demonstrating that the figure of statue emerges in a number of other poems including "The Statue" ("Statuia") (28 December 1903), "To the Pushkin House" ("Pushkinskomu domu") (11 February 1921), and the narrative poem *Retribution* (*Vozmezdie*).[15] While I do not deny the importance of the Pushkinian sculptural myth for Blok and his fellow symbolists, I would argue that Blok did not simply inherit the Pushkinian sculptural myth. He also created his own distinctly feminine *spectral* myth organized around the figure of the ghostly mother who awakens from her deathly slumber and destroys her child. If the genealogy of Blok's sculptural myth can be traced back to Russian romanticism, then Blok's spectral myth, at least, in part owes its genesis to German romanticism.[16]

Blok took up the theme of the spectral mother most directly in 1908 with his translation of the Austrian writer Franz Grillparzer's verse tragedy *Die Ahnfrau*. Composed during a period of reaction that followed the Congress of Vienna, Grillparzer's *Die Ahnfrau* tells the tale an aristocratic Austrian family of Slavic origin that is destroyed by a ghostly ancestress who returns from the grave to avenge her own death at the hands of her husband by killing off the remaining members of her family line. As such, it meshed with Blok's ongoing fascination with the figure of the sleepy mother who awakens to violence as well as with key aspects of his own family history. Blok not only grew up in a household dominated largely by women and an absent father (Chukovsky observes that "[Blok] was encircled by a veritable wall of human warmth consisting of his great-grandmother, grandmother, mama, nanny, and Aunt Katia—too many adoring women perhaps?") but his own family had strong ties to both German and Western Slavic culture.[17] On the paternal side, his family was believed to have descended from russified Germans, and his somewhat estranged father resided in Warsaw. Despite these correspondences, *The Ancestress* (*Pramater'*) (1908) has sometimes been overlooked by scholars because of its status as literary translation rather than original work. Scholars such as Regina B. Thompson and Edmund Hier, who have given the play its due, have focused primarily on the work's relationship to the original German text.[18] Nonetheless, it came to occupy an extremely important place in Blok's creative mythology. As Zara Mints has persuasively shown, it provided Blok with a suitable narrative for understanding the plight of the Russian aristocracy in the revolutionary period.[19] It also supplied him with a ready-made script for an intimate family tragedy that he and his wife were to experience from 1908 to 1909—a script that he would simultaneously follow and resist.

It bears noting that Blok was by no means the only early twentieth-century thinker to become fascinated with Grillparzer's *Die Ahnfrau*. The play, which was first staged in Vienna in 1817 and in Petersburg in 1830, had already experienced somewhat of a revival in Western Europe, particularly because of the ways it meshed with typically fin-de-siècle notions of degeneration.[20] Sigmund Freud was taken in by Grillparzer's play, presumably because it was written by a fellow Austrian and thus had a certain resonance for himself as an Austrian thinker. Freud mentions Grillparzer's play in his writings several times, first in a letter to Wilhelm Fliess dated 15 October 1897 and then later in his *Interpretation of Dreams* (*Die Traumdeutung*) (1900). And in both instances, he embeds his discussion of the text within a larger discussion of the Oedipal tensions inherent within the family romance. Though Blok might have found Freud's discussion of the family romance compelling, convinced as he was that "happiness had grown cold [and] the hearths had been extinguished" (*SS*, 5:70), he does not appear to have become acquainted with the play through the psychoanalyst's commentary, even though *The Interpretation of Dreams* had already appeared in Russian translation in 1904.[21] Instead, he decided to translate *Die Ahnfrau* for the theater of actress Vera Kommissarzhevskaia after the artist Konstantin Somov suggested that he take a closer look at the text.

Blok indicated in a letter to Kommissarzhevskaia that his decision to translate a work by Grillparzer was motivated by his belief that the Austrian playwright's "heroic (perhaps even melodramatic) romanticism could be resurrected on the Russian stage" (*SS*, 8:223). However, his ultimate decision to translate this particular play, rather than Grillparzer's more famous *Medea* (1821), may well have been dictated not only by the fact that the play dealt with the decline of family and culture but also by the fact that it did so in a dreamlike fashion that spoke to both the general symbolist fascination with otherworldliness as well as to his preference for a diffuse form of narration suffused with what Chukovsky has identified as "trancelike vagueness."[22] Whereas in Grillparzer's as well as Euripedes's *Medea* the heroine takes vengeance on her husband, who decided to dissolve their marriage vows and to remarry by murdering their children, in *Die Ahnfrau* the adulterous Ancestress avenges her own death at the hand of her jealous husband by coming back from the grave in the form of a ghost and killing off the family's last remaining male scions.[23] Both plays, then, strictly speaking deal with filicide and the destruction of the family line, but only *Die Ahnfrau* does so in a mystical fashion that deprives the current generation of any complicity in the family's demise and that represents the historical process itself as being driven by the return of repressed feminine forces, that is to say, by the awakening of the specter of the Foremother.

The play's representation of family history as the return of repressed feminine forces clearly resonated with Blok in a way it did not with Freud. In *The Interpretation of Dreams*, Freud, who was allegedly struggling not only with his articulation of the Oedipal complex but also with the writing of his own personal family romance, compares *Die Ahnfrau* rather negatively to Sophocles's *Oedipus*, noting: "If *Oedipus Rex* moves a modern audience no less than it did the contemporary Greek one, the explanation can only be that its effect does not lie in the contrast between destiny and human will, but is to be looked for in the particular nature of the material on which that contrast is exemplified. There must be something which makes a voice within us ready to recognize the compelling force of destiny in *Oedipus*, while we can dismiss as merely arbitrary such dispositions as are laid down in [Grillparzer's] *Die Ahnfrau* or other modern tragedies of destiny."[24] It can be argued that Freud must regard *Die Ahnfrau* as arbitrary, since the image of the terrible foremother operates against the basic concept of mother-son love central to the Oedipal complex, dependent as it is on the incestuous relationship between mother and child, and against his own self-presentation in this text as what Sarah Kofman has identified as his "mother's favorite."[25] Blok, however, whose own relations with his mother were often strained even though they were quite close, is able to imagine a model of family history that can be characterized not only by enmity between fathers and sons but also between mothers and sons.[26] In this respect, Blok's own version of the family romance has much in common with the thought of Carl Jung, who made the ambivalent image of "the loving and the terrible mother" central to his notion of feminine archetypes.[27] While there is certainly no evidence to suggest that Blok had any more familiarity with the writings of Jung than he did with those of Freud, his own reading of this particular play as a reflection of the unconscious forces of history interfaces in compelling ways with Jung's notion of the feminine origins of the collective unconscious.[28]

In fact, Blok goes so far as to identify Grillparzer's *Die Ahnfrau* as the embodiment of the psychic trauma of his entire generation. "In that internal trepidation, with which the juvenile tragedy of Grillparzer is permeated," he opines, "are concealed the reasons why this play came out in so many editions, was translated into all the major European languages, and ran on so many stages. *The Ancestress*, which emerged from the environment of the 'tragedy of destiny' ['tragediia roka'], superseded that environment and became related to such works as E[dgar Allan] Poe's 'Fall of the House of Usher' and H[enrik] Ibsen's *Rosmersholm*" (*SS*, 4:293). And very much like these quintessentially decadent narratives, the entire plot of this play is based on the repression of a family secret—a secret of origins—that comes back to haunt the family. However, it is important to point out that in this play—a play that Blok remarked "bears a very strange title" (nosit ochen' strannoe zaglavie) (*SS*, 4:549)—the family secret is quite literally embodied in the enigmatic and veiled Ancestress. And the Ancestress bears a striking resemblance to the "girlish figure, grasped by silks" (devichii stan, shelkami skhvachennyi) (*SS*, 2:186) from Blok's famous 1906 lyric, "The Stranger" ("Neznakomka") (24 April 1906), despite the fact that the Ancestress is not directly related to this figure.[29]

While the enigmatic female figure of the Ancestress is central to the unfolding of the plot, the emotional focus in this play is, as in many of Blok's own poetic and dramatic works, on the male characters or personae. In Blok's *Ancestress*, which conforms to the plot of the German original quite closely, the drama opens with the old Count Zdenko von Borotin receiving a letter informing him that his last living male relation has just died, leaving the family with no male heirs, save the count himself. Even though the count has a beautiful young daughter named Bertha who could conceivably carry on the family line, the old aristocratic family name seems fated to die out, as the count's only son perished in a drowning accident while still a young child. In a last-ditch effort to ensure the continuation of the ancient family line, if not the family name, the count allows his daughter to betroth the poor, but noble-minded, young Jaromir who recently saved her from an attack by the bandits residing in the forest near the castle. While the count is hopeful about his family's future, Günther, the faithful family servant, is reluctant to believe that this union between Bertha and Jaromir could regenerate the family, because of an ancient curse involving the Ancestress that looms over the household. In a scene highly reminiscent of one from a gothic novel, Günther calls young Bertha's attention to an old family portrait of the Ancestress and then proceeds to tell her why her attempts to save her family are doomed:

> Рода вашего Праматерь,
> В цвете юности и счастья,
> Также—прелесть, также—диво,
> Также Берта, как и вы,
> Принужденная родными
> К нежеланному союзу,
> Не забыла в новом браке
> Прежних радостей любви.
> И в объятиях с любимым
> Раз супруг ее застал,
> И пылая жаждой мщенья
> За позор и преступленье,
> В сердце ей вонзил кинжал.
> Тот кинжал навек прикован
> Здесь, на дедовской стене,
> В память древнего злодейства,
> В память древнего греха.
> Нет Праматери покоя,
> И блуждать осуждена
> До поры, пока не вымрет
> Весь ваш род, зачатый ею,
> И покуда ни один
> Отпрыск свежий, сильный, ярый
> Не останется на старом
> Древе рода Боротин.
> (SS, 4:314–15)

[In the bloom of youth and happiness, your kin's Ancestress, who was also a wonder and a marvel, also Bertha, just like you, was forced by her relatives into an undesired union, and in her new marriage she did not forget the former joys of love. And in the arms of her beloved, her husband found her once, and seething with thirst for vengeance for the shame and the crime, he pierced her heart with a dagger. That dagger has from that time forth been chained here on your grandfather's wall in memory

> of the ancient villainy, in memory of the ancient evildoing. And the Ancestress will have no peace and is fated to wander until that time when the entire kin conceived by her dies, and until not a single fresh, strong, raging offshoot remains on the old family tree of Borotin.]

Although the count persistently discounts the curse as mere superstition, the slumbering Ancestress, who up to this point appears only as an image in a family portrait, awakens and proceeds to haunt the castle in a series of frightening night scenes. Distinguishable from the count's own daughter only by the veil that covers her face, the Ancestress is repeatedly taken by the count for his daughter and by Jaromir for his bride, creating no small amount of havoc in the castle. As the uncanny doublings of the two Berthas become more frequent and the very "order of mimesis" goes awry, it becomes clear to the audience, at least, that the social order surrounding the castle has as well.[30] Suddenly the attacks that the count had to endure from the bandits residing in the forest become more frequent and bloody, resulting in the storming of the castle itself. During this final siege, the count is seriously wounded by one of the bandits who informs him that his daughter's betrothed is none other the count's long lost son, who did not drown, as the family believed, but was stolen by bandits and raised as one of their own. Upon hearing this story, the mortally injured count dies, and his daughter goes insane, unable to tolerate the loss of her father and the incestuous implications of her romance with Jaromir. In the meantime, Jaromir, who is ignorant of the secret of his origins as well as of the ancient curse that hangs over the castle, arranges to meet the Ancestress in the family crypt, having mistaken his foremother for his bride. When he goes to embrace his imagined bride, whom he finds sleeping in the crypt and covered with a veil, he falls into the arms of the Ancestress instead and dies, presumably of suffocation. And, thus, the last remaining male scion of the Borotin family dies in the embrace of the Ancestress—the woman responsible for the conception as well as the demise of the family. The cycle of violence and betrayal out of which the family was born comes to a close, as the Ancestress, the originating womb of the family, is transformed into its tomb, and the family romance ends quite literally in the family plot.[31] The only member of the ancient Borotin family who is permitted to live is the count's daughter, Bertha, who is left alone to roam the halls of the castle in a mad trance, much like the Ancestress herself, revealing herself to be the true daughter of the Ancestress. And thus the feminization of the Borotin household is utter and complete, remaining faithful to the feminine origins of the old Borotin family line.

Die Ahnfrau embodies many features that would allow it to find a receptive home within Blok's own carefully plotted, poetic family romance. Since this play depicts the demise of the family at the hands of an ancestress or foremother, as opposed to an ancestor or forefather, as in Gogol's "A Terrible Vengeance," it permits Blok to give expression to a notion of history based on generational strife, but in a way that directs guilt away from himself and his male characters and that is also consistent with his overriding tendency to present himself as a passive, childlike victim of the inchoate feminine forces of history. And it also responded to his difficult relationship with the feminine. Though it has become somewhat of a critical commonplace to assume that Blok developed an ambivalent attitude toward the feminine only in later works such "The Stranger" and *The Puppet Show* (*Balaganchik*) (1906), which were written after the crisis of 1905 and the devastating love triangle involving his friend Bely and his own wife, the origins of this ambivalence can already be seen in an early lyric such as "I have a premonition of You. The years pass by" ("Predchuvstvuiu Tebia. Goda prokhodiat mimo") (4 June 1901) that helped make his reputation as the poet of the Beautiful Lady.[32] In this poem, which takes its epigraph from a poem by Vladimir Soloviev, Blok's poetic speaker awaits the appearance of the Beautiful Lady—a figure who owes her genesis to Soloviev's Sophia as well as to a German source, Johann Wolfgang von Goethe's *Das Ewig-Weibliche*. But while Blok's lyric speaker expects his Beautiful Lady to make her arrival at dawn's light and not at night like the Stranger or like Grillparzer's Ancestress, he is overcome with fear that she may not appear in her usual benevolent guise. "But I am afraid: You will change your appearance" (No strashno mne: izmenish' oblik Ty) (*SS*, 1:94), Blok's lyric speaker states. What the poetic speaker fears here is exactly what would be the source of horror for the male characters in Blok's *Ancestress*: not only that she will change her appearance but also that she will be unfaithful to the male and his image of her. And here it bears noting that the Russian verbs "to change" and "to be unfaithful," *izmenit'*, are differentiated only by the case that governs them. But while this unfaithfulness, or rather the possibility of unfaithfulness, is the source of great anxiety for the poetic speaker, it is also, arguably, the very thing that prevents this poem and, in fact, it might be argued all of Blok's lyrics, from descending into endless repetition.

Female unfaithfulness ultimately serves a markedly creative function in Blok's poetic universe. Since his lyric speaker can no better imagine a union with his Beautiful Lady than, as we saw in chapter 1, Blok could with his own wife, the only thing that can prevent him from repeatedly figuring eternal waiting and eternal courtship in his poetry is the inclusion of an unfaithful female figure who introduces change. In Blok's case, it is not so much that "all is moved by love" (vse dvizhetsia liubov'iu), as Osip Mandelstam would famously proclaim in his poem "Insomnia. Homer. Taut sails" ("Bessonnitsa. Gomer. Tugie parusa") (1915), but rather that all is moved by adulterous love.[33] Adultery, and more specifically female adultery, is the matrix out of which so many of Blok's works are generated (and it is worth mentioning here that the term "matrix" has an etymological kinship with the Indo-European root for "mother," that is "mater"). But what is particularly striking about *The Ancestress*, and what distinguishes it from most of Blok's own homegrown dramatic works written up to this point (particularly *The Puppet Show* [*Balaganchik*] and *The Stranger* [*Neznakomka*] [1906]) is the way in which it quite literally connects the act of female adultery with the unfolding of history. It is not simply that the Ancestress is unfaithful to her husband, thereby inciting a spiral of violence and revenge, but that, as Blok so explicitly reveals in his July 1908 essay on the play, "The Ancestress" ("Pramater'"), the aristocratic kin was "conceived by her in sin and damnation" (zachatyi eiu vo grekhe i prokliatii) (*SS*, 4:550). Thus, we could say the Ancestress or Foremother gives birth to the family "alone of all her sex," thereby linking her with what would appear to be her direct antithesis, the idealized figure of the Virgin Mary who conceives the Christ child without the aid of an earthly man. In this regard, the tragedy gives expression to that which Blok himself relegated to the backstage or *za kulisami* of his own carefully constructed poetic romance: the origins of its own conception, the primal scene itself, as well as the origins of its demise. In other words, he articulates that which is genuinely *obscene* and thus should by definition be hidden from public view.

Given that the figure of the Ancestress occupies the privileged position of both generating and degenerating force, of loving and terrible mother, it is perhaps not surprising that Blok reserved a very special place for this play within his creative myth. After finishing his initial translation of the play in the spring of 1908 for Kommissarzhevskaia's theater, he was drawn back to the tragedy in 1918, a full century after it was first performed in Vienna, according it particular importance within the realm of both European and Russian history by completing a revised translation of it and composing an extensive introductory essay. In the introduction, Blok acknowledges that *"The Ancestress* is not an eternal tragedy like *Oedipus* or *Macbeth,* but, if it can be phrased this way, it is an *intimate* tragedy [*intimnaia* tragediia], which retains its freshness until that time when humanity ceases to live through the epoch which Grillparzer lived through and which we too had to live through" (SS, 4:293). While it would appear that, as an intellectual educated at the turn of the century, Blok shares Freud's basic appraisal of the aesthetic value of the play (like Freud, he holds *Die Ahnfrau* to be a lesser work than *Oedipus*), what he does not share is Freud's idea that the motivating factors of the play are merely arbitrary ones that have little relevance today. In fact, Blok not only calls attention to the play's intimate or personal nature but also to its special relevance for the situation in modern Russia, noting:

> The history of political reaction in Germany and Austria has preserved for us precious external facts. The tragedy of the soul [tragediia dushi] of the twenty-seven-year-old Austrian poet is completely understandable only in the black days when the *old* still cannot die and wanders, complaining about its tiredness and haunting the living—timidly, stubbornly, at times musically; and the *new* still cannot gain strength and cries with somewhat unexpected tears, like Jaromir, a strong and courageous youth, and perishes in vain like the suicidal Russian youth without "a purpose in life."
>
> All this is not so easy and does not lend itself to a journalistic account [publitsisticheskii uchet]. It would be too easy for us to "superimpose" ["nalozhit'"] the entire tragedy of Grillparzer onto contemporary Russia, to say, for example, that for Russia it symbolizes the slow denigration of the gentry, which played a great role and is withering like an autumnal dahlia "in the gloominess of the dampness of the old gardens." In that would be a portion of truth, but not the whole truth. (SS, 4:294)

Although Blok expresses some reservations about drawing a direct correspondence between the plot of the play and the political situation in Russia, he ultimately finds himself unable to resist the lure of adapting the play to the Russian context. "The deeper Grillparzer delves into his gloomy *mysticism,"* he notes later, "the more awakens in me [prosypaetsia vo mne] the journalistic desire to translate the play into the decline of the Russian gentry; in any event, he who loved it tenderly, whose grateful memory preserved all the wonderful gifts to Russian art and social life in the former century, who clearly understood that it is time to stop crying about the fact that its beneficial juices [blagodatnye soki] have soaked into the native soil never to return—he who knows all this will understand what type of air filled the ancestral castle of Borotin" (*SS*, 4:295). And by the final paragraph of this essay, Blok abandons all of his attempts to exorcise the power of *The Ancestress*, suggesting that "it entered into life [ona voshla v zhizn'] and occupied in life, truthfully, her own not very big, but horrendous place [zhutkoe mesto]; without fail, one more extra wrinkle lies on the forehead of those few who read carefully into it. It is not a 'reactionary' tragedy, but also not an eternal one; perhaps because it was created in an epoch of reaction, when all that was living was weakened by the dead. It is an intimate, *foreboding* tragedy [intimnaia, *predosteregaiushchaia* tragediia]—a work not of a great but of a thoughtful and tortured soul" (*SS*, 4:296).

Blok implicitly identifies the return of Grillparzer's "spectral beauty" (prizrachnaia krasavitsa) from the deathly realm of sleep as an allegory for the Russian revolution of 1917, playing off long-standing associations in his poetry between Russia and a sleeping beauty. Already in 1906 he had imagined Russia as a sleeping princess that was visible to his poetic speaker only in a kind of Lermontovian double dream. In his famous lyric, "Rus" ("Rus'") (24 September 1906), his poetic speaker fears lest he awake the slumbering princess, who he sees in a dream. "You are extraordinary even in dream" (Ty i vo sne neobychaina), he tells her. "I do not touch your garments. I slumber and beyond sleepiness there is a mystery, and in mystery you take your rest, Rus" (Tvoei odezhdy ne kosnus'. / Dremliu—i za dremotoi taina, / I v taine—ty pochiesh', Rus') (*SS*, 2:106). And in presenting Russia as sleeping princess he exhibits yet another similarity with Andrei Bely. In his essay "The Green Meadow" ("Lug zelenyi"), published in *Libra* (*Vesy*) in the fall of 1905, Bely observed that "still not long ago Russia slept. The path of life and death were equally distant from her. Russia became like the symbolic image of the sleeping Pani Katerina [simvolicheskii obraz spiashchei pani Kateriny], whose soul was stolen by the terrible wizard who tortured and tormented her in his alien castle. [. . .] In the colossal images of Katerina and the old wizard, Gogol immortally expressed the languor of the sleeping motherland [spiashchaia rodina]—of the Beauty [Krasavitsa] standing on the crossroads between the mechanistic ghastliness of the West and primordial coarseness."[34] In line with Bely, Blok returns periodically to the image of Russia as a sleeping princess, most notably in the poem "Dreams" ["Sny"] (October 1912), which he included in the *Motherland* (*Rodina*) cycle (1907-16), thereby reinforcing what would become one of the dominant modernist myths.[35]

It bears noting, though, that if in 1906 Blok could still represent Russia as a sleepy fairy princess in "Rus" or, depending on how we choose to read the poem "In the far away light-blue nursery," as a sleeping mother who awakens to find that her only son has become victim to the evil dwarf, he quickly began to detect the stirrings of slumbering Mother Russia. In the November 1908, he observed in his famous essay "The People and the Intelligentsia" ("Narod i intelligentsiia") that "Gogol and many other Russian writers like to imagine Russia as the embodiment of quiet and sleep [voploshchenie tishiny i sna]; but that sleep is coming to an end [no etot son konchaetsia]; the quiet is being replaced by a distant and growing rumble, not like the mixed urban rumble" (*SS*, 5:327).

By the fall of 1908, Blok certainly had good reason to believe that he had sensed the gradual awakening of Mother Russia, embodied in the drama of Grillparzer's *Die Ahnfrau*. If in 1918 *The Ancestress* would prove to be a national tragedy for Russia, then already by the fall of 1908 the play had proven to be a distinctly *"intimate* tragedy" for Blok, one which solidified the connections between the personal and historical family romance. In August 1908, around the very same time that he was scheduled to read his completed translation of the play to Kommissarzhevskaia's acting troupe in preparation for the play's opening in the fall season, the events in his own family life began to take on a strange resemblance to the plot in the play, offering a possible explanation for his insistence in his later essay that *The Ancestress* had "entered into life." At this time, his own wife, who had been on tour with the Meyerhold acting troupe in the provinces, returned home from a spring and summer away from her husband pregnant with a child she had conceived in a liaison with a fellow actor.

Liubov Mendeleeva did not welcome this pregnancy and not only because of the child's paternity. "From early, very early youth," she recalls in her memoirs, "I was absolutely terrified by the thought of having a child. As my wedding day was approaching, I was so worried about the possibility of pregnancy and my whole being so rebelled against it that I decided to have a frank talk with Sasha, who had noticed that I was torturing myself with something incomprehensible. I told him that there was nothing in the world that I hated more than motherhood and that I was so afraid of it that there were moments when I was ready to give up marriage rather than face this possibility. Sasha right then and there quieted all my fears: 'there would be no children.'"[36] Not surprisingly, when Blok's wife did finally learn of her condition in the spring of 1908, she admittedly "firmly decided to terminate [her] pregnancy."[37] She, however, returned home from her tour in the provinces too late to do anything about her condition and after numerous unsuccessful trips to doctors was on the brink of despondency. She reports that Blok "lectured [her]: banality, abomination, let there be a child, since we don't have one, it will be ours."[38] The fact of the child's conception, though, was to remain a carefully guarded secret.[39] And, thus, similar to the way the ancient aristocratic family in Grillparzer's tragedy was "conceived in sin and damnation" by the Ancestress, Blok's own aristocratic family line seemed destined to be carried on thanks to his wife's adulterous liaison.

While there were certainly some striking parallels between Blok's life and the basic plot of *The Ancestress* (namely, the wife's adultery, her conception of a child out of wedlock, and her antipathy toward her future progeny), it is important to point out that Blok does not appear to have viewed the imminent birth of his wife's child as a family tragedy, at least not initially. In her memoirs, *Living Faces* (*Zhivye litsa*) (1925), Zinaida Gippius paints an extremely optimistic and cheerful portrait of Blok at this point in his life. Though she consistently depicts Blok in these memoirs as having an immovable face, more reminiscent of a death mask than the living faces she evokes in her title (in this sense her verbal portrait of Blok appears to be indebted to Somov's famous 1907 portrait of Blok, which depicts his face as mask-like and half-enveloped in shadows [figure 1]), she insists that during this particular period his face was illuminated from within in a way that was uncharacteristic for the poet who normally wore a tragic mask. "There are times," she writes, "when I remember a simple, human Blok with an extraordinarily lucent face [s nebyvalo-svetlym litsom]. In general, I don't remember his smile. If there was one, it was sliding, indistinguishable [skol'ziashchaia, nezametnaia]. But in that period I specifically remember his concerned and tender smile. And his voice was precisely different, warmer. That was when he was awaiting his child and most of all in the first days after his birth" (*ZL*, 29).

It was around this period that Blok began to imagine a much more hopeful future not just for himself but also for Russia. In the early fall of 1908, soon after learning of his wife's pregnancy, he began working on his famous poem "Russia" ("Rossiia") (18 October 1908), which came to

Figure 1. Portrait of Alexander Blok by Konstantin Somov (1907)

occupy a central place in his *Motherland* cycle. Here he presents Russia as simultaneously alluring and unfaithful to the poetic speaker, who, like Christ, must bear his cross for Russia. "I am not capable of feeling sorry for you" (Tebia zhalet' ia ne umeiu), he tells Russia, "and I bear my cross carefully . . . Give up your roguish beauty to whichever enchanter you wish" (I krest svoi berezhno nesu . . . / Kakomu khochesh' charodeiu / Otdai razboinuiu krasu!) (*SS*, 3:254). Though Russia emerges as inconstant, like the Ancestress and so many of the female figures in Blok's poetry, this does not prevent her from fulfilling a maternal role. Drafts of the poem make it clear that Blok considered representing Russia in the final stanzas of the poem as a mother who gives birth to a son. "The mysterious son *grows*" (tainstvennyi syn *rastet*), the poet observes in his drafts. "And 'Russia' humbly awaits what the son will say, and places her entire freedom in him. She waits by the cradle. And the son grows, awakens" (A "Rossiia" smirenno zhdet, chto skazhet syn, i vsiu svoiu svobodu vlozhila v nego. Zhdet u kolybeli. A syn rastet, prosypaetsia) (*SS*, 3:591). Although Blok later abandoned the notion of having Russia give birth to a child in this poem, his willingness to present Russia as a mother suggests that he had entertained a more hopeful narrative for Russia, and perhaps also for himself.

By the late fall and early winter of 1908, however, Blok had begun to give expression to his reservations about the possibility of family happiness in a series of dramatic sketches he recorded in his notebooks. During the middle of the night of the nineteenth and early morning of the twentieth of November, he jotted down the sketch of a plot for a new drama about Russia that involved the same main characters he had dealt with in his play *The Song of Fate* (*Pesnia sud'by*), which he had completed in the spring of 1908 while his wife was on tour with the Meyerhold troupe. Whereas in *The Song of Fate*, Blok focused on the trials and tribulations of a writer named German who left his wife Elena in search of Russia, embodied in the figure of the femme fatale Faina, in this new play, he planned to deal with the consequences of the adulterous liaison, not of the husband with the Russian femme fatale, but of his wife Elena with an unnamed man, playing off of associations, particularly among male modernists, of the figure of Helen with unfaithfulness.[40] According to this sketch, Elena returns home from a trip pregnant with another man's child and her writer-husband willingly accepts his wife's condition and agrees to raise the child. Although Blok concludes this sketch quite optimistically with the statement "but the child grows," he prefaces this dramatic sketch with the description of it as "a (pathological) nightmare" (nochnoi koshmar [patologicheskii]) (*ZK*, 120), suggesting that he had more than a few doubts about his own ability to assume the role of father.

This nightmare would by no means represent the end of Blok's anxiety dreams. On 10 December 1908, Blok recorded the continuation of this family drama. Whereas in the first part of this dramatic dream sketch, he attempted, somewhat unsuccessfully, to repress his own reservations about paternity and to conclude on the optimistic note about the child growing, in this installment he gives full reign to his anxieties about fatherhood. He represents his writer-double not just as a depraved intellect but also as a syphilitic unworthy of the role of father, thereby providing fodder for the notion that he suffered from syphilis:[41]

> She (Elena) is with the nurse.
> Everything is quiet. Suddenly from the adjacent room—his voice: Ah-ah! Ah-ah!
> —What is the matter with you? What is the matter with you [?]
> He runs in, clutching his head.
> —How strange everything is all around me. I had a dream. The curtains were drawn back. Syphilitics were dragging themselves up the mountain. And suddenly—I am there! Save me!
> —If only the child would not hear!
>
> ———
>
> The nightmares are beginning. My mouth can no longer be opened.
>
> ———
>
> They are carrying the one who was injured with a brick.
> —Yes, gentlemen, yes gentlemen. Yes, you see, I will get better.
> It is chance. Nothing happens by chance. You see I am so beautiful and so strong. For what? (*ZK*, 122–23)

However, if in the private realm of his notebooks, Blok sketched the outlines for a decadent drama in which the writer-father would imperil his wife's child with the threat of syphilis rather than outright infanticide, in the more public arena of literary Petersburg, it was the intimate adulterous and filicidial plot of *The Ancestress* that seemed destined to play itself out in his own life, thanks to a little help of fate. Although Kommissarzhevskaia had every intention of opening the theatrical season of her Dramatic Theater with the production of Blok's *Ancestress*, the play's opening was delayed several months, and the elaborate production, which included the costumes and set designs of Alexander Benois and the music of the poet Mikhail Kuzmin, did not open until 29 January

1909, very close to Liubov Mendeleeva's due date.[42] This delay was to hold the potential to become incredibly symbolic for Blok. In a strange confluence of art and life that could perhaps only happen in the very plotted lives of the Russian symbolists, the play's opening coincided with the evening that Liuba was admitted to the maternity ward. Thus, the tragedy of the von Borotin family and the personal drama of the Blok family became temporally linked, setting the stage for *The Ancestress* to become the "*intimate* tragedy" (*intimnaia tragediia*) of which Blok was to speak repeatedly.

This intimacy or semblance thereof was apparently extremely disturbing for Blok. If at other times in the past he had been willing to reveal private aspects of his own domestic life in his drama, such as the complicated triangular relationship that erupted among Bely, Liuba, and himself through the figures of Pierrot, Harlequin, and Columbine in *The Puppet Show* (*Balaganchik*), he reportedly could still be "an extremely modest and secretive poet in his personal life."[43] In this particular instance, he was not only extremely reluctant to reveal the secret surrounding his wife's childbirth (Gippius, for instance, was not privy to the facts of the child's paternity) but he expressed dismay about the ways the play seemed to comment on the events of his private life. Upon his arrival home from the opening, Blok composed a letter to the theater director Fedor Kommissarzhevsky, thanking him for producing his play and apologizing for his decision not to go backstage and congratulate the actors, indicating that his verses had sounded "too intimate" (*slishkom intimnye*). He writes: "Now I have returned from the theater and I send my deep and heartfelt thanks to the much-esteemed Vera Fedorovna [Kommissarzhevskaia] and to you for the production of *The Ancestress*. Imagine that I not only took pleasure in it, but I was interested in what would happen next, although I know the tragedy by heart. . . . I wanted to convey to you personally this and still much more, but I could not go behind the scenes, because I am experiencing very difficult days and am avoiding people. The hours after the raising of the curtain were the very best for me. It was so gratifying to look at your work, at Benois's decorations, and to hear my own verses, which I love, but which today seemed to me to be too intimate for the stage and for Grillparzer" (*SS*, 8:272).

While Kommissarzhevsky's actors were hardly in a position to comprehend the play's intimate nature or to draw comparisons between the plot of Blok's *Ancestress* and the poet's own life, Blok was more than able to do so. In a notebook entry recorded the evening of the play, he frames the description of his wife's entrance to the maternity ward with a mention of *The Ancestress*, thereby merging the plot lines of his family narrative with that of the Borotin family:

> After *The Ancestress* of the 29th of January. The quiet entrance of the maternity ward. Three o'clock in the morning, a relentless smell. Nearby they speak quietly with Liuba and prepare a bath. The midwife talks on the phone with the doctor. And in the distance, upstairs, in the quiet and the semidarkness — (the frenzied distant wail of a woman giving birth [neistovyi dalekii vopl' rozhdaiushchei zhenshchiny].) Or is it a baby crying? Later already — it rings only in the ears. Tiled vaults, cleanliness. The smell gathered in the collar of my fur coat. (*ZK*, 130)[44]

Regardless of the way in which the dramatic plot of *The Ancestress* intersected with the real events of his wife's childbirth, Blok appears to have ignored the fatal implications of this intermingling of life and art once the child was actually born. Liubov Mendeleeva experienced a very difficult and painful labor, and both mother and child remained extremely weak, but Blok tried to be optimistic about the future of the child whom they named Dmitry in honor of Liuba's late father, Dmitry Mendeleev. Dmitry, as Avril Pyman points out, "was also the other name Blok's mother had considered for him and the name is bound up with the dream that this child should grow up as the self he had failed to become," an idea that is supported by Blok's notebook entries from this period.[45] On 2 February 1909, the day of the child's birth, Blok, who had been reading Lev Tolstoy's novel about family life, *Anna Karenina* (1877), copied out the reassuring lines from Konstantin Levin in his notebook: "'But now everything will be on new lines. It is nonsense to say that life will prevent it, that the past prevents it. I must struggle to live a better, a far better, life'" (*ZK*, 131).[46] But try as Blok may to emplot his own life within the more pastoral narrative line of Levin, who would go on to father a child named Dmitry in the novel after the death of his own brother, Blok's and Liuba's lives seemed destined to follow the tragic plot line of Anna, whose adultery, use of birth control, neglect of her children, and repeated association with the figure of the shadow, may have connected her in Blok's mind with the image of the spectral foremother in *The Ancestress*.[47] And as if the tragic implications of *Anna Karenina* and especially *Die Ahnfrau* spilled over into life, on February 10, only eight days after his birth, little Mitia died. Though Blok's aunt, Maria Beketova, suggests in her diary that the doctor was much at fault in the child's death, she does not refrain from presenting Liuba as being highly indifferent to the death of her child and, thus, perhaps somehow responsible. "I am sorry," she writes, "for the [little one], because Liuba is not very sorry. Is it possible that she will shake it off like a cat and even will go on as before? [Blok's mother] Alia is also afraid of that. And I am beginning to be afraid."[48]

In all fairness to Blok's wife, it should be emphasized that it was Blok, not Liuba, who had been drawn to the figure of the filicidal Foremother and to her potential for symbolizing the conditions in Russia following 1905. Once the tragedy of *Die Ahnfrau* had played itself out both on the stage of Kommissarzhevsky's theater and behind the scenes in Blok's own private life, it was Blok who appeared to remain wedded to the fatal consequences of this tragic drama. Though he was genuinely distraught over the death of his wife's child, seeing in this child the potential for rectifying the wrongs of his generation, he seems to have detected a certain logic in the child's death. Not only did it conform to the tragic plot of *The Ancestress*, which had given articulation to his own fears about the viability of his class and generation, but it also appeared to substantiate his long-standing fears about fatherhood. Gippius, for instance, reports in her memoirs that "Blok narrated diligently and in great detail, he explained why [the child] could not live, why he had to die [dolzhen byl umeret']. He told it very simply, but his face was perplexed, unbelieving; having darkened right away, it was frightfully astounded" (ZL, 30).[49] She comes very close to Blok's own earlier premarital view that he should remain childless when she suggests somewhat later in these memoirs that the death of this child may have ultimately been preferable for the poet. She writes: "Perhaps someone will be surprised and will not understand me: What kind of hope was there for Blok in a child? Blok—the father of a family! He the poet, he the eternal knight, and if he was in fact 'immature' [nevzroslyi], then isn't it wondrous—an eternal youth? If the child had remained alive, what would it have given the poet? It would have sooner taken something from him. It would have locked him, if you will, into a family circle [semeinyi krug] . . ." (ZL, 30).

Blok certainly had demonstrated no small amount of resistance to the "family circle," particularly in the difficult period immediately following the events of 1905. In "Stagnation" he had proclaimed: "There is no longer a family hearth. An immense, sticky spider has moved into the sacred and serene place that had been the symbol of the Golden Age. Impeccable manners, calm smiles, quiet evenings—everything is covered in a spider web, and time itself has stopped. Happiness grew cold. The hearths were extinguished. Time is no longer. The doors are opened onto the blizzard-filled square" (*SS*, 5:70). But it was one thing for him to pronounce that the golden age of domesticity was on the wane and that all time had stopped, and it was another thing to see this generational rift so poignantly realized with the figurative stopping of the clock and the death of his wife's child. Shortly after Mitia's death, Blok gave expression to his profound sense of anguish and loss in his poem "On the Death of an Infant" ("Na Smert' mladentsa"), which concludes with the following stanzas:

> Я подавлю глухую злобу,
> Тоску забвению предам.
> Святому маленькому гробу
> Молиться буду по ночам.
>
> Но—быть коленопреклоненным,
> Тебя благодарить, скорбя?—
> Нет. Над младенцем, над *блаженным*,
> Скорбеть я буду без Тебя.
>
> (*SS*, 3:70)

[I will suppress deaf malice; I will commit anguish to oblivion. I will pray to the sacred little coffin at night. But to kneel, to thank You, while grieving? No. I will mourn over the infant, over *the blessed one*, without You.]

Konstantin Mochulsky has read this poem, which appears in the cycle *Retribution* (*Vozmezdie*) (1908–1913), as a "revolt against God, born of despair."[50] In this poem, Blok's lyric speaker takes on God, the father, for allowing the child to die. But if considered in isolation, the poem would appear to operate against the Christological notion of the inevitability of child death, this would hardly seem to be the case when we look at the larger context in which he wrote the poem. While Blok dated this poem February 1909 to emphasize its connection with Dmitry's funeral, Vladimir Orlov reveals that Blok actually completed the poem in March 1909, around the same time he composed his important essay "Gogol's Child" ("Ditia Gogolia").[51]

Written to commemorate the centenary of the writer's birth, this essay credits Gogol, the most unprocreative and, arguably, filicidally inclined of nineteenth-century Russian writers, with being the most fertile.[52] Blok opens the essay with a bold pronouncement:

> If Gogol were living among us now, we would relate to him exactly as the majority of his contemporaries did: with terror, with anxiety, and probably with hostility. That singularly unique person was afflicted with an invincible inner disquiet: sullen, sharp-nosed with penetrating eyes, he was sick and suspicious.
>
> The origins of that disquiet were the artistic throes that were the life of Gogol. Having renounced the wonder of life and a woman's love, this person, like a woman, carried a foetus under his heart—a being sadly focused and apathetic to everything except one thing: not a being, almost not a person, but one naked ear, open only to hear the slow movements, the tugging of the baby. (SS, 5:376)

In this passage, Blok moves seemingly effortlessly from a discussion of Gogol's sharp, wizard-like countenance, reminiscent of that of the filicidal grandfather in his "A Terrible Vengeance," to a description of Gogol as mother. In so doing, he suggests that he sees no disparity between the infanticidal sorcerer and the figure of mother, for he accords Gogol an incredible amount of creative power. He not only credits the writer with the creation of his artistic works but also with having a distinctly erotic relationship with old Russia or Rus. "That very Rus, about whom the Slavophiles shouted and sang entirely, like Corybants, stifling the cries of the Mother of God," he notes later, "flickered to Gogol, like a blinding apparition, in a short creative dream. She gave herself to him in beauty and music, in the whistling of the wind, and in the flight of the mad troika" (SS, 5:378). And, tellingly, he concludes this essay with the promise of the birth of a new Russia—a child: "In the flight to merge with totality, in the music of the world orchestra, in the ringing of the strings and the bells, in the whistling of the wind, in the wails of the violins, Gogol's child was born. He called that child Russia. She looks out at us from the deep-blue abyss of the future and summons us there. What she will grow into we don't know; what to call her we don't know" (SS, 5:379).

What Blok conceived of as an essay commemorating the romantic writer's birth ends up metamorphosing into an announcement of his metaphorical childbirth, and, thus, "Gogol's Child" functions as a kind of literary Annunciation. This is reinforced by the fact that the essay was completed in March, the month that marked the anniversary of the writer's birth and the religious celebration of the Annunciation. In turning the essay into an announcement of Gogol's metaphorical birth, Blok embraces a form of literary couvade.[53] In the context of the literary avant-garde, we can find numerous examples of male writers who adopt the trope of male maternity.[54] But what is so striking about Blok's appropriation of the maternal metaphor in his Gogol essay is its close proximity with the death of his wife's child. After mourning the death of this child, a child with whom he closely identified, Blok once and for all assigns the procreative power of the mother to Gogol, and by extension, to himself. In so doing, he not only links the creative process with the death of a child much more closely than he had done so before but he does so in a fashion that reinforces the notion that new life can emerge from death. And this takes on particular meaning in the context of his evolving spectral myth. After envisioning Russian history and, to a great extent, his own family history in the period immediately following the failed revolution of 1905 as a violent family romance dominated by a ghostly foremother who awakens to enact vengeance upon her kin, Blok envisions a radically different type of narrative for Russia and for himself as a writer.

Blok ascribes to his romantic precursor and implicitly to himself the potential for reversing the deathly narrative of the spectral mother by usurping her procreative power and nurturing the unborn child Russia who resides "in the deep-blue abyss of the future." This image of Russia as unborn child can be related to Blok's own earlier vision of Russia as a slumbering mother, as well as to the figure of the ghostly Ancestress, by virtue of the fact that it too inhabits a liminal space and time divorced from the quotidian. But this unborn child is ultimately a hopeful image that harks back to the happy period when he was awaiting the birth of his wife's child. Even though he may have abandoned the notion of having Russia give birth to a child in his famous poem "Russia," he imagines the male writer giving birth to Russia in "Gogol's Child," thereby inaugurating a new variation on the family romance for Russia and a new role for himself. Instead of identifying with the figure of the victimized son or the reluctant father—something we saw him do alternately in the period leading up to and following 1905—he now imagines himself in the guise of mother, thereby contesting the power of the spectral mother that had held him in thrall. But, as we shall see in the next chapter, Blok would find it difficult to realize this maternal role vis-à-vis Russia in the period immediately following his wife's childbirth.

3

Reproductive Fantasies
Blok and the Creation of *The Italian Verses*

> Long ago it already had been beautifully said that [the poet] should carry [his work] in his heart, like a mother carries her child in her womb [kak mat' rebenka vo chreve]; his own blood should stream into his work, and nothing introduced from without would replace that life-giving stream . . .
> —Ivan Turgenev, "Some Words about the Poems of F. I. Tiutchev" ("Neskol'ko slov o stikhotvoreniiakh F. I. Tiutcheva") (1854)

> The origin of individual poems is mysteriously similar to the origin of living organisms. The poet's thought receives a shock from the external world, sometimes in an unforgettably clear moment, sometimes dimly, like conception in sleep, and for a long time it is necessary to bear the foetus of the future creation, heeding the timid movements of the still weak new life. Everything affects the course of its development—a beam of the horned moon, an unexpectedly heard melody, a book read, a flower's smell. Everything determines its future fate. The ancients respected the silent poet, as one respects a woman preparing to be a mother.
> —Nikolai Gumilev, "The Life of Verse" ("Zhizn' stikha") (1910)

Although his essay on Gogol was overflowing with reproductive metaphors, Alexander Blok did not find the period immediately following the completion of this essay to be particularly productive. Not only did he fail to produce any new poems about Russia for his important

Motherland (*Rodina*) cycle (1907–16) in the six-month period following the completion of the Gogol essay but in his notebook entries from that spring he writes at great length about his growing sense of the discordance of modern life.[1] "The present moment of our intellectual and moral life," he indicates, "is characterized in my opinion by extremes in all spheres: disharmony [neladnost'] (the insanity of alarm or of tiredness) [and] a complete loss of rhythm [polnaia poteria ritma]" (*ZK*, 132). For a poet like Blok this increased sense of disharmony was synonymous if not with the death of poetry, then with the severe inhibition of it. According to Blok, what made Gogol such a prolific writer was his essentially feminine ability to hear the music and rhythms of Russia and of the world orchestra.[2] Perhaps not surprisingly, Blok's growing sense of disharmony coincided with a relative dry spell in his otherwise productive poetic career.[3] In the spring of 1909, Blok suddenly found that he was unable to write with the same relative ease he had in the past, and this was extremely vexing to him. In April he laments to Georgy Chulkov, "Never before have I experienced such a dark streak as in the past month—deathly devastation. [. . .] My writing is going weakly, badly and there is too little of it" (*SS*, 8:282). His only hope of alleviating this creative impasse, he decided, was to leave Russia and his present troubles behind and to immerse himself in Italian art and culture. "There are still no new poems," he wrote to his mother earlier that spring, "but I think in Venice, Florence, Ravenna, and Rome there will be" (*SS*, 8:280).

It is fitting that Blok would have sought refuge in Italy, a place he had visited once before as a child of three with his mother and aunt, as Italy had been a favorite travel destination for Gogol and was for many of the Russian modernists as well.[4] It was also the place that was traditionally viewed as the antipode to Russia in late nineteenth-century literature, especially in the works of Lev Tolstoy.[5] Immersed in *Anna Karenina* (1877) in the winter of 1909 in the period leading up to the birth and untimely death of his wife's child, Blok may have viewed his trip with his wife to Italy after the birth of her child through the lens of Anna and Vronsky's Italian journey. Anna and Vronsky sought a respite from Russian society in Italy shortly after the birth of their child, and it was there that Vronsky was overcome with the sudden urge to study art and to paint Anna, the mother of his child, dressed as an Italian woman. Vronsky, Tolstoy writes, "painted studies from nature under the direction of an Italian professor, and studied Italian life in the Middle Ages. Medieval Italian life had at that time become so fascinating to him that he even began to wear his hat and throw his cloak across his shoulder in a medieval manner which was very becoming to him."[6]

Tolstoy, however, whom Blok had characterized in 1908 as the "sun of Russia" (solntse Rossii) and the repository of all that was good in nineteenth-century Russian culture, seems to have implicitly viewed Anna and Vronsky's Italian vacation as a betrayal not only of their Russian origins but also of genuine art (Tolstoy repeatedly compares Vronsky's attempts to paint as a kind of failed *zhiznetvorchestvo*); Blok, on the other hand, at least initially, envisioned his own trip to Italy as a journey to his second homeland and as a necessary retreat from the discordant sounds of modern Russian life.[7] "Every Russian artist," Blok wrote his mother from Venice, "has the right for at least a few years to block his ears [zatknut' sebe ushi] to all that is Russian and to see his other motherland [drugaia rodina] — Europe and Italy in particular" (*SS*, 8:284). While Blok was by no means deaf to the underground rumblings of European culture, particularly in the wake of the devastating earthquake that had destroyed the cities of Messina and Reggio-Calabria on 28 December 1908, he found in Italy and in Italian Renaissance art, in particular, what he found to be lacking in contemporary Russia: visual pleasures.[8] Whereas in Russia in February he had expressed genuine disdain for the "naive artist" (naivnyi khudozhnik) (*ZK*, 131) in *Anna Karenina* and for modern art in general ("contemporary art," he proclaimed is, "blasphemy [koshchunstvo] in the face of life" [*ZK*, 132]), by May, he had changed his mind. Surrounded by the treasures of medieval and Renaissance culture, Blok developed a true appreciation for the visual arts. "Here one wants to be a painter, not a writer," he declared to his mother. "I would draw a lot if I could" (*SS*, 8:283). Once in Italy, Blok no longer spoke of himself as a poet, but as an artist, and a European artist at that. Just as Vronsky embraced the fashions of the Italian artist, donning the cloak of the medieval artist, Blok makes a point of mentioning in his first letter home from Italy how he now wears a "white Viennese suit and a Venetian panama hat" (*SS*, 8:284).

Though Blok's immediate interest in Italian art might have been compensatory, similar to that of Vronsky who sees the need to reproduce reality only in the wake of Anna's childbirth, it also marked a return to his earlier fascination with the visual arts. As Rachel Polonsky aptly observes, "Blok and Bely came to poetic maturity during the years of the greatest enthusiasm for Pre-Raphaelite tastes and ideas in Russian literary society," and this exerted a profound influence on their early artistic sensibility.[9] In his early essay "Colors and Words" ("Kraski i slova") (1905), for example, Blok had taken up the age-old debate of the relative worth of the sister arts of poetry and painting and had expressed a great deal of respect for artists like Paul Gauguin and Dante Rossetti who also wrote. What Blok appreciated in the visual artist and the artistically inclined poet, such as Alexander Pushkin, was the very quality that was so valorized in the European avant-garde: a childlike apprehension of the world. According to Blok,

> Verbal impressions are more alien to children than visual ones. For children it is pleasing to draw everything that they can; and that which is impossible to draw is unnecessary. In children the word is subordinated to drawing; it plays a secondary role.
>
> A tender and bright color preserves for the artist his childlike receptivity; but adult writers "thirstily preserve in their soul the remnants of this feeling." Desiring to conserve their precious time, they have replaced slow drawing with the swift word; but they have become blind and insensitive to visual reception. It is said that there are more words than colors; but, perhaps, for the elegant writer, for the poet, there are only those words that correspond to colors. After all, it is an amazingly variegated, expressive, and harmonious vocabulary. (SS, 5:20-21)

Blok's travels through Italy in the spring of 1909 provided him with the opportunity to expand his own "variegated, expressive, and harmonious vocabulary" and to return to a child-like apprehension of the world. "Very many of my ideas about art have been clarified and confirmed here," he wrote his mother from Italy. "I have come to understand much about painting and have grown to love it no less than poetry thanks to Bellini and Boccaccio Boccaccino, having completely renounced Titian, Tintoretto, Veronese, and their like (with the exception of a few details)" (SS, 8:283). Blok's preference for Bellini and Boccaccio Boccaccino over the painters of the late Renaissance demonstrates the extent to which his own artistic tastes were informed by those of Ruskin and the other Pre-Raphaelites and differentiated him from his friends Gippius and Merezhkovsky, who had journeyed to Italy at the turn of the century.[10] While Merezhkovsky devoted an entire novel to the biography of Leonardo da Vinci, the artist Walter Pater valorized for his decadent sensibility, Blok declared the Renaissance artist to be the embodiment of that very type of demonic sexuality that he attempted to distance himself from.[11] "Leonardo," Blok opined, "and all that is around him (and he left around him an immense field of many degrees of genius far before his birth and after his death) alarms and tortures me and envelops me in 'native chaos' ['rodimyi khaos']. To the same extent, Bellini, around whom there also has remained much, calms and gratifies" (*SS*, 8:289). And at least one of the reasons Blok was drawn to Bellini and other early Renaissance artists was because of their youthful spirit. "Just as in Venice," he wrote his mother from Florence, "here Bellini and Fra Beato occupy the first place not in their strength, but in the freshness and youthfulness of their art [ne po sile, — a po svezhesti i molodosti iskusstva]" (*SS*, 8:286).

Italian Renaissance art with its focus on images of life and rebirth may have offered Blok the symbols of hope and rejuvenation he so desperately needed at this particular time. It may also have afforded him the opportunity to return to images associated with his own birth as a poet. As Petr Pertsov recalls, Blok's poetic debut had been carefully orchestrated on the pages of the *New Path* (*Novyi put'*) in March of 1903 so as to create the image that he was a poet of the Annunciation, a popular theme in Italian Renaissance painting. "March," Pertsov writes, "seemed to be the most natural, even absolutely necessary month for his debut: March — the month of the Annunciation. [...] For March we decided to collect a sort of artistic entourage for Blok's verses and placed on the pages of his verses four 'Annunciations' — the Leonardo from the Uffizi, a detail — the head of Mary from the same picture, a fresco from Beato Angelico in the Florentine monastery of St. Mark, and an icon from a chapel of the Kiev Cathedral by our own Nesterov."[12] And during his two-month long trip through Italy, Blok kept careful notes of his impressions of various aspects of Italian Renaissance art, devoting particular attention in the early days of his trip to a description of Bellini's numerous representations of Madonna and child as well as to the innumerable paintings of the Annunciation by various Renaissance artists. While in Florence he recorded a detailed list of the various pictures of the Annunciation he had viewed, including the one by Leonardo that had accompanied his poems in 1903:

> Bellini (one), Mantegna (two — 1 small). Giorgione (?). Jacopo Bellini — almost an icon — an oversimplification.
> Alessio Baldovinetti (Florentine XV century) — "The Annunciation."
> The monks draw "The Annunciation" of Leonardo . . . But he understood, it seems, that the spirit is black.[13]
> Lorenzo di Credi — looks like Ge.
> Fra Beato (XIV–XV [century]). The birth of John the Baptist. The Mother (in green) with Vania and five girls (friends) (red, dark blue, yellow) has come to the blessed old man for birth reg-

istration. The mother's stomach is still swollen [Zhivot u materi eshche vspukhshii]. The old man records by the wall beneath the blue sky in the cheerful meadow. In the background there is a half-darkened corridor, and beyond it a glimmer of green (that which I wanted Fra Beato in part had intended). The colors, as usual, are childlike, cheerful, and varied.

Nearby (also a little larger)—"The Annunciation" of Credi. NB. In general—Credi.

Garofolo (Benvenuto di Ferrara)—a new "Annunciation"— Maria is a woman, the angel a half-girl prepared for passion. The choirs of angels are above the blue of the mountains.

Giov. Ant. Boltraffio—the infant—a youth (an intelligent imitation of the teacher). Good. (ZK, 137-38)

Although the trip to Italy presented Blok with many images of fecundity and new life, it also provided him with plenty of reminders of the "deathly devastation" he had felt while still in Russia. Images of death and destruction were to be found everywhere in Italy: not only in the Renaissance paintings about Christ's life but also, most notably, in the various graves and tombs that Blok and his wife saw in Ravenna and in various other towns in northern and central Italy. While in Ravenna, Blok wrote to his mother: "I am very glad that [Valery] Briusov sent us here; we saw Dante's grave, ancient sarcophagi, striking mosaics, and Theodoric's estate. In the field beyond Ravenna amidst roses and wisteria is Theodoric's grave. On the opposite side, there is the most ancient church in which they unearthed in our presence a mosaic floor of the 4th-6th century. It smells damp like in railroad tunnels, and there are tombs everywhere" (SS, 8:284).[14] Blok's conflation of Ravenna's tombs with railroad tunnels implicitly connects the city with the tragic plot of *Anna Karenina*, a text that, as I already mentioned, Blok read prior to his Italian trip.[15] And, gradually, these images of death and decay began to occupy an even more prominent place in the poet's writings. If in early May during the beginning of his Italian journey, Blok's notebook entries focused on images of Christ's conception, already by the end of May his entries had become significantly darker, fixating on the various sepulchers and sarcophagi that were so important in both medieval and Renaissance Italy. On 29 May, he records in his notebook a rather lengthy description of the various sarcophagi he saw in Perugia (the entire description takes up two pages in the published version of his notebooks), noting among other things that one of them contains the remains of a child: "On one [sarcophagus] (a *child's*, the guard says), the top is in the form of an inverted lily. On each of the semi-inclined ones, there are two pillows each. On some of the sarcophagi, there is a gryphon clawing a man (like the calf in Perugia)" (ZK, 143).

These sepulchers and sarcophagi and, in particular, the sarcophagus containing the remains of the child, may have reopened old wounds for Blok connected with the death of his wife's child. It is quite telling that after the entry describing this particular sarcophagus, Blok turns increasingly to the subject of child death. For example, less than two weeks later, between June 11 and 12, while at the Marina di Pisa, he records in his notebook how he awoke "in the middle of the night to the noise of the wind and the sea, under the impression of the revived death of Mitia and of Tolstoy, and of some type of distant silence that returned long ago" (ZK, 145). And right before leaving Italy, having abandoned his earlier plans to travel to Rome, the beloved city of Gogol, because of the heat and exhaustion, Blok was again reminded of children and death. In a letter to his mother written from Milan, he proclaims, "More than ever I see that until death I will not accept or submit to anything from contemporary life. Its disgraceful structure only inspires disgust in me. To remake it is already impossible—no revolution will remake it. *All* people will decay; *a few* people will remain. I love only art, children, and death [Liubliu ia tol'ko iskusstvo, detei i smert']. Russia is for me the same lyrical sublimity. In fact, it does not exist, has never existed, and will never exist" (SS, 8:289).

Based on this letter home to his mother, it would appear that the trip to Italy did not erase Blok's bad memories of the previous winter related to both the death of his wife's child and the sorry state of Russia but in fact had reinforced them. However, although Blok admitted to his friend Evgeny Ivanov in a letter from Italy that his "imagination was tired" (voobrazhenie ustalo) (SS, 8:287), the trip to Italy with its emphasis on "art, children, and death" did manage to cure him of his lingering writer's block. The journey furnished him with the raw material not only for his unfinished impressions of Italy, *Lightning Flashes of Art* (*Molnii iskusstva*) (1909), but also for his *Italian Verses* (*Ital'ianksie stikhi*) (1909), a cycle comprising twenty-three poems about northern and central Italian cities and art. Considered to be among the most classical of Blok's poems, *The Italian Verses* have been the subject of a number of fine studies. Several of these works focus on the intricate formal aspects of the poems, while others examine the ways in which the poems transpose aspects of Italian art and architecture into poetry. What is often missing from these fine analyses, however, is a consideration of how these poems function within Blok's feminine creative myth.[16] Not only do many of them focus on various pictorial representations of the Virgin, Madonna, or Madonna and child but many of the poems about Italian cities and towns also depict the city as a woman or as a mother. And, thus, these poems revisit a theme that gained particular poignancy for Blok in the previous winter—motherhood and, most notably, a form of motherhood that is predicated on the eventual loss of the child.

Maternity is not just a prominent theme in many of the poems; it is also central to the way Blok imagined his own role in the composition of the poems. Whereas in March of 1909, the anniversary of Gogol's birth, as well as the month of Annunciation, Blok credited the romantic writer with giving birth to his creative works and to the idea of Russia, in December of that same year, he claimed to have given birth to his poems about Italy, a place he had referred to earlier as the "other motherland." In a letter composed on 29 December 1909 to Sergei Makovsky, editor of the journal *Apollo* (*Apollon*), he defends his poems against the criticism of his editor, proclaiming: "But *now* I cannot force anything *from myself*. That is the fact of the matter. This is the reason for my answer to you—almost the feeling of a young mother [pochti chuvstvo molodoi materi], when she is told that her child has even some minor defects [takie-to, khot' i melkie nedostatki]; almost a physiological disappointment [pochti fiziologicheskaia dosada]: 'Well, it is okay, I know, but regardless he is so beautiful just the way he is, and even singularly beautiful—"as a matter of principle" ["printsipial'no"] I do not need another'" (*SS*, 8:301–2).[17] With this Blok implies that he is no longer physically able to affect the creative process and that the minor infelicities of his poems are essentially generic and genetic, that is to say, they are part of their internal structure. He emphasizes that his relationship with his verse is highly subjective and physiological rather than objective and cerebral. He foregrounds the feminine and physical nature of the creative process through repeated references to the inner and bodily nature of his writing with terms such as *vnutrenne* and *ot sebia*. But in doing so, he experiences no small amount of anxiety. After employing the childbirth metaphor, he admits rather self-deprecatingly, "Well, here 'Rozanovitis' has already begun" (Nu, tut uzhe poshla "Rozanovshchina") (*SS*, 8:302).

Although he attributes his appropriation of the childbirth metaphor to a literary malady he calls Rozanovitis in honor of the writer Vasily Rozanov, Blok would not be unique in his appropriation of the maternal metaphor. This metaphor would appear to be very apt for a poet who would insist on the combined spiritual and bodily nature of the creative process ("world music," he wrote later, "can only be heard with the entire body and spirit together [vsem telom i dukhom vmeste]" [*SS*, 6:102]), but it had been and would continue to be employed by a number male artists in the Russian context whose poetics differed from Blok's. Writers as diverse as Alexander Pushkin, Ivan Turgenev, Innokenty Annensky, and Vladimir Nabokov invoke the maternal metaphor to discuss their relationship to their artistic labor.[18] But as the feminist scholar Susan Stanford Friedman has argued, the mere popularity of the metaphor should not lead us to conclude that it is a dead figure. She insists that

> Contextual reverberations of the childbirth metaphor ensure that it can never be "dead," merely what Max Black calls "an expression that no longer has a pregnant metaphorical use." The childbirth metaphor has always been "pregnant" with resonance because childbirth itself is not neutral in literary discourse. Whether it appears as subject or vehicle of expression, childbirth has never achieved what Roland Barthes calls "writing degree zero," the language of "innocence," "freed from responsibility in relation to all possible context." The context of the childbirth metaphor is the institution of motherhood in the culture at large. Consequently, the meaning of the childbirth metaphor is overdetermined by psychological and ideological resonances evoked by, but independent of, the text. No doubt, there is variation in the intensity and kind of conscious and unconscious charge that any reader or writer brings to the metaphor. But because it relies on an event fundamental to the organization of culture and psyche, the birth metaphor remains "pregnant" with significance.[19]

Friedman's observation that the childbirth metaphor is "overdetermined by psychological and ideological resonances evoked by, but independent of, the text" aptly describes its status vis-à-vis Blok. Though Barbara Johnson and other feminist critics have suggested that it is somewhat more complicated for women than for men to appropriate the maternal metaphor, since it implies a very real tension between poetry and progeny and books and babies, Friedman suggests that, given the ideological and psychological reverberations of motherhood in Western society, it can also be complicated for men to appropriate the metaphor.[20] This is certainly true if we consider the context in which Blok employs the metaphor. Not only does Blok purport to have given birth to his poems in the very midst of the Christmas season but he does so nine and a half months after the birth and subsequent death of his wife's child. And thus Blok perhaps unwittingly enters into a reproductive rivalry with the Virgin Mary as well as his own wife.

Blok certainly had good reasons to associate his own wife with the Virgin. If his wife's conception of a male child out of wedlock may have allowed him to associate her with the Ancestress or with Anna Karenina, these very same facts may have also compelled him to envision her as the Virgin Mary and himself as a Joseph figure. As Marina Warner observes, in Matthew 1:20 "Joseph [. . .] doubts [Mary's] virtue but does not want to shame her by repudiating her publicly. An angel appears to him and reassures him: 'that which is conceived of her is of the Holy Ghost.'"[21] Although the appearance of the angel erases all thoughts of adultery from Joseph's mind, it does not necessarily efface his feelings of impotency. Similar anxieties surrounding female pregnancy abound in the works of male writers. In *Doctor Zhivago* (1957), for instance, Pasternak's fictional poet gives voice to just such feelings as he awaits his second child. "'It has always seemed to me,'" writes Zhivago, "'that every conception is immaculate and that this dogma, concerning the mother of God, expresses the idea of all motherhood. At childbirth, every woman has the same aura of isolation, as though she were abandoned, alone. At this vital moment the man's part is as irrelevant as if he never had anything to do with it, as though the whole thing had dropped from heaven.'"[22] And because of the peculiarity of his own situation, Blok was very much in a position to see himself as an irrelevant Joseph figure. While awaiting his wife's childbirth, he had imagined his wife as the Virgin and himself as a powerless outsider. On 25 January 1909, he recorded in his notebook, "My wife already does not always have the power and the will to rein me in or to get angry at me (it is terrible to record this). Or is that because any day now there will be a Child and she has gone off in meditation about Him?" (*ZK*, 129). Here Blok reinforces the symbolic nature of this event by referring to his wife's child in uppercase letters, as if to imply that this child is analogous to the Christ child and his wife's pregnancy is similar to Mary's. This religious significance is further reinforced by the fact that this child, like the Christ child, was not fated to live long.

Given the symbolic significance he accords to his wife's childbirth, we have to wonder whether Blok's own claims of poetic maternity in the very midst of the Christmas season were fueled more by feelings of impotency than fecundity. Although Blok's delivery of *The Italian Verses* to his editor marks the most overt way in which poetry replaces progeny in his creative myth, a close examination of the cycle itself suggests that Blok's own attempts to reaffirm life and creativity in the wake of the birth and subsequent death of his wife's child were not entirely successful.[23] In spite of the fact that many of the verses treat the themes of birth and rebirth, Blok framed the poems in a fashion that emphasizes the cycle's tomb-like quality. He chose to begin his *Italian Verses* with an epigraph taken from a Latin inscription on the tower of the Church of Santa Maria Novella in Florence and to close the cycle with the epitaph of Fra Filippo Lippi. Although the epigraph comes from a church tower rather than a tomb, it emphasizes man's inability to escape death, which is personified here as a stealthy woman: "So imperceptibly the age destroys many men. So everything existing in the world comes to an end. Alas, alas, time past cannot be called back. Alas, death herself approaches with a silent step" (Sic finit occulte sic multos decipit aetas / Sic venit ad finem quidquid in orbe manet / Heu heu praeteritum non est revocabile tempus / Heu propius tacito mors venit ipsa pede) (*SS*, 3:98). If, as the inscription suggests, death and destruction are inevitable, then the challenge for the artist becomes how to cheat death, how to create in the advent of inescapable perdition.[24]

This had been arguably Blok's main challenge from the outset. He appears to have made peace with the inevitability of death by embracing a form of poetic creation that relied not just on a Christological model of death and resurrection but also on a model of poetic creation rooted in tombs, catacombs, and the earth's underground. In his late essay "The Collapse of Humanism" ("Krushenie gumanizma") (March–April 1919), he would go so far as to declare that artists "can be called living catacombs of culture" (mozhno nazvat' zhivymi katakombami kul'tury) (*SS*, 6:107), and in doing so he identifies the artist not just as a receptacle of world culture but also as a kind of living tomb. Speaking about the *tombeau*, a poetic genre about dead predecessors made famous by Stéphane Mallarmé, Lawrence Lipking states that "the poet, especially, must speak with a double voice. A destroyer and preserver, he cannot be less than the caretaker of language but cannot be less than original and free."[25] Although in this cycle Blok does not dedicate poems to deceased predecessors, he does devote a fair number of poems to the essentially dead cities of medieval and Renaissance Italy—namely, Ravenna, Venice, Florence, and Siena—and it is in these poems, which will be the focus of my analysis here, that Blok is faced with the challenge of speaking with a double voice, of transforming the tomb, the very bowels of the earth, into a source of creativity and even fecundity.

In confronting this challenge, Blok demonstrates yet another affinity with Gogol, the Russian writer who dared to follow in the footsteps of Dante and to enter into the infernal realms of provincial Russia in the first volume of *Dead Souls* (*Mertvye dushi*) (1842). In Blok's understanding, rather than muting his song, Gogol's willingness to enter into the realm of slumber and death actually served as a source of inspiration. "The more unpopulated, the greener the cemetery," he noted in the final paragraph of his famous Gogol essay, "the louder the song of the nightingale in the birch branches above the graves. Everything ends; only music does not die. 'If music abandons us, what will become of our world?,' so asked the 'Ukrainian nightingale,' Gogol. No, music will not forsake us" (*SS*, 5:379). This idea that creativity can come from death, that the tomb can be transformed into the womb, is an old topos in Western culture that is integral to Blok's vision of poetic creation as the release of sounds from the earth. From very early on in his poetic career, Blok had identified the earth as the source of a special power, not only of the creative forces of music but also of the mother. In his 1906 essay "Stagnation" ("Bezvremen'e"), he was quite explicit about the regenerating potential of the earth, even amid the paralysis of the twentieth century. He had urged: "We will put our ear to our dear native soil [prilozhim ukho k rodnoi zemle i blizkoi] [and ask]: Does the heart of the mother still beat?" (*SS*, 5:82). And for Blok what distinguished Italy from other countries in modern Europe was its proximity to this subterranean realm. In his unfinished prose piece about his Italian journey, *Lightning Flashes of Art*, he reinforces the connections between his journey and a descent into the underworld:

> Travel through a country rich in the past and poor in the present is akin to a descent into Dante's Inferno. From the depth of history's naked crevices emerge eternally pale images, and tongues of dark-blue flame burn your face. It is good if you bring along with you in your soul your own Virgil, who says: "Don't fear. At the end of your journey, you will see The One, who sent you." History startles and oppresses.
>
> Italy is tragic in one sense: in the subterranean rustling of its history, which has resounded never to return. In that rustling can clearly be heard the quiet voice of madness, the mumbling of the ancient Sibyls. Life is right when it shuns that whispering. (*SS*, 5:390)

It is in "Ravenna" (May–June 1909), the first poem of the Italian cycle, more so than anywhere else in the cycle, that Blok hears the markedly feminine whisperings of the earth. Here he comes into contact with the subterranean rumblings not of Mother Russia but of the "other motherland," Italy. It is significant that this encounter occurs in the sleepy provincial town of Ravenna, since this city "preserved better than all other cities early art, the transition from Rome to Byzantium" (*SS*, 8:284) and served as the final resting place for Dante Alighieri, who was exiled from his native Florence:

> Всё, что минутно, всё, что бренно,
> Похоронила ты в веках.
> Ты, как младенец, спишь, Равенна,
> У сонной вечности в руках.
>
> Рабы сквозь римские ворота
> Уже не ввозят мозаик.
> И догорает позолота
> В стенах прохладных базилик.
>
> От медленных лобзаний влаги
> Нежнее грубый свод гробниц.
> Где зеленеют саркофаги
> Святых монахов и цариц.
>
> Безмолвны гробовые залы,
> Тенист и хладен их порог,
> Чтоб черный взор блаженной Галлы,
> Проснувшись, камня не прожег.
>
> Военной брани и обиды
> Забыт и стерт кровавый след,
> Чтобы воскресший глас Плакиды
> Не пел страстей протекших лет.
>
> Далёко отступило море,
> И розы оцепили вал.
> Чтоб спящий в гробе Теодорих
> О буре жизни не мечтал.
>
> А виноградные пустыни,
> Дома и люди—всё гроба.
> Лишь медь торжественной латыни
> Поет на плитах, как труба.
>
> Лишь в пристальном и тихом взоре
> Равеннских девушек, порой,
> Печаль о невозвратном море
> Проходит робкой чередой.
>
> Лишь по ночам, склонясь к долинам,
> Ведя векам грядущим счет,
> Тень Данта с профилем орлиным
> О Новой Жизни мне поет.
>
> (*SS*, 3:98–99)

[All that is momentary, all that is perishable, you have buried in the ages. Like an infant, you sleep, Ravenna, in the hands of a drowsy eternity. Slaves no longer haul mosaics through the Roman gates. And the gilding burns out in the walls of the cool basilicas. From the slow kisses of the dampness the coarse vault of the tombs is gentler where the sarcophagi of holy monks and empresses turn green. Silent are the burial halls; shady and cold their thresholds so that the black glance of blessed Galla, having awakened, would not burn through the stone. The bloody trace of military battle and offense is forgotten and erased so that the resurrected voice of Placidia would not sing of passions of years past. The sea has retreated into the distance, and the roses have encircled the rampart so that Theodoric, asleep in his tomb, would not dream of the storm of life. And the vineyard desert, homes, and people—all are tombs. Only the bronze of the solemn Latin sings on the slabs like a trumpet. Only in the fixed and quiet gaze of Ravenna's maidens, at times, does sadness about the irretrievable sea pass by in a timid sequence. Only at night, leaning over the valleys, keeping count of the coming centuries, does Dante's shade with its aquiline profile sing to me of New Life.]

Blok opens this poem about the town of Ravenna, a place he had characterized elsewhere as "a city for rest and a quiet death" (gorod dlia otdykha i tikhoi smerti) (*SS*, 8:294), with an apostrophe. Addressing the town as one would a woman, he states: "All that is momentary, all that is perishable, you have buried in the ages" (Vsë, chto minutno, vse chto brenno, / Pokhoronila ty v vekakh). Here Blok associates Ravenna with an enveloping female space not unlike that which he associates with many of the women in his poems. Yet in spite of the fact that he clearly figures Ravenna as a feminine space that buries everything in the ages, the city does not ultimately emerge in this poem as an all-enveloping tomb or as the suffocating mother figure that we met in Blok's *Ancestress (Pramater')* (1908) and in so many of his early Petersburg poems but rather as a safe maternal space, which does not so much bury as preserve its inhabitants in time. There is a certain etymological connection between the Russian verbs to "to bury" (pokhoronit') and "to preserve" (sokhranit'), a connection that is only reinforced by the imagery evoked in the remaining lines of the stanza.[26] If in the first two lines of the poem, the city emerges as a capacious maternal space, a womb/tomb that preserves/buries everything in its wake, in the second two the city metamorphoses into a small child that slumbers in the hands of eternity, an image that emphasizes new life rather than death and suffocation: "Like an infant, you sleep, Ravenna, in the hands of a drowsy eternity" (Ty, kak mladenets, spish', Ravenna, / U sonnoi vechnosti v rukakh).

The idea that a place might function simultaneously as mother and child and as womb and tomb is not an unusual one within Blok's poetics and is entirely consistent with his general tendency throughout much of his poetry to present the maternal semiotic not only as a fluid relationship between mother and child but also between life and death.[27] While Blok's editor Sergei Makovsky was not at all surprised by the representation of Ravenna as both mother and child, he was upset by the specific manner in which Blok chose to describe this relationship. Years after the poem's first publication, Makovsky felt compelled to correct the poetic "child" that Blok had decidedly allowed to go off into the world in what he considered to be a less than perfect form. "The infant," Makovsky states, "sleeps in the arms [na rukakh] of its mother, not 'in her hands' ['v rukakh']. The entire visual image is incorrect because of this 'blunder' ['oploshnost']."[28] Though visual imagery certainly plays a key role in this poem, as well as in many of the poems of the Italian cycle, Makovsky's insistence that this particular relationship between mother and child must conform to the traditional visual image of the Madonna and child—an insistence motivated perhaps in part by Makovsky's training as art critic—ignores key verbal and rhythmic aspects of the poem, as well as their thematic resonances. In his sensitive reading of the poem, Gerald Pirog suggests that there is an inner logic to Blok's usage of "in the hands" (v rukakh). "The figurative entombment in *both* time and atemporality," Pirog observes, "will effect the sense of the word 'grob' and its cognates throughout the poem by establishing an equivalence among all locative or quasi-locative constructions with *v vekax* and *v rukax večnosti.*"[29]

By depicting Ravenna not only as enveloping everything "in the ages" but also as simultaneously being enveloped "in the hands of eternity" (*"v rukakh"* as opposed to *"na rukakh"* ["in the arms"]), Blok emphasizes that the city is cut off from the rest of the modern world and exists in a time and space all its own. Simultaneously dead and asleep, the city is, if not actually bewitched or *zakoldovannyi,* then at least caught in a catatonic state not unlike that which he had earlier ascribed to Russia. In his 1906 poem "Rus" ("Rus'") he had presented Russia as a sleeping fairy princess, similar to the slumbering Pani Katerina from Gogol's "A Terrible Vengeance" ("Strashnaia mest'") (1832). "You are extraordinary even in dream. I do not touch your garments" (Ty i vo sne neobychaina. / Tvoei odezhdy ne kosnus') (*SS,* 2:106), he noted. And it is not difficult to see in

Blok's vision of Russia as a woman in deathly slumber confirmation of Poe's notion that "the death [. . .] of a beautiful woman is, unquestionably, the most poetical topic in the world."[30] Death becomes Ravenna, just as deathly sleep becomes Russia; it makes her softer, more feminine, and less rapacious. "From the slow kisses of the dampness," he notes, "the coarse vault of the tombs is gentler" (Ot medlennykh lobzanii vlagi / Nezhnee grubyi svod grobnits). In other words, death mitigates the passions that were dominant in Ravenna's history from Roman through Byzantine times. And Blok demonstrates this by burying deep within the poem's central stanzas, stanzas four through six, a description of how death prevents the passions and violence of history from being awakened. Among other things, he notes that the black glance of blessed Galla Placidia will no longer burn through stone, the resurrected voice of this woman will no longer sing of passions of years past, and the Ostrogoth king Theodoric will no longer dream of the storms of life.[31]

For Blok, this compulsion to contain passion and violence, particularly of Ravenna's most famous female inhabitant, Galla Placidia, "sister, spouse, and mother of Roman emperors" and "widow of an Ostrogoth ruler" (SS, 3:527), may in fact be linked to his inability to reconcile female passions with the maternal semiotic that predominates in the first stanzas of the poem. In a letter to Briusov, which he penned in October 1909, after his return home from Italy, Blok conflated the image of Galla Placidia with the portrait of an Egyptian girl he had seen in the Alexandrian room of the archaeological museum in Florence, a girl he had regarded as the epitome of the obverse of the maternal. In his *Lightning Flashes of Art*, he devotes an entire section to the "gaze of the Egyptian girl" (vzgliad egiptianki), noting:

> Her eyes gaze in such a fashion that they triumph over her entire face; they probably triumph over the body and everything around them [pobezhdaiut, veroiatno, i telo i vse okruzhaiushchee]. There is in them complete indifference and stubbornness of aspiration beyond the concepts of modesty, shame, or insolence; the only thing that you can say about those eyes is that they look and will look as they looked in life. To envision them closed, partly closed, or sleepy is not possible; in them there is neither tiredness, nor maternity [ni materinstva], nor joy, nor sadness, nor desire. All that you can see in them is dull insatiable hunger [glukhaia nenasytnaia alchba]; hunger to the grave, and in life and beyond the grave it is all the same. Neither a Roman emperor, nor a barbaric Hyperborean, nor an Olympian god can give to that hunger any approximation of fulfillment. The

eyes gaze just as terribly, blankly, and languorously as the lotus smells. They gaze from one century to the next, from one era to the other.

The eyes are outlined with dark circles. One (the left, as always) is less noticeable than the other. That is the physiological peculiarity of all passionate natures, which comes from constant stress, from a vain craving to find and to see what does not exist in this world [to, chego net na svete]. (SS, 5:399)

While Blok is certainly able to acknowledge the role of passions, and more specifically female passions in the unfolding of history, he clearly feels more comfortable with "the fixed and quiet gaze of Ravenna's maidens" (pristal'nyi i tikhii vzor / Ravennskikh devushek) than with the hungry gaze of the Egyptian girl, who like Gippius's lyric speaker in her early poem "Song" ("Pesnia") (1893), desires "what does not exist in this world." With her passions and desires, the Egyptian girl's double, Galla Placidia, emerges in "Ravenna" as a femme fatale rather than as the placid figure that her name would seem to invoke. And Blok intimates that it is better to let a sleeping Galla Placidia lie. In his poem, all of Ravenna conspires to ensure that she will not awaken: "Silent are the burial halls; shady and cold their thresholds so that the black glance of blessed Galla, having awakened, would not burn through the stone. The bloody trace of military battle and offense is forgotten and erased so that the resurrected voice of Placidia would not sing of passions of years past" (Bezmolvny grobovye zaly, / Tenist i khladen ikh porog, / Chtob chernyi vzor blazhennoi Gally, / Prosnuvshis', kamnia ne prozheg. // Voennoi brani i obidy / Zabyt i stert krovavyi sled, / Chtoby voskresshii glas Plakidy / Ne pel strastei protekshikh let).

Although Blok demonstrates a certain reluctance here to awaken the passions and the song of Galla Placidia, this does not mean that he merely shuts his ears to the sounds of history. Elsewhere he insists that "contemporary culture listens to the voice of the ore deep in the bowels of the earth [golos rudy v glubokikh zemnykh nedrakh]" (SS, 5:391).[32] And Ravenna, a city that he tacitly identified with the underground realm of the railroad, certainly provided him with the opportunity to listen to the underground rustling of history, rustling that for him constituted the raw material of poetry. In one of his final essays, "On the Calling of the Poet" ("O naznachenii poeta") (10 February 1921), he notes that "the poet is the son of harmony; and he is given some kind of role in world culture. Three tasks are entrusted to him: first, to free sounds from the native inchoate elements in which they reside; second, to bring those sounds into harmony, to give them form; third, to transport that harmony into the external world" (SS, 6:162). And Blok clearly succeeds at this in "Ravenna." Here he descends into the subterranean realm of Ravenna, into mother earth, and from this deathly maternal realm he manages to bring out not so much "the resurrected voice of Placidia" (voskresshii glas Plakidy) as the fully formed artistic sounds of the earth. Amid destruction, he is able to hear and give voice to that which others may not hear, the sounds of harmony and art. As he puts it: "And the vineyard desert, homes, and people—all are tombs. Only the bronze of the solemn Latin sings on the slabs like a trumpet" (A vinogradnye pustyni, / Doma i liudi—vsë groba. / Lish' med' torzhestvennoi latyni / Poet na plitakh, kak truba).

The poet's relationship with the subterranean sounds of Ravenna resembles not only the son's relationship with the mother but also in a sense the relationship between a midwife and laboring woman. This is something that is poignantly realized in the poem's ninth and final stanza, where Blok resurrects the image and the song of Ravenna's most famous adopted son, Dante Alighieri. Among the images of death and destruction, Blok notes: "Only at night, leaning over the valleys, keeping count of the coming centuries, does Dante's shade with its aquiline profile sing to me of New Life" (Lish' po nocham, sklonias' k dolinam, / Vedia vekam griadushchim schet, / Ten' Danta s profilem orlinym / O Novoi Zhizni mne poet). And by summoning the shade of Dante from the depths of Ravenna, Blok also heralds the birth of the self in this poem. As Lucy Vogel has observed, "it is at this point, when Blok and Dante meet face to face, so to speak, that the reader becomes aware of the identity of the persona in the poem and recognizes one of the stances often assumed by the poet himself—that of the prophet of a new era."[33] The fact that both Dante and his double, the poetic persona, emerge in the poem's ninth and final stanza is not without significance. That the two poetic sons, Dante and Blok, appear side by side in the poem's ninth stanza not only recalls the transformative power of the number for Dante but also reinforces the childbirth imagery invoked in the poem's first stanza, with the nine stanzas perhaps corresponding to the nine months of gestation.[34] In other words, Blok does not just hear the words of Dante's *La Vita Nuova*, but he comes into being at this stage in the poem, and this process of poetic self-creation is the direct result of his engagement with the rhythms and sounds of mother earth.

Blok's symbolic birth in this poem would appear to be intimately connected to his own desire to see himself as child. In his important essay "On the Present State of Russian Symbolism" ("O sovremennom sostoianii russkogo simvolizma") (March–April 1910), which he wrote not long after completing the poems for the Italian cycle, he urged his contemporaries to remember that they contained within themselves the potential for the renewal and the rebirth of their childlike selves.[35] He implores them: "We have lived through the madness of other worlds, prematurely requiring a miracle; the same, you see, occurred with the people's soul [narodnaia dusha]: it prematurely demanded a miracle, and its lilac revolutions turned it into ashes." He continues: "There is something indestructible in the soul—there where it is an infant. In one place in the funeral service for infants, the deacon stops pleading, and says simply: 'You gave a *true promise* that *blessed infants* would be in Your Kingdom' ([E]st' neistrebimoe v dushe—tam, gde ona mladenets. V odnom meste panikhidy o mladentsakh d'iakon perestaet prosit', no govorit prosto: "Ty dal *nelozhnoe obetovanie,* chto *blazhennye mladentsy* budut v Tsartsvii Tvoem") (SS, 5:435).[36] If ever Blok would appear to confirm this truth, it would be in his *Italian Verses.* Though Blok often identifies with the position of child in his poems, it is in the *Italian Verses,* and in the cycle's city poems in particular, that Blok reinforces the childlike status of his poetic speaker. Here he not only envisions the subterranean realms of the city of Ravenna as a womb-like space from which the poet can emerge like a newborn child but he also imagines Italy, the land of the Renaissance, as a place where the poet can experience his own reincarnation.

This would not be the first time he expressed fascination with the idea of reincarnation or Nietzschean self-begetting. In one of his notebook entries dating from 1906, he opines, "More and more often with me there is physical exhaustion. Probably it is the same as with pregnant women [u beremennykh zhenshchin]: the curse for carrying the foetus [prokliatie za noshenie ploda]; for me it is the curse of rebirth [pererozhdenie]. It is impossible to call upon Dionysus in vain—in this is the entire appeal of Bacchus in the words of V[iacheslav] Ivanov. If I am not transformed [preobrazhus'], then I shall die in languor" (ZK, 84). But it can be argued that he fulfills this promise of transformation most fully in the wake of his wife's childbirth. Most notably, in the three poems about Venice in his Italian cycle, he imagines the self first as a Christ figure, then as John the Baptist, and finally as an unborn child. That Blok should envision the watery city of Venice as a site of transformation is by no means unusual given the importance of Venice in the Russian cultural imagination, particularly for Petersburg poets. St. Petersburg with its canals and the architecture of Bartolomeo Francesco Rastrelli had frequently been imagined as the northern Venice, a point that was not lost on Blok. In a letter to Briusov, Blok noted, "Venice is situated in a special place, almost outside of Italy; one can love her like Petersburg; Venice relates to Italy as Petersburg does to Russia" (*SS*, 8:293). Based on his correspondence, it would appear Blok had certainly experienced his arrival in Venice as a spiritual homecoming. "I reside in Venice," he wrote his mother, "already completely as if in my own city; and almost all the customs, galleries, churches, the sea, the canals are my own, as if I have been here for a very long time. Our rooms look out onto the sea, which is visible through the flowers on the windows. If you look from the Lido, the entire north is edged with snowy heights, a portion of which we traversed. The water is completely green. This is all familiar from books, but it is very new; however, the novelty is not shocking, but calming and refreshing" (*SS*, 8:283).[37]

Although Blok speaks of the soothing qualities of Venice in the letter home to his mother, he depicts the act of reincarnation within the Venice poems themselves as anything but calm and reassuring, thereby acknowledging that childbirth, that initial cleavage between mother and child, is fraught with tension and violence. In the first Venice poem (9 May 1909), he depicts his relationship with the city not as a homecoming but as a painful leave-taking that appears to coincide with his poetic speaker's death:

> С ней уходил я в море,
> С ней покидал я берег,
> С нею я был далёко,
> С нею забыл я близких . . .
>
> О, красный парус
> В зеленой да́ли!
> Черный стеклярус
> На темной шали!
>
> Идет от сумрачной обедни,
> Нет в сердце крови . . .
> Христос, уставший крест нести . . .
>
> Адриатической любови—
> Моей последней—
> Прости, прости!
>
> (*SS*, 3:102)

[With her I went away into the sea, with her I abandoned the shore, with her I was far away, with her I forgot those close to me . . . Oh, red sail in the green distance! Black glass beads on a dark shawl. Walking from the gloomy Mass with a bloodless heart . . . Christ, exhausted from carrying his cross . . . To my Adriatic love—my final one—farewell, farewell!]

In a departure from the maternal city-poem "Ravenna," Blok opens this impressionistic poem not with a direct address to the city but with a song of the city. In the poem's first stanza, which recalls an Italian song or canzone, Blok seems to conflate Venice with a seductress who forces him to forsake the shore and his loved ones.[38] Blok's poetic speaker states: "With her I went away into the sea, with her I abandoned the shore, with her I was far away, with her I forgot those close to me . . ." (S nei ukhodil ia v more, / S nei pokidal ia bereg, / S neiu ia byl dalëko, / S neiu zabyl ia blizkikh . . .). What is significant here is not just the fact that the lyric speaker is swept away by his Venetian love but also the manner in which he is swept away—she exercises power over him, something that is reinforced by the repeated use of the anaphora "with her." Still, although she exerts control over the poetic speaker, this does not apparently prevent him from revering Venice. In fact, in the following stanza, which differs markedly from the first in structure, the poetic speaker addresses some of the city's major charms: "Oh, red sail in the green distance! Black glass beads on a dark shawl" (O, krasnyi parus / V zelenoi dáli! / Chernyi stekliarus / Na temnoi shali). Through the reference to contrasting colors, the black beads, and the dark shawl, Venice emerges here as a femme fatale who bears a striking resemblance to the gypsy Carmen that Blok would immortalize in the 1914 *Carmen* (*Karmen*) cycle. But unlike Carmen, Venice is portrayed here not as a passionate woman who is doomed to die at the hands of her jilted lover but rather as a passionate woman who is fated to witness the death or departure of her beloved.

While it has become somewhat of a commonplace to speak of death in Venice, Blok appears to associate the city not just with death but also, as the reference to the city's black beads and dark shawl intimate, with mourning. If the theme of mourning is merely hinted at in the second stanza through the reference to black attire, then it is more fully developed in the third stanza, where Blok rather elliptically refers to someone who "walks from the gloomy Mass with a bloodless heart" (Idet ot sumrachnoi obedni, / Net v serdtse krovi.) While it is not entirely clear who departs from the evening mass, since Blok has chosen not to include the third-person pronoun, he does appear to associate Venice in a more general way with mourning through the reference to the bloodless heart of the churchgoer.³⁹ In fact, this image of the bloodless heart paves the way for the appearance of "Christ, exhausted from carrying his cross" (Khristos, ustavshii krest nesti) in the final line of this stanza. Vogel has perceptively noted that "here once again Blok chose to reveal his own forlorn and dejected state by identifying himself with Christ."⁴⁰ And Avril Pyman has suggested that the figure of Christ here "seems to beg association with the poet-Christ 'carefully' bearing His cross in the love poem of the previous autumn: 'Rossíya.'"⁴¹ Certainly, Blok does seem to repeat an eroticized scene of martyrdom that he had played out earlier on native soil. However, if in the earlier poem, Russia, epitomized by an unfaithful peasant woman, was responsible for the poet's martyrdom, then in this poem Venice appears to be at least partly the cause of the poet's suffering. Venice does not simply sweep the poetic speaker away; she is the death of him. And in the last stanza, the dying poetic speaker bids Venice a final farewell: "To my Adriatic love—my final one—farewell, farewell!" (Adriaticheskoi liubovi— / Moei poslednei— / Prosti, prosti!). Significantly, the expression that the poet employs to express his leave-taking is not *proshchai* but *prosti*, a word that connotes a final farewell and request for forgiveness before death.

The poet's relationship with the city is no less complicated in the second Venice poem (August 1909), where he envisions himself this time not as a Christ figure, but as Christ's precursor, John the Baptist, who becomes the victim of Herod's daughter Salome. Venice, the southern obverse of the poet's native St. Petersburg, is transformed into a site where Blok can imagine the biblical narrative of history as unfolding in reverse order. And as in the earlier Venice poem, the action takes place at the water's edge:

> Холодный ветер от лагуны.
> Гондол безмолвные гроба.
> Я в эту ночь—больной и юный—
> Простерт у львиного столба.
>
> На башне, с песнию чугунной,
> Гиганты бьют полночный час.
> Марк утопил в лагуне лунной
> Узорный свой иконостас.
>
> В тени дворцовой галлереи
> Чуть озаренная луной,
> Таясь, проходит Саломея
> С моей кровавой головой.

> Всё спит—дворцы, каналы, люди,
> Лишь призрака скользящий шаг,
> Лишь голова на черном блюде
> Глядит с тоской в окрестный мрак.
> (*SS*, 3:102–3)

[Cold wind from the lagoon. Silent coffins of gondolas. This night I—ill and young—am prostrate by the lion's pillar. On the tower the giants beat out the midnight hour with an iron song. Mark has drowned his intricate iconostasis in the moonlit lagoon. In the shadow of the palace gallery, barely illuminated by the moon, stealthily Salome walks by with my bloody head. Everything is asleep—palaces, canals, people. Only the gliding step of the specter, only the head on the black plate looks with anguish into the surrounding darkness.]

Here the poet's fatal encounter with Salome à la John the Baptist occurs in a hallucination he has at the bewitching hour of midnight. Ill and prostrate by the lion's column in St. Mark's Square, a square that, as Pirog has observed, had traditionally served as a place of execution, the lyric speaker gradually imagines the city of Venice with its lagoon, clock tower, and square as an ominous nocturnal landscape filled with images of death and destruction.[42] The gondolas abandoned in the lagoon for the night become floating coffins; the two figures on the clock tower in St. Mark's Square become giants who beat out the midnight hour; and St. Mark's Square becomes a man named Mark who drowns the city's portals in the depths of the moonlit lagoon. The poet's oneiric transformation of the city of Venice into a site of death sets the stage for the emergence of the image of Salome with the poet's head on a charger from her actual place on the mosaic lunettes of the baptistery of St. Mark's Basilica into the palace gallery: "In the shadow of the palace gallery, barely illuminated by the moon, stealthily Salome walks by with my bloodied head" (V teni dvortsovoi gallerei, / Chut' ozarennaia lunoi, / Taiais', prokhodit Salomeia / S moei krovavoi golovoi).[43] Like the floating coffins, giants, and torturer Mark, which set the scene for Salome's quasi-theatrical appearance, we must assume that the figure of Salome does not actually exist but is rather a figment of the speaker's diseased imagination. In his sickly state, he mistakes the shadows in the palace gallery for the elusive figure of Salome and the full moon against the black sky for his own severed head on a black charger.

By focusing on Salome's spectral quality in this poem, Blok differs considerably from other modernist writers in his presentation of this biblical figure. In sharp contrast to Gustave Flaubert, Gustave Moreau, Joris-Karl Huysmans, Stéphane Mallarmé, and Oscar Wilde, Blok does not dwell here on the unveiling of Salome's body as she performs the dance of seven veils for Herod in exchange for John the Baptist's head. Having decided to discard an earlier stanza that presents her as a "dancer in a transparent tunic" (pliasun'ia v tunike prozrachnoi) (SS, 3:530), he instead refers only to "the gliding step of the specter" (prizraka skol'ziashchii shag).[44] In so doing, he de-eroticizes and disembodies the modernist Salome, foregrounding her shade-like quality and her closeness to death, which is personified as a stealthy woman in the cycle's epigraph.[45] But if Blok's gliding spectral Salome has little kinship with the full-bodied dancing Salome of the European modernists, she does bear a striking likeness to the specter of the Ancestress that had haunted Blok throughout the previous year.[46] As in Blok's translation of Grillparzer's *Die Ahnfrau* and some of his earlier Petersburg poems, the emergence of this spectral female figure in the poem coincides with the male figure's loss of agency and eventual death. Whereas in the first stanza, the poet, though ill, still has the strength to utter the first person pronoun "I" ("This night I—ill and young—am prostrate by the lion's pillar" [Ia v etu noch'—bol'noi i iunyi— / Prostert u l'vinogo stolba]), once the figure of Salome emerges from the shadows of the gallery onto the stage-like space of St. Mark's Square, the speaker's power is significantly reduced, the "I" of the speaker becoming a mere pronoun ("my bloody head" [moia krovavaia golova]). By the final stanza, once Salome's ghastly status is fully revealed (it is here that she is called a specter or *prizrak*), even this trace of the poet's subjectivity disappears, as "[his] bloodied head" is severed from him grammatically through erasure of the personal pronoun: "Only the head on the black plate looks with anguish into the surrounding darkness" (Lish' golova na chernom bliude / Gliadit s toskoi v okrestnyi mrak). It bears noting, though, that the poet's loss of his head—and the scattering of his "I"—does not prelude his power to speak. Similar to the poet Orpheus, who continues singing his mournful songs even as his severed head floats down the River Hebrus, Blok's poetic speaker is able to continue his poem about the Venetian Salome, even after his own imagined beheading.[47] Salome may be a deathly shade, but she is still the poet's muse, and it is of her that he is compelled to sing.

This was by no means the first time that Blok had expressed interest in the femme fatale Salome. In October 1906, Blok had discussed the related figure of Herodias in his essay "Poetry of Charms and

Incantations" ("Poeziia zagovorov i zaklinanii"). Typically understood to be the wife of Herod and the mother of Salome, Herodias was often conflated with her daughter by the modernists. Stéphane Mallarmé, for example, entitled his dramatic poem about Salome *Herodias* (*Hérodiade*) allegedly "in order to differentiate her from the Salome [he would] call modern or exhumed, with her archaic *fait-divers*."[48] In his initial discussion of Herodias in his 1906 essay, Blok attributed to her the ability to dance, the activity most frequently associated with Salome by European modernists.[49] He also implicitly associated her dance with illness, thereby playing off long-standing cultural associations of dance with illness.[50] "Herodias," he notes, "is a dancer, an evil wife [plasun'ia—zlaia zhena]. In medieval miniatures, she is represented dancing and gyrating at Herod's feast, like a wandering minstrel [skomorokh]. According to Ukrainian belief, a diabolic poison grew from the corpse of Heriodias—shag tobacco [tabak tiutiun]. The fever-shaker [likhoradka-triasavitsa], which forces a person to contort and shake, was linked with the frenzied dance of Herodias; according to Catholic belief, Herodias had several dancing daughters; according to old Bulgarian [belief] (the Bogomil priest Hermes) and Russian belief, the shakers [triasavtsy] were Herod's daughters" (*SS*, 5:64).

While Blok's initial fascination with the "dancer, an evil wife" may have been sparked by feelings of helplessness in the face of his wife's own inconstancy (an inconstancy that, as we have seen, he simultaneously encouraged and resented), his decision to take up the subject of Herodias's deathly daughter, Salome, seems to have been influenced by theatrical performances of the Salome story in Petersburg in the previous fall as well as by representations of Salome he saw in Venice and other cities while on vacation in Italy.[51] During the fall of 1908, there were several unsuccessful attempts to stage productions of the story both by Ida Rubinstein and Nikolai Evreinov.[52] On 27 October 1908, Blok was present at the dress rehearsal of Evreinov's production of the story, in which his lover Natalia Volokhova played the title role. For Blok, then, the theme of Salome was not just connected to the trip to Italy, which he and his wife took following the birth of her child, but also coincided with the time in Petersburg in which he was awaiting the birth of his wife's child. Taken in this context, Blok's implicit identification with the John the Baptist in his Venice poem may be connected to feelings of insecurity and even impotency he might have experienced in the face of his own wife's childbirth.

Blok presents his poetic ego in this poem not just as beheaded or figuratively castrated but also as young and ailing, a fact that can give rise to speculation that this poem, like the "pathological nightmare" of the previous year, discussed in chapter 2, gives expressions to fears that his impotency was connected to illness. The source of the poet's hallucinations—his deadly muse—would appear to be the spectral Salome, the daughter of Herodias whose frenzied dance is linked with the "fevershaker [likhoradka-triasavitsa], which forces a person to contort and shake." Salome may not be presented as dancing in this final version of this poem, but the illness associated with her fatal dance has perhaps already infected the poetic speaker. The connections among illness, Salome, the beheading of John the Baptist, and song are somewhat tenuous in this poem, but Blok would intertwine them more explicitly in "Neither Dreams nor Reality" ("Ni sny, ni iav'") (19 March 1921), which he worked on quite extensively in March 1909.[53] In this essay, which opens with a description of singing peasants who spread syphilis throughout the neighboring villages, Blok implicitly identifies with a tired soul who is at once Christ, attended by the fallen woman Mary Magdalene, and a headless John the Baptist, who has fallen prey to Salome:

> The tired soul took a seat at the threshold of the grave. Again it is summer, again the almond is blooming on the steep slopes. Mary Magdalene walks by with a vessel, Peter with keys; Salome carries a head on a platter; her lilac and gold dress is so wide and heavy that she must throw it back with her foot.
> —My soul, where is your body?
> —My body continues to roam the land, trying not to lose its soul, having lost it already long ago. (SS, 6, 171)

Because of the way in which Blok frames this dream sequence with the mention of the introduction of syphilis into the countryside, we have to wonder whether for Blok the John the Baptist theme is not tied up with feelings of impotency caused by either the presence of or fear of the contagious disease. If this is the case, then the second Venice poem would appear to be doubly anxious: not only does it possibly point to the poet's feelings of impotency in the wake of his wife's pregnancy but it links this powerlessness to the deathly daughter of Herodias, a fatal woman whose erotic dance, though not represented in the final version of Blok's Venetian poem, may be the cause of the poet's fever. And, thus, once again, Blok's poetic alter ego comes out the loser as a result of his encounter with the all-powerful feminine figure, one who has the power of creation and destruction.

Blok was not the only male modernist to express fascination with the story of Salome and John the Baptist after the birth of a child. Mallarmé actually conceived the idea for his work about Salome after his wife gave birth to their first child, Geneviève, in 1864. And the proximity of these two births—poetic and real—was to be the source of significant creative anxiety for the French poet. In "Gift of the Poem" ("Don du poème") (1883), which he completed in 1865 shortly after his daughter's birth, Mallarmé pits his newly conceived poem *Herodias* against his wife's baby girl. "I bring you the child of an Idumaean night, / Black, and with featherless wings bled white" (Je t'apporte l'enfant d'une nuit d'Idumée! / Noire, à l'aile saignante et pâle, déplumée), he writes, tacitly referring to the girl child Herodias, which he conceived shortly after the birth of his daughter. Halfway through this poem about the process of poetic creation, though, his lyric speaker cries out in utter despondency: "O mother cradling your infant daughter, / Welcome the birth of this untimely monster" (Ô la berceuse, avec ta fille et l'innocence / De vos pieds froids, accueille une horrible naissance).[54] In referring to his poem as an untimely monster, Mallarmé reveals his own feelings of impotency and helplessness in the wake of his wife's pregnancy. Judging from the persistence of his writer's block, it would appear that he never recuperated from the sense of helplessness. The French symbolist would spend the next twenty years trying to finish his work about Salome.

Though Blok, at times, found himself unable to bring specific projects to completion (such as his long narrative poem *Retribution* (*Vozmezdie*), which I take up in the next chapter), he was as a rule exempt from the type of writer's block that Mallarmé (and Flaubert, another admirer of Salome) famously suffered from. In contradistinction to Mallarmé, Blok was able not only to bring his Salome poem to fruition but also to imagine himself transcending his role as Salome's victim. After portraying himself as an ailing and headless John the Baptist in the second Venice poem, he is capable, if only for a brief instant, of imagining his future rebirth in the third and final Venice poem (26 August 1909):

> Слабеет жизни гул упорный.
> Уходит вспять прилив забот.
> И некий ветер сквозь бархат черный
> О жизни будущей поет.
>
> Очнусь ли я в другой отчизне,
> Не в этой сумрачной стране?
> И памятью об этой жизни
> Вздохну ль когда-нибудь во сне?

Кто даст мне жизнь? Потомок дожа,
Купец, рыбак, иль иерей
В грядущем мраке делит ложе
С грядущей матерью моей?

Быть может, венецейской девы
Канцоной нежной слух пленя,
Отец грядущий сквозь напевы
Уже предчувствует меня?

И неужель в грядущем веке
Младенцу мне—велит судьба
Впервые дрогнувшие веки
Открыть у львиного столба?

Мать, что́ поют глухие струны?
Уж ты мечтаешь, может быть,
Меня от ветра, от лагуны
Священной шалью оградить?

Нет! Всё, что есть, что было,—живо!
Мечты, виденья, думы—прочь!
Волна возвратного прилива
Бросает в бархатную ночь!
  (SS, 3:103–4)

[The stubborn hum of life weakens. The tide of worries recedes. And through the black velvet some kind of wind sings of a future life. Will I awaken in another homeland, not in this gloomy country? And will I ever in a dream breathe in the memory of this life? Who will give me life? Will the descendent of a doge, a merchant, fisherman, or priest in the future darkness share a bed with my future mother? Perhaps my future father, having captivated the ear of a Venetian girl with the sound of his tender canzone, already has a premonition of me through the tunes? And in the future century will fate command me, the infant, for the first time to open my trembling eyelids near the lion's pillar? Mother, what do the muffled strings sing? Do you perhaps dream of protecting me from the wind, from the lagoon, with your sacred shawl? No! Everything that is, that was—exists! Dreams, apparitions, thoughts—be gone! The wave of the returning tide throws [them] into the velvety night!]

In sharp contrast to the earlier Venice poems, Blok presents the city here not as a site of loss and leave-taking or a place of death and sacrifice but as a place of sanctuary and of rebirth. The tides of Venice do not sweep the poetic speaker away to distant lands, far from friends and kin, but instead wash away his cares. "The stubborn hum of life weakens," writes Blok, and "the tide of worries recedes" (Slabeet zhizni gul upornyi / Ukhodit vspiat' priliv zabot). Whereas Venice was previously associated with "black glass beads on a dark shawl" (Chernyi stekliaris / Na temnoi shali), the typical attire of not just a woman in mourning but also the femme fatale, she is now presented as much softer and more maternal. The "cold wind" (kholodny veter), which presaged the poet's death at the hand of Venice-Salome in the second Venice poem, metamorphoses in this poem into the velvety night air that foretells of the speaker's rebirth and of Venice's newfound maternal role: "And through the black velvet some kind of wind sings of a future life" (I nekii vetr skvoz' barkhat chernyi / O zhizni budushchei mne poet). The waters and winds of Venice, long associated in the modernist consciousness with death and degeneration, are transformed into life-giving forces in this poem. And Venice, often considered by Russian poets as the southern European double of St. Petersburg, becomes a site for the poet's imagined rebirth, outside of the confines of the Russian empire. That Blok should envision the Venetian lagoon as a site of rebirth is perfectly in keeping with certain poetic representations of birth. Speaking about the origins of poets, Harold Bloom notes, "the Incarnation of the Poetic character, if an inland matter, takes place near caverns and rivulets, replete with mingled measures and soft murmurs, promises of an improved infancy when one hears the sea again."[55] Venice with its ebbs and tides not only evokes the sounds of the poet's native Petersburg but also seems to mimic the sounds of the amniotic fluids inside of the womb, and therefore, this poem, much like the earlier poem "Ravenna," suggests the enclosed feminine space of maternity. And like "Ravenna," this poem speaks of new life. But whereas "Ravenna" reinforces the potential of new life, this poem immediately begins to question the efficacy of the promise of new life. The poet insists on asking not only where he will be reborn but whether he will be born again at all: "Will I awaken in another homeland, not in this gloomy country? And will I ever in a dream breathe in the memory of this life?" (Ochnus' li ia v drugoi otchizne, / Ne v etoi sumrachnoi strane? / I pamiat'iu ob etoi zhizni / Vzdokhnu l' kogda-nibud' vo sne?).

The poet's skepticism about the possibility of his own rebirth gives way to concerns about his own origins, as the central stanzas of the poem are transformed into a kind of primal scene.[56] Here he does not imagine how he was conceived, as in the classic case of the primal scene, but rather how he will be conceived, thus marking the potential, if we see this poem in terms of the religious symbolism of the earlier poems, of a second coming. Blok makes explicit in these central stanzas what was more concealed in his earlier translation of *Die Ahnfrau*: a fascination with his origins and more specifically with the nature of the primal scene itself. But whereas in his translation of *Die Ahnfrau*, as in the German original, the primal scene was repressed, taking place offstage prior to the unfolding of the dramatic sequence, in this poem, the foretelling of the primal scene, of the story of the poet's own conception, occupies center stage. It bears noting, however, that this proleptic vision of the poet's reconception and rebirth remains shrouded in mystery. In envisioning his own rebirth in Venice, the poet longs to know not just whether he will be reborn but who will be his father. And thus this poem about Venice can be said to circle around problems that might have bothered a poet whose own childhood was disrupted by divorce and characterized by the absence of a strong paternal figure in the home.[57]

It has often been stated that the issue of paternity is inherently more vexing than that of maternity, because of the very nature of human reproduction. The act of giving birth itself can confirm the identity of the mother, but it does not elucidate the identity of the father. And this is a poem that clearly revolves around issues not only of legitimacy but also of origins and more specifically the identity of the father. But perhaps equally as vexing to the poetic speaker as the identity of his future father is the nature of his future mother: Will she fulfill her promise of protecting and preserving her child from the elements, like the Mother of God, or will she forsake him? In the poem's penultimate stanza, Blok seems to suggest that she will fulfill this promise in asking: "Do you perhaps dream of protecting me from the wind, from the lagoon, with your sacred shawl?" (Uzh ty mechtaesh', mozhet byt', / Menia ot vetra, ot laguny / Sviashchennoi shal'iu ogradit'?). This image of Venice as a comforting, maternal site bearing a shawl or veil reminiscent of the protective veil of the Virgin is, however, abruptly broken in the poem's final stanza, which resounds with a stark "no." The dream of new life, articulated in the previous stanzas, is abruptly shattered or, more accurately, swept away in this final stanza: "No! Everything that is, that was—exists! Dreams, apparitions, thoughts—be gone! The wave of the returning tide throws [them] into the velvety night!" (Net! Vsë, chto est', chto bylo—zhivo! / Mechty, viden'ia, dumy—proch'! / Volna vozvratnogo priliva / Brosaet v barkhatnuiu noch'!).

Venice, then, ultimately refuses to make complete the metamorphosis from a femme fatale to a mother figure, from the femme fatale with the dark shawl to the *Mat'- Pokrov*, and the speaker fails to enact the rebirth he so desperately longs for in the poem. It is possible to read in this poem and, indeed, in many of the other city poems of the Italian cycle, an attempt on Blok's part to work through not only his own relationship with his mother, with whom he had traveled to Italy as a young boy, but even more importantly his relationship with his wife, who had recently and all too briefly been a mother herself. It would appear that Blok remained intensely resentful of Liuba's seeming indifference to maternity; that he should might seem unusual given his own complicated relationship to childbearing. Soon after his arrival home from Italy, he penned a rather strange sketch of an unidentified woman in his notebooks. He reminisces: "When I fell in love with those eyes, motherhood [materinstvo] flickered in them—some type of dampness, incomprehensible submission. But it all was an illusion. Probably even Cleopatra was able to reflect motherhood [umela otrazit' materinstvo] in the apathetic sea of her eyes" (ZK, 159). Though it remains unclear whether he is talking about his wife or another woman, one thing is clear here: the woman he describes has betrayed what he sees as her maternal role.

Not surprisingly, the image of the neglectful mother or inimical female figure appears frequently in *The Italian Verses*. Not only does Blok identify Galla Placidia with a penetrating gaze that defies maternity in "Ravenna," the poem that is most overtly about the maternal semiotic, but he accuses many of the cities, all of which bear feminine names in both Russian and Italian, of being unfaithful. In the first poem, "Florence" ("Florentsiia") (May–June 1909), for example, he depicts Florence, the home city-state of Dante, not as an enveloping maternal figure but as a female Judas who casts out her most famous native son. There is enmity in his heart and perhaps a desire to enact revenge for Dante's poor treatment when he states: "Die, Florence, Judas, disappear into the eternal darkness! In the hour of love I will forget you; in the hour of death I will not be with you!" (Umri, Florentsiia, Iuda, / Ischezni v sumrak vekovoi! / Ia v chas liubvi tebia zabudu, / V chas smerti budu ne s toboi!) (SS, 3:106). And in the poem's second stanza, he envisions her as a woman who has lost her first bloom of beauty: "Oh, Bella, laugh at yourself, you are no longer beautiful! Your features are distorted by a rotten sepulchral wrinkle" (O, Bella, smeisia nad soboiu, / Uzh ne prekrasna bol'she ty! / Gniloi morshchinoi grobovoiu / Iskazheny tvoi cherty!) (SS, 3:106). By figuring Florence as covered in rotten grave-like wrinkles, he presents her as the antithesis of Ravenna, the womb-like tomb, which serves as Dante's final resting place. In his opinion, Florence has let herself become a victim of European decay: "Your automobiles wheeze, your houses are monstrous, you have surrendered yourself to pan-European yellow dust" (Khripiat tvoi avtomobili, / Tvoi urodlivy doma, / Vseevropeiskoi zheltoi pyli / Ty predala sebia sama!) (SS, 3:106). Because of her willingness to give herself over to modernity and more specifically to commerce, Florence is doomed to eternal death. As he puts it: "You alarm the magnificent Medicis, you stomp on your lilies, but you cannot resurrect yourself in the dust of the mercantile crush!" (Ty pyshnykh Médichei trevozhish', / Ty topchesh' lilii svoi, / No voskresit' sebia ne mozhesh' / V pyli torgovoi tolchei!) (SS, 3:106).[58] Florence does emerge in a slightly more positive light in the subsequent Florentine poems where he envisions the city as a "tender iris" (iris nezhnyi) (SS, 3:107); nevertheless, inherent in Blok's depiction of Florence is a high degree of ambivalence.

Blok's lyrical journeys throughout Italy, the "other motherland," take on great symbolic significance for the poet: they reflect on his complicated relationship to Mother Russia in the difficult period following 1905, as well as to the figure of the mother, a figure who we know for Blok could represent both coddling and suffocation. Time and again, Blok presents the cities of Italy as being somewhat empty and even tomb-like spaces that are anything but inviting either to the poetic speaker or to the child of the poem, figures who are often tacitly conflated in the cycle. And perhaps one of the most ambivalent poems of the entire cycle is "Siena" (7 June 1909), the one poem of the cycle where he associates the city with a church. Though the church is traditionally figured as a maternal space (hence the popularity of churches named in honor of the Mother of God), the Gothic church in this poem is presented as the very antithesis of the enclosed feminine space we would normally associate with the maternal:

В лоне площади пологой
Пробивается трава.
Месяц острый, круторогий,
Башни—свечи божества.

О, лукавая Сиена,
Вся—колчан упругих стрел!
Вероломство и измена—
Твой таинственный удел!

От соседних лоз и пашен
Оградясь со всех сторон,

> Острия церквей и башен
> Ты вонзила в небосклон!
> (*SS*, 3:113)

[In the lap of the gently sloping square, the grass breaks through. The moon is a sharp crescent; the towers are candles of divinity. Oh, cunning Siena, all of you is a quiver of taut arrows! Treachery and infidelity are your mysterious destiny! Walled off on all sides from neighboring vines and fields, you thrust the spikes of your churches and towers into the firmament!]

Blok presents the Gothic city of Siena in highly phallic terms, reminiscent, in some ways, of the language he uses to describe the city in *Lightning Flashes of Art*. "Sharp towers," he notes in his travelogue, "are everywhere you look—refined, light, like all Italian Gothic, refined to the extreme and so tall, as if they are whirling up to the very heart of God. Siena plays more brazenly with Italian Gothic—an old infant [staryi mladenets]" (*SS*, 5:395). In the poem, architecture alone does not produce the impression of sharpness; nature also plays a role in emphasizing Siena's phallic qualities: the grass breaks through the lap of the square and a sharp crescent moon hangs over the city, while church towers cut into the sky. But here the city's realization of the extremes of Italian Gothic does not take on the playful quality of an "old infant" (staryi mladenets) but rather the bellicose nature of a female warrior. In the poet's imagination, the city is transformed into an arrow-wielding Amazon who is unfaithful and hence threatening to the male speaker: "Oh, cunning Siena, all of you is a quiver of taut arrows! Treachery and infidelity are your mysterious destiny" (O, lukavaia Siena, / Vsia— kolchan uprugikh strel! / Verolomstvo i izmena— / Tvoi tainstvennyi udel!). This threat to the masculine realm is realized when Siena thrusts the spikes of her churches and towers (tserkvi i bashni), both of which are grammatically feminine entities in Russian, into the masculine firmament (nebosklon).

Though we might reason that the bellicose nature of Siena—and of her churches—puts her in a perfect position to defend her inhabitants and her children, this logic does not appear to be borne out in the final stanzas of the poem. Here Blok describes the Madonnas, who fill Siena's churches, as no more maternal than her architecture. These Sienese Madonnas do not project a reassuring maternal gaze that emanates comfort and warmth; instead, they squint ominously into the darkness:

> И томленьем дух влюбленный
> Исполняют образа,
> Где коварные мадонны
> Щурят длинные глаза:
>
> Пусть грозит младенцу буря,
> Пусть грозит младенцу враг,
> Мать глядится в мутный мрак,
> Очи влажные сощуря!...
> (SS, 3:113)

[And the holy images fill the enamored spirit with languor, where the treacherous madonnas squint with their long eyes: Let the storm threaten the infant; let an enemy threaten the infant; the mother gazes into the murky darkness, squinting her damp eyes!..]

In his discussion of the poem, Pirog suggests that this image of the Madonnas with their elongated eyes represents Blok's attempt to recall the particular style of Byzantine painting associated with the Sienese school. Pirog refers to the passage from Blok's *Lightning Flashes of Art,* where the poet indicates that "in the long-eyed Madonnas [of the Sienese school] there is a terrible cunning; whether they look at the child, or nurse him, or humbly accept the Annunciation of Gabriel, or simply focus their gaze on the empty space—invariably, some type of crafty, feline tenderness shows through" (SS, 5:395). Certainly, the squinting Madonnas both in the poem and in Blok's travelogue do evoke certain qualities of Byzantine painting. I do not want to deny that there is a mimetic quality to Blok's depiction of the icons of the Madonna in this poem, but what is significant about Blok's verbal portraits of the Madonnas in "Siena," as well as in his *Lightning Flashes of Art,* is their emotional quality: the Madonnas are portrayed not only as cunning but also as failing to reflect back the gaze of the child. The Madonna "gazes into the murky darkness, squinting her damp eyes" (gliaditsia v mutnyi mrak, / Ochi vlazhnye soshuria). And the squinting of these Sienese Madonnas suggests a comparison with perhaps the most ambivalent and complicated mother figure in Russian literature, Anna Karenina. Toward the end of Tolstoy's novel, after Anna has forsaken her first child, Serezha, for Vronsky and decided not to bear any more children, Dolly observes how Anna begins to squint or screw up her eyes—a gesture that for Tolstoy betrays her inclination to dissemble and to neglect what he sees as her natural, maternal role.[59]

There is little that is canonical about Blok's presentation of the Madonna in "Siena" or, for that matter, in any of the other poems in the cycle. Elsewhere in the Italian cycle, he goes so far as to accuse the Madonna of perfidiousness. "Your eyes," he writes, "are lowered humbly, your shoulder is covered with a veil... You appear to many to be sacred, but you, Maria, are perfidious ..." (Glaza, opushchennye skromno, / Plecho, zakrytoe fatoi ... / Ty mnogim kazhesh'sia sviatoi, / No ty, Mariia, verolomna ...) (*SS*, 3:116). Though there has been a tendency among some Blok scholars to stress the objective aspect of these poems and to focus on the themes of Italian art and history and Russian history in them, I would claim that the repeated emphasis throughout them on the ambivalent figure of the mother or the city as woman suggests Blok's attempts to work out his complicated relationship to the issue of motherhood, an issue that had been all too real for him in the previous year. Blok projects his own ambivalent feelings about maternity and the problems of life and death onto Ravenna, Venice, Florence, Siena, and the other sites he depicts in the cycle. Consequently, Italy emerges quite literally as "the other motherland," a phantasmic space that allows the poet to explore the range of tensions and emotions that can exist between mother and child.

The mother-son dyad is crucial for Blok in these poems, as it is for many male writers. In fact, the French theorist Roland Barthes has gone so far as to claim that "the writer is someone who plays with his mother's body (I refer to Pleynet on Lautréamont and Matisse): in order to glorify it, to embellish it, or in order to dismember it, to take it to the limit of what can be known about the body."[60] In *The Italian Verses*, however, Blok portrays the mother and the maternal body in anything but utopian terms, implicitly identifying his poetic speaker with a fearful child and a host of other disempowered male figures, such as John the Baptist. Not only does he implicate the mother figure in violence, neglect, or wrongdoing in the poems "Siena" and "Florence" but in other poems such as those about Venice he presents the city as a watery grave where the poet-child is doomed either to death or to an impossible birth. Once the center of medieval and Renaissance culture, Italy emerges in these poems as a decadent space, populated by dead children and equally dead art. In producing such an image of Italy, Blok appears to have failed to appropriate the positive maternal role he had assigned to his romantic precursor in "Gogol's Child" ("Ditia Gogolia") (1909). Even though Blok had compared the creative process of his Italian poems to childbirth in a letter he wrote to his editor, this cycle with its emphasis on death and destruction ultimately seems to refute his claims of artistic fecundity. Moreover, here Blok gives birth not to the idea of Russia but to the concept of the "other motherland," Italy. Thus, in a creative sense, Blok would appear to be guilty of a kind of infidelity, much like his own wife and so many of the female figures that grace his poems. He would, however, return to the theme of Russia in his later poetic cycles as well as in his narrative poem *Retribution*, the subject of chapter 4. In this text, which he began working on shortly after his father's death, Blok once again takes up more directly the problem of the Russia's family romance, placing an emphasis this time on the tensions between father and son rather than on those between mother and child.

4

A Time of Troubles
Blok and the Disruption of Poetic Succession

Пимен. Укрывшихся злодеев захватили
И привели пред теплый труп младенца,
И чудо—вдруг мертвец затрепетал.—
"Покайтеся!"—народ им завопил:
И в ужасе под топором злодеи
Покаялись—и назвали Бориса.
[*Pimen.* The villains, who had hidden, were captured and brought before the child's warm corpse, and miraculously the corpse suddenly began to tremble. "Confess!" the people cried out to them. And in horror beneath the axe, the villains confessed and named Boris.]
Alexander Pushkin, Boris Godunov (1831)

Solness. If old Knut Brovik had owned the house, it never would have burned down so conveniently for him—I'm positive of that. Because he doesn't know how to call on the helpers, or the servers either. [...] So you see, Hilda—it *is* my fault that the twins had to die.
Henrik Ibsen, The Master Builder (1892)

Blok's Italian cycle would appear to represent his most direct attempt to work out the tensions between poetic production and human reproduction. Nevertheless, he continued to be preoccupied by family problems and to address them in his works—although now in a somewhat different way. In spite of the fact that he persisted in asserting that he was better off childless, he began to show signs of regret about his own inability to be a good family man. Already thirty years old, he compared himself rather unfavorably to those of his contemporaries who had managed to assume the traditional adult roles of husband and father. In a letter to Boris Bugaev (Andrei Bely), dated 6 June 1911, he expresses no small amount of regret about the fact that he could not lead the type of life of their friend and Blok's second cousin, Sergei Soloviev. "Sweet Serezha," he remarks, "is a brilliant man, a future scholar of philology, my brother in spirit and blood, a magnificent patriarch, a progenitor of his kin (and I am a destroyer) [velikolepnyi patriarkh, prodolzhatel' roda (a ia istrebitel')]" (SS, 8:345). At least in part, Blok's vexation about his own inability to carry on his family line appears to have been brought on by the death of his own father, Alexander Lvovich Blok, in Warsaw on 1 December 1909. Though Blok had little consistent contact with his father growing up (his parents divorced shortly after his birth and his father resided in Warsaw), he was upset by his death and in later years "remember[ed] him intimately" (pomn[il] ego krovno) (SS, 7:12). With the demise of his father, Blok not only found his favored status as child in jeopardy (arguably one can retain the status of child only as long as one's parents remain living) but also found himself in the unenviable position of being the last male member of his particular line of the Blok family.

It was shortly after the death of his father that Blok began working on his semiautobiographical narrative poem *Retribution* (*Vozmezdie*), which, according to his own statements, treats "the links in a single chain of a kin" (zven'ia edinoi tsepi roda) (SS, 3:297) and was inspired, in part, by Alexander Pushkin's novel in verse *Eugene Onegin* (*Evgenii Onegin*) (1833).[1] In his decision to dedicate himself not only to the composition of a poetic family chronicle of sorts but also to a long poetic form, analogous in some ways to Pushkin's novel in verse, we can discern in Blok a concern with origins that would seem to confirm his own need, now that he was on the cusp of middle age, to engage in a process that Lawrence Lipking has identified as "summing-up."[2] In his important book *The Life of the Poet: Beginning and Ending Poetic Careers* (1981), Lipking argues that, in an effort to secure their legacy as poets, myriad poets from ancient to modern times turn to longer poetic forms as they approach the height of their poetic powers.[3] While Blok certainly had from the very outset of his poetic career evinced an inclination toward narrative, dedicating much of his energy to the composition of poetic cycles, his decision at this particular time in his poetic career to write a long poem, devoted to the subject of the family, is completely in line with what Lipking has seen as the modern poet's turn to the long narrative poem or, as he rather loosely terms it, the "modern 'epic.'"[4] As Lipking observes, "the modern 'epic' is dominated by one story and one story only: the life of the poet."[5]

For Blok, though, this decision to tell the story of the life of the poet or, more accurately, the story of the poet's family, was fueled less by the sense of well being which can overtake the poet in his middle years, that feeling of harmony about which Lipking speaks, than by a sense of urgency rooted in the times. As Virginia Woolf famously proclaimed, "on or around December 1910, human nature changed." And this statement was no less true for the Russian symbolist poet than it was for the Bloomsbury writer. In 1910 Blok was forced not only to confront his own mortality, now that his father had recently died and he could no longer consider himself a child, but also his growing anachronism as a poet. 1910 was a watershed year in Russian culture, marked by the deaths of several important cultural figures for the symbolist generation—Vera Kommissarzhevskaia, Lev Tolstoy, and Mikhail Vrubel—as well as by a crisis in Russian symbolism.[6] And as much as Blok may have attempted, in his essay on the symbolist crisis, to convince himself and his fellow symbolists that they could regenerate themselves and their poetic movement from within by resurrecting the infant in their souls, he could not help but feel his own youth slipping away. This feeling was only exacerbated by the appearance of two new poetic groups, the acmeists and futurists, both of whom were intent each in their own way in doing away with their symbolist precursors.[7]

The tensions between "fathers and sons" about which Ivan Turgenev had written in a social and political sense now began to play themselves out in the arena of modernist poetry. And for the first time in his poetic career, Blok was forced to confront the possibility of his own obsolescence as a poet. "We know one thing," he wrote later, "that the breed [poroda] which comes to take the place of another [idushchii na smenu druguiu] is new; that which it replaces is old; we observe eternal changes in the world; we ourselves participate in the succession of breeds; our participation is for the most part inactive [bezdeiatel'no]; we degenerate [vyrozhdaemsia], we grow old, we die; rarely is it active: we occupy some place in world culture and we ourselves facilitate the formation of new breeds" (SS, 6:161–62). But while the vicissitudes of modern Russian history may have forced Blok to come to terms with the contentious nature of poetic history, as we have already seen, long before Harold Bloom would articulate his theory of the "anxiety of influence," this did not make Blok any more willing to give up the fight and to cede his place to the new generation of poets. His immediate reaction to the appearance of "new breeds" was to try to stake out his own legacy as a poet and as a man in ways that were extremely tangible. Blok not only undertook the composition of *Retribution*, a narrative poem that told the story of an aristocratic family similar to his own against the background of Russian history, but he also began the renovation of his family home in Shakhmatovo with the inheritance money he received from his father's estate upon his death. The latter undertaking was no easy feat. In letters to his mother, he documents both the joys and the difficulties of the process of house building. "The renovations drag on," he writes, "but God willing they will be finished by St. Peter's day" (*SS*, 8:310). Elsewhere Blok compares the task of organizing a brigade of thirty workers for the renovations to babysitting. "House construction" (domostroitel'stvo), he complains in another letter to his mother, "is a very difficult nightmare [ves'ma tiazhelyi koshmar]; however, the results can make up for all the troubles of looking after thirty grown-up children" (*PABR*, 2:90).

If the actual physical process of house construction was trying, then the process of poetic house building that he undertook in *Retribution* was no less arduous, particularly for a poet whose entire artistic stance had been antithetical to the very notion of good housekeeping.[8] "There is nothing easier [for the writer] than losing contact with the soil [kak poteriat pochvu] [and] undertaking only 'household affairs' ['domashnie dela']" (*SS*, 5:369), he wrote in his important essay "The Soul of a Writer" ("Dusha pisatelia") (February 1909). "The internal 'beat' [vnutrennyi 'takt'] of the writer, his *rhythm*, can only be formed through the presence of the road [nalichnost'iu puti]" (*SS*, 5:370). Not surprisingly, given his avowed preference for travel over homesteading, Blok proceeded rather slowly on *Retribution*. After sketching out his ideas for his poetic family chronicle in 1910, Blok began working the following year on what was eventually to become the third section of the poem, which treats his hero's response to his father's death and is based heavily on Blok's own trip to his father's funeral in Warsaw. This process, though, of coming to terms with the death of the father, and in a sense the imminent demise of his own family line, was by no means easy for Blok and marked one of the most unproductive and difficult periods in his creative life, save the period following *The Twelve* (*Dvenadtsat'*) (January

1918) and *The Scythians* (*Skify*) (30 January 1918).[9] As Konstantin Mochulsky has observed, "in 1911 the poet wrote only two poems; he wrote no prose at all. All his creative energy was absorbed by *Retribution*."[10]

Already by January of 1911, though, Blok had completed a draft of the section of the poem dealing with the hero's relationship with his deceased father, subtitling it a "Warsaw Poem" ("Varshavskaia poema") and dedicating it to his half sister Angelina from his father's second marriage. However, he was not satisfied with the poem and spent the months that followed revising it and expanding its focus to include more about the life of the son. As he struggled with the plot of the poem, he made the process of revision and expansion of the work a "family affair," turning to his mother for advice on how to conclude it. On 3 December 1911, two years after the death of his own father, Blok decided on the advice of his mother that the poem should end with "the 'son' being raised on the bayonets of the barricade" (*SS*, 7:99). For Blok the idea that the son should die in the revolution accorded well with his notion of the tragic, romantic nature of his family. "Against the background of each family," he noted in this same year, "arises its own rebellious offspring [miatezhnye otrasli] — as a reproach, a warning, a revolt. Perhaps they are worse than others. Perhaps they themselves are doomed to perish. They disturb and destroy their own kind, but they are *right* by virtue of their newness [*pravy* noviznoiu]. They assist in the evolution of man. Usually, they are themselves barren [besplodny]. They are the last [poslednie]. Everything ends with them. They have no exit from their own revolt — neither in love, nor in children, nor in the formation of new families [ni v liubvi, ni v detiakh, ni v obrazovanii novykh semei]" (*SS*, 3:464).

From very early youth, Blok had expressed little faith that he or any members of his class could be good family men and, in this sense, his praise of his second cousin Serezha Soloviev was an exception to the rule. Tolstoy wrote that "all happy families resemble one another, but each unhappy family is unhappy in its own way." For Blok, at least, all happy families resembled one another in that they were not like the Blok family in terms of class or disposition. While at his estate in Shakhmatovo in May 1910, he contrasted his old aristocratic family somewhat negatively with that of the peasantry. "We are moneyed and childless people" (my — liudi denezhnye i bezdetnye), he wrote, "while thievish Egorka will take the wool from sheep for his children, warm up his children with hay, give his children eggs from unfed chickens" (*ZK*, 171). In his own mind, what prevented him and his family from leading a happy home life was its inherently romantic and rebellious nature, that demonism that had characterized Lermontov, Gogol, Dostoevsky, and, more recently, Vrubel. This is something that emerges very clearly in his cycle *What the Wind Sings About* (*O chem poet veter*) (1913), which immediately precedes his unfinished poem *Retribution* in the major Soviet edition of his collected works. As he writes in one of the lyrics from this cycle, "Dear friend, even in this quiet house a fever seizes me. I cannot find a place in the quiet house by the peaceful fire!" (Milyi drug, i v etom tikhom dome / Likhoradka b'et menia. / Ne naiti mne mesta v tikhom dome / Vozle mirnogo ognia!) (*SS*, 3:286). But while he may have found it difficult in this particular poem to envision his lyric speaker penned in by the confines of a "quiet house" (tikhii dom), he does affirm the importance of home at the end of the poetic cycle. As David A. Sloane has pointed out, in the cycle's final poem, all the trials and tribulations that the poet has experienced are revealed to have happened elsewhere in a dream: "All that was in the dark Carpathians, in distant Bohemia..." (Bylo to v temnykh Karpatakh, / Bylo v Bogemii dal'nei...) (*SS*, 3:290).[11] And in this figural return from the Carpathian mountains—the setting for Gogol's "A Terrible Vengeance" ("Strashnaia mest'") (1832) as well as for a more recent gothic tale, Bram Stoker's *Dracula* (1897)—back home to Russia, the lyrical persona confirms Blok's own long-standing belief that there's no place like home. "I am also a vagabond [brodiaga]," he would state later, "but I always came home from everywhere. Without a home you lose yourself [Bez doma vy sami sebia poteriaete]."[12] And Blok's ties to hearth and home has been duly noted. "The more tempestuous and painful Blok's inner life was," Georgy Chulkov observes, "the more insistently he strove to create coziness and order in his home. Blok had two lives—one routine, domestic, quiet; the other erratic, unsettled, intoxicated. *In Blok's home there was order*..."[13]

For Blok, 1913 may have been the most tempestuous and homeless year in the period leading up to the Bolshevik revolution and civil war. This year witnessed growing international tensions that would eventually lead to world war and increasing cultural tensions between the symbolists and the acmeists and futurists, which only served to strengthen his sense of displacement. It was in early February of this year, on the fourth anniversary of Mitia's death and the third anniversary of Kommissarzhevskaia's death, that Blok made his famous antisymbolist statement cited earlier: "It is time to untie my hands. I am no longer a schoolboy. No more symbolisms—I am alone. I answer for myself *alone*—and I can still be younger than the 'middle-aged' young poets, who are burdened by progeny and acmeism" (*SS*, 7:216). Though Blok appears with this statement to renounce all personal and poetic ties, it should be noted that less than two weeks after making it he expresses his intention to extend his own fictional narrative of his family in *Retribution* into the future and to have his hero, whom he based heavily on himself, father a child. This would appear not only to confirm Chulkov's observation that Blok had two selves—one domestic, the other unsettled—but also to suggest that Blok's rivalry with the acmeists was both poetic and deeply reproductive. Now that he was approaching middle age, Blok found it difficult to fathom that he would not leave anything for posterity, except his poetry, and he decided that he must produce a child, if only within the world of his poems. But in attempting to prove himself to be as fecund as the acmeists, Blok apparently did not wish to replicate what he saw as their essentially bourgeois family values. The child of a broken marriage himself, Blok could not envision his poetic alter ego's kin growing up in a nuclear family setting like the traditional families of old; instead, he would grow up in isolation without knowledge of his father, much as Jaromir had in Grillparzer's *Die Ahnfrau*.[14] According to Blok's expanded plan for the poem, dating from this period, the plot would unfold as follows:

> PROLOGUE. ("Life without beginning and without end")
> CHAPTER I. Petersburg at the end of the 70s. The Turkish war and March 1st. That is the background. The family and the appearance in it of the "demon." Growing bored, he takes his young wife off to Warsaw. In a year she returns: "pale, tortured, a golden-haired child in her arms" ["bledna, izmuchena, rebenok zolotokudryi na rukakh"].
> CHAPTER II. Petersburg in the 90s. The Tsar. Troikas, *veuve Clicquot*. The education of the son at the mother's. Youth, visions, spring dust, romance (still successful). *The first mazurka*. The approach of the revolution, news of the imminent death of the father.
> CHAPTER III. Arrival in Warsaw. The death of the father. Ennui, frost, night. *The second mazurka*. "Her" arrival. A son is conceived [zachat syn].
> CHAPTER IV. Return to Petersburg. Red dawns, black nights. His death (already unsuccessful). The barricade.
> EPILOGUE. *The third mazurka*. Somewhere in a *poor* room, in some city, a child grows. Two leitmotifs: one life continues, like an infantry, hopelessly. The other the mazurka. (*SS*, 3:461)

Though Blok did not remain wedded to these specific chapter divisions, eventually determining that the poem should comprise a prologue, three chapters, and an epilogue, he did remain committed to this basic generational framework and most notably to the notion that the hero—the son—should father a son of his own.[15] What is different about his revised plan for the poem is his intention that this child should grow up not in an urban setting (Blok had, after all, identified the city as filled with possible dangers for the child in his poems dating from as early 1904) but in the Polish countryside and that this child like the son in the earlier sketch for the poem should die a martyr. In the preface, which he affixed to the poem in 1919, he makes this point clear. "In the epilogue," he writes, "there should be represented an infant [mladenets], who is held and cradled in the lap of a simple mother, lost somewhere in the expansive Polish clover fields, unbeknownst to anyone and not knowing about anything. But she cradles and nurses her son, and the son grows: He already begins to play; he begins to repeat after the mother: 'I will go meet the soldiers . . . I will throw myself on their bayonets . . . And for you, my freedom, I will ascend the black scaffold'" (SS, 3:299). The notion that hope for the future would be embodied in a child produced by a peasant woman was by no means new for Blok. As mentioned earlier, during his wife's pregnancy, Blok had conceived the idea in his famous poem "Russia" ("Rossiia") (18 October 1908) that Russia, embodied in the poem by a peasant woman, would give birth to a child. Although Blok eventually abandoned his attempt to have Russia bear a child in this poem, his drafts make it clear that the child was to serve as a source of power for Russia. And if in his Russia poem it is unclear whether Blok's lyric speaker would actually father it, as Russia's inconstancy toward the speaker is clearly emphasized, in *Retribution* his hero would play an active role in its creation. This child, born of the aristocrat and the Polish peasant woman, would ostensibly serve as the basis for positive social change in the Slavic lands, redressing the age-old tensions between Russia and Poland, which he imagines in the poem as a downtrodden woman. (In the poem's third chapter, he notes: "The country—beneath the burden of insults, under the yoke of an impudent force—lowers its wings like an angel, loses its shame like a woman" [Strana—pod bremenem obid, / Pod igom naglogo nasil'ia— / Kak angel, opuskaet kryl'ia, / Kak zhenshchina, teriaet styd] [SS, 3:340].) Thus, in spite of Blok's own resistance to family feelings, his hero and alter ego would fulfill his destiny as one of *"the harbingers of something better"* (*predvestniki luchshego*) (SS, 3:464), if not by raising, then by fathering a child. In conceiving the idea of the child as a symbol for social change in the new era, Blok would appear to provide a creative model for his poetic successor Boris Pasternak. At the conclusion of his novel about the revolution, *Doctor Zhivago,* Pasternak permits the poet-doctor Yury Zhivago to live on through Tania, the love child he unknowingly produces with Lara during the tempestuous years of the civil war.[16]

Unlike his poetic successor, though, Blok was unable to realize his own alter ego's potential as the progenitor of the child of the revolution. Although he continued to work on *Retribution* intermittently up until his death in August 1921, he never completed the poem. Significantly absent from Blok's completed fragment of the poem is the articulation of the next generation, the hero's son, except in the preface that he affixed to the poem in 1919. In terms of its incompleteness, Blok's poem occupies a place in his oeuvre not unlike that which *Herodias* occupies in Stéphane Mallarmé's. And like Mallarmé, Blok at times struggled desperately to bring his poems to fruition.[17] Although Blok's *Retribution* differs considerably from Mallarmé's *Herodias* in its revolutionary sprit and epic scope, Blok does evoke the theme of Salome—a theme that, as we have seen, was intimately connected for Mallarmé as well as for Blok with feelings of creative impotency. And now when Salome makes her appearance in the opening lines of the poem's prologue, which Blok completed in early March 1911, she is depicted in typical decadent guise as a dancer:

> Но песня—песнью всё пребудет,
> В толпе всё кто-нибудь поет,
> Вот—голову его на блюде
> Царю плясунья подает;
> Там—он на эшафоте черном
> Слагает голову свою;
> Здесь—именем клеймят позорным
> Его стихи ... И я пою,—
> Но не за вами суд последний,
> Не вам замкнуть мои уста!..
>   (*SS,* 3:302)

[But the song will still remain a song; in the crowd someone always sings; look the female dancer presents his head on a charger to the tsar; there he lays down his head on the black scaffold; here they brand his poems with a disgraceful name ... And I sing, but you do not have the final judgment. You will not seal my lips! ..]

In his appropriation of the Salome myth in this poem, Blok would seem to imply that he or more specifically the poetic speaker will not succumb to muteness, that malady which would plague many of the fictional poets in Mikhail Bulgakov's unfinished masterpiece about the disastrous effects of revolution on the creative writer, *The Master and Margarita* (*Master i Margarita*) (1929-40), and which would be intimately connected with the myth of Salome and John the Baptist. Like John the Baptist, several of the writers in Bulgakov's novel lose their head, either in a literal or figurative sense, and thus become victims of history and of the revolution.[18] Blok, however, suggests that his poetic speaker will not become a victim of history, which he configures here and elsewhere as a markedly a feminine force through reference to the dancer Salome. If in this passage the figure of the poet succumbs to the desire of Salome and places his head on the scaffolding, then his double, the poetic speaker, claims that he will continue to compose his song, refusing to fall prey to creative impotence, that figurative castration which for Mallarmé became so intimately connected with Salome's double, Herodias. In his avowed refusal to fall silent, Blok clearly distinguishes himself from his French precursor.

Whereas Mallarmé seemed unable to envision the creative process as anything other than angst ridden, referring to his source of inspiration as the "Modern Muse of Impotence" (Muse moderne de l'Impuissance), Blok was not a poet inclined to romanticizing writer's block, nor was he a poet who frequently suffered from the condition that was so intimately associated in France with Mallarmé and Flaubert and in Russia with Gogol. Blok imagined such creative impasses as a sign of weakness, something that he makes abundantly clear in his 1915 autobiographical sketch in which discusses the creative habits of both sides of his family, the Beketovs and the Bloks. After extolling the literary productivity of his mother and aunts, Blok turns to a consideration of his father's relative failure in the sphere of publishing.[19] "In his entire life," he notes, "he published only two small books (not counting his lithographed lectures)" and over the last twenty years of his life "he labored over an essay devoted to the classification of the sciences. A talented musician, an authority in belles lettres, and a subtle stylist, my father considered himself a student of Flaubert [uchenik Flobera]. The latter was the primary reason why he wrote so little and failed to complete the major work of his life: he was unable to put his continually evolving ideas in the compact forms which he sought [v te szhatye formy, kotorykh iskal]. In that search for compact forms there was something spasmodic and terrible [chto-to sudorozhnoe i strashnoe], as there was in his entire spiritual and physical appearance" (*SS*, 7:12).

Considering his own failure to complete *Retribution*, Blok would appear to have more in common with his father and the figure of the silenced poet in the poem's prologue than his earlier statements would imply. Although Blok worked on *Retribution* on and off over a span of twelve years, rather than the twenty that Alexander Lvovich reportedly spent working on his essay on the categorization of the sciences, this would seem to represent a clear instance in which, to quote Blok's important Pushkin essay, "a son may not resemble his father in any respect, except in one secret trait; but [this trait] makes the father and son resemble each other" (syn mozhet byt' pokhozh na otsa ni v chem, krome odnoi tainoi cherty; no ona-to i delaet pokhozhimi otsa i syna) (*SS*, 6:161). And in his 1919 preface to *Retribution*, Blok speaks about the genesis of his poem in terms that are highly spasmodic and, hence, reminiscent of his father's creative process. "The plan [for the poem]," he claims, "appeared to me in the form of concentric circles, which became tighter and tighter [vse úzhe i úzhe], and the smallest circle, having compressed itself to the limit, began again to live a life of its own, to burst open and to disperse into the surrounding environment, and in time to act on the periphery" (*SS*, 3:297). Through this description, Blok suggests that the structure of his poem conforms to the Dantean vision of hell as a series of concentric circles—a locus where the body is presented as perpetually in pain. And he lays bare the physicality of the process of composition. "Such was the life of the draft," he notes, "which appeared to me [kororyi mne risovalsia]. In my consciousness and my words, I attempt to convey it now; then it existed primarily in a musical and muscular understanding [v poniatii muzykal'nom i muskul'nom]. Not for nothing do I speak about muscular consciousness, because at that time the entire movement and development of the poem was for me tightly connected with the muscular system's development" (*SS*, 3:297).

This is also one of the rare instances in which Blok speaks about the poetic process in highly masculine and bodily terms, reminiscent of the discourse of both acmeism and futurism. Nikolai Gumilev, one of the major theoreticians of the acmeist or Adamist movement, would employ similar terminology in the title of his essay "The Anatomy of a Poem" ("Anatomiia stikhotvoreniia") (1921).[20] And Blok's own reliance throughout the preface on this highly physiological description of the poetic process might be seen as the last, fatal attempt of an aging poet to exert his power over the new generation of poets and in particular over the acmeists who frequently envisioned themselves as newborn Adams. Although Blok's relationship with the futurists changed over the years, with his initial praise eventually giving way to critique, he remained consistent in his criticism of the acmeist poets as a whole.[21] In his late essay "'Without Divinity, without Inspiration'" ("'Bez bozhestva, bez vdokhnoven'ia'") (April 1921), Blok weighs the acmeists quite negatively on Pushkin's scales. "If only they would untie their hands," he writes, "and become if only for a moment rough, uncouth, even deformed, and in this regard more like their motherland, a country crippled, burned by sedition [sozhzhennaia smutoi], destroyed by ruin! But no, they do not want to and are unable to; they want to be distinguished foreigners [znatnye inostrantsy], members of trade organizations and guilds" (SS, 6:183-84). According to Blok, the acmeists lacked that poetic fist or *kulak* that he had earlier credited the futurists with possessing and that he purports to wield in the poem's preface. "Through systematic handiwork," he informs the readers of *Retribution*, "the muscles first develop on the arms, the biceps, so they are called, and then next—gradually—the more subtle, refined, and sparse network of muscles on the chest and the back under the wings. Such a rhythmical and gradual growth of muscles should have formed the rhythm of the entire poem" (SS, 3:297).

Blok makes references in the preface to his own ability to embrace the "masculine current" (muzhestvennoe veian'e) (SS, 3:296) of the time, tracing the highly physiological discourse of his own poem to his interest in French wrestling.[22] But he also repeatedly undercuts his own masculinity and sense of potency through his acknowledgment of the terrifying effects of history on people and, by extension, on the writer.[23] "In short, the world whirlpool [mirovoi vodovorot]," he maintains, "sucks almost the entire person into its funnel. Barely even a trace remains of the personality; if it continues to exist, it becomes unknown, disfigured, crippled. There was once a person—and now he is no longer; there remains only worthless, limp flesh and a rotting little soul" (SS, 3:298).[24] And there is ample evidence to suggest that by the time that he composed the preface to his poem, Blok may not only have begun to see his own aging body as transforming into "worthless, limp flesh" but also to have held out little hope that he would leave anything for posterity except "a rotting little soul." Although Blok apparently intended his hero and alter ego to sow his seed one "passionate and sinful night in the lap of some quiet and feminine daughter of a foreign people" (v strastnuiu i greshnuiu noch' v lono kakoi-to tikhoi i zhenstvennoi docheri chuzhogo naroda) (SS, 3:299), this seed, we must conclude, bore no fruit, as the child of the revolution never actually materialized in the poem proper.

One would be hard pressed to find another text in Blok's oeuvre that is so infused with images of impotence — the spilled seed, the drowning subject, the decapitated poet — all of which operate against his ostensible intention to extend the narrative of his kin or *rod* into the future.[25] This is something that can be observed even in those sections of the poem, which he penned prior to 1917, after which point he reportedly did "not [feel] the need or the inclination to complete a narrative poem filled with revolutionary presentiments in years when the revolution had already occurred" (*SS*, 3:295). Already in the first chapter of his poem, which was completed in the spring of 1916, Blok's speaker laments: "The twentieth century... is even more homeless; even more dreadful is the gloom of life. (Even blacker and more enormous is the shadow of Lucifer's wing)" [Dvadtsatyi vek... Eshche bezdomnei, / Eshche strashnee zhizni mgla / (Eshche chernee i ogromnei / Ten' Liutsiferova kryla]) (*SS*, 3:305). And this sense of homelessness was not lost on Blok's friends and contemporaries. Bely, for instance, remarked that "the kinship theme in Blok is melancholy in the narrative poem *Retribution* [Unyla v poeme "Vozmezdie" tema roda u B.]; these verses are wonderful, but what kind of sense is there in them when they represent 'hopeless heaviness' ['bezprosvetnaia tiazhest']."[26] And Kornei Chukovsky asserted that "like all his other works, Blok's *Retribution* is a poem about doom. It contains Blok's depiction of his parents' house in the process of slowly falling apart."[27] They seemed surprised that the poem is gloomy, but we have to question, given Blok's long-standing beliefs about his own family, whether this poem could have ever been anything other than about inevitable doom. In 1915, Blok wrote a letter to Vladimir Kniazhin in which he admitted: "I would be afraid if I had children.... Let one of the Blok lines at least end with me — there is little good in them."[28] And while there is a big difference between actually bearing children and representing the birth of a child in a poem, it would seem that Blok had no easy time extending his fictional family narrative into the future.

The antiprocreative streak was, as we have seen, deeply entrenched in Blok, and one of the ways in which it manifests itself in this work is in violence directed toward children. Blok not only evinces a desire to figuratively kill off the new generation of poet-children — his younger poet-cousins, as it were, the acmeists and futurists — through a virtuoso display of his poetic muscle in the poem's preface but he also identifies this work with that of the quintessentially decadent and even infanticidally inclined artist Henrik Ibsen. Blok opens the poem with an epigraph taken from Ibsen's play *The Master Builder* (1892), which reads:

"Youth is retribution" (Iunost'—eto vozmezdie) (*SS*, 3:295). Through this reference to Ibsen's play, Blok clearly suggests that he envisions himself under attack by youth and identifies with the fate of the play's main character, the master builder Solness.[29] But in identifying with Solness, Blok also implicitly links his creative process with infanticide. Solness does not simply die at the hands of youth, embodied in the play by the figure of Hilda, but he dies without leaving any heirs, and he supposedly does so as matter of choice.[30] Solness claims that he willingly sacrificed all hopes of family happiness for the opportunity to excel at his art. "For this chance to build homes for others," he tells Hilda, "I've had to give up—absolutely give up any home of my own—a real home, I mean, with children."[31] And he bears no small amount of guilt for his sacrifice of family happiness, believing himself to have willed the death of his twins in a fire for the sake of his art. He implores Hilda, the embodiment of youth: "Don't you believe me, Hilda, that there are certain special chosen people who have a gift and power and capacity to *wish* something, *desire* something, *will* something—so insistently and so—so inevitably—that at last it *has* to be theirs? Don't you believe that?"[32]

Retribution, then, is no less connected than some of his earlier works to the theme of the death of a child and the end of the family line. The ghost of the dead child quietly enters this poem through the epigraph from *The Master Builder*; it also haunts the poem's preface, which Blok first read publicly at the Petersburg House of Arts (Dom iskusstv) in July 1919.[33] Here Blok locates the genesis of the poem in early 1910s, which witnessed a number of catastrophic events, among them the murder of a child, Andrei Yushchinsky, in Kiev that sparked the infamous Beilis affair. By the time of the composition of the prologue, the accused killer, Mendel Beilis, had been acquitted of the trumped-up charges of murdering the child for the purposes of ritual sacrifice, but Blok relays the anti-Semitic rumors that circulated around the death of the child.[34] "In Kiev" (V Kieve), he notes, "the murder of Andrei Yushchinsky occurred, and the question was raised about the use of Christian blood by the Jews" (proizoshlo ubiistvo Andreia Iushchinskogo, i voznik vopros ob upotreblenii evreiami khristianskoi krovi) (*SS*, 3:296). By locating the origins of his poem in a year dominated by the blood libel, Blok appears to take a rather conservative position here, reinforcing the vision of history marked by child death and the disruption of the family line that informs the poem.[35] And through this reference to the rumors about the draining of the child's blood, he also anticipates the vampire motif associated with the era more generally and with his hero's father in the main chapters of the poem.

Olga Matich has persuasively argued that the poem's fascination with vampirism is linked to the "epoch's preoccupation with genealogy that assumes particularly monstrous form in Stoker's novel [*Dracula*]." As she observes, "the vampire's bite, which depletes its victims of physical vitality, transports them into life on the verge of death. The sexual fiend poisons the victim's bloodline, spreading contagious vampirism, which, as critics have shown, was a fin-de-siècle metaphor for syphilis. Stoker himself in all likelihood died from it, as probably did Blok."[36] Certainly, this poem, obsessed as it is with vampirism and the deathly figure of Salome—a figure that, as I demonstrated in the last chapter, Blok repeatedly associated with illness—can productively be read as articulating the fears of Blok's generation, if not of Blok himself, of the threat of syphilis. But in focusing not just on the contagion of the bloodline but also on the spilling of blood, this work is very much concerned as well with the social and political violence that threatened to destroy the next generation.

In very real terms, a bloody model of history was playing itself out on the stage of Russian history. The murder of Andrei Yushchinsky was just the very beginning of a period of bloodletting that culminated in war, revolution, and, finally, the civil war. In July 1918—a year prior to his reading of the preface to *Retribution* at the House of Arts—Tsar Nicholas II, Tsarina Alexandra, and all of their children were killed by the local Bolsheviks in Ekaterinburg. And in the preface, Blok may be making subtle references to the deposition or "uncrowning" of the Romanov family when he notes that "the cost of [the development of the generations] is the loss finally of those eternally lofty characteristics, which in their own time sparkled, like the best diamonds in the crown of man [kak luchshie almazy v chelovecheskoi korone] (like, for example, humane characteristics, virtues, impeccable honesty, high morality, etc.)" (*SS*, 3:297-98). But while Blok may have believed in the inevitability of revolution, this does not mean that he did not mourn the death of the old era.

In the poem's preface, he implicitly links the period following the end of the Romanov dynasty to the Time of Troubles, that period of intense strife spurred on by the death or murder of the tsarevich Dmitry, heir to the throne, during which a number of pretenders to the throne emerged, resulting, in turn, in the founding of the Romanov Dynasty.[37] Blok does this most directly by reinforcing the poem's connections to Pushkin's play *Boris Godunov* (1831) and perhaps also to Modest Mussorgsky's opera *Boris Godunov* (1869).[38] Whereas Pushkin's *Eugene Onegin*—one of the alleged inspirations for *Retribution*—is marked by its famous lyrical digression or *otstuplenie* on society dancing and women's feet, *Retribution* is characterized by a more dangerous and tragic dance structure that would implicitly associate it with Pushkin's play and even Mussorgsky's opera about political and generational strife—the dance of Maryna Mniszek, the wife of the False Dmitry.[39] "The entire narrative poem," Blok states, "should be accompanied by the distinct leitmotif of 'retribution'; this leitmotif is the *mazurka*, the dance which carried Maryna on her porch, dreaming about the Russian throne, and Kostiushka with his right hand extended toward the heavens, and [Adam] Mickiewicz at the Russian and Parisian balls" (*SS*, 3:299). Maryna Mniszek by virtue of her dancing merges with the Salome figure whom we encounter in the prologue, a figure that Blok had earlier associated with her mother Herodias, "the dancer, the evil wife." Like Salome's dance of the seven veils, alluded to within the poem's prologue, Maryna's mazurka is a fatal dance that leaves at least one male victim in its wake. Not only was Maryna's waltz toward Moscow and the Russian throne made possible because of the death (or murder) of the tsarevich Dmitry but this dance, in turn, unwittingly ensured that her husband, the False Dmitry, would suffer a similar fate—execution.

The story of Maryna Mniszek and the False Dmitry would seem to have particular relevance for Blok at this point in Russian history. Russia had just witnessed the end of the Romanov dynasty and the outbreak of civil war and war with Poland and thus appeared to be repeating certain aspects of her bloody medieval past. In his essays dating from this period he frequently likens the period to the Time of Troubles. For example, in "On a List of Russian Authors" ("O spiske russkikh avtorov") (December 1919), he notes that "our entire past is presented for judgment to the generations of people succeeding us and differing much from us, because an upheaval greater than the one we are experiencing now has not been known in Russian history for at least two hundred years (since Peter), or even for three hundred years (the Time of Troubles [Smutnoe vremia])" (*SS*, 6:136). But while the theme of the Time of Troubles appears to have had particular historical resonance in 1919, Blok seems to have envisioned early twentieth-century Russian history in analogous terms considerably earlier. As early as October 1911, Blok indicated that his poetic alter ego should be named Dmitry. "Allow, finally, the 'hero' to be incarnated" (Puskai, nakonets, 'geroi' voplotitsia), he notes. "Let him be called *Dmitry* (as they wanted to name me)" (Pust' ego zovut *Dmitriem* [kak khoteli nazvat' menia]) (*SS*, 3:462). In deciding to name his hero and alter ego Dmitry, Blok would appear to identify not only with his wife's deceased child but also perhaps with the historical figure of Dmitry, something that is entirely in line with the poem's Polish themes as well as his abiding interest in other Western Slavic themes dating back to *Die Ahnfrau*.[40]

In identifying with Dmitry — the child-victim par excellence in Russian history — Blok appears to have experienced a kind of anxiety of authorship that we might characterize as an "impostor complex."[41] Not only must he deal with a theme that had been treated by a myriad of Russian writers and artists including the father of modern Russian literature, Alexander Pushkin, but he must do so in a fashion that reinforces his role as the ultimate child-victim within the family romance of Russian history. This task was complicated by the fact that with the appearance of the new groups of postsymbolist poets, Blok no longer had claims on the position of the youngest child in the family romance of Russian modernism. He would also not be the only Russian modernist poet to fashion himself as Dmitry. As Gregory Freidin has convincingly demonstrated, Osip Mandelstam identified with the martyred tsarevich Dmitry — and perhaps with the False Dmitry as well — in the poem "In a sledge lined with straw" ("Na rozval'niakh, ulozhennykh solomoi"); he dedicated it to Marina Tsvetaeva in 1916, and in so doing, Freidin argues, he was not just playing off of cultural associations with the name "Marina" but reinforcing a modernist paradigm of the son as martyred child that could be traced back to Merezhkovsky's novel *The Antichrist: Peter and Alexis* (*Antikhrist: Petr i Aleksei*) (1905).[42] By 1919, then, at which point Blok made manifest the Time of Troubles theme in his poem's prologue, it would appear that he was destined to inhabit no role other than the False Dmitry, and, hence, the emphasis on Maryna Mniszek's mazurka in the poem's preface and on the figure of the poet "lay[ing] his head on the black scaffold" in the presence of the dancer. However, Blok's authenticity is called into question less by the fact that the younger poet had laid claims to the role of Dmitry (Blok does not seem to be either aware of or concerned with Mandelstam's assumption of the role of Dmitry and perhaps of the False Dmitry as well in his poem to Tsvetaeva) than by the fact that his wife's child had, in a sense, already fulfilled the role in the years of reaction following 1905. Blok may have claimed that Dmitry was the name his parents had intended to call him, but in reality this name — and all the historical associations that went along with this name—were conferred not on him but on his wife's deceased child.

Although Blok does not actually refer to his hero by the name of Dmitry or, for that matter, by any other name in the completed sections of the poem, he does present him as very much a victim of history, and more specifically as a potential victim of family violence.[43] If in the poem's preface, he hints at a possible kinship between the hero and the historical figure of Dmitry, in the poem proper, most of which he composed prior to the preface, he associates his hero much more directly with another child-victim whose fate is also connected with the Russian-Polish borderlands, Pani Katerina's son in Gogol's "A Terrible Vengeance." Dating back to the revolution of 1905, Blok had evinced a fascination with the cycle of abuse and murder in Gogol's tale. But if in many of his earlier works, Blok tended to deviate from the gendered dynamic of the Gogolian tale, focusing in some works, at least, on the manner in which the abused mother-daughter inflicts violence on her child, in his narrative poem Blok remains much more faithful to the plot structure of the Gogolian original, detailing how the paternal figure is responsible for ruining the life not only of the mother but also the child. Drawing on the conventions of the gothic, which clearly inform Gogol's text, Blok compares the entry of his hero's future father into the home of his maternal grandparents, the Beketovs, to the arrival of a "odd stranger" (neznakomets strannyi) (SS, 3:319), and he associates him not only with the figure of Byron but also with the far more demonic figure of the Gogolian wizard.[44] Like the Gogolian wizard, Blok's fictional father is associated with the potential for child killing, if not with the act per se. In the stanzas that immediately follow the appearance of this demonic stranger into the Beketov household, Blok intimates that this prospective suitor is a potential murderer by linking him with a hawk who feeds on young nestlings:

> Встань, выйди по́утру на луг:
> На бледном небе ястреб кружит,
> Чертя за кругом плавный круг,
> Высматривая, где похуже
> Гнездо припрятано в кустах . . .
> Вдруг—птичий щебет и движенье . . .
> Он слушает . . . еще мгновенье—
> Слетает на прямых крылах . . .
> Тревожный крик из гнезд соседних,
> Печальный писк птенцов последних,
> Пух нежный по́ ветру летит—

> Он жертву бедную когтит...
> И вновь, взмахнув крылом огромным,
> Взлетел—чертить за кругом круг,
> Несытым оком и бездомным
> Осматривать пустынный луг...
> Когда ни взглянешь,—кружит, кружит...
>
> Россия-мать, как птица, тужит
> О детях; но—ее судьба,
> Чтоб их терзали ястреба.
>
> (SS, 3:319)

[Get up, go out in the morning to the meadow. In the pale sky, a hawk circles, sketching smooth circle after circle, looking for where a nest is concealed the worst in the shrubs... Suddenly, bird twittering and movement... He listens... and a moment later flies down on straight wings... A warning cry from the neighboring nests, the sad squeak of the last fledglings, fine down flies in the wind, and he claws the poor victim... And again, flapping his enormous wing, he flies up, sketching circle after circle. With an insatiable and homeless eye, he looks around the deserted meadow... Whenever you look, he is circling, circling... Mother-Russia, like a bird, grieves for her children; but it is her fate that the hawks will tear them to pieces.][45]

After casting a shadow on the suitor's intentions in this passage and drawing an implicit connection between the family romances of the Beketovs and Bloks and of Russia proper, Blok goes on to describe the courtship and subsequent marriage of the hero's mother to the hero's father in terms highly reminiscent of "A Terrible Vengeance." Though Blok departs from the incestuous plot of the original, configuring the demon-suitor as a stranger rather than as a member of the family, he persists in viewing his hero's parents in the context of the Gogolian tale. In this text, the hero's mother does not fall in love with her young suitor but is seduced by his charms and magic potions, much as the father-wizard seduced his daughter in Gogol's story. As Blok notes: "He charmed the youngest daughter with his beauty. He promised her a kingdom (not owning one). And she believed him, growing pale ... He transformed her native home into a prison (although this home did not resemble a prison at all...)" (On krasotoiu / Men'shuiu doch' ocharoval. / I tsarstvo [tsarstvom ne vladeia] / On obeshchal ei. I emu / Ona poverila, bledneia... / I dom ee rodnoi v tiur'mu / On prevratil [khotia nimalo / S tiur'moi ne skhodstvoval sei dom...]) (SS, 3:324). And if the courtship of the hero's father and mother is compared to the seduction of Pani Katerina, then their marriage and ensuing physical union, is described as a cross between the union of Lermontov's demon with the princess Tamara and that of count Dracula with one of his female victims.[46] In what appears to be a poetic reenactment of the primal scene, the poet describes the union of the hero's mother with the father demon as a vampiric attack: "(And in an instant he shakes his sickly wing, descends stealthily on the meadow, and drinks the live blood of the shaking victim, who is frightened out of her mind . . .) — This is the love of that vampiric century which turned into cripples those worthy of the calling of human being!" ([Seichas — bol'nym krylom vzmakhnet, / Na lug opustitsia besshumno / I budet pit' zhivuiu krov' / Uzhe ot uzhasa — bezumnoi, / Drozhashchei zhertvy . . .] — Vot — liubov' / Togo vampirstvennogo veka, / Kotoryi prevratil v kalek / Dostoinykh zvan'ia cheloveka!) (SS, 3:325). The young wife does, however, finally manage to escape from the clutches of her demon-husband, though she is certainly the worse for wear. Like one who has had all of her lifeblood drained from her, she returns home "thin, worn out, pale . . . And in her arms lies a child" (Khuda, izmuchena, bledna . . . / I na rukakh lezhit rebenok) (SS, 3:327).

In Gogol's tale, Pani Katerina's resistance only makes the father-wizard more intent on enacting revenge, which he does by killing her son and then her husband, Danilo, and Blok intimates that the demon-husband in his poem may react to his wife's abandonment in a similar way. Though Blok never completed the poem's second chapter, which was to deal with the hero's upbringing, he does open it with the Gogolian wizard, thereby casting a shadow on the son's education. The first stanza of the second chapter begins: "In those distant, obscure years, slumber and darkness reigned in our hearts. Above Russia, Pobedonostsev stretched his owl wings, and it was neither day or night, but just a shadow of enormous wings; he traced a magic circle around Russia, looking into her eyes with the glassy gaze of the wizard" (V te gody dal'nie, glukhie, / V serdtsakh tsarili son i mgla: / Pobedonostsev nad Rossiei / Proster sovinye kryla, / I ne bylo ni dnia, ni nochi / A tol'ko — ten' ogromnykh kryl; / On divnym krugom ochertil / Rossiiu, zaglianuv ei v ochi / Stekliannym vzorom kolduna) (SS, 3:328). Even though Blok opens this chapter on the hero's education with a description of Konstantin Pobedonostsev rather than his hero's own father, he establishes an affinity between the two by associating them both with sorcery. That Blok should identify the reactionary legal scholar and procurator of the Holy Synod with paternal authority has a certain logic, given that Pobedonostsev had personally undertaken the supervision of the education of Nicholas II and that he had shared with Blok's own father the vocation of law.

While it becomes apparent in the third chapter that the son manages to escape the clutches of father, who shares a certain kinship with the evil wizard Pobedonostsev, and to survive into adulthood, the notion that the father may succumb to violence continues to haunt the child even after the death of the father. The third chapter opens with the hero, the demon's son, traveling to Warsaw to visit his dying father. Although the son arrives only after his father has already died, he continues to see him, even in death, as a potential threat. As Blok's hero gazes on the corpse of his father, he decides to retrieve his ring, and it is at this point, when he is bent over the corpse of his father, that he realizes the extent to which his father embodied an evil force:

> Ушли родные. Только сын
> Склонен над трупом... Как разбойник,
> Он хочет осторожно снять
> Кольцо с руки оцепенелой...
> (Неопытному трудно смело
> У мертвых пальцы разгибать).
> И только преклонив колени
> Над самой грудью мертвеца,
> Увидел он, *какие* тени
> Легли вдоль этого лица...
> Когда же с непокорных пальцев
> Кольцо скользнуло в жесткий гроб,
> Сын окрестил отцовский лоб,
> Прочтя на нем печать скитальцев,
> Гонимых пó миру судьбой...
> Поправил руки, образ, свечи,
> Взглянул на вскинутые плечи
> И вышел, молвив: "Бог с тобой".
>
> (SS, 3:334–35)

[The relatives left. Only the son is bent above the corpse... Like a robber, he wants to carefully remove the ring from the torpid hand... (It is difficult for an inexperienced person to bravely unbend the fingers of the dead). And only having kneeled over the very chest of the dead man did he see *what kind of* shadows fell along that face... When from the unyielding fingers the ring slipped into the rigid casket, the son crossed his father's brow, reading on it the stamp of wanderers, chased across the world by fate... He straightened his hands, the icon, the candles, looked at the protruding shoulders and left, saying: "God be with you."]

A Time of Troubles

There is an abounding fear in this work that the dead father will be roused and will inflict violence on the child, and thus the hero's father can be seen both as a vampire who might awaken from the dead and as a Pushkinian statue that may come to life and wreak havoc on the hero (with the rigor mortis of the corpse making the dead father appear like a statue).[47] And an elaborate ritual is performed to ensure that the demon-father will not be awakened from the dead. The poetic speaker observes: "A woman decorated his raised shoulders with flowers; then on the ribs of the coffin an irrevocable strip of lead was placed (so that, having been resurrected, he could not get up)" (Tsvetkami dama ubrala / Ego pripodniatye plechi; / Potom na rebra groba leg / Svinets poloskoiu besspornoi / [Chtob on, voskresnuv, vstat' ne mog]) (SS, 3:335). Although this act may ensure that the father will not be roused from his grave, it does not prevent memories of the father from haunting the hero. During the funeral services, the son is unable to shake memories of his demonic father and of their shared kinship: "In the soul of the child, he left difficult memories: he never knew his father. They met only accidentally, living in separate cities, so alien in all their paths (except perhaps the most secret ones)" (V dushe rebenka ostavlial / Tiazhelye vospominan'ia — / Otsa on nikogda ne znal. / Oni vstrechalis' lish' sluchaino, / Zhivia v razlichnykh gorodakh, / Stol' chuzhdye vo vsekh putiakh / [Byt' mozhet, krome samykh tainykh]) (SS, 3:336). An inclination toward violence would appear to be the one of the secret things that bound father and son together. Though the father may have been inclined toward vampirism, the son could also extract blood from his father:

> Сын помнит: в детской, на диване
> Сидит отец, куря и злясь;
> А он, безумно расшалясь,
> Вертится пред отцом в тумане . . .
> Вдруг (злое, глупое дитя!) —
> Как будто бес его толкает,
> И он стремглав отцу вонзает
> Булавку около локтя . . .
> Растерян, побледнев от боли,
> Тот дико вскрикнул . . .
>   Этот крик
> С внезапной яркостью возник
> Здесь, над могилою, на "Воле", —
> И сын очнулся . . . Вьюги свист;
> Толпа; могильщик холм ровняет;
> Шуршит и бьется бурый лист . . .
>   (SS, 3:337)

[The son recalls: The father sits in the child's room on a sofa, smoking and growing irritable; and becoming naughty, he senselessly turns about in front of his father in a fog ... Suddenly (an evil, stupid child!), as if the devil urges him, he plunges a pin right into his father near his elbow ... Upset, white from the pain, he cried out wildly ... That cry appeared with sudden clarity here above the grave at "Liberty," and the son awoke ... The whistle of the whirlwind; the crowd; the grave digger is evening out the mound; the brown leaf rustles and beats about ...]

Unable to come to terms with the legacy of his father, and with the sickly blood ties that bind father and son, the hero begins to wander through Poland. His wanderings are framed by the appearance of the horseman of Pan-Moroz. While the city of Warsaw quietly sleeps, Pan-Moroz, who resembles the horseman from both Pushkin's *Bronze Horseman* and Gogol's "A Terrible Vengeance," gallops throughout the city, sowing vengeance:[48]

> Жизнь глухо кроется в подпольи,
> Молчат магнатские дворцы ...
> Лишь Пан-Мороз во все концы
> Свирепо рыщет на раздольи!
> Неистово взлетит над вами
> Его седая голова,
> Иль откидные рукава
> Взметутся бурей над домами,
> Иль конь заржет—и звоном струн
> Ответит телеграфный провод,
> Иль вздернет Пан взбешённый повод,
> И четко повторит чугун
> Удары мерзлого копыта
> По опустелой мостовой ...
> И вновь, поникнув головой,
> Безмолвен Пан, тоской убитый ...
> И, странствуя на злом коне,
> Бряцает шпорою кровавой ...
> Месть! Месть!—Так эхо над Варшавой
> Звенит в холодном чугуне!
>
> (*SS*, 3:340–41)

[Life tightly conceals itself underground; the magnates' palaces are silent ... Only Pan-Moroz fiercely roams about the open plain in all directions! Furiously his gray head flies up above you, or his folded sleeves wave up in storms above the houses, or his steed neighs, and the telegraph wire answers with a ring of strings, or the enraged Pan pulls up his rein, and the cast iron clearly echoes the blows of his frozen hoof on the deserted pavement ... And again having hung his head, Pan-Moroz, exhausted with anguish, is silent ... And wandering on his evil steed, he rattles his bloody spur ... Vengeance! Vengeance! So the echo rings out in the cold cast iron above Warsaw!]

Though Pan-Moroz never actually meets up with the hero-son the way that the Bronze Horseman does with Evgeny in Pushkin's Petersburg poem, there is an inkling that the appearance of this rider is, in part, connected to the travels that the hero embarks on after attending his father's funeral. While Blok had originally intended that his hero's wanderings would bring him into contact with the simple Polish woman who would conceive his child and possibly even spur him on to revolutionary deeds, this is not the way he envisions the final meeting between the Polish woman and his hero in the drafts of the remaining portions of the third chapter, which he worked on during the last months of his life. Instead, the hero's travels lead him into the Polish countryside in the middle of winter. Lost in a blizzard, he meets up with a simple girl named Maria from the Carpathian Mountains who offers him solace from the cold. Similar in some ways to the child in Dostoevsky's "The Boy at Christ's Christmas Party" ("Mal'chik u Khrista na elke") (January 1876), an important text for Blok dating back to the period following the events of 1905, he literally falls prey to Pan-Moroz. But unlike this child, Blok's hero does not die alone but in the embrace of the Polish woman Maria, whose name, Zara Mints has suggested, recalls the Polish girl in Gogol's *Taras Bulba* (*Taras Bul'ba*) (1835) who is indirectly responsible for Andrei's death at the hands of his own father.[49] But while the name of Maria may reinforce the idea of the son's own betrayal if not of his father, then of his fatherland, it is also a name which has far less inimical associations. Vladimir Orlov has observed that the name Maria may refer to the victimized heroine in Pushkin's "Poltava" (1829).[50] And, perhaps even more importantly, given Blok's reliance throughout so many of his works on a Christian imagery, the name recalls the Mother of God. In line with the religious associations of the name, the son's death in the arms of Maria can be seen as reminiscent of a pietà:

И он умирает в ее объятиях. Все неясные порывы, невоплощенные мысли, воля к подвигу, [никогда] не совершенному, растворяется на груди этой женщины.

> Мария, нежная Мария,
> Мне пусто, мне постыло жить!
> Я не свершил того . . . . .
> Того, что должен был свершить.
> (SS, 3:473)

[And he is dying in her arms. All the unclear aspirations, unfulfilled thoughts, the will for a heroic deed, which is [never] completed, dissolve on this woman's breast. Maria, tender Maria, living is empty and repellent for me! I did not complete what ..... what I should have completed.]

Blok's final lines, "I did not complete what ... what I should have completed" (Ia ne svershil togo ..... / Togo, chto dolzhen byl svershit'), ring prophetic. Although he had conceived of *Retribution* as a poem that would trace the story of his family and of Russia into the future, Blok found it no easier in this poem than in any of his earlier works to envision a harmonious relationship between the generations and to effect a smooth line of succession from father to son. While it can be surmised that the hero's final erotic embrace with Maria results in the conception of a son who will fulfill those ideals that die with the hero, it is telling that Blok never actually completed those sections of the poem dealing with the birth of the child. Blok's seeming inability to realize this child stems as much from the dynamics of the poem as from his own illness. If within the completed chapters of the poem, Blok configures the family romance of the fictitious Blok family as a rewriting of Gogol's "A Terrible Vengeance" or even Bram Stoker's *Dracula*, replete with violence and infanticidal tendencies, then within the preface that he attached to the poem in 1919, he emphasizes the way the poem itself—and modern Russian history—is animated by a dance of death akin to that which fueled the Time of Troubles—the mazurka of Maryna Mniszek. And it is the fatal dance of Maryna, rather than the regenenerative powers of Maria, that appear to predominate in this poem, turning it into a modernist vision of the Time of Troubles. And much like Pushkin's and Mussorgsky's versions of the Time of Troubles, this poem is haunted by child death.

Even though Blok may have conceived of *Retribution* as a homage not just to his biological father but also, to some extent, to his spiritual father Pushkin, this poem ends up turning into one about the death of the son and of the demise of the family. And as a poem about the end of his family line, it resonated with the events in civil-war-era Russia. There is some evidence to suggest that Blok emphasized the connections between the recent events in Russian history and the plot of his poem by the ways he staged readings of the text. In September 1920, two years after the assassination of the tsar and his family in Ekaterinburg, Blok read excerpts from *Retribution* at the House of Arts; the poet Maria

Shkapskaia also was scheduled to read, and at Blok's urging, she read a poem about the murder of a male heir to the throne. Shkapskaia's reading of the poem reportedly produced outrage from Gumilev, one of the poets whom Blok had earlier accused of being "burdened by progeny and acmeism." The poet Nadezhda Pavlovich recalls that "Gumilev was disturbed that Shkapskaia publicly read her poem, 'Louis XVII,' where she spoke of the legal and internal justice of the death of the dauphin, the son of the executed Louis XVI. The poem resounded topically; it spoke of the fate of the successor to the throne, Alexis, the son of Nicholas II. Blok had included the poem in the literary evening and insisted that Maria Mikhailovna read it."[51]

That Blok would have been drawn to Shkapskaia's poem about the death of the heir to the throne comes as no surprise when we consider the disruptive model of generational history that predominates in *Retribution* as well as some of his earlier writings. From very early on in his poetic career, Blok had expressed skepticism about the idea that there could be a smooth transition between the generations, particularly with the end of the golden age of domesticity, which for him coincided with the events of 1905. And after 1917, he appears to have resigned himself to the idea that this end of the golden age of domesticity had become a reality. Pavlovich reports that "at that time there were daily accounts about the fact that children would be taken from their mothers for a communist upbringing. M. M. Shkapskaia and I went to [Blok's mother] Alexandra Andreevna who was upset by this prospect. Shkapskaia was upset; for her it was a question of a personal nature. Alexander Alexandrovich did not enter into the conversation for some time, and then unexpectedly he said: 'But perhaps it would have been better for me if . . . they had taken me in their own time . . .'"[52] Distraught by the rumors that such a policy was to be instituted, Pavlovich composed the short poem: "An orchard has apple trees, a woman has children, but I have only songs, and that pains me" (U sada—est' iabloni, / U zhenshchiny est' deti, / A u menia tol'ko pesni, / I mne—bol'no).[53] Blok responded to Pavlovich's four-line poem with one of his own which took a radically different position on the idea of the breakup of the family and was consistent with his strife-ridden vision of history. In what can be seen as a quintessentially modernist restatement of the Latin phrase "ars longa, vita brevis" as well as a gloss on his own antigenerative poetics, Blok proclaims poetry to be more permeable and pleasurable than progeny:

> Яблони сада вырваны,
> Дети у женщины взяты,
> Песню не взять, не вырвать,
> Сладостна боль ее.
>
> (SS, 3:375)

[The orchard's apple trees are torn out, the children are taken from the woman, a song cannot be taken or torn out, its pain is delightful.]

II

Writing against the Body
Gippius and the Problem of Lyric Embodiment

Дано мне тело—что мне делать с ним,
Таким единым и таким моим?

За радость тихую дышать и жить,
Кого, скажите, мне благодарить?
[I am given a body—what should I do with it so singular and so uniquely mine? For the quiet joy of breathing and living who, tell me, am I to thank?]
>   Osip Mandelstam, "I am given a body—what should I do with it?" ("Dano mne telo—chto mne delat' s nim?") (1909)

На нас тела, как клочья песни спетой . . .
В небытие
Свисает где-то мертвенной планетой
Всё существо мое.

В слепых очах, в глухорожденном слухе—
Кричат тела.
Беспламенные, каменные духи!
Беспламенная мгла!
[Bodies hang on us like the tatters of a song sung . . . My whole being is suspended somewhere in nonbeing like a dead planet. In blind eyes, in deaf-born ears, bodies yell. Flameless, stone spirits! Flameless darkness!]
>   Andrei Bely, "Bodies" ("Tela") (1916)

Каменной глыбой серой,
С веком порвав родство.
Тело твое—пещера
Голоса твоего.

[Like a gray monolith, having severed ties with the age. Your body is the cave of your voice.]

        Marina Tsvetaeva, "The Sibyl" ("Sivilla") (6 August 1922)

5

Style "Femme"
Gippius and the Resistance to Feminine Writing

Я не знаю зачем упрекают меня,
Что в созданьях моих слишком много огня,
Что стремлюсь я навстречу живому лучу
И наветам унынья внимать не хочу.
Что блещу я царицей в нарядных стихах,
С диадемой на пышных моих волосах,
Что из рифм я себе ожерелье плету,
Что пою я любовь, что пою красоту.
Но бессмертья я смертью своей не куплю,
И для песен я звонкие песни люблю.
И безумью ничтожных мечтаний моих
Не изменит мой жгучий, мой женственный стих.
[I don't know why they reproach me that there is too much fire in my creations, that I rush to greet the living ray, and I don't want to hear the slander of dejection. That I sparkle like a queen in my elegant verses with a diadem in my luxurious tresses, that I weave a necklace for myself from rhymes, that I sing of love, that I sing of beauty. But I will not buy immortality with my death, and for my songs I like sonorous songs. And my burning, my feminine verse will not betray the madness of my petty reveries.]

    Mirra Lokhvitskaia, "I don't know why they reproach me" ("Ia ne znaiu zachem uprekaiut menia") (1898)

Zinaida Gippius certainly shared with her younger contemporary, Alexander Blok, a resistance to traditional marriage and procreation.¹ In her correspondence with the longtime object of her affections and member of the Merezhkovsky ménage, Dmitry Filosofov, she claimed that "the ancestral instinct [was] not in [her]" (rodovogo chuvstva vo mne net) (*IIA*, 72), and that "the [sexual] act [was] oriented backward, downward, into the family and the birth of children" (akt obrashchen nazad, vniz, v rod, v detorozhdenie) (*IIA*, 67). But while she openly eschewed the generative impulse in her correspondence, as well as in her philosophical writings, she organized her poetic myth in a radically different manner than Blok and did not choose to make the relinquishment of family ties and domesticity the focal point of her poetic works. If Blok struggled throughout much of his poetic career against the burdens of progeny and domesticity, making it one of the dominant themes of his poetry, then Gippius, as a woman poet, was engaged in a battle against burdens of a much more essential variety in her verse—that of the body and more specifically the female body—in an effort to be accepted as a serious poet and thinker within the male-dominated Russian symbolist movement, a movement that like its French counterpart put a great emphasis on the ethereal and the otherworldly.

However, in Russian symbolism, women were accorded a much more central role than they were in French symbolism, running salons and even publishing in the major journals and periodicals.² Nonetheless, there was still a tendency among the major practitioners of the movement to envision woman as muse rather than writing subject and to conflate her with the figure of the eternal feminine, which came to Russia via the German romantics and was valorized in the writings of Vladimir Soloviev, an important figure for the symbolists.³ It was partly for this reason that some women writers such as Poliksena Solovieva, the sister of Vladimir Soloviev, opted to mask their sex in their writings. Solovieva not only employed masculine verbal forms in her verse, forms considered to be unmarked in Russian, but she also used the pseudonym "Allegro," which would conceal her female sex as well as her connection to Soloviev, who was in large part responsible for the cult of the feminine among the symbolists. This is not to imply that it was impossible for women to gain critical acclaim in modern Russia by writing as women. In fact, one of the most popular turn-of-the-century poets, Mirra Lokhvitskaia, wrote in an unabashedly feminine and sensuous fashion that did not prevent her from gaining entry into literary circles or from receiving the prestigious Pushkin Prize twice, including once posthumously. Indeed, it might be argued that it was Lokhvitskaia's willingness to embrace her femininity that made her so popular, paving the way for the emergence later of a figure such as Anna Akhmatova.[4]

Gippius, however, chose an artistic path that was diametrically opposed to that of Lokhvitskaia and Akhmatova and that was in certain respects more akin to that of Solovieva with whom she had a close friendship.[5] Whereas Lokhvitskaia called attention to her feminine style of writing, referring to her poetry as "my burning, my feminine verse" (moi zhguchii, moi zhenstvennyi stikh) and casting herself as overtly feminine in her poetry, Gippius resisted identifying with the feminine in her verse or with a mode of writing that the French feminists subsequently identified as *écriture féminine* or writing the female body.[6] Not only did she draw inspiration for her verse from Charles Baudelaire and the (male) metaphysical tradition in Russian poetry but she made the conscious decision to mask her sex in her writing.[7] She chose to write, in her own words, "like a *human being*, and not just like a woman" (kak *chelovek*, a ne tol'ko kak zhenshchina), as if to imply that writing like a woman was somehow inferior to writing as a human being.[8] In an attempt to hide or de-emphasize her sex, she frequently used the unmarked (masculine) voice in her poetry rather than the feminine voice a female poet typically used, and she consistently employed the androgynous or unmarked signature, Z. N. Gippius, for her poetry rather than Zinaida Gippius or Zinaida Gippius-Merezhkovskaia, which would mark her not simply as a woman but as the wife of Dmitry Merezhkovsky.[9] As she explicitly informed the writer Nina Berberova somewhat later in life, "my signature is, of course, Z. Gippius. I have never in my life signed as 'Zinaida'" (*PBKh*, 8).[10]

Yet, in spite of her suppression of "Zinaida" and many of the feminine associations that went along with this signature, Gippius's writing was often perceived in stereotypically feminine terms. Critics in the popular press insisted on employing the terms "female writer" (zhenshchina-pisatel'nitsa) and "poetess" (poetessa) to describe her.[11] For example, in an article entitled "Contemporary Women Writers" ("Sovremennye zhenshchiny-pisatel'nitsy"), which appeared in M. O. Volf's journal *The Herald of Literature* (*Vestnik literatury*) in August 1901, Vladimir Novoselov classifies Gippius as one of many women writers or *zhenshchiny-pisatel'nitsy*, a label that clearly reinforces the authors' femininity through the redundant pairing of the word *zhenshchiny* or women with the already gender-marked *pisatel'nitsy* or female writers. In keeping with this general tendency to view the authors as women first and then as writers, Novoselov not only refers to Gippius as "Madame Gippius" (G-zha Gippius) but also characterizes her poetry in stereotypically feminine terms, this in spite of her predilection for the masculine voice and for metaphysical subjects in much of her poetry. He indicates that "Z. N. Gippius is an original female writer, whose talent is brilliant, yet capricious [darovanie iarkoe, no kapriznoe]. No one has works that are as uneven as Mme. Gippius." He continues: "She has things that are delightful, bearable, and just plain impossible" (U nee est' veshchi prelestnye, snosnye i priamo nevozmozhnye).[12] We must wonder whether Novoselov would have used the words "capricious" (kapriznoe) or "impossible" (nevozmozhnoe) to describe a male poet's talent, for these are epithets that are generally employed not to describe creative gifts but rather to characterize what is traditionally seen as a difficult female character. By identifying Gippius's poetical works in such a fashion, Novoselov insinuates that Gippius writes in that very manner she eschewed, that is to say like a woman.

Novoselov was by no means unique in his tendency to read a woman's poetry in terms of stereotypical assumptions about the nature of women or the female sex. Other critics who published in the popular press at the turn of the century also participated in what Sandra M. Gilbert has termed the fetishization of the femininity of the female poet.[13] When Gilbert speaks of the fetishization of the female poet, she refers to the obsession among members of the critical establishment with locating a feminine style of writing and style of dress in the female writer, regardless of whether the writer in question defined herself as a poet or a poetess or engaged in cross-dressing or dressed in traditionally feminine garb. While Gilbert locates this tendency within an early twentieth-century Anglo-American context, a similar phenomenon existed in Russia at the turn of the century. Interestingly enough, in the Russian context this fetishization of the femininity of the female author sometimes manifested itself as an outgrowth of the turn-of-the-century fascination with the romantic notion of the eternal feminine, as well as of the 1860s discussions about the so-called woman question or *zhenskii vopros*—a discourse that was originally intended to liberate women from exploitation.[14]

Perhaps one of the biggest proponents of the latter was Kornei Chukovsky. In his book on modernism, *Faces and Masks* (*Litsa i maski*) (1914), Chukovsky enters into an imaginary dialogue with Gippius in which he accuses her of fabricating her poetic texts like a seamstress. "How monotonous and poor" (Kak odnoobrazno i bedno), he notes. "It is as if [your poems] were fabricated on a machine in bundles by the dozens. You fabricate more and more" (Kak budto na mashinke sfabrikovano tselymi pachkami, diuzhinami. Vy zhe fabrikuete eshche i eshche).[15] Here Chukovsky implicates her in the typically feminine activities of sewing and fabricating rather than writing, suggesting that the machine she employs to produce her art is not the typewriter or "writing machine" (pishushchaia mashinka) but the sewing machine or *shveinaia mashinka*. He invites such an interpretation when he refers to her creative process as fabrication and also perhaps when he speaks of the creative product as bundles or *pachki*. The Russian word *pachki* can refer to bundles of printed material as in *pachki pisem* or *pachki gazet* as well as to bundles of material, namely the ballerina's costume or tutu. While Chukovsky clearly has the former meaning in mind, he implicitly borrows his metaphors from the realm of the factory when he accuses Gippius of producing her poems by the bundles.

By figuratively locating her within the factory, he reduces her creativity to little more than a mode of mass production. Furthermore, he calls attention to the sexualized nature of this process. Not only is the implied instrument of her labors, the sewing machine, grammatically feminine in Russian but it can be perceived as a mechanized representation of the female body and sexuality because of its ability to produce endlessly. Perhaps the best example in Russian culture of this conflation of the sewing machine with the female body can be found in Nikolai Chernyshevsky's novel *What Is to Be Done?* (*Chto delat'?*) (1863), a work with which Chukovsky and his entire generation was well acquainted. In the novel, the heroine, Vera Pavlovna, enters into a Platonic marriage with Lopukhov, a member of the radical intelligentsia of the 1860s, rather than allowing herself to be prostituted in a figurative sense by accepting the marriage proposal of a wealthy man whom she does not love. Finding her marriage to Lopukhov to be unfulfilling, she decides to channel her energies into opening up a sewing factory that employs destitute women and ex-prostitutes. In this role as mistress (or madame) of the sewing factory, Vera Pavlovna enables the young women to replace their female bodies with the feminine sewing machine as the instrument of their livelihoods, allowing them to convert unproductive female sexuality into productive female labor.[16]

In Chernyshevsky's text, the sewing machine emerges as a necessary harness for unbridled female energy and sexuality. With the repetitious up-and-down motion of the needle, the sewing machine replaces the repetitive motion of the sexual act with productive labor, transforming sewing into a sublimated form of sexual activity. Chukovsky, it would appear, was at least implicitly aware of the cultural associations of sewing with a displaced or sublimated form of sex, for in the paragraph immediately following his discussion of how Gippius fashions or fabricates her poetic texts, he accuses her of engaging in the related activity of *slovobludie*, which could be translated as either verbal promiscuity or verbal masturbation.[17] In an interchange that is more akin to that between a judge and an accused than that between the critic and writer, Chukovsky implores Gippius: "What is this? 'Modesty of shamelessness,' 'beginning end,' 'passionate impassion,'—what is this in your works? Is it simply verbal promiscuity, *façon de parler*, or a genuine heartfelt feeling" (Chto zhe eto takoe? "Skromnost' besstydstva," "nachal'ynyi konets," "strastnoe besstrastie,"—chto zhe eto takoe u vas? Prosto li slovobludie, *façon de parler*, ili podlinnoe krovnoe chuvstvo)?[18] And with this Chukovsky extends his identification of sewing with sex, taking it from the thematic level to the linguistic level, employing the French expression, *façon de parler*, meaning in a manner or style of speaking, to refer directly to her verbal fabrication.

Identifying Gippius's poetic process with both verbal fabrication and *slovobludie*, Chukovsky would seem to view Gippius, the female symbolist poet, through the cultural lens of the prostitute-seamstresses in Chernyshevsky's novel.[19] Yet I should like to emphasize that while Chukovsky implicitly draws on the representation of the feminine presented in Chernyshevsky's novel, the underlying assumption in his appropriation of it—that the creative model of the female artist is necessarily synonymous with the impure and obscene form of female fabrication—was by no means confined to perceptions of the feminine offered up in Russian literature and culture. In fact, Elisabeth G. Gitter has convincingly demonstrated that female creativity was frequently associated with female sexuality in Victorian novels and popular literature, which are filled with images of golden-haired spinners and seamstresses, and in Sigmund Freud's purportedly scientific writings on femininity.[20]

In his notorious public lecture "Femininity" ("Die Weiblichkeit")(1933), Freud offers as scientific fact notions about female creativity that are similar to those Chukovsky offers as subjective critical judgment in his essay on Gippius. In this lecture, Freud maintains that there is an inherently sexual and even perverse nature to the traditional arts of the distaff side. "It seems," he opines, "that women have made few contributions to the discoveries and inventions in the history of civilization; there is, however, one technique which they may have invented—that of plaiting and weaving. If that is so, we should be tempted to guess the unconscious motive for the achievement. Nature herself would seem to have given the model which this achievement imitates by causing the growth at maturity of the pubic hair that conceals the genitals. The step that remained to be taken lay in making the threads adhere to one another, while on the body they stick into the skin and are only matted together. If you reject this idea as fantastic and regard my belief in the influence of lack of a penis on the configuration of femininity as an *idée fixe*, I am of course defenseless."[21]

Freud suggests that the primary motive behind female plaiting and weaving is not to create an object of art or even ornamentation but rather to compensate for women's supposed genital deficiency. He insists that women engage in the activities of plaiting and weaving in an attempt to imitate what he perceives as the natural plaiting or weaving of the pubic hair that conceals the absent (female) penis. With this interpretation, he not only calls attention to the ostensibly compensatory and inferior nature of female creativity but he also reduces female creativity to little more than a sexual perversion, since this discussion interfaces almost perfectly with his earlier remarks on fetishism. In his article "Fetishism" ("Fetischismus"), completed in 1927, several years before his public lecture on femininity, Freud explains that female hair and clothing, that is, the products of feminine plaiting and weaving, frequently serve as penis substitutes or fetish objects for the adult male, since they veil the female body, concealing the absent (maternal) penis that the adult male like "the little boy once believed in and—for reasons familiar to us—does not want to give up."[22] If in the early essay, Freud presents fetishism as the male perversion par excellence, then by 1933 he appears to implicate women in this perversion, for in his lecture on femininity he identifies the feminine arts of plaiting and weaving as unconsciously motivated by a desire to fashion or fabricate a substitute for the so-called absent (female) penis, something that has led Roland Barthes to assert that Freud "institutionally [devolves] fetishism onto women."[23]

In his insistence on the inherently sexual and fetishistic nature of female creativity, Freud is not too different from Chukovsky. Both Freud and Chukovsky assume that female creativity is a mere fabrication or imitation of nature. And both enact what might be termed "downward displacement" in their interpretation of female creativity: Freud aligns the feminine activities of plaiting and weaving with the inherently onanistic activity of the plaiting and weaving of the pubic hair, while Chukovsky aligns Gippius's writing with *slovobludie*.[24] Though Chukovsky's comments are much less overtly anatomical than Freud's, his critique of Gippius may ultimately be more shocking because of the manner in which it appears to transform the 1860s writer's representation of feminine labor and creativity against a woman writer. To be sure, not all appropriations of the writings of the 1860s by critics of women writers were nearly as negative or bodily as that of Chukovsky. However, in the final analysis, many of these early twentieth-century critics tended to fetishize the femininity of the female author either by accusing the female author of engaging in the traditionally feminine act of fabrication, as Chukovsky does, or by trying to isolate the essence of the writer's feminine soul or *zhenskaia dusha*.

Pavel Krasnov participates in the latter tendency. In his review of A. N. Salnikov's book, "Our Contemporary Poetesses" ("Nashi sovremennye poetessy"), published in *The Herald of Literature* in 1905, Krasnov draws on the writings of another 1860s radical critic, Dmitry Pisarev, in his discussion of female creativity.[25] In the opening paragraph, Krasnov defines his task as a literary critic in terms of a somewhat idiosyncratic restatement of Pisarev's views on femininity. "One of the eternally interesting questions," Krasnov maintains, "has to be the question of the spiritual differences of the sexes. Does there exist a specifically feminine soul that does not resemble the masculine soul, and does this femininity consist, as Pisarev maintained, in the combination of weakness, stupidity, and coquettishness, or are there some specifically feminine traits which are not destroyed even in that instance when a woman ceases to be weak and stupid, that is to say when she possesses a unique development and talent?"[26] Although Krasnov purports to be more enlightened than his precursor, who he claims identified femininity as "a combination of weakness, stupidity, and coquettishness" (kombinatsiia slabosti, gluposti i koketskva), Kransov's views on women's poetry ultimately serve to reinforce stereotypes about the true essence of the "female soul" (zhenskaia dusha). At the end of his review of Salnikov's book, which is devoted to a study of women poets as disparate as Allegro, Gippius, Lokhvitskaia, and Teffi, Krasnov concludes with the sweeping generalization that all women's poetry in Russia is united by a preoccupation with "passivity" (passivnost') and "coquettishness" (koketstvo), and in so doing he ends up sounding very much like the Pisarev he describes in the beginning of his essay.[27]

Krasnov does not, however, end his review here. As if his final judgment about the femininity of women's poetry in Russia were not convincing enough, he leaves the reader of his review with one final image to ponder. At the end of his review he includes a page containing a series of photographs of the women writers featured in Salnikov's book. The photographs of the women are purposefully arranged so as to create the illusion that they are from a page in a personal photograph album. This style of framing the women's portraits creates an air of intimacy that would not normally be accorded to male writers and is symptomatic of just that type of fetishization of the female author that Gilbert has identified in early twentieth-century criticism. The images of these women writers do not suggest they are poets; rather their arrangement turns them into just a series of elegant female figures designed for viewing pleasure. Framed as beautiful objects for the (male) gaze, the photographs of the women poets become the ultimate fetish objects. Fashionable and forever silent, these female artists appear to exude the very sentiment, passivity, and coquettishness that Krasnov ascribes to their poetry.[28]

Gippius would probably not have looked favorably on such a trivial representation of herself as one of many pretty young women in a photograph album, let alone on her early critics' insistence on referring to her as a "poetess" (poetessa) and "woman writer" (zhenshchina-pisatel'nitsa). She not only resisted being identified in print as a woman writer by employing a genderless signature but also reportedly shunned all official affiliations with women writers. In later years, she reportedly told the émigré writer Irina Odoevtseva, "Once in Petersburg they approached me for poems for a women's salon album and I told them: I do not form affiliations on the basis of sex! [po polovomu priznaku ne ob"ediniaius'!]."[29] In addition, she argued virulently against such sectarianism in print. In an article entitled "On the Female Sex" ("O zhenskom pole") (1923), Gippius, writing under the male pseudonym of Lev Pushchin, argues against the then-critical preoccupation with the gender of the female artist.[30] She calls for a genderless criticism, stating: "Art does has not deserve to be considered either with the female or with the male sex. Art does not acknowledge two measures [male and female], but only one — its own." Believing that art is by definition ungendered, she goes on later in this same article to refute the very categories of "women's poetry" (zhenskaia poeziia) and "women's art" (zhenskoe iskusstvo). "In every 'live woman,'" she holds, "there is something else besides the 'female sex.' And creativity belongs to just this portion of 'the besides.' Only to this portion. It is true that this portion is typically not large. The prevailing 'feminine' may crush this portion or it may paint it in its own colors . . . It is unwise that we, not understanding this, proclaim pell-mell: 'female sex' = 'woman.' And having dreamed up such an absurd concept as 'female creativity,' we write about 'women's poetry' or about nonexistent 'women's art.'"[31]

But perhaps one of the greatest paradoxes of Zinaida Gippius is that in spite of her insistence that there was no such thing as "women's poetry," she seemed more than willing to indulge her critics' and contemporaries' expectations and play a feminine role. And in this regard, she evinced some similarities with Mirra Lokhvitskaia. But whereas Lokhvitskaia fashioned herself as overtly feminine in her poetry, calling attention to how "[she] sparkle[d] like a queen in [her] elegant verses with a diadem in [her] luxurious tresses" (bleshchu ia tsaritsei v nariadnykh stikhakh, / S diademoi na pyshnykh moikh volosakh), Gippius, for the most part, confined her feminine self-fashioning to the realm of the salon, transforming her very self into a work of art and inviting the fashion critiques of her contemporaries.[32] According to Akim Volynsky, editor of *The Northern Herald* (*Severnyi vestnik*), "Gippius was not only a poetess by profession. She was herself poetic through and through [Ona sama byla poetichna naskvoz']. She dressed in a somewhat provocative and sometimes even loud manner. But there was great fantastical beauty in her toilet all day long. The cult of beauty never forsook her either in the abstract or in life. In the evening having let down the massive shades in the study of Muruzi House on Liteiny [Prospect], she would sometimes let down the current of her rather sylph-like hair. She would take a tortoise shell comb and comb through her hair calling forth sparks of magnetic light. There was in this an everlasting intoxicating eroticism."[33]

By all accounts, Gippius's penchant for calling attention to her body and hair continued even in later years while in exile in Paris. Nina Berberova, for instance, offers a description of Gippius's entrance into a Parisian literary salon that approximates the description of the fashion model's entrance onto the runway. And Berberova spares no words in her critique of Gippius's fashion sense, remarking: "She always liked the color pink, which was not becoming to her dark red hair, but she had her own criteria and what in another woman might have appeared strange became with her a part of her very self. A half-transparent silk scarf streamed around her neck, her thick hair was arranged in a complex hairdo."[34] This description sounds more like the advice we would find in the "Dos and Don'ts" section of a twenty-first century fashion magazine than a literary memoir: Redheads should never wear pink! Berberova's description of Gippius's salon fashion is not at all unusual.

Gippius's clothing and hairstyles became the subject of discussion in the writings of contemporary writers and critics alike including those of Sergei Makovsky, Vladimir Zlobin, and Irina Odoevtseva.[35] At times, this obsession with her fashion deteriorated into an almost clinical form of fetishism. Ivan Bunin, for instance, allegedly went so far as to speculate about the intimate contents of Gippius's closet. Berberova recalls in her memoirs how he "jokingly said that in her commode lay forty pairs of pink silk panties and in her closet hung forty pink petticoats."[36]

If we are to believe Gippius's contemporaries, this fetishistic fascination with her clothing and hair (not to mention her lingerie) was by and large the product of her own design. In *On the Parnassus of the "Silver Age"* (*Na Parnase "Serebrianogo veka"*) (1962), Sergei Makovsky maintains that "she dressed in a fashion that was not customary in writers' circles and not how they dressed in 'society,' in a very unique manner with the obvious intention of being noticed. She wore dresses of her 'own' design that either clung to her like scales or had ruches and flounces. She loved beads, chains, and fluffy scarves. Need I even mention her famous lorgnette? [. . .] And her 'makeup'! When she grew tired of her braid, she concocted a hairdo that gave her a ridiculously unkempt look with curls flying about in every direction. In addition, there was a time she dyed her hair red and made herself up in an exaggerated fashion ('proper' ladies in those days in Russia abstained from 'maquillage')."[37]

Judging from Makovsky's account, Gippius's sense of style did not just overstep the boundaries of good taste but represented a parody of the very notion of femininity. Much like the female impersonator, who does not simply dress in a feminine manner but takes cultural notions of femininity to a parodic extreme, Gippius made herself up in a highly provocative, playful, and "exaggerated fashion," which was at times extremely off putting. According to her personal secretary, Vladimir Zlobin, "she was a strange being, almost like someone from another planet. At times she seemed unreal, as often happens with people of very great beauty or excessive ugliness. Brick-red rouge covering her cheeks and dyed red hair which looked like a wig. She dressed elaborately in shawls and furs (she was always cold) in which she would become hopelessly entangled. Her costumes where not always successful and did not always befit her age and rank. She could turn herself into a scarecrow."[38] In my opinion, she did not transform herself into a scarecrow but rather into a parody of the very image of the poetess that was fetishized in the popular press. And this impersonation of the poetess was so parodic and extreme as to incite speculation that she was not a woman. Berberova, for one, claims that "she artificially worked up in herself two features of her personality: poise and femininity. Within she was not poised and she was not a woman."[39]

Though Gippius's penchant for provocative feminine fashions might appear, at first glance, to have contradicted her desire to write "like a *human being*, and not just like a woman" and to be perceived accordingly, I would argue that just the opposite was the case. In a cultural climate where the female artist was constantly being presented as feminine, Gippius seems to have found that one of the best ways to uncover this cultural production of the female artist, aside from arguing for a genderless criticism in print using a male pseudonym, was by dressing herself up in an extremely feminine manner. In doing so, she did not simply reproduce the accepted cultural notion that the female artist should necessarily be feminine and stylish; she reproduced these notions with a crucial critical difference by adopting a subversive discursive strategy that the French feminist theorist Luce Irigaray would term female mimicry or *mimétisme*. Irigaray's translators Catherine Porter and Carolyn Burke define her concept of mimicry as "an interim strategy for dealing with the realm of discourse (where the speaking subject is posited as masculine), in which the woman deliberately assumes the feminine style and posture assigned to her within this discourse in order to uncover the mechanisms by which it exploits her."[40]

Gippius mimicked "the feminine style and posture assigned to her" by fashioning herself in an ultrafeminine manner in the salon for all her critics and contemporaries to see and by playfully acknowledging that she wrote in a style consonant with her provocatively feminine salon demeanor. Though she persisted in masking her gender in her verse, she developed an entire critical vocabulary that centered on feminine fashion and style.[41] In her informal, off-the-cuff letters to writers and critics (many of whom, incidentally, were male), Gippius would sometimes compare the creative process to the production of feminine *couture* and *coiffure*, playing into the critics' fetishization of the female author. In a letter to Georgy Adamovich, for instance, she humors the young poet and critic, conceding that the caustic tone of one of her texts can be attributed to her feminine style—to the sharp pins she holds in her mouth as she tailors one of her designs. As she tells him: "You are, in essence, very correct. This is a foul nature—a mouth filled with pins—and it is necessary to acknowledge this in order to make the necessary corrections to this foul nature (*style 'femme'*)" (Vy, v sushchnosti, ochen' pravy: eto skvernaia priroda—rot, napolnennyi bulavkami,—i sleduet eto soznavat', chtoby delat' k takoi skvernoi prirode [style "femme"] nuzhnye korrektivy) (*IIA*, 418).

Here she plays into the expectations that her discourse, the discourse of the female artist, is not only overtly fashionable and feminine but also that it is marked by sexual excess. This description of her authorial voice as a "mouth filled with pins" (rot, napolnennyi bulavkami) resonates with the excesses of "gender" (rod) and "sex" (pol) through paronomastic wordplay. This "mouth" (rot) is not simply "filled with pins" (napolnennyi bulavkami) but "oversexed" (na-pol-nennyi), the result of a "foul nature" or sex (skvernaia pri-rod-a) that Gippius in typical turn-of-the-century fashion identifies as synonymous with feminine style or *style "femme,"* as she terms it in French. And there is some indication that this *style "femme,"* this feminine style and posture, was quite literally assigned to her within the critical discourse of the period. If we are to believe Adamovich, it was not Gippius herself, but Pavel Miliukov, editor of the newspaper *The Latest News* (*Poslednie novosti*), who originally identified Gippius's sharp tongue with the accouterments of feminine fashion. In one of his essays on Gippius, Adamovich recalls Miliukov telling her, "I am too old and too busy to watch for all of the hairpins with which you decorate each of your articles!" (Ia slishkom star i slishkom zaniat, chtoby usledit' za vsemi shpil'kami, kotorymi vy kazhduiu svoiu stat'iu ukrashaete!). To this Gippius reportedly replied, "Just think. I have hairpins! I!" (Nu, podumaete, u menia shpil'ki! U menia!).[42] If this interchange actually occurred, then when Gippius told Adamovich that she had pins in her mouth, she was quite literally mimicking the feminine style that was assigned to her by one of the leading members of the critical establishment of the Parisian émigré community.

It bears noting, though, that Irigaray's concept of mimicry does not demand that the female artist literally mime the critique of the male critic. Whether Adamovich's account of the discussion between Gippius and her editor is true or apocryphal has little bearing on the fact that she mimicked and parodied the prevailing critical and cultural notions of the female poet. She not only acknowledged speaking as if with pins in her mouth, fashioning what might be seen as the female equivalent for the English expression "to speak with a forked tongue," but she playfully referred to texts as clothing or *odezhda* and to writing as a process of feminine fashioning.[43] In one of her letters, for example, she admits, "G. has a hook in her hands, instead of a pen, and she is crocheting from bad wool" (U G. kriuchek v rukakh, vmesto pera, da i viazhet-to ona iz skvernoi shersti) (*IIA*, 399), referring to herself in the third person by her own hook-like Russian initial "Г." Although writers and critics as far back as the Renaissance have been known to speak of poetic style in terms of dress and hair, Gippius's playful designation of texts as clothing and hair, the prototypical fetish objects according to Freud, takes on special significance in light of Gippius's own notorious obsession with her clothes and hair.[44] In instances such as this letter, Gippius transforms herself into both the subject and the object of her own self-fashioning. And she lays bare this process when she notes elsewhere that "Z. Gippius is inclined to weave [...] designs endlessly, but, at a certain moment, A. Krainy [her male critical alter ego] arrives and calmly rips them apart" (Z. Gippius sklonna plesti [...] uzory do bezkonechnosti, no v izvestnyi moment prikhodit A. Krainii i spokoino ikh rvet) (*IIA*, 171). Thus, Gippius fashions herself not just as a modern-day Penelope, both cunning and devious, but also as the feminine "Merezhkovskaia." The designs that Gippius mentions refer to texts (the word "text" is related etymologically in Russian as well as in English to the word "textile" [compare the Russian words *tekst* and *tkan'*]) and also perhaps to the feminine self, Merezhkovskaia.[45] The poet's feminine married surname, Merezhkovskaia, can be paronomastically related to the Russian word *merezhka*, which can refer to "a loop in a net and in knitting."[46]

In addition to playfully admitting to engaging in feminine fashioning in some of her later correspondence, she dedicated several poems in her first book of verse to the related themes of weaving, webs, strings, and nets, including "Grizelda" ("Grizel'da") (1895), "Autumn" ("Osen'") (1895), "Dust" ("Pyl'") (1897), "The Seamstress" ("Shveia") (1901), "The Thread" ("Nit'") (1901), "Nets" ("Merezhi") (1902), and "The Spiders" ("Pauki") (1903).[47] The predominance of such themes in her early verse should not lead us to conclude that she was comfortable with her femininity or her body. In fact, I would suggest that the very opposite was the case. A testament to this is the fact that Gippius often refers to the feminine self in the third person, envisioning herself the way her detractors and critics would see her (e.g. "This is a foul nature—a mouth filled with pins—and it is necessary to acknowledge this in order to make the necessary corrections to this foul nature [*style 'femme'*]," "G. has a hook in her hands, instead of a pen, and she is crocheting from bad wool," and "Z. Gippius is inclined to weave [...] designs endlessly, but, at a certain moment, A. Krainy arrives and calmly rips them apart"). In such instances, she evinces a tendency to position the feminine self as object, rather than as subject, thereby distancing the feminine self from the speaking subject that she positions as inherently male.[48]

A similar distancing strategy can be seen in some of her early poems about feminine creativity, which often lack the element of parody or mimicry of her later critical exchanges. For example, in her early poem "The Seamstress" ("Shveia"), one of several poems she wrote using a female persona, Gippius describes the feminine art of sewing as a backbreaking activity, and she effectively disassociates this creative activity from the feminine "I" through the grammar of the poem:[49]

> Уж третий день ни с кем не говорю...
> А мысли—жадные и злые.
> Болит спина; куда ни посмотрю—
> Повсюду пятна голубые.
>
> Церковный колокол гудел; умолк;
> Я всё наедине с собою.
> Скрипит и гнется жарко-алый шелк
> Под неумелою иглою.
>
> На всех явлениях лежит печать.
> Одно с другим как будто слито.
> Приняв одно—стараюсь угадать
> За ним другое,—то, что слито.
>
> И этот шелк мне кажется—Огнем.
> И вот уж не огнем—а Кровью.
> А кровь—лишь знак того, что мы зовем
> На бедном языке—Любовью.
>
> Любовь—лишь звук... Но в этот поздний час
> Того, что дальше,—не открою.
> Нет, не огонь, не кровь... а лишь атлас
> Скрипит под робкою иглою.
>   (*Stikh*, 119-20)

[It's already the third day that I speak with no one... And my thoughts are greedy and evil. My back hurts; wherever I look there are light-blue spots. The church bell rang; grew silent; I am all by myself. The hot-scarlet silk squeaks and bends beneath the inexperienced needle. A seal is stamped on all phenomena. It is as if one is merged with the other. Having accepted one, I try to divine the other beyond it, that which is hidden. And it seems to me that the silk is—Fire. And now no longer fire—but Blood. And blood is only a sign of that which we call in our impoverished tongue—Love. Love is only a sound... But in this late

hour I will not reveal that which is further. No, not fire, not blood
... but only satin squeaks under the timid needle.]

While this poem differs significantly in tone from her parodic statements about feminine self-fashioning, it does share with them a tendency to treat the woman as the object of vision or the surveyed rather than as a viewer or surveyor. This emphasis on the woman as object, rather than subject, corresponds with the complicated subject position of the woman in this poem. Although it is clear from the presence of the first person verbal form ("I speak" [govoriu]) in the first line of the poem that the speaking subject and the seamstress are one and the same, Gippius resists identification of the "I" of the poem with the activity of sewing through her exploitation of Russian grammar. It can be assumed that she describes how sewing results in the back pain of the poetic speaker when she states "my back hurts" (bolit spina), but in doing so she refrains from using the Russian construction "U menia" that would directly identify the backbreaking activity of sewing with the speaker. And in the following stanza, this disassociation of the speaker from the activity of sewing is even more apparent. Rather than describing outright the manner in which the speaker of the poem engages in the act of sewing, she makes reference to the incessant scratching of the unskilled needle against the hot silk: "The hot-scarlet silk squeaks and bends beneath the inexperienced needle" (Skripit i gnetsia zharko-alyi shelk / Pod neumeloiu igloiu). Though the needle is clearly wielded by the seamstress, in this poem it is the needle, not the seamstress, that is the actual agent.

In her refusal to directly connect the speaker with the activity of sewing in this poem, Gippius might be seen as resisting the typically feminine role of woman in history and, in particular, in religious history. In religious painting and poetry, there exists a long tradition of depicting Mary sewing or engaged in needlework as she awaits the Annunciation. Sewing is thus intimately intertwined with Mary's essentially biological role in the act of creation, and it signals her receptivity to this role in world history.[50] Gippius herself would draw on this representation of sewing and of the female self in her later poem "Good News" ("Blagaia vest'"), which she completed in March, the month of the Annunciation, in 1904 and that she included in her second volume of poems:

Дышит тихая весна,
Дышит светами приветными...
Я сидела у окна
За шерстями разноцветными.

Подбирала к цвету цвет,
Кисти яркие вязала я . . .
Был мне весел мой обет:
. В храм святой завеса алая.

И уста мои твердят
Богу Сил мольбы привычные . . .
В солнце утреннем горят
Стены горницы кирпичные . . .

Тихо, тихо. Вдруг в окне,
За окном,—мелькнуло белое . . .
Сердце дрогнуло во мне,
Сердце девичье, несмелое . . .

Но вошел . . . И не боюсь,
Не боюсь я Светлоликого.
Он как брат мой . . . Поклонюсь
Брату, вестнику Великого.

Белый дал он мне цветок . . .
Не судила я, не мерила,
Но вошел он на порог,
Но сказал,—и я поверила.

Воля Господа—моя.
Будь же, как Ему угоднее . . .
Хочет Он—хочу и я.
Пусть войдет Любовь Господняя . . .
(*Stikh*, 145-46)

[The quiet spring breathes, breathes with welcoming lights . . . I sat by the window at my multicolored woolens. I matched color to color, and knit bright tassels . . . My vow was cheerful to me: a scarlet curtain for the sacred church. And my lips repeat the customary prayers to the God of Powers . . . In the morning sun, the brick walls of the chamber burn . . . Quiet, quiet. Suddenly in the window, beyond the window, whiteness glimmered . . . My heart shook in me, my virginal, cowardly heart . . . But he came . . . And I am not afraid. I am not afraid of the Light-faced One. He is like my brother . . . I will bow down to my brother, the herald of the Great One. He gave me a small white flower . . . I did not judge, did not measure, but he came to the threshold, but he spoke—and I believed. The will of God is mine. Let that be which suits Him best . . . If He wants something—then I also want it. Let God's Love enter . . .]

But if in this poem, Gippius clearly aligns her speaker with the Virgin Mary and associates female handiwork with positive erotic potential by virtue of it proximity to the Annunciation, then in "The Seamstress" not only is the speaker revealed to be a rather ordinary seamstress but sewing itself is presented in a much more ambivalent light owing to its inability to precede or prepare for an extraordinary event. As in "Good News," Gippius implicitly connects sewing with eroticism in the fourth stanza of "The Seamstress" which reads: "And it seems to me that the silk is—Fire. And now no longer fire—but Blood. And blood is only a sign of that which we call in our impoverished tongue—Love" (I etot shelk mne kazhetsia—Ognem. / I vot uzh ne ognem—a Krov'iu. / A krov'—lish' znak togo, chto my zovem / Na bednom iazyke—Liubov'iu). But while these lines suggest that sewing carries with it the potential for an erotic and even religious act of creation, in this poem sewing ultimately fails to fulfill its positive potential. In the end, there is no transformation, no miracle: "Love is only a sound . . . But in this late hour I will not reveal that which is further. No, not fire, not blood . . . but only satin squeaks under the timid needle" (Liubov'—lish' zvuk . . . No v etot pozdnii chas / Togo, chto dal'she,—ne otkroiu. / Net, ne ogon', ne krov' . . . a lish' atlas / Skripit pod robkoiu igloiu). By returning to the way the fabric (now not precious silk, but only satin) squeaks under the timid needle, Gippius reinforces the notion that female handiwork is a debased from of creativity—one that lacks the power to occasion any kind of spiritual transformation. Further, she clearly divorces the woman in the poem from the activity of sewing.

Despite this obvious disassociation between the agent and activity of sewing in "The Seamstress," it can be inferred that the speaker of the poem is synonymous with the seamstress. However, in her famous poem "The Spiders" ("Pauki") (1903), which she also included in her first volume of poems, Gippius makes the disassociation of the speaker of the poem from the related activity of weaving more pronounced, demonstrating even more ambivalence toward traditional female creativity. For this reason, "The Spiders" deserves even greater attention. In this poem, the now unmarked poetic speaker looks on in horror as four spiders go about the seemingly sinister activity of weaving their webs:

> Я в тесной келье—в этом мире.
> И келья тесная низка.
> А в четырех углах—четыре
> Неутомимых паука.
>
> Они ловки, жирны и грязны.
> И всё плетут, плетут, плетут . . .

> И страшен их однообразный
> Непрерывающийся труд.
>
> Они четыре паутины
> В одну, огромную, сплели.
> Гляжу—шевелятся их спины
> В зловонно-сумрачной пыли.
>
> Мои глаза—под паутиной.
> Она сера, мягка, липка.
> И рады радостью звериной
> Четыре толстых паука.
> (*Stikh*, 139)

[I am in a cramped cell in this world. And the cramped cell is low. And in the four corners are four tireless spiders. They are nimble, greasy, and dirty. And they still weave, and weave, and weave ... And terrible is their monotonous unbroken labor. They have woven four webs into one enormous one. I look: their backs are stirring in dusk's putrid dust. My eyes are beneath the web. It is gray, soft, sticky. And the four fat spiders are happy with a beastly happiness.]

Scholars have typically interpreted "The Spiders" not as a poem about the creative process but rather as a metaphysical poem about the bleak condition of "this world" (etot svet). For instance, in her book *Paradox in the Religious Poetry of Zinaida Gippius* (1972), Olga Matich compares the anxiety of the lyrical "I" in the poem to that of Dostoevsky's character Svidrigailov as he contemplates eternity. She contends that the "frighteningly *pošlij* picture of life, which Gippius frequently associated with a confining cell ('kel'ja'), is reminiscent of Svidrigajlov's (*Crime and Punishment*) vision of eternity."[51] D. S. Mirsky also reads the Dostoevsky sub-text as central to Gippius's poetic vision, if not to "The Spiders" in particular. He notes that "in *Crime and Punishment*, Svidrigailov wonders if eternity is not but a 'Russian bath-house with cobwebs in every corner.' Mme. Hippius took up the idea and perhaps her best poems are variations of this theme."[52] Indeed, in "The Spiders," the speaker's vision of "this world" as a "cramped cell" (tesnaia kel'ia) with "four tireless spiders" (chetyre neutomimykh pauka) in "four corners" (v chetyrekh uglakh) does echo Svidrigailov's vision of eternity not as a vast space but as "a single little room—a bathhouse in one of our backwater villages, something like that, sooty, spiders in all the corners" (odna komnatka, edak vrode derevenskoi bani, zakoptelaia, a po vsem uglam pauki).[53]

Yet despite the shared imagery of these two visions (the confining room, the dirty surroundings, the spiders in the corners), I do not believe that the intertextual connections between Gippius's poem and Svidrigailov's dream provide the only key to the poem. Instead, I would suggest that the intertextual allusions to Svidrigailov's dream function as a veil or fetish (note that the term *intertextualité*, coined by the French feminist Julia Kristeva, is derived from the Latin suffix *inter-* and the noun *textus* and thus could be said to connote interweaving) that creates the illusion that the poem corresponds to the metaphysical vision of Svidrigailov while concealing the poem's possible connections to issues of female creativity. Since the time of the ancients, spider weaving has been associated with a distorted and lesser form of female creativity. Most notably, in Ovid's *Metamorphoses*, the young weaver Arachne is punished severely by Athena not just for creating a tapestry superior to her own but also for deigning to mock the gods in her tapestry.[54] As a result of this abuse, Arachne hangs herself, but Athena takes pity on her, allowing her to live not as a woman but as a spider. And thus Arachne is able to pursue her former art but in a markedly debased form. The young weaver, who had formerly produced lush and extravagant tapestries that rivaled those of the gods, is reduced to producing her web from her own bodily secretions. The figure of Arachne therefore has frequently been associated with a highly corporealized and even sexualized mode of female creativity.[55] There is evidence that Gippius herself identified on some level with the figure of Arachne. She compared textuality not just to weaving but specifically to web weaving. As she notes in her *Contes d'amour* (1893–1904): "It is strange but true: I can only write letters to a person with whom I feel a corporeal thread, *my own*" (Stranno, no tak: mogu pisat' pis'ma tol'ko k cheloveku, s kotorym chuvstvuiu telesnuiu nit', *moiu*) (*Dnev*, 1:53).[56]

Though the connection between Gippius's poem "The Spiders" and the myth of Arachne is not immediately apparent, there is some indication already in the first stanza that the poem should not be read solely in the context of Svidrigailov's dream. In the first two lines of the poem, the speaker states: "I am in a cramped cell in this world. And the cramped cell is low" (Ia v tesnoi kel'e—v etom mire. / I kel'ia tesnaia nizka). While the confining cell in which the speaker is located appears to point to the "little room" in Svidrigailov's dream, it is revealed in the very first line of the poem that this room is located not in eternity but "in this world" (v etom mire). This difference in the topos of the speaker's vision points to the fact that "The Spiders" may represent a rewriting or revision of Svidrigailov's dream. This fact, however, is veiled over in the last two lines of the first stanza, which describe the speaker's cell in terms similar to those used to describe Svidrigailov's bathhouse. Indeed, if we were to limit our reading of the poem to the first stanza alone, we could characterize it more or less as a translation of Svidrigailov's vision into poetic form.

However, in the second stanza of the poem, Gippius begins the process of rewriting or revising Svidrigailov's vision. This is underscored by a shift in the viewpoint of the speaker of the poem. Whereas in the first stanza, the speaker has a panoramic view of the cell that encompasses the four corners of the room where the four spiders are located, already by the second stanza the speaker has a much more limited viewpoint that is confined to a close-up of the "four tireless spiders" (chetyre neutomimykh pauka) at work. And it is here that the poem, which formerly corresponded with Svidrigailov's vision in terms of imagery as well as viewpoint, begins to explore, in extreme, almost fetishistic detail, the creative aspect of the spiders' labor—something that is not at all touched on in Svidrigailov's dream. Now the spiders, described as "nimble, greasy, and dirty" (lovki, zhirny, i griazny), are shown to be able to produce endlessly in an almost machinelike fashion. As the speaker indicates in line 6, "And they still weave, and weave, and weave ..." (I vse pletut, pletut, pletut...). The spiders' seemingly endless productivity, which is emphasized by the threefold repetition of the word "weave" (pletut) as well as by the use of ellipses, is abhorrent, even anxiety-producing, to the speaker of the poem. As the speaker indicates: "And terrible is their monotonous unbroken labor" (I strashen ikh odnoobraznyi / Nepreryvaiushiisia trud).

There is sufficient evidence to suggest that the speaker's horror or anxiety in the presence of the spiders' creative labor or *trud* points to the author's anxiety about the creative process. The term that Gippius uses to qualify the spiders' unbroken labor, monotonous or *odnoobraznyi*, is the same term that she herself employs to describe the product of her creative labors, her poems, in "The Necessary Thing about Verses" ("Neobkhodimoe o stikhakh"). In this essay, which served as the preface to her first volume of poems, Gippius characterizes her poems as "very isolated, peculiar, and, in their peculiarity, monotonous" (ochen' obosoblennye, svoestrunnye, v svoestrunnosti, odnoobraznye) (*Stikh*, 72), anticipating, as it were, the "monotonous unbroken labor" (odnoobraznyi nepreryvaiushiisia trud) of the spiders.[57] In the poem, the spiders engage in "unbroken labor" that quite literally involves the pulling of strings or threads from their bodies as they form their webs. This is a truly "monotonous" or "uniform" activity that entails the constant repetition of *obraz*, that is, form, to produce the geometrical structure of the web.

Rhymed poetry comprises by its very design a web-like structure. The presence of rhyme in a poem forces us to read the poem not only from left to right but also up and down, mimicking the horizontal and vertical motions necessary to create the warp and weft of a tapestry. This is a structural element of poetry that Vladimir Mayakovsky lays bare in his poem "Order No. 2 to the Army of the Arts" ("Prikaz No. 2 armii iskusstv") (1921) in which he imagines "little futurists, imagists, acmeists entangled in the cobweb of rhymes" (futuristiki, / imazhinistiki, / akmeistiki, / zaputavshiesia v pautine rifm).[58] And in "The Spiders" an analogy can be drawn between the creative labor of the author of the poem and the "unbroken labor" of the four spiders of the poem. This is particularly apparent in lines 9 and 10, where the speaker observes: "They have woven four webs into one enormous one" (Oni chetyre pautiny / V odnu, ogromnuiu, spleli). If we examine the poem closely, we realize that it is composed of four smaller texts or stanzas that form the poem proper. This accords well with existing ideas about textuality. The notion of the text as a web or netting is a common trope. In *The Pleasure of the Text* (*Le plaisir du texte*) (1973), Roland Barthes asserts that the word "text" means "tissue" and that during the process of writing "the subject unmakes himself, like a spider dissolving in the constructive secretions of its web." This leads him finally to proclaim that "were we fond of neologisms, we might define the theory of the text as an *hyphology* (*hyphos* is the tissue and the spider's web)."[59]

Gippius, as we have seen, occasionally referred in her comments to fellow writers and critics to the production of the text in analogous terms as the sewing or weaving of little nets or designs. In such informal interchanges, the industry of feminine fashioning is imagined in playful, parodic terms; in this poem, though, the production of the web (text) is figured in a highly sexualized and even grotesque fashion. Here the "four fat spiders" (chetyre tolstykh pauka), described as "happy with a beastly happiness" (rady radost'iu zverinoi), engage in a creative act akin to the sexual act itself. In lines 11 and 12, the speaker of the poem looks on, like a reluctant voyeur, to see the spiders' backs quivering as they engage in the highly sexualized activity of weaving: "I look: their backs are stirring in dusk's putrid dust" (Gliazhu—sheveliatsia ikh spiny / V zlovonno-sumrachnoi pyli). This description of the backs of the spiders moving up and down, as well as the reference to the foul-smelling dust, evokes an image of the creative process that is not the least bit positive or redeeming. Indeed, at a certain point in the poem, the creative process of weaving is represented as a source of fear and anxiety for the speaker. The speaker's fear and disgust concerning the creative process increases throughout the poem as s/he comes in closer proximity to the spider's web. In the fourth and final stanza, the speaker, who in the first stanza had the power to pronounce the pronoun "I," practically merges with the spider's web, denoted by the feminine Russian noun *pautina*. As s/he notes: "My eyes are beneath the web. It is gray, soft, sticky" (Moi glaza pod pautinoi. / Ona sera, miagka, lipka). "Gray" and "sticky" are appropriate terms to describe the web that is produced from the constructive secretions of the spiders' body as well as, perhaps, the freshly written text or poem that emerges from the nib of the fountain pen, particularly before it has dried. And, thus, the speaker's horror in the face of the spiders' web may be read as symptomatic of Gippius's own creative anxiety in the face of female authorship. As in a nightmare, though, the symbols of her anxiety — the spider and the web — are magnified and multiplied. Gippius's poetic speaker and alter ego must confront the reality of a corporealized form of female creativity through the contemplation not of one but four spiders weaving their webs in each corner of the room, and thus the horror surrounding Arachne's fate becomes virtually inescapable.[60]

Gippius's implicit identification with the highly decadent and implicitly feminine figure of the spider was not lost on her contemporaries.[61] In 1907, several years after the "The Spiders" appeared in print, Mitrich (Dmitry Togolsky) published a caricature of Gippius in one of the St. Petersburg journals that depicted her as a fashionable femme fatale on the verge of metamorphosis into spider woman (figure 2). In this caricature, reminiscent of the illustrations of the British decadent Aubrey Beardsley, Gippius is presented in two guises: as figure and shadow that translate into woman and spider woman. In the figure itself, she is depicted wearing an elaborate bouffant-style topknot and clad in one of her notoriously elegant and extravagant dresses complete with ruches and a long swirling hemline. In her mouth, she has a cigarette holder. In her left hand, she clutches her infamous lorgnette; in her right hand, she dangles a spider. This spider, which may be read as an allusion to her poem "The Spiders," is more than just another accouterment of feminine fashion like the lorgnette and the cigarette holder; it is the alter ego of Gippius herself. In the shadow cast from the figure, she metamorphoses, as it were, from the fashionable and elegant poetess into a spider-like

Figure 2. Caricature of Zinaida Gippius by Mitrich (Dmitry Togolsky) (1907)

creature: the lorgnette Gippius holds in her left hand in the figure appears in the shadow as a phallic string or thread that Gippius pulls with both hands from the center of her body.[62]

Temira Pachmuss indicates in her early book on the poet that a copy of the caricature was found in Gippius's personal archive, a fact that would suggest that Gippius liked the caricature enough to keep it.[63] In many respects, this caricature would appear to be deeply at odds with Gippius's avowed desire to write "like a *human being*, and not just like a woman" and to be viewed accordingly by the literary establishment. But if in poems such as "The Seamstress" and "The Spiders," she self-consciously distances herself from the highly corporealized and sexualized mode of feminine fashioning, then in the world of literary St. Petersburg and later Paris she was more than willing to identify herself with the highly sexualized figure of the salon poetess. In so doing, she was not so much valorizing essential femininity as attempting to unmask or unveil the production of the female artist as necessarily fashionable and feminine. However, in her attempt to subvert this production of the female artist, Gippius often reproduced some of the negative stereotypes of femininity of the day, something that has led one scholar to dub Gippius "an unwitting and unwilling feminist."[64] As a case in point, when Gippius compares her own feminine writing style to a mouth filled with pins, she not only evokes the highly negative stereotype of woman as a devouring female or *vagina dentata* but also refers outright to her own foul nature or *skvernaia priroda*. And this is just one of the many ways she evinces a problematic relationship with the female body and self that, at times, borders on misogyny. In Gippius's case, misogyny was intimately intertwined with her tendency to appropriate the subject position not just of the male but more specifically that of the dandy. This might seem to be a contradiction in terms since, as one scholar so eloquently puts it: "In spite of his 'effeminate' habits and tastes a dandy is masculine, radically masculine. In fact, in Baudelairean terms a woman can never be a dandy because her relationship to 'loi' and 'espirit' is totally different."[65] But, as chapter 6 suggests, this extreme form of masculinity would not deter her from appropriating the typical posture and vantage point of the dandy. In fact, it provided her with a very accommodating cultural model for writing against the female body and sex.

6

The Dandy's Gaze
Gippius and Disdainful Desire for the Feminine

> The demonic woman differs from your typical woman first and foremost in her manner of dress. She wears a black velvet cassock, a chain on her forehead, a bracelet on her leg, a ring with an opening for "a cyanide tablet that will be brought to her without fail the following Tuesday," a stiletto behind her collar, rosary beads on her elbow, and a portrait of Oscar Wilde on her left garter.
>
> She also wears ordinary items of the female toilet, but not in those places where they are meant to be. So, for instance, the demonic woman allows herself to wear a belt only on her head, an earring on her forehead or neck, a ring on her thumb, and a watch on her leg.
>
> Nadezhda Teffi, "The Demonic Woman"
("Demonicheskaia zhenshchina") (1914)

Zinaida Gippius was by no means the only Russian modernist to call attention to the performative nature of femininity. Nadezhda Teffi, the younger sister of the intensely popular turn-of-the-century poet Mirra Lokhvitskaia, made the fashionable woman of literary Bohemia the subject of her parodic sketch "The Demonic Woman." Early twentieth-century readers could very well have understood the demonic woman to have been a caricature of Gippius. Referred to as the

"White She-Devil" (Belaia D'iavolitsa) by members of the Holy Synod of the Russian Orthodox Church and later as a "witch" (ved'ma) by Leon Trotsky, Gippius displayed many of the parodic extremes of the demonic woman.[1] She not only wrote deeply religious poems that she likened to prayers but she also dedicated numerous poems to the subject of the devil.[2] And in addition to oscillating between the sacred and profane in her poetry, she willingly transgressed the divisions between the male and female genders. She adopted an ultrafeminine salon demeanor that parodied stereotypical notions of femininity, and she challenged cultural notions of gender division altogether by employing a masculine persona in much of her poetry and by styling herself like a female dandy. Most notably, in the famous 1906 portrait by Léon Bakst (figure 3), she appears in an elegant white jabot and black riding jacket and britches, wearing the "disdainful expression" (prezritel'noe vyrazhenie) that was one of the defining characteristics of the dandy.[3]

If a possible relationship between Teffi's demonic woman and Gippius is concealed behind the pretense that the demonic woman represents a social type rather than a particular individual, the connection becomes more plausible upon comparison of Teffi's literary sketch with her later description of the poet. In her portrait of the poet, Teffi depicts a Gippius who is no less flamboyant or dandified than her demonic woman. Not only does Teffi's Gippius wear items of the female toilet in those places where they are not meant to be worn; she also appropriates items from the male toilet that could very well have come from the dandy's dressing table, if not from that of Oscar Wilde himself. "[Gippius] dressed very strangely," Teffi recalls. "In her youth, she played at being original [Ona original'nichala]. She would wear a man's suit, an evening gown with white dolman sleeves, and wrap a ribbon with a broach around her forehead. In time her play at being original turned into something ridiculous. She would drape a pink ribbon with a monocle around her neck and throw the cord around her ear so that the monocle would dangle against her cheek."[4] As this account shows, Gippius did more than simply dress in men's wear, which was popular among early twentieth-century women writers as diverse as Allegro, Vita Sackville-West, and Gertrude Stein; she directly associated herself with the androgynous figure of the dandy or aesthete through her choice of accessories.[5] Though she did not wear a badge of dandyism on her garter in the form of a portrait of Oscar Wilde, she did wear it draped around her neck in the form of a monocle on a ribbon and much to the consternation of her Russian contemporaries. As her personal secretary

Figure 3. Portrait of Zinaida Gippius by Léon Bakst (1906)

Vladimir Zlobin notes, "in Paris, people got used to her, to her monocle, her voice like a sea bird's, her purplish, death-like face powder. But in Russia, after all, it was considered bad taste to use makeup and rouge, especially the way she did. No wonder that in St. Petersburg she had the reputation of being almost a Messalina or, at least, of being extremely affected."[6]

By donning an eyepiece, Gippius entered into a long dandy tradition in Russia of employing eyewear for the purpose of shock and public outrage.[7] As Yury Lotman points out in his essay "Russian Dandyism" ("Russkii dendizm") (1994):

> An important role in the behavior of the dandy was played by eyeglasses—a detail which came from the fops of the preceding epoch. Even in the eighteenth century eyeglasses took on the characteristic of a fashionable detail of the toilet. A look through glasses was equivalent to staring straight at a stranger, that is to say a daring gesture [derzkii zhest]. Decorum of the eighteenth century in Russia prohibited younger people or people of lower rank from looking through glasses at someone of a higher rank: it was considered to be rude [eto vosprinimalos' kak naglost']. Delvig recalled that in the Lycée they were prohibited from wearing glasses and that because of this all women seemed to him like beauties. To this he added ironically that when he graduated from the Lycée and procured a pair of glasses, he was extremely disenchanted.[8]

The dandy's eyewear may have had an even more complicated semiotic function than Lotman discusses here. Besides serving as a sign of the dandy's rudeness, his proclivity for snubbing society, it also became a sign of his ambiguous gender and of his self-perception. On the one hand, the fop's stylish eyewear was employed to objectify others, to control them with his gaze. And on the other hand, the dandy's interest in fashionable eyewear was the sign of his narcissism, of his desire to be the object of others' gaze and, hence, of his desire to assume the role of visual object generally associated with women in Western culture.

And if in the eighteenth century, in the embryonic stages of dandyism, the fop's glasses were turned toward those of higher status, in the nineteenth century, the dandy's lorgnette and opera glasses were often turned toward women with whom the dandy identified on certain points. Lotman notes that in the Pushkin era

> A specific trait of dandified behavior consisted of looking in the theater through opera glasses not at the stage, but at the balconies where the ladies were sitting. [Eugene] Onegin emphasizes the dandyism of this gesture by looking "askance" ["skosias'"], which was considered impertinent:
>
>> He directs his double lorgnette askance
>> At the balconies of unacquainted ladies ...
>
> And looking at unacquainted ladies in such a fashion was considered to be twice as rude.
> The female equivalent of "daring optics" ["derzkaia optika"] was the lorgnette, if it were not turned to the stage:

> Toward her were directed
> Neither the jealous lorgnettes of ladies,
> Nor the lenses of stylish connoisseurs.[9]

According to Gippius's contemporaries, she was not averse to employing "daring optics" of her own. In addition to wearing a monocle on the street, Gippius employed a lorgnette in the salon, to much the same ends as the dandies of the previous century. She would reportedly stare rudely at her interlocutors through her fashionable lorgnette so as to emphasize her aristocratic superiority. So integral was this visual play to her salon theatrics that Sergei Makovsky notes in his famous verbal portrait of her: "Is it even necessary to remind you of her infamous lorgnette? It was not without affectedness that Z. N. would bring it up to her nearsighted eyes and look right at her interlocutor. With this gesture she emphasized her absent-minded arrogance."[10] Perhaps because at the turn of the century lorgnettes were no longer carried by young men but primarily by aristocratic ladies, Gippius's lorgnette frequently became associated with her bourgeois femininity rather than with her androgyny or dandyism in the minds of her contemporaries.

Sergei Esenin, for instance, in his famous "letter of sorts (on an issue known to all)" (vrode pis'ma [na obshcheizvestnoe]) (1925) sarcastically dubs Gippius the "lady with the lorgnette" (dama s lornetom) and recounts how she stared at him through her lorgnette as she accused him of "being affected" (krivliat'sia) for wearing peasant felt boots or *valenki*.[11] For Esenin, the peasant poet, Gippius's lorgnette becomes a symbol not just of her femininity but of her bourgeois femininity. (And his description of the confrontation of the "lady with the lorgnette" with the peasant in *valenki* anticipates the courtroom scene in Vsevolod Pudovkin's film *Mother* (*Mat'*) (1926), where the bourgeois lady with a lorgnette looks on as Pavel Vlasov receives his sentence.) While I do not dispute the class implications of Gippius's lorgnette that Esenin brings out in his letter, I believe that the gendered implications of her lorgnette deserve a second look. The lorgnette, as I mentioned earlier, was employed by the dandy as well as the society lady in the nineteenth century and became a sign of both the dandy's narcissism and effeminacy and his disdain or *prezrenie* for the feminine. And it is only by the early twentieth century that the lorgnette or, more accurately, double lorgnette is coded as almost exclusively feminine.

However, the lorgnette Gippius carried apparently differed significantly from those employed by society ladies at the turn of the century.

As Irina Odoevtseva points out in her memoirs *On the Banks of the Seine* (*Na beregakh Seny*) (1983), Gippius did not carry the ladies' double lorgnette but the dandy's single lorgnette or quizzing-glass. "There was a lot I didn't discern in [Gippius]," Odoevtseva observes, "and a lot I didn't understand. I didn't even realize that her lorgnette didn't have two lenses as was customary, but only one lens, that it was not a lorgnette, but a unique object in its own right. A monocle on a stick must have been made by special order. In those distant years, monocles were still in style—elegant older gentlemen or snobbish youth wore them. But, of course, not ladies. A lady in a monocle or with a monocle was completely unthinkable (Dama v monokle ili s monoklem byla sovershenno nemyslima)."[12] The double take that Odoevtseva does when she learns that Gippius carried a monocle on a stick rather than the proper ladies' lorgnette is understandable. This small detail of her toilet reveals that Gippius fancied herself not just as a "lady with a lorgnette" (dama s lornetom), as Esenin would have us believe, but also as a "dandy with a monocle" (dendi s monoklem).[13]

In styling herself in such a fashion, Gippius emphasizes her androgynous nature in a very complex way. The dandy, or aesthete, as he was alternatively known, was, after all, an overwhelmingly male cultural figure in spite of his effeminacy, something that would make Gippius's identification with the figure extremely complicated. "The dandy is a he," insists Jessica Feldman in her discussion of the modernist dandy.[14] And while the dandy appropriates typically feminine characteristics such as a fetishistic interest in his toilet, he typically guards himself from complete absorption into the feminine realm through his rude behavior toward women. As a gendered being, the dandy is characterized by a crucial divide that is mirrored by the androgynous split in his very gaze. The dandy typically disdains women and rudely objectifies then in his gaze. Yet he likes to present himself as an object of society's gaze, thus adopting a position that has typically been identified as feminine in Western culture. In other words, the dandy is split between two modes of his androgyny or bisexuality—between (feminine) object and (masculine) subject. "Dandyism," Feldman insists, "exists in the field of force between two opposing, irreconcilable notions about gender. First, the (male) dandy defines himself by attacking women. Second, so crucial are the female characteristics to the dandy's self-creation that he defines himself by embracing women, appropriating their characteristics. To begin with the attack. The 'actual' dandy courts women in order to cut them. If never allowing the slightest bit of power over one means living a solitary (or celibate) life, so be it."[15] And the extreme manifestation of the dandy's ambivalence toward the female flesh, especially in the early twentieth century, would seem to be not celibacy but same-sex male love.

A prime example of this particular praxis of dandyism would be Oscar Wilde in the British context and Sergei Diaghilev and his largely male coterie in the World of Art (Mir iskusstva) in the Russian context, a group with whom Gippius had very close contact at the turn of the century.[16] Gippius, together with her husband Dmitry Merezhkovsky, entered into a mystical ménage à trois with Dmitry Filosofov, a member of the World of Art and the cousin and one-time lover of Diaghilev. She also emphasized her affinity with the androgynous figure of the dandy or aesthete in complex ways throughout her art and life. She adopted the dandy's fashionable eyewear and she appropriated his disdainful posture. In identifying with this figure that was "masculine, radically masculine," Gippius added yet another split to what Feldman has identified as the gender divide of dandyism, since she identified with a male cultural figure who simultaneously borrowed from and rejected the feminine.[17] This was a complicated gender identification for Gippius as a woman poet to make, but she made it, and it was central to her self-fashioning. It helps to explain how, on the one hand, she could have eschewed femininity in her writing and, on the other hand, could have identified with an ultrafeminine pose that positioned the feminine in a highly ambivalent light.

Dandyism informed Gippius's writing in a myriad of ways. She wrote much of her literary criticism using the male pseudonyms Anton Krainy (Anton "the Extreme") and Tovarishch German (Comrade Herman) among others, and she frequently imbued her critical writings with the sarcastic and biting tone of the dandy. Her contemporaries were often inclined to regard this tone as inherently caddy and feminine. As we saw in the last chapter, Miliukov accused Gippius of figuratively "sticking pins" (podpuskat' shpil'ki) in her critical writings, and in doing so, he emphasizes the fashionable and feminine nature of her critical voice. But the narcissism and vanity that Miliukov implicitly associates with her critical voice may just as easily be categorized as dandified. (After all, as one poet puts it, "Dandy's a gender of the doubtful kind; / A something, nothing, not to be defined; / 'Twould puzzle words its sex to ascertain, / So very empty, and so very vain.")[18] These traits were central to the critical sensibility of the prototypical fin de siècle dandy, Oscar Wilde.[19] And Gippius may well have had the sexually ambiguous figure of the dandy in mind when she crossed the line of gender demarcation and wrote her critical essays as a man. If there is a hint of Wildean dandyism in Gippius's critical voice, then her appropriation of literary dandyism becomes even more apparent in some of the writings she dedicated to the subject of love and of courtship at the turn of the century.

At this time, Gippius was engaged in the writing of a "*special* diary" (*spetsial'nyi* dnevnik) (*Dnev*, 1:35) entitled *Contes d'amour* (1893-1904). In these memoirs, she does not just reveal a basic ambiguity about her gender that is characteristic of "a gender of a doubtful kind"; she also appropriates many of the dandy's stereotypical romantic patterns. She apparently indulges in a series of unconsummated romances with various men, and at least one woman, and much like the dandy she evinces views about women and more specifically the female body that are misogynistic. Though Gippius writes her *Contes d'amour* as herself, without any overt literary mask, she is highly conscious of the extent to which her "tales of love" are implicated in fiction, and thus they demonstrate one of the salient characteristics of the dandy text—the overt aestheticization of life. Gippius purposefully calls attention to the constructedness and even literary quality of her memoirs through the very choice of the title, *Contes d'amour* or *Tales of Love*. And she repeatedly makes reference to the events of her life as *skazki liubvi* or "tales of love," thereby comparing her love life to a plotted amorous fiction. She further reinforces the fictionality of her tales by somewhat ironically referring to the "'little facts'" (faktiki) of her love life. Thus, she not only calls into question the truthfulness of the events she represents but she also self-consciously blurs the boundaries between life and art and fact and fiction.

Lydia Ginzburg has shown that such distinctions are particularly fluid in the genre of autobiography. "Sometimes," she notes, "only the most tenuous line separates autobiography from the autobiographical tale or novel. The actual names of the characters may be changed, the resulting conventionality at once removing the work to another category, wherein the author obtains the right to invent."[20] Gippius plays upon the fluidity of the boundaries between fact and fiction, life and art, in *Contes d'amour* in ways that may be said to be distinctly symbolist. Olga Matich has shown that in the symbolist period the differences between documentary text and literature were all but effaced by the writers' obsession with life creation or *zhiznetvorchestvo*. "Diaries with a fragmentary lyrical structure resembling poetry," Matich observes, "assumed a central place in symbolist literary practice in general. Gippius, whose *Contes d'amour* or diary of 'love affairs,' reflected her ideology, considered diaries and letters of equal importance with poetry. The diary could be seen as the archetypal symbolist text, blurring the boundaries between art and life, as well as transforming the life text into art."[21]

In fact, Gippius went quite far in blurring the boundaries between life and art and "transforming the life text into art." She did not simply efface the boundaries between fact and fiction within her *Contes d'amour*. More than two decades later, in 1927, Gippius published a novel entitled *The Memoirs of Martynov* (*Memuary Martynova*) in the émigré journal *The Link* (*Zveno*) in which she rewrites many of her own personal "tales of love" from the point of view of her dandified male narrator, Ivan Martynov.[22] Reminiscent of Gippius herself, the fictional memoirist Ivan Martynov makes an early appearance in his own "tales of love" in the guise of a page. Interestingly enough, whereas Gippius referred to her actual diary of love affairs as "tales of love," she decided to call the fictionalized version of these tales "memoirs," further disrupting the generic distinctions between the autobiography and autobiographical tale. I bring up the interrelationship between Gippius's *Contes d'amour* and her *Memoirs of Martynov* not only because it demonstrates the fluidity in documentary and artistic genres, typical of Gippius and the symbolists' writing in general, but also because it points to the fluidity in genders in Gippius's writing. The fact that she could easily translate her "tales of love" into dandified male memoirs demonstrates the extent to which maleness and dandyism always already informs her *Contes d'amour*, albeit in an inverted form. In fact, it is only the feminine grammatical gender of Gippius's voice in her "tales of love" that prevents it from being a true dandy text.

The very manner in which Gippius frames her *Contes d'amour* links her amorous pursuits with the image of the male lover found in Western fiction. On 6 May 1901, Gippius affixed an epigraph consisting of a lyrical fragment written by Viktor Burenin, author of among other things the exotic society tale, "A Romance in Kislovodsk" ("Roman v Kislovodske") (1888).[23] And if anything, this quotation emphasizes her affinity with an inverted or feminine Don Juan figure.[24] The epigraph reads: "She sought encounters and always went back, and because of this, she never met with anyone even once" (Ona iskala vstrech—i shla vsegda nazad, / I potomu ni s kem, ni razu, ne vstrechalas') (*Dnev*, 1:35).[25] Following this epigraph, Gippius adds the question: "Why??," inviting the reader of her memoirs to search for an answer in the text that follows. If we were to read the epigraph according to typical gender stereotypes of women, we would probably proclaim that "she" displays the typical behavior of the frigid woman, who desires yet is incapable of sexual consumption. However, if we were to shift the gender of the subject in the epigraph from "she" to "he," as Gippius herself would later do in *The Memoirs of Martynov*, we would not say that he is frigid but rather that he emphasizes the coldness toward the opposite sex that is characteristic both of the actual dandy who frequently leads "a celibate (or solitary) life" and also of the man suffering from a Don Juan complex. Perhaps one of the greatest paradoxes of the figure of the Don Juan is that despite the number of his conquests, he evinces a certain resistance to having an enduring relationship with a woman. For this very reason, in "Don Juan, or Loving to Be Able To," an essay in her *Tales of Love*, Julia Kristeva asks: "But what makes Don Juan chase and run? What is he looking for?"[26] The questions that Kristeva poses here regarding the mystery of Don Juan are just the questions that Gippius poses about herself in the epigraph to her *Contes d'amour*: "What makes her chase and run? What is she looking for?"

Gippius does not answer the questions concerning the mystery of Don Juan that she tacitly alludes to in her epigraph, nor does she directly identify with the figure of Don Juan himself. However, in 1926, not long before she published her *Memoirs of Martynov*, she published a poem entitled "Don Juan's Answer" ("Otvet Don-Zhuana ") in the journal *The New House* (*Novyi dom*) in which she attempts to solve the mystery of Don Juan's serial romances and perhaps of her own female Don Juanism:

> Дон Жуан, конечно, вас не судит,
> Он смеется, честью удивлен:
> Я—учитель? Шелковистый пудель,
> Вот, синьор, ваш истинный патрон.
>
> Это он умеет с "первой встречной"
> Ввысь взлетатъ, потом идти ко дну.
> Мне—иначе открывалась вечность:
> Дон-Жуан любил всегда одну.
>
> Кармелитка, донна Анна... Ждало
> Сердце в них найти одну—Ее.
> Только с Нею—здешних молний мало,
> Только с Нею—узко бытие...
>
> И когда, невинен и беспечен,
> Отошел я в новую страну,—
> На пороге Вечности я встречен
> Той, которую люблю—одну.[27]
>
> (*Stikh*, 352–53)

[Don Juan, of course, does not judge you. He laughs, honestly surprised: Am I the teacher? A silky poodle—here, señor, is your true patron. It is he who is able from "the first woman he meets" to fly to the heights, then sink to the bottom. Eternity opened up to me differently: Don Juan always loved the one. The Carmelite, Donna Anna . . . His heart waited to find in them the one—Her. Only with Her are the earthly lightning bolts insufficient. Only with Her is existence narrow . . . And when, innocent and carefree, I went away to a new land, on the threshold of Eternity, I was met by Her whom I love—the one.]

If in the poem Gippius identifies through her masculine poetic speaker with the figure of Don Juan, she does so more indirectly in her *Contes d'amour*. In her diary, she employs the feminine "I" for her narrative voice, thereby emphasizing the documentary quality of her writing. Yet the gender of her narrative voice notwithstanding, she exhibits the behavior associated not only with Don Juanism but also dandyism. As a text, her memoirs are informed by an androgynous or bisexual divide characteristic of the dandy, since there is a crucial split or divide between the gender Gippius employs to tell her tale and the way in which she tells it. Though she writes her "tales of love" essentially as a woman, she relies heavily on the conventions of the dandy's or rake's notebook. Gippius makes it clear in the text of her memoirs that she has selected a "little black book" (chernaia tetrad') (*Dnev*, 1:35) to contain her diary of "love affairs," recalling the little black book employed by rakes to document their conquests. She also devotes the entire second entry of her "tales of love" to nothing short of a Don Juan list of love affairs she had with various men during her youthful days in the Caucasus. The fact that Gippius locates her early romantic affairs in the Caucasus is significant, for in the Russian imagination the Caucasus are intrinsically associated with Pechorin, the hero of Mikhail Lermontov's novel *A Hero of Our Time* (*Geroi nashego vremeni*) (1840) and one of the prototypical Russian literary dandies. Ostensibly, Gippius chooses to disassociate herself from Pechorinism by censoring out her descriptions of those affairs that display her former rakish behavior, indicating: "I am leaving out all of my Tiflis 'suitors,' everything, where there is only primitive vainglory, which I only afterward disguised to myself, calling it 'the desire for power over people' ['zhelanie vlasti nad liud'mi']" (*Dnev*, 1:36). Nonetheless, Gippius does not decline from masquerading her Casanova-like behavior in front of the reader. She spares no details of the other young suitors she snubbed, making reference to her cold indifference and reproaches.

In fact, in *Contes d'amour* Gippius thrives on maintaining aesthetic distance from the object of her affection. She mediates the descriptions of her love affairs through the cultural lens of the ambivalent lover, be it in the guise of the Don Juan or the dandy. And she also reveals the elaborate lengths to which she would go in order to maintain distance. For instance, in one of the very first love affairs that she describes in any detail in her memoirs, she is not even a major actor in the romance but instead engages in what François Roustang terms in *The Quadrille of Gender: Casanova's "Memoirs"* (*Bal masqué de Giacomo Casanova*) (1984) "the game of substitution."[28] Declining to actively pursue the object of her affections, Gippius decides to live and love vicariously through an imagined "rival" who will play out for her the romantic role she is too ambivalent to enact. She recalls: "At fifteen, at the dacha outside of Moscow, falling in love with the landlord's son, a beautiful red-bearded Master (of what?). By the way, I did not dream of mutual affection [o vzaimnosti ne mechtala] but wanted him to fall in love with [my cousin] Annette" (*Dnev*, 1:36). This tendency to distance her desire is more than a girlish whim; it becomes a sustained romantic pattern in these memoirs. Gippius either creates an imagined rival through whom she loves vicariously, or she diffuses her desire by pursuing two love objects simultaneously who, in turn, become rivals. In such instances, Gippius orchestrates a triangulation of desire that René Girard terms "mimetic."[29] While Girard demonstrates that the presence of a rival, be it real or imagined, confers value on the love object and incites desire, for Gippius this desire is incited particularly because the configuration of the love triangle creates and maintains distance between the actors in the romance.

Gippius, much like Don Juan, moves from lover to lover, traversing almost as many geographic as personal boundaries. In her diary, we can trace her travels to Moscow, the Caucasus, St. Petersburg, Taormina, Rome, Florence, and finally back to St. Petersburg. It is in the romantic setting of Taormina, which she calls "the white and light-blue city of the most comical form of love—homosexuality" (belyi i goluboi gorod samoi smeshnoi iz vsekh liubvei—pederastii) (*Dnev*, 1:60), where she meets the one person with whom she could conceivably fall in love, her Donna Anna, so to speak—the homosexual Henri Briquet.[30] Effeminate and highly aesthetic, Briquet might be said to represent, in a sense, an inverted image of Gippius herself.[31] She describes her first encounter with Briquet in Taormina in an entry that was written in St. Petersburg and, hence, is separated from the event by both time and distance. She recalls:

> In the enormous empty hall of the Reifs' villa (I love such rooms, big and empty), there is the tall, slender figure of Briquet with unbelievably blue eyes and a tender face. Very, very handsome. About 24 years old, no more. Irreproachably elegant, although, there is something another woman might call affected [pritvornoe], but for me—no, it is feminine. It is pleasing to me, and on the outside I sometimes like gay men ([Wilhelm von] Gloeden is old and comically unbalanced). I like the illusion of possibility: a suggestion of bisexuality. He seems to be both a man and a woman. That is very close to me. That is to say, that which *appears*. Well, in actuality, it ends ... [Mne nravitsia tut obman vozmozhnosti: kak by namek na dvupolost', on kazhetsia i zhenshchinoi i muzhchinoi. Eto mne uzhasno blizko. To-est', to, chto *kazhetsia*. Ved', v sushchnosti, konchaetsia eto ...] (*Dnev*, 1:61–62)

Gippius is not only attracted to but clearly identifies with the effeminate and dandified quality that Alan Sinfield defines as central to homosexual identity at the fin de siècle.[32] Tall, slender, elegant, and androgynous, Briquet is the very epitome of the early twentieth-century dandy. And the very terms that Gippius employs to describe Briquet recall the established language of dandyism. When Gippius identifies Briquet as "appearing" or *kazhetsia*, she hits on a very important element of the dandy found in one of the seminal treatises or handbooks of dandyism. Jules-Amédée Barbey d'Aurevilly, in one of the first and most influential books on dandyism, *On Dandyism and George Brummell* (*Du Dandysme et de George Brummell*) (1845), determines the ability to seem or to appear to be something as central to the dandy as it is to women. "*To appear is to be* for Dandies as for women" (*Paraître*, c'est *être*, pour les Dandys comme pour les femme), Barbey insists.[33] Whether Gippius, who spent time in France and spoke French, was familiar with Barbey's treatise on dandyism is not known.[34] However, the fact that she, like Barbey, identifies Briquet's ability "to seem" as integral to his being is highly suggestive. Equally telling is the manner in which she identifies with his undefinable, androgynous qualities, noting "that is very close to me" (eto mne uzhasno blizko).

In many ways, Gippius's meeting with Briquet is a kind of epiphany. In her lyrical descriptions of him, she does not just extol his qualities, finding in him the figure of the male muse, but she also defines herself in relationship to him.³⁵ She gives new meaning to the term "mimetic desire," as she identifies with Briquet's dandified proclivity for appearances as well as with his related dandified quality of defying fleshiness and corporeality. Briquet possesses a subtlety of personality that is antithetical to the womanly fleshiness that she eschews and that, as we have seen, she would refer to elsewhere as "a foul nature (*style 'femme'*)." She notes: "And his soul truly is not without subtlety. (It is amazing how in the majority of cases, the body recalls the soul in its form. How meaty women are! And how much baser they are than men! I am speaking about the majority, of course. And I am not thinking about myself, truly" (A dusha, v samom dele, ne bez tonkosti. [Udivitel'no, kak v bol'shinstve sluchaev, telo po forme napominaet dushu! Kak zhenshchiny miasisty! I naskol'ko oni grubee muzhchin! Govoriu o bol'shinstve, konechno. I ne dumaiu o sebe, iskrenno]) (*Dnev*, 1:62).

Once again, Gippius does not mention dandyism in her discussion of either Briquet's or her own soul. Nevertheless, her description of Briquet and by implication herself is informed by the ethos of dandyism. If in the earlier description of her spiritual double, Gippius would reflect the dandy's tendency to define himself "by embracing women" or femininity, in this passage she articulates the dandy's related yet seemingly antithetical tendency to cut or snub woman.³⁶ The manner in which Gippius praises her twin soul as being devoid of female fleshiness recalls Baudelaire's famous distinction between dandy and woman. In one of his more misogynistic statements, the French poet contends:

> La femme est le contraire du dandy.
> Donc elle doit faire horreur.
> La femme a faim et elle veut manger. Soif, et elle veut boire.
> Elle est en rut et elle veut être foutue.
> Le beau mérite!
> La femme est *naturelle*, c'est-à-dire abominable.
> Aussi est-elle toujours vulgaire, cest-à-dire le contraire du dandy.
>
> [Woman is the opposite of the dandy. Thus she must inspire horror. Woman is hungry and she wants to eat. Thirsty, and she wants to drink. She is in heat and she wants to be fucked. What fine merit! Woman is *natural*, that is to say, abominable. Thus she is always vulgar, that is to say, the opposite of the dandy.]³⁷

While Gippius's meditations on the self and soul are not nearly as misogynistic as Baudelaire's definition of the dandy, they do reflect her tendency in these memoirs to internalize the ethos of dandyism and to disassociate herself from the feminine and the womanly. Yet try as she may to fashion herself in imitation of her beloved, she realizes that she cannot have a real romance with Briquet unless he turned out to be, as she terms it, "a *special* homosexual" (*spetsial'nyi* pederast) (*Dnev*, 1:62). The fact that she cannot have a real romance with him is, no doubt, a large part of her initial attraction to Briquet. Ultimately, though, Briquet fails to fulfill his function as male muse, and, like the figure of Don Juan in her later poem "Don Juan's Answer," Gippius once again flies to the heights only to sink to the bottom, as her lyric flights of fancy give way to disillusionment. "I guess, anyway," she observes, "I will not truly fall in love, because he is, both outwardly and inwardly, only a close caricature of the being, who if he actually existed would please me *completely*. No, it is not worth it. But I want love around me, not in him, but toward him" (pozhalui, vse-taki ne vliublius' khorosho, potomu chto on—vneshne i vnutrenno—tol'ko blizkaia karikatura na sushchestvo, kotoroe, esli b zhilo, moglo by mne *do kontsa* nravit'sia. Da, ne stoit. Khochu liubvi, khotia by okolo menia, ne v nem—k nemu) (*Dnev*, 1:62).

And as with the earlier romances she describes, Gippius reverts once again to a "game of substitutions." She convinces her friend, Madame Reif, to pursue her affections for Briquet. And, at least, on the surface Reif would appear to present the perfect understudy for such a role. As Gippius writes:

> Madame Reif is a caricature also—of me (but not a close one). Here is a description of her. You judge.
> A rather tall blonde, an elongated thin face. Very light eyes, which can see nothing, a lorgnette on a ribbon, an ever-changing expression, a quickness of movements. She speaks of beauty and of God. (Only she was 25 years old, and I was 28 at the time.) (*Dnev*, 1:63)

Allowing her "caricature" to take on the active role, Gippius assumes the role of Madame Reif's "confidante" (konfidentka). She realizes the unlikelihood that Briquet will return Madame Reif's affections or fulfill what she sees as Reif's "hysterical desire" to conceive a child by Briquet.[38] Nonetheless, she proclaims: "Let those two caricatures . . . not love each other, since if he could love a woman, he would probably love me. But let her love him!" (Pust' eti dve karikatury . . . ne liubiat drug druga, ibo esli b on mog liubit' zhenshchinu—on liubil by menia, veroiatno,—a pust' ona liubit ego!) (*Dnev,* 1:63). And for Gippius, who has been obsessed with maintaining aesthetic distance throughout her *Contes d'amour*, this courtship of the two caricatures may indeed represent the pinnacle of "mimetic desire" and of amorous fictionality.

She does not just find a substitute for her ideal object of affection. She also finds a substitute for herself in the courtship process. By enacting the role of confidante, Gippius receives vicarious pleasure from the romance she has orchestrated or, more accurately, authored. Her role here ultimately is not unlike that of the reader of her amorous fictions, who can gain pleasure from eavesdropping on another's love affairs.

The complicated narrative web she weaves in her "tales of love" does not, however, end here. The romance that Gippius authors between the two caricatures, Briquet and Madame Reif, produces a sufficient amount of "love around [herself]" that she in turn falls in love. This time the object of her affections is Elizabeth von Overbek, a young musician Gippius meets at the Reifs' villa in Taormina. Their relationship begins to unfold when the young woman hands over her mother-of-pearl cane to Gippius to admire:

> Martha began speaking with the baroness. The little English girl had a strange, beautiful cane in her hands with mother-of-pearl incrustations.
> "Show me your cane," I said.
> And when she stretched it out to me, I had an inexplicable feeling without words: You see I can do whatever I want with this creature [sushchestvo]. It is mine. Later came words, much later. (*Dnev*, 1:65)

Though Gippius does not explain what this scene means, we might interpret the baroness's passing of the mother-of-pearl cane to Gippius symbolically as the transference of the (female) phallus that the child presumes the all-powerful mother to wield. After all, it is after receiving the cane — and the power it appears to bestow — that she is endowed with the desire and power to pursue a romance with the young Englishwoman and to enact the active role of lover. And in her later *Memoirs of Martynov*, Gippius reenacts this scene almost verbatim, giving the role formerly played by her in her *Contes d'amour* to her eponymous hero. Thus, in her more fictionalized account, she quite obviously codes her behavior as masculine. In a later entry of her *Contes d'amour*, Gippius would describe her affair with the baroness as "[her] 'exploit'" (moi "podvig") (*Dnev*, 1:67), thereby making her identification with the dandy complete. In her subsequent "tales of love," Gippius's love objects are men rather than women; nevertheless, her relationship with them is not significantly different. True to the spirit of her epigraph, Gippius chases and runs, courts and cuts, identifying in reverse with the ethos of dandyism and Don Juanism.[39] But in her diary, as opposed to her "Don Juan's Answer," she never reveals what or who she is searching for. When her male muse makes a fleeting appearance in the figure of Henri Briquet, he turns out to be no more real than any of the other cast of characters that inhabit her *Contes d'amour*, beginning with the Tiflis "suitors" that she describes ironically using quotation marks. Throughout these memoirs, Gippius thrives on maintaining distance from the object of her affection and in ensuring that her affairs remain unconsummated.

The sublimated economy of desire that informs Gippius's *Contes d'amour* played a central role in her early lyrics as well. If in her *Contes d'amour* Gippius manifests her androgyny by mimicking Don Juan and courting and cutting both men and women, in her lyric poetry she demonstrates her androgyny most frequently by adopting an unmarked or masculine lyrical "I" and wooing a female addressee.[40] In imagining the poetic speaker as masculine and the addressee as feminine, Gippius would appear to be working within the traditional forms of the love lyric, particularly as practiced by Alexander Blok and other male members of the symbolist movement. Yet as traditional as some of Gippius's love lyrics might seem to be especially from a formal perspective, her female authorship calls into question their heterosexual nature. Russian modernist scholars Konstantin Azadovsky and Alexander Lavrov point out that several of the love lyrics in her first volume of collected poems, namely "Stairs" ("Lestnitsa") (1897), "Circles" ("Krugi") (1899), and "A Walk Together" ("Progulka vdoem") (1900), can be read as documenting Gippius's relationship with the young baroness who makes a brief appearance in her *Contes d'amour*.[41] Though these poems are extremely sympathetic, treating the themes of separation and loss, not all of the love lyrics that Gippius addressed to a real or imagined feminine other are nearly as positive.[42] She often assumed a libertine posture in her early love lyrics that I see as intimately connected to the dandified and rakish stance she occupies in her *Contes d'amour*. But if in her *Contes d'amour* she typically merely depicts the object of her affection with no small amount of irony and, at times, snobbery, then in some of her early love lyrics she instead directly addresses the object of her affection in this fashion.[43]

In several of the love lyrics in her first volume, Gippius's presumed masculine poetic speaker addresses the feminine object of her desire as if "talking through his lorgnette." By this I mean that the masculine speaker addresses the feminine object of desire with the downward gaze or *prezrenie* that both Lotman and Feldman have identified as central to the dandy's posture.⁴⁴ This type of love lyric, which we might call a dandy lyric, deviates significantly from the traditional love lyric in terms of the articulation of desire, something that is not surprising given the dandy's complicated gender identification. If in the traditional male love lyric, which can be traced back to Dante Alighieri and Francesco Petrarch, the masculine speaking subject articulates longing for the absent feminine object of desire, in Gippius's dandified love lyrics, the masculine speaking subject expresses ambivalence toward the present feminine object of desire. Simultaneously attracted to and repulsed by the feminine addressee, the dandified speaker is neither completely heterosexual nor completely homosexual but something in between. This indeterminacy is further complicated by the fact that the sex of the author does not coincide with the gender of the speaker of the poem, making it possible to read Gippius's lyrics not just as dandy lyrics but also as masked lesbian love poems.

Gippius's 1903 poem "The Kiss" ("Potselui") is perhaps the most representative of her indeterminate, dandified love lyrics. Hoping to add an air of scandal to her first volume of poems, Gippius sent "The Kiss" to Valery Briusov along with the following instructions: "I am exhausted by the monotonous integrity of my poems. [. . .] I ask that you place the proposed happily perverse poem [veselo-izvrashchennoe stikhotvorenie] in the most illuminated spot possible. What a shame that it cannot follow [my poem about] the Christian according to Ephrem of Syria!"⁴⁵ A far cry from "monotonous," Gippius's "Kiss" rivals Briusov's notorious one-line poem "Oh, cover your pale legs" ("O, zakroi svoi blednye nogi") (1894) in terms of its erotic quality. However, if Briusov's one-liner is shocking for its overtly sexual overtones, Gippius's "Kiss" is shocking for its sexual indeterminacy. In "The Kiss," nothing much happens nor, we are led to believe, will much ever happen given the profound ambivalence of the masculine poetic speaker toward the female addressee:

> Когда, Аньес, мою улыбку
> К твоим устам я прлиближаю,
> Не убегай пугливой рыбкой,
> Что будет—я и сам не знаю.
>
> Я знаю радость приближенья,
> Веселье дум моих мятежных;
> Но в цепь соединю ль мгновенья?
> И губ твоих коснусь ли нежных?

> Взгляни, не бойся; взор мой ясен,
> А сердце трепетно и живо,
> Миг обещанья так прекрасен!
> Аньес... Не будь нетерпилива...
>
> И удаление, и теснота
> Равны—в обоих есть тревожность,
> Аньес, люблю я неизвестность,
> Не исполнение,—возможность.
>
> Дрожат уста твои, не зная,
> Какой огонь я берегу им...
> Аньес... Аньес... и только края
> Коснусь скользящим поцелуем...
> *(Stikh*, 126)[46]

> [When, Agnès, I bring my smile closer to your lips, don't run off like a scared little fish. What will happen I myself don't even know. I know the joy of drawing closer, the gaiety of my rebellious thoughts. But will I connect the moments in a sequence? And touch your tender lips? Look up. Don't fear; my gaze is clear, and my heart is palpitating and alive. The moment of promise is so wonderful! Agnès... Don't be impatient... Both separation and closeness are the same; in both there is alarm. Agnès, I love uncertainty. Not fulfillment, but possibility. Your lips tremble, not knowing what flame I spare them... Agnès... Agnès... I will touch only the edge with a sliding kiss...]

Sibelan Forrester has read this poem as representing "a somewhat extreme case of masculinization in Gippius's speaker and stereotypical femininity of her addressee in an erotic context."[47] Building on Forrester's reading, I would argue that the extreme masculinization of Gippius's poetic speaker derives from the dandified posture of the lyric speaker. The speaker of the poem, who reveals his masculine gender through the use of the phrase "I myself" (ia sam) at the end of the first stanza, displays the ambivalence toward the feminine that Feldman has identified with the complicated masculine figure of the dandy. The speaker refuses to satisfy the feminine addressee's or, for that matter, the implied female reader's desire to see the kiss completed or consummated. Instead, the speaker lords over the feminine addressee, Agnès, the power to satisfy her with a kiss or to deny her satisfaction. He taunts and tantalizes Agnès, much like a woman might tease a man, displaying a fair amount of scorn or *prezrenie* for the feminine object of his affection.

The speaker's disdain for the feminine addressee is evident from the poem's inception, where he addresses her as if looking down on her, if not literally then figuratively. In the first two lines of he poem, he rather coldly tells Agnès how exactly he intends to kiss her. In an unusual turn of phrase, he expresses his intention to bring not his lips or *usta* but his smile or *ulybka* to Agnès's lips. This description of a kiss as the union of a smile with lips is no less jarring in Russian than it would be in English and underlines the inherent inequality of this kiss and the superior stance of the speaker, for this proposed kiss will not mark the meeting of two sets of lips, of two analogous body parts, but of the speaker's somewhat smug and disdainful gesture, his smile, with Agnès's lips. He smiles on Agnès in the first few lines of this poem not like a man in love but like a dandy in awe of his power over a woman. In this gesture, we can detect the "disdainful expression" (prezritel'noe vyrazhenie) that would become the earmark of Gippius, the page and female dandy. Like a true dandy, the speaker courts Agnès just to cut her. And the rite of courtship is inseparable from the speaker's contempt for the feminine object of his affections.

He does not just tell the feminine addressee, Agnès, how he will kiss her, but how he expects her to react to the kiss, to his desire. He addresses her as one would speak to a child, chastising: "Don't run off like a scared little fish" (Ne ubegai puglivoi rybkoi). In so doing, he denies her the possibility of controlling her own desire — of accepting or resisting his advances. He implicitly places Agnès in a subservient role that is consonant with various literary and etymological associations with her name. Agnès is, after all, the name of the young ward in Molière's play *The School for Wives* (*L'École des femmes*) (1662), whom the main character, Arnolphe, is invested in keeping ignorant.[48] In her discussion of the poem, Forrester indicates that "the non-Russian name An'es (French Agnès), which lacks the standard Russian feminine noun ending -a, is repeated five times in five stanzas, and repetition may defamiliarize it as a name, letting the reader recall that etymologically it means 'lamb.'"[49] Indeed, the French name Agnès is derived from the Latin word for lamb and the Greek word for humble and meek, as is the Russian word for lamb, *iagnenok*.[50] And the speaker reinforces Agnès's meekness by invoking her name again and again as well as by comparing her expected reaction to his advances to the inhuman squirming of a "scared little fish" (puglivaia rybka).

Given the reluctance of the speaker to actually kiss Agnès, we have to question whether he is not the true meek one in this poem. Immediately after asserting his knowledge and superiority over the feminine addressee in the first three lines of the poem, he admits: "What will happen I myself don't even know" (Chto budet—ia i sam ne znaiu). Tellingly, the speaker reveals his uncertainly about how or if the kiss will be consummated at that very moment when he asserts his masculinity through the use of the emphatic expression "I myself" (ia sam) in the final line of the first stanza. Uncertainty or ambivalence many not be part of the accepted cultural stereotypes of masculinity; they are, however, as we know from Feldman's discussion, the defining characteristics of the masculine cultural figure of the dandy.

In a statement that would seem to come straight from the dandy's diary, the speaker begins the next stanza: "I know the joy of drawing closer, the gaiety of my rebellious thoughts" (Ia znaiu radost' priblizhen'ia / Vesel'e dum moikh miatezhnykh). After admitting at the end of the previous stanza that he did not know what would become of his desire for Agnès, the speaker ostensibly attempts to assert his "knowledge" and certainty here with the bold pronouncement "I know" (ia znaiu). Yet, once again, the speaker's "knowledge" falls short, especially in the biblical sense of the word. Here the speaker reveals knowledge of the process of courtship, of "getting closer" (priblizhen'e), not of the product of courtship, that is, consummation. Given that his courtship results in celibacy, the speaker, like the cultural figure of the dandy, is clearly not merely ambivalent about the feminine object of his affections. For him courtship is a pleasure primarily of the mind not the body, much as it would seem it was for Gippius. Significantly, he defines courtship as "the gaiety of [his] rebellious thoughts" (Vesel'e dum moikh miatezhnykh), recalling the rebellious yet ultimately solipsistic stance of the romantic hero. And since thoughts hold more erotic appeal than actions, he questions whether, in fact, he will ever consummate his desire for Agnès: "But will I connect the moments in a sequence? And touch your tender lips?" (No v tsep' soediniu l' mgnoven'ia? / I gub tvoikh kosnus' li nezhnykh?).

The questions at the end of the second stanza serve not only to reveal the speaker's insecurity and ambivalence toward sexuality but also to taunt the feminine addressee with the possibility of fulfillment of desire. The speaker lords over Agnès the power he has to fulfill her desire or to leave her unfulfilled. He challenges her: "Look up. Don't fear; my gaze is clear, and my heart is palpitating and alive" (Vzgliani, ne boisia; vzor moi iasen. / A serdtse trepetno i zhivo). It is perhaps no accident that the speaker demands that Agnès look up at him, as he has been looking down on her, at least, metaphorically, since the beginning of the poem. The speaker looks on Agnès with disdain or *prezrenie,* which in Russian emphasizes the visual metaphor through the presence of the word *zrenie* or sight. His clear gaze or *vzor* is that of the dandy who does not feel a need to interact directly with women but is content to observe them as if through a lorgnette.

The speaker succeeds in prolonging his detached, dandified view of the feminine addressee through the very language of the poem. Language and, in particular, the language of poetry may be viewed as a vehicle of seduction and physical intimacy, but it can just as well be viewed as a medium for delaying or avoiding physical contact and keeping the object of desire at arm's length. To be sure, one can kiss and tell or even tell and kiss, as the speaker purports to do here, but the two activities cannot be done simultaneously. And if earlier in the poem the speaker employs language and speech to seduce Agnès, to tell her how he will kiss her, now halfway through the poem he uses language to resist contact and launches into a romantic cliché to create physical distance between the addressee and himself: "The moment of promise is so wonderful!" (Mig obeshchan'ia tak prekrasen!) Besides employing such clichés, the very stuff of bad love poetry, to maintain distance, the speaker employs language effectively to silence Agnès and her desire. He warns: "Agnès . . . Don't be impatient . . ." (An'es . . . Ne bud' neterpeliva . . .). And this marks the third time within the course of the poem that the speaker employs a negative imperative to essentially silence Agnès and to negate her feelings. (Recall that earlier, he cautions: "Don't run off like a scared little fish" and "Don't fear.")

The speaker's negation, silencing, and objectification of the feminine addressee may be tied to the dandy's desire to avoid intimacy with women. The romantic credo of the speaker, like the dandy, is essentially noninvolvement or even celibacy. As he states: "Both separation and closeness are the same; in both there is alarm" (I udalenie, i tesnost' / Ravny—v oboikh est' trevozhnost'). Here the speaker quite clearly associates closeness or *tesnost',* a euphemism here for physical closeness or intimacy, with separation or *udalenie.* Disavowing intimacy, the speaker states his preference for distance and indeterminacy: "Agnès, I love uncertainty, not fulfillment, but possibility" (An'es, liubliu ia neizvestnost', / Ne ispolnenie,—vozmozhnost').

And to the bitter end, he persists in resisting the feminine addressee's desire to complete the kiss. Once again, in the final stanza, he tantalizes Agnès with the possibility of desire fulfilled, addressing her condescendingly: "Your lips tremble, not knowing what flame I spare them..." (Drozhat usta tvoi, ne znaia, / Kakoi ogon' ia beregu im...). The poem ends, much as it began, with a statement of what the speaker intends to do in the future, and with desire deferred. He notes: "Agnès ... Agnès ... I will touch only the edge with a sliding kiss ..." (An'es ... An'es ... i tol'ko kraia / Kosnus' skol'ziashchim potseluem ...). In place of the flame of passion, suggested in the second line of the stanza, the speaker vows only to bring a "sliding kiss" (skol'ziashchii potselui) to the edge of Agnès's lips at some point in the future. And by slipping away in such a manner, the speaker reveals himself to be somewhat of a cold fish if not the actual "scared little fish" (puglivaia rybka) of the poem, and thus this poem reflects the fluid gender identity characteristic of dandyism.

"The Kiss" is slippery in other respects as well. Like the infamous kiss in Chekhov's 1887 story of the same title, Gippius's "Kiss" eludes any one single meaning or interpretation. In the case of Gippius's poem, the kiss is markedly off-center or ec-centric (i.e., a kiss on the edge or *krai* reminiscent of Gippius's own "A. Krainy") and is as perplexing to the reader of the poem as the kiss in the dark is to Chekhov's hero Riabovich, who is a recipient and hence also reader of kisses in Chekhov's tale.[51] Like Riabovich, the reader of Gippius's "Kiss" must question not only what the kiss means but, most importantly, who is doing the kissing. Gippius does not just leave the reader in the dark as to the identity of the speaker; she intentionally misleads the reader. While the masculine gender of the speaker and his romantic inclinations makes it appear that he is a dandy, we also cannot rule out that the dandy-speaker in the poem is a she in male guise. Gippius, as we saw earlier, identified herself quite directly with the cultural figure of the dandy by adopting not only his posture but his gaze as well. And I would suggest that "The Kiss" is a clear example where we find Gippius "talking through her lorgnette," that is to say, appropriating the perspective of the dandy to romance another woman, to write a masked lesbian love lyric.[52]

Gippius provides several textual clues that this dandy lyric may be read as a lesbian love lyric in disguise. Through the guise of the dandy-speaker, she praises a type of intimacy that does not coincide with the masculine norm, a norm that puts the emphasis on consummation. I would suggest that the uncertainly or the unknown the speaker gives voice to in "Agnès, I love uncertainty, not fulfillment, but possibility" (An'es, liubliu ia neizvestnost' / Ne ispolnenie,—vozmozhnost') may be interpreted not just as the unknown physical act of love but also as love between two women—a love that has typically been silenced in the Russian literary tradition. Through innuendo the speaker in the poem expresses preference for a type of sexuality that could be more typically defined as feminine with its valorization of possibility or *vozmozhnost'* over fulfillment or *ispolnenie*, its privileging of foreplay over consummation. Moreover, the poem is characterized by a slipperiness that may be said to evoke the slipperiness involved in the meeting of two lips in a kiss and the markedly fluid economy of female sexuality. Notable in this regard is the fact that the speaker repeatedly makes reference to the addressee's lips, using both the poetic term *usta* as well as the more usual term *guby* to describe them. Lips in Russian as in English may refer both to the mouth as well as the female sex. Also highly suggestive is the manner in which the poetic speaker compares Agnès to a "little fish." In popular culture, the female sex has often been compared to the fish. A prime example of this implicit comparison can be found in the Western mythological figure of the mermaid, where the woman's lower body—her sex—is metamorphosed into a fish tail.

The French feminist Luce Irigaray employs feminine bodily imagery, reminiscent of that found in Gippius's poem, in her articulation of a theory of feminine writing or *écriture féminine*.[53] Irigaray valorizes feminine writing for its fluid economy and compares women's language to "two lips which speak together," a form of desire that simultaneously evokes self-pleasure and same-sex love. In spite of the presence of Irigarayan imagery in the poem, namely the two lips (those of the speaker and addressee) and the economy of fluids, Gippius's poem, it seems to me, resists this type of reading, for the author does not valorize romantic relationships between two women. She self-consciously presents the possibility of love between two women through the lens of a dandified speaker, who lords his power over the woman. And as a markedly unequal relationship, this poem not only defies the *écriture féminine* of Irigaray but also, it should be noted, Gippius's own theory of the inherent equality of the kiss. In her important essay, "Amorousness" ("Vliublennost'") (1904), she accords the kiss special meaning. In other words, for Gippius a kiss is not just a kiss. She holds that "the kiss, that stamp of the closeness and equality of two 'I's, belongs to amorousness" (potselui, eta pechat' blizosti i ravenstva dvukh "ia,"—prinadlezhit vliublennosti). However, "desire and passion greedily stole the kiss from [amorousness] a long time ago when she was still sleeping, and adapted [the kiss] for themselves, changing it and staining it with their own colors" (*Dven*, 1:262). In her own poem, the kiss is portrayed in highly ambivalent terms and clearly lacks the equality or *ravenstvo* that she claims to be the hallmark of a true kiss.

In her article "Laid Out in Lavender: Perceptions of Lesbian Love in Russian Literature and Criticism of the Silver Age, 1893-1917" (1993), Diana Burgin argues that many Russian modernist women writers expressed ambivalence about romantic relations between women. She notes that despite the central role that sexuality played in the writings of the period, openly lesbian love lyrics were not being written.[54] Women writers often felt compelled to rely on disguise to present lesbian themes in their works:

> Lesbian writers employ camouflage tactics most frequently in personal forms, especially love lyrics. These tactics may include expressing Lesbian relationships in allegorical terms (for example, a love between two personified feminine abstract nouns) and changing the sex of the Lesbian speaker or, less commonly, that of her female addressee, from female to male. The use of the last two devices "heterosexualizes" Lesbian love lyrics and makes them innocent (nevinnye) as Russians are wont to say, but it also diminishes their sexual and affectional particularity. The latter evolves from the emotional, spiritual, and erotic interaction of two women apart from whatever gender roles these women may or may not choose to play in the relationship. In my opinion the Lesbian poet who in her writing disguises her love for another woman as the love of a man for a woman in an effort, however understandable in a homophobic society, to "normalize" that love always risks distancing herself from her specific sexuality and making the lyrical expression of her sexuality in that sense less authentic. She also plays right into the widely held heterosexist stereotype of the "mannish" Lesbian and of Lesbian relationships as perforce pale imitations of heterosexual ones.[55]

I would suggest that Gippius both fits into and elides this categorization. She certainly does rely on "camouflage tactics" in "The Kiss." However, the camouflage or clothing she dons is not in keeping with that of the typical heterosexual male, as Burgin would suggest, but with that of the dandy, whose own gender and sexuality are highly ambivalent. In adopting the style or stance of the dandy, Gippius does not so much normalize or heterosexualize lesbian relationships as complicate them. By identifying with the dandy, Gippius wittingly or unwittingly displays her own ambivalence not just toward the other woman in the poem, the female addressee, but also toward her feminine self. And given Gippius's own tendency to present herself as an object of vision, both in the salon and in poems such as "The Seamstress" ("Shveia")

(1901) and even "The Spiders" ("Pauki") (1903), we cannot rule out the fact that she may have identified not only with the poem's speaker but also with the poem's addressee. Read in such a fashion, the poem would appear to reflect the way Gippius would like to be kissed and thus would be inherently narcissistic, but narcissistic in a way that involves an ambivalent attitude toward the female self.[56]

Perhaps Gippius's ambivalence about both the female self and the female other can best be seen in her poem "The Ballad" ("Ballada"). Like "The Kiss," this poem was written in 1903 and appeared in her first collection of poems. Gippius dedicated "The Ballad" to Poliksena Solovieva, who was herself a lesbian who wrote veiled lesbian love lyrics by employing a masculine lyrical "I" and the sexually ambiguous pen name Allegro. In dedicating the poem to Solovieva, Gippius may have been entering into a polemic with her about the nature of erotic relationships. In "The Ballad," Gippius once again adopts a masculine lyrical "I" to express desire for a feminine love object, this time for a mermaid or a *rusalka,* and, in doing so, she can be seen as writing both within and against the male poetic tradition:

Мостки есть в саду, на пруду, в камышах.
Там, под вечер, как-то, гуляя,
Я видел русалку. Сидит на мостках,—
Вся нежная, робкая, злая.

Я ближе подкрался. Но хрустнул сучок—
Она обернулась несмело,
В комочек вся съежилась, сжалась,—прыжок—
И пеной растаяла белой.

Хожу на мостки я к ней каждую ночь.
Русалка со мною смелее:
Молчит—но сидит, не кидается прочь.
Сидит, на тумане белея.

Привык я с ней, белой, молчать напролет
Все долгие, бледные ночи.
Глядеть в тишину холодеющих вод
И в яркие, робкие очи.

И радость меж нею и мной родилась,
Безмерна, светла, как бездонность;
Со сладко-горячею грустью сплелась,
И стало ей имя—влюбленность.

Я—зверь для русалки, я с тленьем в крови.
И мне она кажется зверем...

> Тем жгучей влюбленность: мы силу любви
> Одной невозможностью мерим.
>
> О, слишком—увы—много плоти на мне!
> На ней—может быть—слишком мало...
> И вот, мы горим в непонятном огне
> Любви, никогда не бывалой.
>
> Порой, над водой, чуть шуршат камыши,
> Лепечут о счастье страданья...
> И пламенно-чисты в полночной тиши,—
> Таинственно-чисты,—свиданья.
>
> Я радость мою не отдам никому;
> Мы—вечно друг другу желанны,
> И вечно любить нам дано,—потому,
> Что здесь мы, любя—неслиянны!
> (Stikh, 137–38)

[There is a boardwalk in the garden, on the pond, in the reeds. There once strolling toward evening I saw a mermaid. She sat on the boardwalk all tender, timid, and angry. I crept up closer. But a twig snapped; she turned around timidly, gathered herself tight into a bundle—jump—and melted like white foam. I go to the boardwalk to her every night. The mermaid is bolder with me. She is silent, but she sits and does not flee. She sits in the fog, showing up white. I have grown accustomed to being silent with her, the white one, through all the long pale nights. To gazing into the silence of the waters growing cold and into her bright, timid eyes. And happiness has been born between her and me, immeasurable, light, like bottomlessness. It became intertwined with bittersweet sadness, and its name became amorousness. I am a beast to the mermaid, I with decay in my blood. And she seems to me a beast... The more amorousness burns we measure the strength of our love with impossibility alone. Oh, alas, there is too much flesh on me! On her perhaps too little... And here we burn in an incomprehensible flame of a love that has never been. At times, above the water, the reeds rustle a little, prattling about the happiness of suffering... And flamingly chaste, mysteriously chaste, are our meetings in the midnight silence. I will not give up my happiness to anyone; we are eternally desirable to each other, and it is our lot to love eternally, because here we love without merging!]

At first glance, "The Ballad" would not appear to have much in common with Gippius's "Kiss." "The Kiss," with its dandified speaker and essentially innocent (or ignorant) female addressee, has many of the markings of the society tale, while the fairy-tale-like romance in "The

Ballad" between the masculine speaker and the mermaid is seemingly far removed from salon society and the codes of dandyism. Nonetheless, the poem can be read not only as treating many of the themes and imagery found in "The Kiss" but also as transforming and metamorphosing them.[57] The manner in which the masculine speaker in "The Ballad" chases the skittish mermaid recalls the way in which the dandy-speaker in "The Kiss" pursues the frightened Agnès. If in "The Kiss" the speaker envisions Agnès with her lips pursed like a "scared little fish," then, I would suggest, in "The Ballad" the poetic speaker implicitly sees the feminine other in the beastly guise of half-woman, half-fish, and thus the image of the mermaid in this poem is more in keeping with the Western mythological figure of the mermaid than with the Russian *rusalka*.[58] In this poem, the mermaid is repeatedly depicted as running off "like a scared little fish," as retreating to her habitat, the feminine realm of water and fluids: "She turned around timidly, gathered herself tight into a bundle—jump—and melted like white foam" (Ona obernulas' nesmelo, / V komochek vsia s"ezhalas', szhalsas'— pryzhok— / I penoi rastaiala beloi). Not only does she melt "like white foam," returning like an imperfect Aphrodite to her watery origins, but "she sits in the fog, showing up white" (ona sidit na tumane, beleia). She is metaphorically and metonymically associated with water and fluids (the white foam, the fog); she is also fluid in the sense that she cannot be possessed.

Indeed, it is the slipperiness or elusiveness of the feminine other that the masculine speaker finds most alluring. Like the dandy-speaker in the earlier poem, the poetic speaker prefers aesthetic distance from the feminine other to interaction with her. (And we can imagine how standing on the boardwalk the poetic speaker must look down on the mermaid.) As the speaker notes, "I have grown accustomed to being silent with her, the white one, through all the long pale nights. To gazing into the silence of the waters growing cold and into her bright, timid eyes" (Privyk ia s nei, beloi, molchat' naprolet / Vse dolgie, blednie nochi. / Gliadet' v tishinu kholodeiushchikh vod / I v iarkie, robkie ochi). Looking rather than touching is the privileged sense and means of apprehension in this poem, just as it is in "The Kiss," the title of the poem notwithstanding. It affords the poetic speaker the necessary distance to achieve true love. And it is because of this distance, not in spite of it, that love arises between the poetic speaker and the mermaid: "And happiness has been born between her and me immeasurable, light, like bottomlessness. It became intertwined with bittersweet sadness, and its name became amorousness" (I radost' mezh neiu i mnoi rodilas' / Bezmerna, svetla, kak bezdonnost'; / So sladko-goriacheiu grust'iu splelas', / I stala ei imia—vliublennost'). Ironically, happiness can be "born" (rodit'sia) specifically because the distance between poetic speaker and mermaid, between man and beast, so to speak is undefinable and "immeasurable" (bezmerna). It does not fit any prescribed form of love. And the speaker continually makes reference to the fact that this love cannot be measured. "The more amorousness burns," he notes, "we measure the strength of our love with impossibility alone" (Tem zhguchei vliublennost': my silu liubvi / Odnoi nevozmozhnost'iu merim). And the impossibility that the speaker refers to here is of course the impossibility of consummation: "And it is our lot to love eternally, because here we love without merging!" (I vechno liubit' nam dano,—potomu, / Chto zdes' my, liubia—nesliianny!).

The impossibility of man uniting with the mermaid is a very old topos in Western folklore and literature. The feminine mythological figure of the mermaid is highly sexualized yet unattainable. Even if, as in this poem, the mermaid overcomes her skittishness in the presence of man, the abnormality of her anatomy makes consummation of the male's desire for her impossible: the parts simply do not fit. The speaker alludes to the physical impossibility of a union, when he states: "Oh, alas, there is too much flesh on me! On her perhaps too little" (O, slishkom—uvy—mnogo ploti na mne! / Na nei—mozhet byt'—slishkom malo). In rendering the topos of the inconsumable love of man and mermaid, Gippius adds a new twist to the old myth. She infuses the folkloric theme with the ethos of dandyism by portraying her masculine poetic speaker as being as skittish as the feminine other. Her poetic speaker knowingly pursues a feminine other that is unattainable, thus affording him the opportunity to preserve, to quote Feldman again, his "solitary (if not celibate) life." While revealing a dandified ambivalence toward the feminine other, the poetic speaker also suggests his implicit identity with the feminine. In the sixth stanza, the speaker describes himself in the very same terms he uses to describe the feminine other in the poem. He notes: "I am a beast to the mermaid, I with decay in my blood. And she seems to me a beast . . ." (Ia—zver' dlia rusalki, ia s tlen'em v krovi. / I mne ona kazhetsia zverem . . .). Though femininity and effeminacy fit into the equation of dandyism, beastliness certainly does not. The manner in which in this passage Gippius configures both the masculine poetic speaker and the mermaid as beastly recalls the way she imagined woman as antithetical to the dandified Briquet, her male muse and masculine alter ego in *Contes d'amour:* "How meaty women are! And how much baser they are than men! I am speaking about the majority, of course. And I am not thinking about myself, truly." And it can be argued that it is at this point in the poem where the womanliness of the masculine poetic speaker is unmasked and the possible lesbian subtext of the poem is revealed.

While in many respects Gippius's "Ballad" can be seen as transferring or translating the erotic dynamic in "The Kiss" into another setting, it also does something very different. If in the earlier poem, Gippius's masculine poetic speaker retains his disdain for and dandified posture toward the female addressee throughout the poem, in "The Ballad" the dandified posture of the masculine speaker breaks down, as he betrays a beastliness that is contrary to the very ethos of dandyism outlined by Gippius in her *Contes d'amour* as well as by Baudelaire in his famous disquisition on dandyism and womanhood. And it is at this point that we can see the difficulty inherent in Gippius's stylization of herself as female dandy. In order to fashion herself as a cultural figure that is virulently masculine, in spite of his effeminacy, Gippius is faced with the daunting task of repressing her own feminine self, and more specifically the female body. In "The Ballad," the very manner in which her poetic speaker becomes contaminated with the qualities not only of the woman but more notably of the inhuman mermaid may be read as both symptomatic of the return of the repressed feminine as well as indicative of her dandified relationship with woman. For Gippius, as for the Baudelairean dandy, the feminine in its embodied and incarnated form is almost always negative.[59] This does not mean, however, that she did not valorize the feminine in the abstract. In fact, like many of her male contemporaries, Gippius did participate in the valorization of the eternal feminine, but as we shall see in the next chapter, she did so in her own idiosyncratic way.

7

Eternal Feminine Problems
Gippius, Blok, and the Incarnation of the Ideal

And woman must obey and find a depth for her surface. Surface is the disposition of woman: a mobile, stormy film over shallow water.

        Friedrich Nietzsche, *Thus Spoke Zarathustra*
        (*Also sprach Zarathustra*) (1883–85)

В невозмутимом покое глубоком,
Нет, не напрасно тебя я искал.
Образ твой тот же пред внутренним оком,
Фея–владычица сосен и скал!
[No, not in vain I searched for you in the imperturbably deep calm. Your image is the same in the mind's eye—a fairy mistress of the pines and crags.]

        Vladimir Soloviev, "On Lake Saima in Winter"
        ("Na Saime zimoi") (December 1894)

Но разве мог не узнать я
Белый речной цветок,
И эти бледные платья,
И странный, белый намек?
[But really could I not recognize the white river flower, and these pale dresses, and the strange white hint?]

        Alexander Blok, "The fogs concealed You"
        ("Tebia skryvali tumany") (May 1902)

Despite the fact that Zinaida Gippius was ambivalent about her own femininity, she devoted a fair number of works to a consideration of the feminine ideal and thus can be profitably discussed within the context of the second-generation Russian symbolists and their cult of the eternal feminine.[1] Nearly a decade before Alexander Blok made his debut as the poet of the Beautiful Lady, Gippius dedicated several short stories to the issue of the embodiment of the feminine, taking up a philosophical problem that had been raised by Vladimir Soloviev and that would become central to the poetics of Blok and his generation. Following in the tradition of Soloviev and anticipating the works of the younger generation of symbolists, Gippius tended to identify in these early works with a masculine subject rather than the feminine ideal, presenting the events in the story through the lens of a male narrator or character who encounters the earthly embodiment of the eternal feminine. But while the gendered dynamic of some of her early works was remarkably similar to that of Soloviev and his male successors, Gippius differed significantly from them in terms of her intense skepticism about the idea that this divine feminine principle could be successfully incarnated in a woman of flesh and blood. This skepticism appeared to increase following her acquaintance with Blok and his poetry, culminating in a polemic with him about the embodiment of the ideal. What seemed to disturb Gippius most about Blok and his relationship with his ethereal, otherworldly ideal was that he appeared to betray it by marrying the woman who had ostensibly served as the muse for his *Verses about the Beautiful Lady* (*Stikhi o Prekrasnoi Dame*) (1901-2).

Although Gippius may have perceived Blok's decision to marry or incarnate his muse as a betrayal of the mystical, sublimated relationship that had characterized the poet's relationship with his Beautiful Lady in his early poems, it was not out of keeping with the philosophy of Vladimir Soloviev. In line with the tradition of courtly love, which informed his writings, Soloviev became romantically involved with two married women, Sophia Khitrova and Sophia Martynova, who both bore the first name of his divine feminine principle. And he did make it clear in his philosophical writings that the eternal feminine or the divine Sophia could conceivably be embodied in a real woman, albeit in a lesser form.[2] As he wrote in his famous treatise *The Meaning of Love* (*Smysl liubvi*) (1892-94), "The heavenly object of our love is only one, always and for all humans one and the same—the eternal Divine Femininity. But seeing that the task of true love consists not in merely doing homage to this supreme object, but in realizing and incarnating it in another lower being of the same feminine form, though of an earthly nature, and seeing that this being is only one of many, then its unique significance for the lover of course *may* also be transient."[3] The notion that the feminine ideal could be realized or incarnated in a woman of flesh and blood was central to his poetics. In his poem "Three Meetings" ("Tri svidaniia") (1898), which he composed only a few years after *The Meaning of Love*, he details his three encounters with the divine Sophia: first with an actual nine-year-old girl in a Moscow church, then in a vision in the British Museum, and finally in all her glory in the sands of Egypt. Though Soloviev's poetic account of his three meetings with Sophia is informed by no small amount of self-parody, he never falters in his belief that she does exist or that she has the potential to positively change the world.

Like many of her contemporaries, Gippius was deeply influenced by the poetry and philosophy of Soloviev, but she differed significantly from him in terms of the way she imagined the feminine in her works. For instance, in "The Apple Trees Blossom" ("Iabloni tsvetut"), an early short story that first appeared in *Our Time* (*Nashe vremia*) in 1893, she takes issue with the idea that an encounter with the earthly embodiment of Sophia or the eternal feminine will necessarily exert a positive force on man. This brief, first-person narrative recounts the trials and tribulations of a sensitive young musician named Volodia who encounters an unfamiliar young girl in the apple orchard near his family's country estate and begins to meet with her in the garden, much to the dismay of his controlling mother. From the very outset, the appearance of the young girl gives him cause for hesitation. After being startled by a strange and seemingly inexplicable rustling sound, he spies an unfamiliar young girl in unusual attire. He observes: "her clothing was very strange, unlike the typical dresses of young ladies. It seemed to me to be at once masquerade-like and completely simple [. . .]. It was a wide dress from soft white material, but it was equally wide at the top and hemline (now I saw her entirely, because I was standing by the fence on the other side), with a narrow dark-red belt. I understood why there was such a strange rustling when she walked: her dress ended with a long train, and not even a train, but simply a piece of material which fell at the back, careless and beautiful. The sleeves were narrow and long, almost to her fingers" (*Soch*, 292).

Though the strange young girl identifies herself as Marfa Koreneva, a girl from the neighborhood, she prefers to go by the sobriquet Marta and true to the possible seasonal associations of this variation on the name "Martha," she begins to take on mysterious qualities for Volodia. "She seemed beautiful to me," he remarks, "like sky through the trees, like tender, fragrant air, like pink clouds near the setting sun" (*Soch*, 293). And his initial identification of Marta with the forces of nature does not seem to be misplaced. Marta informs Volodia that she has an intimate connection with nature and can sense when the apple trees will blossom, a fact that appears to be supported by the manner in which her attire seems to change in tandem with nature. At their second meeting in the orchard, Volodia notices not only that her red belt is now gold but also that the color of her dress has changed. "Perhaps," he notes, "the sun cast its rays in a unique fashion; perhaps, it was my imagination, but it seemed to me that today her clothing was tinted slightly pink, like the blossoms of an apple tree" (*Soch*, 294).

Volodia's growing infatuation with Marta does not go unnoticed by his mother, who had hitherto been the center of his universe. Overcome by jealousy, she forbids him from seeing Marta. Right before Volodia and his mother are scheduled to return to their home in Moscow and the apple blossoms are about to open, his mother goes out to the neighbors' house and leaves him alone in the house, forbidding him to see Marta. Against the wishes of his mother, Volodia meets Marta in the apple orchard. During this meeting, he observes changes in her that appear to correspond with those in nature. "She seemed paler to me than she was before," he notes. "But her dress, this time I couldn't doubt it, was not white, but slightly pink" (*Soch*, 299). It is at this moment, on the verge of the opening of the apple blossoms, that, for the first time, he has a truly mystical experience. As he notes: "Never before, never stronger did I feel that I was—'together with her,' and that there was happiness in this, if this could last" (*Soch*, 300). After "everything around [them] grew clearer and colder, the sky turned green, and the twilight descended" (*Soch*, 300), Marta announces that it is time for the apple blossoms to open, but Volodia, overcome with angst about his mother's prohibition, informs her that he is going away with his mother and leaves Marta and the garden.

In the very final section of the story, Volodia tells of the disastrous consequences of this final encounter with Marta in the apple orchard — consequences that might tempt us to read the apple orchard not as the setting for a miracle but as the Garden of Eden and the site of man's fall from grace. Immediately after Volodia's clandestine meeting with Marta in the garden, Volodia's mother falls gravely ill, and he believes that she did so on purpose. "She, mother," he notes, "did it all intentionally in order to take her revenge on me, I know. True, she did grow thin and weak that very evening, but I know that it was out of intense hatred for me" (*Soch*, 301). After his mother's death, he moves to St. Petersburg without even inquiring about Marta. Though he continues to play music, as he had during his stay in the country, and even makes a living as a musician, he becomes disillusioned by the way in which his present life fails to live up to the brief moments that he had with Marta in the garden. In the final lines of the story, Volodia contemplates suicide, thinking: "It is so terrible, so ugly . . . How far I am from Marta! But am I really going to? No, no I shall only try, nobody will know, but I will try" (*Soch*, 302).

"The Apple Trees Blossom" demonstrates that it can be extremely difficult and even dangerous for the artist or sensitive man to attempt to translate the feminine ideal into reality, and in so doing it would seem to foretell of the sometimes disastrous attempts of the symbolists to try to realize the feminine ideal in their beloved. Gippius puts forth a similar message about the difficulties of attempting to embody the ideal in "Miss May" ("Miss Mai"), another early short story that first appeared in *The Northern Herald* (*Severnyi vestnik*) in 1895.[4] This story, which opens just before Easter, is about a refined young aristocrat named Andrei who is engaged to a young woman named Katia. Though Andrei believes himself to be in love with Katia, he begins to question his feelings for her once he comes in contact with a mysterious stranger named May Ever, the English cousin of one of Katia's friends. When Andrei first sees Miss May, he doesn't know whether she is a real woman or a vision, so ethereal and disembodied is she and so unlike his more earthly and voluptuous Katia:

> At the railing of the balcony right in front of the door, an unfamiliar tall girl in a white dress stood and looked at Andrei. She was silent, and Andrei was silent, because it occurred to him that again this only seemed to be and that in general there was some kind of terrible misunderstanding. Suddenly from the first glance he noticed and understood everything about her, perhaps because she was almost all in one light color and seemed solid and simple as if she were cut from one piece. Andrei noticed that her white dress was of a light and almost transparent silk fabric, everything from the top to the bottom was in innumerable pleats and gathers as if it were wrinkled. And the pleats did not fall straight, but dragged slightly behind and stirred from the barely perceptible wind in the garden, now ascending now descending like soap foam. Her extremely long and thin neck

extended from that foam imperceptibly; it was the same color as her dress, and it also seemed transparent like fine Chinese porcelain when it is looked at in the sun—only here there was a barely perceptible pinkish cast of life. Her light-golden hair, which was not thick and was without the slightest red or gray tint, was combed back smoothly. But the shorter hairs stuck out to the side and loosely and lightly curled around her ears and temples. Her face, transparent like her neck without the shadow of rouge, was calm. Her gray eyes, set wide apart, were framed by curly eyelashes that were slightly darker than her hair. Her eyebrows, which were darker still, rose up evenly and simply. Her pink lips were tightly pursed.

After that first moment of fear and surprise, Andrei knew that here there was no miracle of any kind, that the girl was not a ghost or a hallucination, but simply a live girl—and nonetheless she seemed to be a miracle to him, because she was not reminiscent of a live and ordinary girl. In order to touch her, it was necessary to take one and a half steps, but it seemed that to do so it was necessary to traverse the abysses of the heavens and the clouds and that it was better not even to attempt to touch her, so strange was the impression that the transparency of her face gave. (*Soch*, 313-14)[5]

In spite of his initial resistance to approach this woman, who resembles the earthly embodiment of Aphrodite with her white dress with its foam-like swirling hemline, Andrei does manage to speak to her. And over the course of his stay at Katia's estate, he repeatedly meets with Miss May in the garden where they converse about their feelings. Gradually, he begins to forget about his fiancée, Katia, feeling "no pangs of conscience, not even the smallest amount of guilt in front of his fiancée, so distant was she from him and so incomparable were their relations with his present ones" (*Soch*, 329). Whereas his relations with Katia were ordinary, earthly, and sexualized, his relations with Miss May were of a spiritual order. Andrei, the narrator reveals, "discovered a soul in himself—and immediately gave it entirely to the girl in the white dress, whom he barely knew and from whom he barely heard any words. She said that 'this' would come of its own accord—and in all probability there was truth in her words" (*Soch*, 329).

While Andrei understands that his relationship with Miss May is radically different from that which he had with Katia, he insists that it must ultimately assume a similar form. In an attempt to incarnate the love he feels for Miss May, he proposes marriage to her. She, however, admits to never having had the desire to marry. "Love is one thing, and marriage is another" (Liubov'—odno, a brak—drugoe), she tells him. "I have no inclination toward marriage" (Ia k braku nikakoi sklonnosti ne imeiu) (*Soch,* 334). And in her final meeting with him in the garden, before she announces her departure, she insists that the love they once knew—that unfettered, free, and sublimated love that marked their initial meetings—is no longer:

> —Yes. It's like this. I am not saying that you didn't love me. But our love has passed. Everything good in our love has passed. Now it is necessary to break up. Weren't you happy from this love? Were there real moments of great happiness? Tell me! When the lime trees were blooming, do you remember? When you were afraid to kiss me? Were there?
> —Yes, there were, whispered Andrei.
> —Well, there, and now everything has passed. The lime trees cannot open again, and those best moments cannot be. You confuse that which cannot be confused. You conflate love—that which is from God—with a wedding, with a union, with habit, with ties, which are from people [Ty liubov', to, chto ot Boga, svodish' na svad'bu, na soedinenie, na privychku, na sviazi, kotorye ot liudei]. Perhaps, even a wedding can be good, but I will not undertake it. I am hot and stuffy, and it's difficult for me. I love only love. Forgive me. One need not grumble if something is over. That's how it should be. You see it once was ... (*Soch,* 336)

Shortly after Miss May delivers this speech, the narrator informs us that "lightning without thunder illuminated the trees in the garden and the sky with a shaking gray spark. Andrei saw the white dress of May for the last time, and it appeared to his exhausted and weary soul that it was a vision like all of his love" (*Soch,* 336). And, thus, Miss May vanishes from the scene forever, like a May rain. "Miss May" does not, however, end here, but concludes with a coda that serves to reinforce the idea that marriage requires a different kind of love than that espoused by Miss May, Andrei's vision of the eternal feminine. After doubting his love for Katia during Miss May's visit, Andrei finds himself involved in a very earthly, ordinary, but nonetheless satisfying married relationship with Katia. While he had formerly rejoiced in the manner in which kissing Miss May "he felt some type of cold in her, not even cold, but coolness, as if it were wind from evening spring water" (*Soch,* 335–36), he now takes pleasure in the very earthly kisses of his very corporeal wife. In the very last paragraph of the story, the narrator informs us that "he bent his head down and kissed her. She happily responded to him, and Andrei again involuntarily thought how soft and pleasant her lips were and how entirely sweet she was" (*Soch*, 338).

Although Gippius allows Andrei to find marital bliss with Katia, it is clear that the type of love she sanctions is the ephemeral chaste love that Andrei and Miss May share in the garden amongst the blooming lime trees. And of the two main female characters in the story Miss May is certainly the one closest to Gippius in spirit. Although Gippius may have been inclined to flaunt her femininity in the salon and to cross-dress like a dandy, she was also known to dress in white and to reinforce her own eternal femininity. This is a detail that has been duly noted by her contemporaries. In a diary entry dating from December 1901, Valery Briusov recalls that while Gippius and her husband were visiting him in Moscow, she inquired: "I don't know your Moscow customs. May one go anywhere in white dresses? Otherwise I don't know what I'll do. My skin somehow won't take any other color . . ."[6] It was also in Moscow at the photography studio of Otto Renar that Gippius had the famous photograph taken of herself in a long flowing gown of thin white woolen fabric that made her appear every bit as ethereal and disembodied as her fictional Miss May. In this portrait (figure 4), the whiteness of her gown not only blends with the pallor of her skin, giving her the same haunting appearance as her fictional character, but her dress sweeps dramatically to one side producing the illusion that she is enveloped in foam. In other words, similar to her own Miss May, Gippius appears in this photograph in the guise of the eternal feminine or Aphrodite Uranus.[7]

But if Gippius styled herself as Aphrodite in this famous early photograph, she was nonetheless intensely skeptical about the idea that the eternal feminine could be adequately embodied in a woman of flesh and blood. She had already gone on record about the difficulty of successfully embodying or incarnating the eternal feminine in some of her early short stories, and she soon became very critical of certain aspects of the Blokian idea of the Beautiful Lady. Even though she was an early supporter of Blok and his poetry, helping him to make his literary debut on the pages of *The New Path* (*Novyi put'*) in March of 1903, she appeared to take on the very idea of the Beautiful Lady quite directly in her early parody "Love for an Unworthy One" ("Liubov' k nedostoinoi").[8] Composed in 1902, shortly after she had become acquainted with Blok and his poetry, this poem does not so much question the concept of the Beautiful Lady as the tendency among male poets and Blok in particular to conflate the Beautiful Lady with their beloved. The poem begins in

Figure 4. Photograph of Zinaida Gippius taken at the Moscow studio of Otto Renar (circa 1900)

a traditional enough fashion with the poetic speaker paying homage to his Beautiful Lady:

> Ах! Я одной прекрасной дамы
> Был долго ревностным пажом,
> Был ей угоден... Но когда мы
> Шли в парк душистый с ней вдвоем—
> Я шел весь бледный, спотыкался,
> Слова я слышал, как сквозь сон,
> Мой взор с земли не подымался...
> Я был безумен... был влюблен...
> И я надеялся... Нередко
> Я от людей слыхал о том,
> Что даже злостная кокетка
> Бывает ласкова—с пажом.
> Моя ж мадонна—молчалива,
> Скромна, прелестна и грустна,
> Ни дать ни взять—немая ива,
> Что над водами склонена.
> О, ей—клянусь!—я был бы верен!
> Какие б прожили мы дни!..
> И вот, однажды, в час вечерен,
> Мы с ней у озера,—одни
> Длинны, длинны ее одежды,
> Во взгляде—нежная печаль...
> Я воскресил мои надежды,—
> Я всё скажу! Ей будет жаль...
> Она твоим внимает пеням,
> Лови мгновения, лови!..
> Я пел, склонясь к ее коленям,
> И лютня пела о любви,
> Туман на озеро ложится,
> Луна над озером блестит,
> Всё живо... Всё со мной томится...
> Мы ждем... Я жду... Она молчит.
> Туман качается, белея,
> Влюбленный стонет коростель...
> Я ждать устал, я стал смелее
> И к ней: "Мадонна! Неужель
> Не стоит робкий паж привета?
> Ужель удел его—страдать?
> Мадонна, жажду я ответа,
> Я жажду ваши мысли знать".
> (*Stikh*, 294-95)

[Ah! For a long time I was the jealous page of one beautiful lady. I pleased her... But when we walked into the fragrant park together, I, all pale, walked, tripped. I heard her words as if in a dream; my gaze did not stir from the ground ... I was crazy ... I was in love ... And I hoped ... Not infrequently I had heard from people about how even a malicious coquette could be affectionate with a page. My madonna was quiet, humble, beautiful, and sad, exactly like a mute willow bowed over the waters. Oh, I swear, I would have been faithful to her! What days we would spend! .. And then one day in the evening hour, we were alone by the lake. Long, long were her garments. There was tender sadness in her glance ... I resurrected my hopes: I will tell all! She will be sorry ... She will heed your songs. Seize the moment, seize! ... I sang, bending toward her knees. And the lute sang about love. A fog descends on the lake; the moon sparkles above the lake; everything is alive ... Everything languishes with me ... We wait ... I wait ... She is silent. The fog rolls in, turning white; the corncrake in love wails ... I grew tired of waiting and became bolder. I said to her: "Madonna! Doesn't a timid page deserve your attention? Can it be that his lot is to suffer? Madonna, I thirst for an answer. I thirst to know your thoughts."]

While the basic scenario in this parodic poem is analogous to that of Blok's poems with the masculine poetic speaker paying homage to his feminine ideal, the situation changes abruptly in the following section of the poem where the beautiful lady, designated here in the lower case rather than the upper case as in Blok's poetry, is called on to speak. Rarely does the Beautiful Lady talk in Blok's early poetry. And when one of her various earthly manifestations is permitted to break her silence, such as the woman in the third pair of lovers in *The Puppet Show* (*Balaganchik*) (1906), it is not unusual for her to be presented as simply echoing the thoughts and sentiments of her beloved. So central is repetition to Blok's treatment of the feminine here that Peter Barta has read the play as a variation on Ovid's myth of Echo and Narcissus and therefore as a key text in the Russian symbolists' reworking of this particular tale of metamorphosis.[9] Blok was by no means only turn-of-the-century writer to associate the ideal woman with the figure of Echo. For instance, in *Eve of the Future Eden* (*L'Eve future*) (1886), Villiers de l'Isle-Adam's fictional Thomas Edison constructs a female automaton named Hadaly who readily plays Echo to his friend Lord Ewald's Narcissus. Hadaly, whose name we are told means "ideal" in Persian, perfectly simulates not only the outward form of Ewald's lover, Alicia, but also her voice, which is based on a recording of Alicia's voice. Further,

Hadaly is programmed so that the simulated voice perfectly mimes the sentiments of Lord Ewald.[10] However, in opposition to Hadaly, who merely mimes the words of her beloved, or to Blok's Beautiful Lady, who is typically struck by muteness, Gippius's madonna does not remain silent, nor does she mimic the thoughts of her poet-page. Instead, she reveals herself to have a mind of her own:

> Она взглянула . . . Боже, Боже!
> И говорит, как в полусне:
> "Знать хочешь мысли? Отчего же!
> Я объясню их. Вот оне:
> Решала я . . .—вопрос огромен!
> (Я шла логическим путем),
> Решала: нумен и феномен
> В соотношении—каком?
> И всё ль единого порядка—
> Деизм, теизм и пантеизм?
> Рациональная подкладка
> Так ослабляет мистицизм!
> Создать теорию—не шутка,
> Хотя б какой-нибудь отдел . . .
> Ты мне мешал слегка, малютка;
> Ты что? смеялся? или пел?"
>
> (*Stikh*, 295)

[She glanced . . . God, God! And she says as if half in a dream: "You want to know my thoughts? Of course! I will explain them. Here they are: I was working on . . . an enormous problem! (I took a logical route.) I pondered in what relation are noumenon and phenomenon? And is everything of the same order—deism, theism, and pantheism? How a rational underside weakens mysticism! To create a theory is no joke, even some part of it . . . You bothered me somewhat, little one. What's with you? Were you laughing? Or singing?"]

Gippius takes a bold step here when she allows her beautiful lady to talk back. The fact she can converse eloquently about noumenon and phenomenon, not to mention deism, theism, and pantheism, is a testament to her earthly and intellectual existence, and this is greatly upsetting to her poet-page. It is because she refuses to play the role of silent lady to the garrulous poet-page that he designates her as unworthy or *nedostoinaia*. Immediately after receiving an earful of his madonna's thoughts on metaphysics, Gippius's poet-page offers the following warning to his contemporaries:

> Мрачись, закройся, месяц юный!
> Умолкни, лживый коростель!
> Пресéкнись, голос! Рвитесь, струны!
> Засохни, томный розанель!
> И ссохолось всё, и посерело,
> Застыл испуганный туман.
> Она—сидела как сидела,
> И я сидел—как истукан.
> То час был—верьте иль не верьте,—
> Угрюмей всяких похорон...
> Бегите, юноши, как смерти,
> Философических мадонн!
>
> (*Stikh*, 295)

[Be gloomy, hide, young moon! Be silent, lying corncrake! Cut yourself off, voice! Break, strings! Dry up, languid geranium! And everything dried up and turned gray; the frightened fog froze. She sat as she was sitting, and I sat like a statue. The hour was, believe it or not, gloomier than any funeral... Lads, flee from philosophizing madonnas as from death!]

This playful warning may be read as Gippius's attempt to caution Blok and the younger generation of poets against conflating their beloved with the feminine ideal well before the cult of the Beautiful Lady was in full swing.[11] If in some of her earlier stories, she called attention to the difficult or even disastrous consequences of attempting to incarnate the ideal, here she takes what might be seen as a more overtly feminist stance and reveals the Beautiful Lady to have thoughts of her own. And it is highly likely that her contemporaries would have seen the "philosophizing madonna" in this poem as a not-so-so veiled reference to Gippius herself.[12] Though she may have worn the long white garments that were associated with the eternal feminine, she did not shy away from making her own intellectual or philosophical views known, nor did she play second fiddle to her husband Dmitry Merezhkovsky when it came to philosophical matters.[13] In fact, her personal secretary Vladimir Zlobin maintains that "the guiding male role [in intellectual matters] belonged not to him, but to her. She was very feminine and he masculine, but on the creative and metaphysical planes their roles were reversed. She fertilized, while he gestated and gave birth. She was the seed, and he the soil, the most fertile of all black earths."[14]

Gippius's resistance, then, to the symbolist tendency to incarnate the feminine ideal is evident not only in her refusal to position herself or her own "beautiful lady" as silent muse but also in the very specific way she reacted to her friend Blok's decision to marry Liubov Mendeleeva, the woman who had served as the muse and prototype for the image of the Beautiful Lady in his early poetry. Gippius and her husband, as noted in chapter 1, reportedly did not approve of Blok's decision to marry his real-life muse.[15] And after the wedding, doubts apparently continued to linger about the effect that marriage would have on Blok's poetry. In a letter written to Boris Bugaev (Andrei Bely) on 20 November 1903, Blok reports: "One of the Petersburg poets wrote me: 'A legend is being spread about you that, having married, you have stopped writing poetry.' Mme. Merezhkovskaia, it seems, decided this earlier. What does it mean? Mme. Merezhkovskaia created a complicated theory about marriage, told me about it one spring evening, but at that time I liked the spring evening more, didn't listen to the theory, understood only that it was complicated. And now I have gotten married, again I write poetry, and that which was formerly sweet remains sweet" (*SS*, 8:69).

Although Gippius may have believed that marriage would not accord well with Blok's poetry, it would appear, given Gippius's own early stories, that it was much more likely that his marriage would not accord well with her poetics, which were diametrically opposed to attempts to realize the feminine ideal. Both "Miss May" and "The Apple Trees Blossom," though written in the early to mid-1890s after her own marriage to Merezhkovsky, can be read as cautioning against the very attempts to incarnate the feminine ideal that would be central not only to Blok's relations with his wife but also to those of so many of his contemporaries. Shortly after Blok's wedding to Liubov Mendeleeva, Andrei Bely and Sergei Soloviev gave Gippius and other skeptics of the possibility of the realization of the eternal feminine much to think about by creating a veritable cult around Liubov Mendeleeva. In her memoirs, Blok's aunt Maria Beketova indicates that the so-called Blokites or *blokovtsy* insisted against better judgment in seeing Blok's bride as the earthly embodiment of the Beautiful Lady from his poetry. "They positively gave Liubov Dmitrievna no peace," she notes, "forming mystic conclusions and generalizations on the basis of her gestures, movements, hairdo. It was enough for her to don a bright ribbon, sometimes simply to wave her hand, and already the 'Blokites' looked at each other with a meaningful expression and uttered aloud their conclusions. It was not possible to get angry at this, but somehow it grew tiring and the atmosphere became heavy."[16]

Gippius was apparently not a direct witness to any of these antics; however, it is likely that rumors of the Blokites' behavior reached her in St. Petersburg. In her memoirs *Living Faces* (*Zhivye litsa*), which she completed in 1924, shortly after her emigration from Russia, she makes mention of Blok's disappearance from Petersburg life immediately following his wedding and of his extended contact with Bely and Soloviev on his Shakhmatovo estate.[17] "That entire summer," she writes, "I did not correspond with Blok. In the fall someone told me that, having married, Blok left for Shakhmatovo, that his wife was some type of astonishing beauty [kakaia-to udivitel'naia prelest'], that Boria Bugaev and Serezha Soloviev (the son of Mikhail and Olga Soloviev) were guests at their place for a long time" (ZL, 19). Once Gippius picks up her narrative about the fall of 1903 and winter of 1904, we get the sense that she may have had an inkling of some of the dramatic goings on at Shakhmatovo that centered around Blok's bride. She goes to elaborate lengths to establish that marriage had not changed Blok much, describing in some detail a conversation that purportedly took place between herself and the poet that centered around the question of Blok's position on the issue of the embodiment of the feminine ideal:

> And our conversation was the same [as before his wedding]. I only brought up one direct question that was in essence completely unnecessary:
> —Is it not true that in speaking about Her you never think, cannot think about some real woman?
> He even lowered his eyes as if he were ashamed that I could pose such questions:
> —Well, of course not, never.
> And I became ashamed [I mne stalo stydno]. Such a danger for Blok, even having married, could not exist. What was I suspecting him of! It was necessary to see that marriage had changed him . . . perhaps even too little.
> As we were saying goodbye:
> —You don't want to introduce me to your wife?
> —No. I don't want to. It isn't necessary. (ZL, 19-20)

If Gippius were as ashamed as she purports to have been about posing this rather indiscreet question about the embodiment of the eternal feminine, it is highly unlikely that she would have replicated this dialogue in her memoirs for her contemporaries and future readers to see. In this case, her professed shame may be the result of her somewhat playful attempt to mask over her philosophical differences with Blok rather than an accurate reflection of her own reaction to this social situation. In December 1904, Gippius published a rather harsh critique of Blok's *Verses about the Beautiful Lady* in *The New Path*, the same journal where Blok had made his poetic debut. Among other things, she criticizes him for his imprecise representation of the Beautiful Lady. "She, She, everywhere She," Gippius writes, "and the songs of her knight are so wonderful in all their monotony that you don't know which one delineates who she is? Of course, *not* the earthly lady of medieval knights; perhaps, the 'Maiden of the Rainbow Gates' of Vladimir Soloviev? The eternal feminine? Sophia-Wisdom? It's all the same. We don't know, and it is unlikely that her knight knows. He doesn't know, moreover, what to say."[18]

But if Blok remained unsure about what to say about the Beautiful Lady, then Gippius certainly had her own answers. In 1906, after the appearance of her review of Blok's *Verses about the Beautiful Lady* and well after her reported conversation with him about his belief in the incarnation of the Beautiful Lady, she published a cycle of poems entitled *Waterslide* (*Vodoskat*) in *Libra* (*Vesy*), in which she compares her soul to the feminine forces of nature, thus participating in the Solovievian tradition of presenting one of the hypostases of the eternal feminine or Sophia as the world soul as embodied in nature.[19] In her second volume of verse, which she published with Musaget in 1910, she included the poems from this cycle and dedicated three of them, "She" ("Ona"), "A Waterslide" ("Vodoskat"), and "A Thunderstorm" ("Groza") directly to Blok.[20] In *Living Faces*, she offers an explanation for the dedication of the poems. She explains that while Blok was looking through the manuscript of her second volume of poems, she told him to "select the ones [he liked] best of all" and "[she would] dedicate them [to him]" (*ZL*, 29). Here, she attributes very little significance to the poems Blok chose. "He selected a few, one after another," she notes. "Whether he selected good or bad ones I don't know. In any event, he selected those which were dearer than the others" (*ZL*, 29).

While Gippius clearly de-emphasizes the importance of the dedication in her memoirs, we must not forget that she penned these memoirs in emigration after her final break with Blok following his publication of *The Twelve* (*Dvenadtsat'*) (January 1918), where he took a radically different position on the Bolshevik revolution from Gippius. Even though she may not have originally intended to dedicate these lyrics to Blok, her decision to include the dedication in her second book of verse alters the way in which these poems are read and perceived. If in and of themselves these poems function as apostrophes to the poet's soul, this apostrophic quality is further complicated by the inclusion of the dedication. In dedicating these poems to Blok, Gippius is, as it were, baring her soul to the male poet. And the fact that the first of the poems Gippius dedicates to Blok is entitled "She" (1905) is of particular interest since Blok had already distinguished himself as the poet of the Beautiful Lady:

> Кто видел Утреннюю, Белую
> Средь расцветающих небес,—
> Тот не забудет тайну смелую,
> Обетование чудес.
>
> Душа, душа, не бойся холода!
> То холод утра,—близость дня.
> Но утро живо, утро молодо,
> И в нем—дыхание огня.
>
> Душа моя, душа свободная!
> Ты чище пролитой воды,
> Ты—твердь зеленая, восходная,
> Для светлой Утренней Звезды.
> (*Stikh*, 165–66)

[He who has seen the Morning White One among the flowering heavens will not forget the brazen secret, the promise of miracles. Soul, soul, don't fear the cold! It is the morning cold [that indicates] the nearness of the day. But the morning is lively, the morning is young, and in it is the breath of fire. My soul, my free soul! You are cleaner than spilled water. You are the green rising firmament for the bright Morning Star.]

In her discussion of Blok's complicated relationship with Gippius, Avril Pyman insists that in this poem "Gippius reminds him of the Beautiful Lady."[21] In many ways, Gippius does seem to associate her soul if not with the Beautiful Lady per se, then with the Solovievian world soul as embodied in nature. The poem opens with the promise of a miracle: "He who has seen the Morning White One among the flowering heavens will not forget the brazen secret, the promise of miracles" (Kto videl Utrenniuiu, Beluiu / Sred' rastsvetaiushchikh nebes,— / Tot ne zabudet tainu smeluiu, / Obetovanie chudes). Gippius employs extremely vague and mystical language, reminiscent of that of Soloviev and the early Blok, to describe this mysterious event. Though the event she is referring to is the rising of the morning star, Venus, she resists using specific astronomical terminology to refer to this natural occurrence. Instead, she likens the appearance of the morning star to the arrival of the Beautiful Lady or the divine Sophia by referring to the star, Venus, with the capitalized feminine substantive adjectives, *Utrenniaia, Belaia*. After describing the potential of this natural event in the first stanza, the speaker turns inward toward self and soul in the next stanza: "Soul, soul, don't fear the cold! It is the morning cold [that indicates] the nearness of the day. But the morning is lively, the morning is young, and in it is the breath of fire" (Dusha, dusha, ne boisia kholoda! / To kholod utra,—blizost' dnia. / No utro zhivo, utro molodo, / I v nem—dykhanie ognia). If in this middle stanza Gippius expresses the apprehension that her speaker's soul, designated by the feminine noun *dusha,* experiences vis-à-vis this event, already by the third and final stanza the soul appears to have found a place for herself in this miraculous, natural occurrence. "My soul, my free soul!" (Dusha moia, dusha svobodnaia!), the speaker states. "You are cleaner than spilled water. You are the green rising firmament for the bright Morning Star" (Ty chishche prolitoi vody, / Ty—tverd' zelenaia, voskhodnaia, / Dlia svetloi Utrennei Zvezdy). Not only does Gippius associate the soul with the feminine nouns *voda* and *tverd'*, but she presents the soul as the very ground or *tverd'* necessary for the appearance of the Morning Star or *Utrenniaia Zvezda*, also a feminine noun in Russian. In providing the necessary ground for Venus, the poet's soul functions as a kind of earthly double for the star, Venus, and thus her relationship to Morning Star approximates that of the earthly world soul to the more ethereal divine Sophia.

In this poem, Gippius does more than imagine her soul as the earthly embodiment of the feminine ideal; she symbolically offers her soul to Blok through the inclusion of the dedication and, in such a fashion, she engages in no small amount of coquettishness with the male poet. The gift of self and soul that she extends to Blok appears to be the perfect gift for the poet of the Beautiful Lady. But perhaps like all gifts, this poem has a dangerous underside. J. Hillis Miller has observed that "*Gift* in German means poison. To receive or give a gift is a profoundly dangerous or equivocal act. One of the French words for gift, *cadeau,* comes from the Latin *catena,* little chain, rings bound together in a series. Every gift is a ring or a chain, and the gift-giver or gift-receiver enters into the endless ring or chain of reciprocal obligation which [Marcel] Mauss has identified as universally present in 'archaic' or 'civilized' societies."[22] In Gippius's case, the gift she proffers is dangerous not because it engenders the need for Blok to produce another gift in return, in accordance with the rules of reciprocity outlined by Mauss, but rather because the gift of the poet's soul is not as innocuous as it appears to be at first glance. Similar in some ways to the gift of the Trojan horse, Gippius's soul is not as benevolent as it first seems, and this is revealed in the other poem, entitled "She" ("Ona") (1905), which precedes the poem by the same title dedicated to Blok:

> В своей бессовестной и жалкой низости,
> Она, как пыль, сера, как прах земной.
> И умираю от этой близости,
> От неразрывности ее со мной.
>
> Она шершавая, она колючая,
> Она холодная, она змея.
> Меня изранила противно-жгучая
> Ее коленчатая чешуя.
>
> О, если б острое почуял жало я!
> Неповоротлива, тупа, тиха.
> Такая тяжкая, такая вялая,
> И нет к ней доступа—она глуха.
>
> Своими кольцами она, упорная,
> Ко мне ласкается, меня душа.
> И эта мертвая, и эта черная,
> И эта страшная—моя душа!
>   (*Stikh*, 165)

[In her dishonest and pathetic lowliness, she is like dust, gray like the dust of the earth. And I am dying from her proximity, from her indivisibility with me. She is scaly, she is prickly, she is cold, she is a snake. She has wounded me with her abhorrent burning knobby scales. Oh, if I had felt the sharp stinger! She is sluggish, dumb, quiet. She is so heavy, so listless. And there is no getting to her; she is deaf. With her rings, she, the impudent one, snuggles up to me, suffocating me. And that dead, and that black, and that awful one is my soul.]

If in the other, more demure "She" poem, Gippius implicitly identifies the "she" of the poem with the appearance of the morning star, and hence the arrival of the eternal feminine or the Beautiful Lady, in this poem she indirectly identifies "her" with an earthy incarnation of the feminine, one which is not the least bit reassuring or positive. Just as in the poem to Blok, though, Gippius's poetic speaker does not immediately make it apparent that the "she" of the poem's title refers to the poet's soul. But if in the poem to Blok Gippius's speaker reveals already in the first line of the second stanza that the subject of the poem is the poet's soul or psyche, in this poem this revelation is delayed until the very conclusion of the poem. In fact, if we were to limit ourselves to reading all but the last line of the poem, we might accuse Gippius's speaker, who is clearly revealed to be masculine in the penultimate stanza, of evoking all of the characteristics of the castrating woman, who is suffocating, fleshy, snakelike, and phallic—serpentine qualities that Temira Pachmuss has suggested are reinforced by the undulating metrical structure of the poem.²³ However, when we read the last line of the poem, we have to question whether Gippius is merely appropriating misogynistic male discourse, as she would do in some of her dandified poems, or subverting it by applying this serpentine language not to a female being but to her soul—an entity that in Western metaphysics is generally configured in completely opposite terms. This subversion is further complicated by the fact that Gippius evokes an implicit identification between the self and soul in the poem's final line.

The presence of the two "She" poems side by side forces us to question whether Gippius believes the soul to be the earthly embodiment of the eternal feminine or a corporealized, phallic woman, a duality, incidentally, that is reinforced by her own proclivity for presenting the self in the salon sometimes as an ethereal and androgynous woman in white, sometimes as a parody of the fashionable woman. If in the first poem that she dedicated to Blok, in which images of whiteness and purity predominate, there is little question that she presents the self in positive terms, then in the next poem she addresses to Blok, "A Waterslide" (1905), she presents the soul in much more ominous terms, terms that suggest that the feminine principle has been contaminated by her demonic double. Whereas in the first poem to Blok, she implicitly compares her soul to drops of pure water ("You are cleaner than spilled water" [Ty chishche prolitoi vody]), in this poem she presents her psyche as metamorphosing into an icy waterslide:

> Душа моя угрюмая, угрозная,
>   Живет в оковах слов.
> Я—черная вода, пенноморозная,
>   Меж льдяных берегов.
>
> Ты с бедной человеческою нежностью
>   Не подходи ко мне.
> Душа мечтает с вещей безудержностью
>   О снеговом огне.
>
> И если в мглистости души, в иглистости
>   Не видишь своего,—
> То от тебя ее кипящей льдистости
>   Не нужно ничего.
>
>   (*Stikh*, 169)

[My sullen, menacing soul resides in chains of words. I am black water, foamy and frozen, between two icy shores. You, with your petty human tenderness, don't come near me. My soul dreams with prophetic impetuousness about the snowy fire. And if in the haziness of my soul, in its prickliness, you do not see your own, then its seething iciness doesn't need anything from you.]

Here Gippius configures the soul in highly negative terms reminiscent of those employed by Friedrich Nietzsche to describe woman's soul in *Thus Spoke Zarathustra* (*Also sprach Zarathustra*) (1883–85). Unlike Nietzsche, though, she does not call attention here to the shallowness of her soul; instead, she refers to its complicated depths. She opens with the statements: "My sullen, menacing soul resides in chains of words. I am black water, foamy and frozen, between two icy shores" (Dusha moia ugriumaia, ugroznaia, / Zhivet v okovakh slov. / Ia — chernaia voda, pennomoroznaia, / Mezh l'dianykh beregov). Whereas in this first stanza she presents the self and soul as terrible and menacing, in the next stanza she enacts a warning to the reader, as well as implicitly to the poem's addressee, Blok: "You, with your petty human tenderness, don't come near me. My soul dreams with prophetic impetuousness about the snowy fire" (Ty s bednoi chelovecheskoiu nezhnost'iu / Ne podkhodi ko mene. / Dusha mechtaet s veshchei bezuderzhnost'iu / O snegovom ogne). Implicit in the soul's dream of the snowy fire is a desire to suffer like the souls in the icy ninth ring of Dante's *Inferno*.[24] Intent on doing so in solitude, the soul requires nothing from anyone. As the lyric speaker states in the final stanza: "And if in the haziness of my soul, in its prickliness, you do not see your own, then its seething iciness doesn't need anything from you" (I esli v mglistosti dushi, v iglistosti / Ne vidish' svoego, — / To ot tebia ee kipiashchei l'distosti / Ne nuzhno nichego). With this final statement, Gippius seems to proclaim to the reader, and more importantly to the poem's addressee, Blok, that she refuses to change or to be the type of soul or *dusha* that he expects.

In "A Thunderstorm" (1905), the final poem she dedicates to Blok in this collection, Gippius goes one step further in debunking her previous identification of the soul with the eternal feminine. Here the icy waters of her soul about which she speaks in the second poem to Blok are transformed into a full-fledged storm:

Моей души, в ее тревожности,
Не бойся, не жалей.
Две молнии, — две невозможности,
Соприкоснулись в ней.

> Ищу опасное и властное,
>   Слиянье всех дорог.
> А всё живое и прекрасное
>   Приходит в краткий срок.
>
> И если правда здешней нежности
>   Не жалость, а любовь,—
> Всесокрушающей мятежности
>   Моей не прекословь.
>
> Тебя пугают миги вечные...
>   Уйди, закрой глаза.
> В душе скрестились светы встречные,
>   В моей душе—гроза.
>   (*Stikh*, 172)

[Don't fear, don't pity my soul in its alarm. Two flashes of lightning—two impossibilities—have adjoined in it. I seek the dangerous and the powerful, the merging of all roads. And all that is alive and wonderful arrives in short time. And if the truth of earthly tenderness is not pity, but love, do not contradict my all-shattering rebelliousness. Eternal moments frighten you... Go away, close your eyes. In my soul opposing lights have crossed; in my soul there is a thunderstorm.]

Here Gippius urges her addressee neither to fear nor to pity her soul. Drawing on the type of chaotic imagery inherent in much of the poetry of the nineteenth-century Russian poet Fedor Tiutchev, Gippius presents the soul as an unsettling place that can combine opposites: "Two flashes of lightning—two impossibilities—have adjoined in it" (Dve molnii,—dve nevozmozhnosti, / Soprikosnulis' v nei).[25] There is something intensely passionate about the way she describes the longings of this soul. As she states: "I seek the dangerous and the powerful, the merging of all roads" (Ishchu opasnoe i vlastnoe, / Slian'e vsekh dorog). And this synthesis—or merging of opposites—is deeply erotic: "And all that is alive and wonderful arrives in short time" (A vsë zhivoe i prekrasnoe / Prikhodit v kratkii srok). Through this combination of opposites, she recalls the erotic dynamic of her earlier poem "Electricity" ("Elektrichestvo") (1901), which opens: "Two threads are twisted together, the ends bared. Now 'yes' and 'no' are not merged, not merged but entwined" (Dve niti vmeste svity, / Kontsy obnazheny. / To "da" i "net"—ne slity, / Ne slity—spleteny) (*Stikh*, 111). And as in "Electricity," the merging of opposites in this poem is equated if not with sex, then with love. As she notes: "And if the truth of earthly tenderness is not pity, but love, do not contradict my all-shattering rebelliousness" (I esli pravda zdeshnei nezhnosti / Ne zhalost', a liubov',— / Vsesokrusha-iushchei miatezhnosti / Moei ne prekoslov'). Significant here, though, is the very pointed notion that love, or the eternal feminine or world soul, does not manifest itself in pity, or even tenderness, but in rebelliousness—in the violent forces of nature. And she makes this clear in the final stanza of the poem: "Eternal moments frighten you . . . Go away, close your eyes. In my soul opposing lights have crossed; in my soul there is a thunderstorm" (Tebia pugaiut migi vechnye . . . / Uidi, zakroi glaza. / V dushe skrestilis' svety vstrechnye / V moei dushe—groza). With this final proclamation, Gippius urges the reader and by extension Blok not to bother her soul or, in other words, not to fool with Mother Nature.

Together "She," "A Waterslide," and "A Thunderstorm" constitute a powerful dialogue with the poet of the eternal feminine not just about the nature of the self and soul but also about the nature of the feminine world soul.[26] These three poems, which are distributed throughout Gippius's second book of poetry, make up a kind of mininarrative about the nature of the poet's psyche. If she begins this story of her soul by comparing it to freshly spilled water, she concludes by likening it to a violent lightning storm, and in such fashion she reveals that even the eternal feminine or world soul as embodied in nature can be uninviting and inherently dangerous. This depiction of the soul or *dusha* in such violent and passionate terms is further complicated by the fact that she pairs the first and arguably most innocent of these poems about the female psyche with a demonic double poem "She," which depicts the soul in a highly corporealized fashion. Gippius's complicated relationship with the feminine is well reflected in these poems to Blok as well as in a number of other poems in her second volume such as "To Her" ("K Nei") (1905), "The Feminine 'It doesn't exist'" ("Zhenskoe 'Netu'") (1907), "He to Her" ("On-Ei") (1907), and even "Creature" ("Tvar'") (1907). Nonetheless, her preoccupation with the issue of embodiment of the feminine would not be confined to the early part of the century; it would appear throughout the poetry she composed in emigration well after the heyday of the cult of the eternal feminine.[27]

In her final collection of poetry, *Radiances* (*Siianiia*), which she published in Paris in 1938, she demonstrates the extent to which the problem of femininity continued to have a powerful hold on her. In this volume, she included an undated poem entitled "Femininity" ("Zhenskost'") in which she presents the female soul in highly negative terms reminiscent of her infamous "She" poem:

> Падающие, падающие линии...
> Женская душа бессознательна,
> Много ли нужно ей?
>
> Будьте же, как буду отныне я,
> К женщине тихо-внимательны,
> И ласковей, и нежней.
>
> Женская душа—пустынная,
> Знает ли, какая холодная,
> Знает ли, как груба?
>
> Утешайте же душу невинную,
> Обманите, что она свободная...
> Всё равно она будет раба.
> (*Stikh*, 265)

[Falling, falling lines... The female soul is unconscious. Is there much that it needs? Be, as I shall be from now on, quietly attentive toward woman, both more affectionate and more tender. The female soul is deserted. Does it know how cold it is? Does it know how coarse? Comfort the innocent soul; deceive her that she is free... Regardless, she will be a slave.]

From the very first lines of this poem it becomes apparent that "femininity" (zhenskost'), at least in its earthly incarnation, is not something to be revered. Rather than putting the feminine on a pedestal, Gippius debases it, presenting it here as "falling, falling lines" (padaiushchie, padaiushchie linii). Although it does not appear that Gippius was familiar with Freud's famous question, "What do women want?," her poem's next lines recall Freud's association of woman with the unconscious. Her unmarked poetic speaker observes: "The female soul is unconscious. Is there much that it needs?" (Zhenskaia dusha bessoznatel'na, / Mnogo li nuzhno ei?). And, in many regards, her poetic speaker assumes a posture in this poem analogous to that of a (male) thinker or philosopher who purports to have unlocked the secrets of the female psyche. Throughout it, the speaker addresses not the female soul but another individual like himself, dispensing advice on how to deal with the unconscious female soul. The speaker implores: "Be, as I shall be from now on, quietly attentive toward woman, both more affectionate and more tender" (Bud'te zhe, kak budu otnyne ia, / K zhenshchine tikho-vnimatel'ny, / I laskovei i nezhnei). But even though the lyric speaker calls for attentiveness toward woman, he does not have much respect for the female soul. As he states: "The female soul is deserted. Does it know how cold it is? Does it know how coarse?" (Zhenskaia dusha—pustynnaia, / Znaet li, kakaia kholodnaia, / Znaet li, kak gruba?). In his insistence on the emptiness and coarseness of the female soul, Gippius's poetic speaker reveals, once again, an inclination toward dandyism. The only way to deal with woman is to condescend to her. As Gippius's poetic speaker instructs in the poem's final lines, "Comfort the innocent soul; deceive her that she is free . . . Regardless, she will be a slave" (Uteshaite zhe dushu nevinnuiu, / Obmanite, chto ona svobodnaia . . . / Vse ravno ona budget raba).

This may be among the most overtly misogynistic poems that Gippius or, for that matter, any Russian poet ever wrote about the female soul. And Gippius may very well have had this poem in mind when, in one of her late letters, she urged her friend Swedish artist Greta Gerell: "Don't think that I think badly about the feminine. I have written and thought much about 'woman.' If women are sometimes unwitting, irresponsible, etc., the true 'eternal feminine' is lofty and saintly. [Ne croyez pas que je pense mal du "féminin." J'ai beaucoup écrit et pensé de la "femme." Si les femmes sont souvent inconscientes, irresponsables, etc., le vrai "éternel-féminin" est grand et saint.] I also have a poem about it which I will send to you one day" (*IAA*, 549). The specific poem Gippius promised was "The Eternal Feminine" ("Vechnozhenstvennoe"), which she originally dedicated to Nina Berberova and published in *The New Ship* (*Novyi korabl'*) in 1928. In her final collection, *Radiances*, Gippius placed "The Eternal Feminine" ("Vechnozhenstvennoe") immediately after the poem "Femininity":

    Каким мне коснуться словом
        Белых одежд Ее?
    С каким озареньем новым
        Слить Ее бытие?
    О, ведомы мне земные
        Все твои имена:
    Сольвейг, Тереза, Мария . . .
        Все они—ты Одна.
    Молюсь и люблю . . . Но мало
        Любви, молитв к тебе.
    Твоим—твоей от начала
        Хочу пребыть в себе,
    Чтоб сердце тебе отвечало—

> Сердце—в себе самом,
>   Чтоб Нежная узнавала
>   Свой чистый образ в нем...
> И будут пути иные,
>   Иной любви пора.
> Сольвейг, Тереза, Мария,
>   Невеста-Мать-Сестра!
>   (*Stikh*, 266)

[With what word should I touch Her white garments? With what new illumination can I merge Her being? Oh, all Your earthly names are known to me: Solweig, Thérèse, Mary ... All of them are You alone. I pray and love ... But there is insufficient love and prayers to You. Masculinely Yours—femininely Yours from the beginning, I want to subsist in myself, so that my heart will respond to You—my heart in itself, so that the Tender One will recognize Her pure image in it ... And there will be other paths, time for another love. Solweig, Thérèse, Mary—Bride-Mother-Sister!]

As the juxtaposition of the poems "The Eternal Feminine" and "Femininity" would seem to suggest, Gippius's skepticism about the feminine in its earthly form, as embodied in a particular woman, does not obviate her belief in the eternal feminine in its ideal Trinitarian and ultimately androgynous incarnation as Bride-Mother-Sister.[28] In fact, the very opposite would appear to be the case.[29] What serves as the impetus for this beautiful poem about the eternal feminine, designated in the poem as a neuter substantive adjective rather than a feminine noun, is the lyric speaker's inability to grasp the eternal feminine—something made all the more palpable by the opening questions: "With what word should I touch Her white garments? With what new illumination can I merge Her being?" (Kakim mne kosnut'sia slovom / Belykh odezhd Ee? / S kakim ozaren'em novym / Slit' Ee bytie?). Although these questions might appear to foreground the speaker's anxiety about approaching the topic of the eternal feminine—a topic that has been the subject of so much love poetry in the Western tradition—it can be argued that it is her inapproachability—her inability to be contained within any single woman—that Gippius finds most attractive and that occasions her speaker's androgynous response to the eternal feminine, a kind of bisexual splitting into a masculinely-femininely being. As her speaker reveals to the eternal feminine, "Masculinely Yours—femininely Yours from the beginning, I want to subsist in myself, so that my heart will respond to You" (Tvoim—tvoei ot nachala / Khochu prebyt' v sebe, / Chtob serdtse tebe otvechalo).

Gippius's simultaneous idealization of the eternal feminine and resistance to the feminine in its corporeal form might seem to reflect her complicated feelings about her own femininity and her own female body. However, this can also be interpreted as part of her ongoing philosophical reaction against the cult of the eternal feminine. What she clearly objected to was not the idolatry of the feminine in its ideal form but rather the tendency of so many of the male symbolists, particularly of the second generation, to attempt to conflate real women with the eternal feminine, to contain the feminine. As much as she may have been inclined toward theatricality and playing different female roles, ranging from the parody of the stylish woman to the eternal feminine clad in white, she clearly reacted against the tendency of male poets to identify woman in all of her corporeality with the eternal feminine. And she felt strongly enough about this philosophical issue to revisit the problem of the eternal feminine in the poems she published in emigration almost two decades after the death of the poet of the eternal feminine.

Her dialogue with Blok and his coevals about the cult of the eternal feminine represents just one of the many ways she resisted the tendency of so many of her contemporaries to attempt to incarnate the feminine ideal. In addition to taking on the problem of female embodiment in her works about the feminine, she also addressed the problem through her elaborate presentations of the self in salon society, first in St. Petersburg and later in emigration in Paris. Unlike most of her contemporaries, who seemed intent on conflating art and life, text and body, Gippius readily assumed various, often contradictory, gendered roles in her life and art that made it difficult to determine the true nature of her identity and of her body. In so doing, she not only resisted her contemporaries' attempts to read her as a gendered body but she demonstrated her own trouble with the issue of embodiment. So crucial, in fact, was the topic of embodiment to Gippius's self-fashioning that she would dedicate the final years of her life to the composition of a long narrative poem that, among other things, addresses the very problem of how to read her as a gendered body. It is this poem that is the subject of the final chapter.

8

Body Trouble
Gippius and the Staging of an Anatomy of Criticism

So they resolved to get the views of wise
Tiresias. He knew both sides of love.
For once in a green copse when two huge snakes
Were mating, he attacked them with his stick,
And was transformed (a miracle!) from man
To woman; and spent seven autumns so;
Till in the eighth he saw the snakes once more
And said "If striking you has magic power
To change the striker to the other sex,
I'll strike you now again." He struck the snakes
And so regained the shape he had at birth.
Ovid, Metamorphoses

"You all think that it's a boy," [Peredonov] said screwing up his eyes sardonically, "but it's no boy, it's a girl, and some girl she is!"
Fedor Sologub, The Petty Demon (Melkii bes) (1907)

He stretched himself. He rose. He stood upright in complete nakedness before us and while the trumpets pealed Truth! Truth! Truth! we have no choice but confess—he was a woman.
Virginia Woolf, Orlando: A Biography (1928)

The surprise that Virginia Woolf's fictional biographer experiences in reading the body of the poet in *Orlando: A Biography* is in many ways similar to that experienced by Zinaida Gippius's critics and contemporaries. Though Gippius never appeared as a new female Adam the way that Orlando does halfway through Woolf's fictional biography, she did evince an antipathy toward her own femininity and the female body that confounded her critics' and contemporaries' attempt to read and interpret her as a gendered body. Gippius, as we have seen, not only frequently employed the masculine persona in her writing and engaged in cross-dressing in the salon, but she also manifested a genuine skepticism about the possibility of embodying the eternal feminine in her writings. Yet, at the same time, she willingly flaunted her femininity in the salon, appearing sometimes as the earthly incarnation of Aphrodite Uranus and at other times in ultrafeminine clothing that approximated that of the female impersonator. Perplexed by Gippius's willingness to assume such contradictory gendered identities, many of her early critics and contemporaries insisted that they must have been rooted in a physiological cause.[1] And, therefore, rather than analyzing the ways in which she constructed these different identities, they set out to determine what Michel Foucault would ironically refer to in quotation marks as her "'true' sex."[2]

This tendency to make the body of Gippius the subject of a literal "anatomy of criticism" would appear, at first glance, to be distinctly at odds with the active resistance she put up to the issue of embodiment in her writings. Nonetheless, this mode of reading predominates in the works of her critics and contemporaries. As a case in point, Sergei Makovsky begins his essay on Gippius in *On the Parnassus of the "Silver Age"* (*Na Parnase "Serebrianogo veka"*) (1962) with the "theory" that she was not a normal woman in the physical sense. He prefaces his reading of her poetry with a reading of her body that focuses on her sexual ambiguity. He recalls:

> She was about thirty at the time, but it seemed that she, so very thin and svelte, was much younger. She was of average height, slim-hipped without the suggestion of a chest, and with small feet... Pretty? Oh, without a doubt. "What a captivating youth!" one thought at first glance. A sweet, proudly turned-up little head, elongated slightly squinting grayish-green eyes, a bright expressively formed mouth turned up at the corners, and a rarely proportioned little figure made her look like an androgyne from a canvas of Sodoma. In addition, she did her thick, gently wavy bronzish-red hair into a long braid as a sign of her virginity (in

spite of her ten-year marriage) . . . A most telling detail! Only she could come up with the idea of flagrantly flaunting the "purity" of conjugal life (which for her took on a very unusual form).[3]

Simon Karlinsky has suggested that "like several other memoirists, Makovsky hints that Gippius was physically a hermaphrodite and was biologically incapable of engaging in heterosexual relations."[4]

Makovsky was not the only one to suggest that Gippius may have been a hermaphrodite or, in any case, was not a "normal" woman. Rumors of the poet's supposed anatomical idiosyncrasies circulated throughout the memoirs of Andrei Bely, Nikolai Berdiaev, and Nina Berberova among others. In *The Beginning of the Century* (*Nachalo veka*) (1933), Bely contributes to the myths about Gippius's sex, when he calls attention to her wasp-like figure devoid of hips and breasts and her highly unusual mode of self-presentation. "Z. Gippius," he maintains, "was just like a wasp of human proportions, if not like the figure of a 'seductress' (from the pen of Aubrey Beardsley); a clump of distended red hair (or she let it down to her heels) covered her small and somewhat crooked little face; powder and the sparkle of a lorgnette in which was installed a greenish eye; she ran her fingers through her cut-glass beads, staring at me, sticking out her flaming lip, shedding powder; from her little forehead hung a stone like a glittering eye on a black pendant; from her breastless chest rattled a black cross; the buckle on her little boot dazzled me with sparkles; one leg rested on top of the other; she tossed the train of her tight-fitting white dress; the charm of her bony, hipless frame reminded one of a communicant cunningly captivating Satan."[5]

Though Bely emphasizes Gippius's androgynous appearance, he does not present her as the embodiment of spiritual androgyny that was idealized at the turn of the century but rather as a highly eroticized and predatory figure verging on the monstrous.[6] An equally uncomplimentary portrait of the poet emerges in Berdiaev's autobiography *Self-Knowledge: An Experiment in Philosophical Autobiography* (*Samopoznanie: Opyt filosofskoi avtobiografii*) (1949). Possibly influenced by Gippius's own depiction of her soul as snakelike in her famous poem "She" ("Ona") (1905) ("She is scaly, she is prickly, she is cold, she is a snake" [Ona shershavaia, ona koliuchaia, / Ona kholodnaia, ona zmeia] [*Stikh*, 165]), Berdiaev emphasizes the poet's serpentine nature in his verbal portrait of her.[7] He remarks: "I was always struck by her snakelike coldness. She was devoid of human warmth. Clearly it was the result of the intermingling of female and male natures, and it was difficult to determine which predominated."[8] When Berdiaev refers to Gippius's "snakelike coldness" (zmeinaia kholodnost') and the "intermingling of female and male natures" (peremeshannost' zhenskoi prirodoi s muzhskoi), he is clearly intimating that she was physically hermaphroditic rather than spiritually androgynous.[9] And key here is his usage of the word "nature" or *priroda*. In his earlier work *The Meaning of the Creative Act* (*Smysl tvorchestva*) (1916), he had differentiated between androgyny and hermaphroditism on the basis of their relationship with nature and the natural; he specified that "androgyny [was] man's likeness to God, his ascent above nature," while "hermaphroditism [was] a bestial *nature-bound* mixing of the sexes that [had] not been transformed into a higher form of being."[10] Thus, once again, Gippius, the woman poet, emerges as a freak of nature or *urod* in the works of her contemporaries.

If in Berdiaev's autobiography Gippius appears essentially as the embodiment of the figure of the hermaphrodite from *The Meaning of the Creative Act*, then she fares little better in Nina Berberova's literary memoirs, *The Italics Are Mine* (*Kursiv moi*) (1969), something that is all the more striking given that Berberova and Gippius shared the same difficult fate of being émigré women writers.[11] Here Berberova offers a detailed description of Gippius's ultrafeminine clothing and hairstyles only to suggest that this feminine fashion belied the sex that lay below. Berberova begins with a description of Gippius's hair, panning slowly downward to her arms and legs, noting: "She always liked the color pink, which was not becoming to her dark red hair, but she had her own criteria and what in another woman might have appeared strange became with her a part of her very self. A half-transparent silk scarf streamed around her neck, her thick hair was arranged in a complex hairdo. Her thin small hands with unpainted fingernails were dry and impersonal, her legs (to display them she always wore short dresses) were beautiful like the legs of a young woman of times past."[12] At this point in her description, Berberova shifts her gaze inward to Gippius's lingerie and then abruptly upward to her notorious jewels, remarking: "Bunin jokingly said that in her commode lay forty pairs of pink silk panties and in her closet hung forty pink petticoats. She had some old jewels, chains, and pendants, and sometimes (though not that evening) she appeared with a long emerald teardrop on her forehead, suspended on a thin chain between her eyebrows."[13] And it is here that Berberova in a vaguely Freudian act of interpretation infers that the long emerald teardrop Gippius wore on her forehead represented merely an "upward displacement" of the jewels which lay below, for she directly juxtaposes her description of Gippius's jewels with the daring revelation: "There can be no doubt she artificially worked up in herself two features of her personality: poise and femininity. Within she was not poised. And she was not a woman."[14]

Berberova's proclamation that "she was not a woman" might sound similar to the fictional biographer's claims in Woolf's *Orlando* that "he was a woman" or even to some of the outrageous headlines that can be found in today's grocery store tabloids. Nonetheless, in spite of its similarity to fiction, this is a view that continues to be widely discussed by scholars and critics even today. Both Simon Karlinsky in his introduction to Zlobin's memoirs and S. N. Saveliev in his recent study on Gippius feel compelled to address rumors about the poet's supposed hermaphroditism. S. N. Saveliev even brings to light the humorous detail that Gippius's husband purportedly received an anonymous note via post, proclaiming: "Aphrodite has taken revenge on you by sending you a wife-hermaphrodite" (Otomstila tebe Afrodita, poslav zhenu—germafrodita).[15] Yet while Saveliev and Karlinsky are careful to point out that the idea that she was a hermaphrodite was largely myth, other scholars have been much less critical of the literary gossip of the period.[16] In the course of my own research on Gippius, I have encountered several scholars who have insisted that I should keep the "facts" of the poet's anatomy in mind in working on the poet. For example, one scholar informed me: "Gippius probably wasn't a woman. She never had children, and she probably didn't have female sexual organs." And another cautioned me to bear in mind: "It is not to be ruled out that she was a hermaphrodite" (Eto ne iskliucheno, chto ona byla germafroditom).[17]

In "Transcending Gender: The Case of Zinaida Gippius" (2005), Olga Matich has recently articulated a similar desire to know more about the poet's body. She concludes her discussion of Gippius's attempts to transcend gender with the statement: "The question that remains — one that has been raised behind closed doors for years — is whether her body could be penetrated sexually." She then goes on to enumerate many of the above-cited myths about Gippius's supposed anatomical abnormalities, and she also mentions a number of additional ones. Yury Felzin, she notes, "supposedly told another émigré writer, Vasilii Yanovsky, the following story: '[W]ell-informed people tell me that Z[inaida Nikolaevna] has some sort of anatomical defect.' Chuckling condescendingly, he added, '[T]hey say that D[mitrii Sergeevich] likes to look through the keyhole.'" This piece of literary gossip, in turn, leads Matich to ponder: "What did Merezhkovsky spy on? If Gippius indeed was a hermaphrodite, it gives a new twist to the cigarette holder that was an inseparable part of her phallic image. It also gives an ironic twist to Trotsky's tongue-in-cheek description of Gippius as a witch with a tail in *Art and Revolution*. It's a nasty joke to be sure, but his claim that he could not say anything definite 'about the length of her tail' because it was hidden from sight has clear sexual connotations, especially in the Freudian 1920s."[18] Matich is somewhat more skeptical of the literary gossip than most of Gippius's early critics and contemporaries. Nonetheless, she does appear to hold onto the belief that knowledge about the poet's body would provide invaluable insight into the poet when she invites her own readers to imagine the anatomical detail that allegedly fueled Merezhkovsky's voyeurism.

By implying that it is necessary to know the workings of Gippius's body in order to understand her body of works, Gippius's critics and contemporaries would appear to espouse a type of criticism that is distinctly at odds with poststructuralist notions about the role of the author in the text and the *corps* in the corpus of works. As Svetlana Boym has persuasively argued in her book *Death in Quotation Marks: Cultural Myths of the Modern Poet* (1991), poststructuralist theorists such as Roland Barthes, Michel Foucault, and Paul de Man certainly did their part in celebrating not only the death of the author with the capital "A" but also, in the case of Barthes, the decomposition of the dead author's body.[19] In his seminal essay, "The Death of the Author," Barthes suggests that the nature of writing is such that it is not proper for the critic to discuss the author, let alone the body of the author. "Writing," he maintains, "is the destruction of every voice, of every point of origin. Writing is that neutral, composite, oblique space into which our subject slips away, the negative where all identity is lost, starting with the very identity of the body writing."[20] By positing that the act of writing precipitates not just the death of the author but also, by extension, the decomposition of the body of the author, he implies that critical interest in the body is tantamount to critical necrophilia. Yet while the early Barthes clearly condemns this type of criticism, the late Barthes willingly indulges in critical practice — or rather malpractice — on the body of the author. In *The Pleasure of the Text* (*Le plaisir du texte*) (1973), Barthes, while still upholding the death of the author "as an institution," celebrates the reader's desire for the very figure of the author.[21] In this sense, he succumbs to the very seductions of the dead author's body that he earlier held were to be shunned by the critic.

It bears noting, though, that in Russian intellectual circles this critical insistence on resurrecting the dead poet's body does not carry the same taboo that it does in the West because a radically different notion of authorship from that of Western modernism emerged in the Russian modernist context. To a great extent, Barthes's theory of the death of the author was indebted to the poetics of purity espoused first by the symbolist Stéphane Mallarmé and later developed by Paul Valéry.[22] As Mallarmé writes in "The Crisis of Verse" ("Crise de vers") (1886), "work that is pure involves the disappearance of the poet's voice, which cedes the initiative to words, propelled by the shock of their bumping together. They kindle reciprocal reflections like a trail of fire on precious stones, replacing the hard breathing of bygone lyric inspiration or the individualistic shaping of the phrase."[23] If French symbolism reached its apotheosis with the pure poetry of Mallarmé, then Russian symbolism was, for all its ambivalence about the body and sexuality, invested in a mode of authorship that was distinctly bodily in its preoccupation with the merging of art and life known as *zhiznetvorchestvo*.[24] Recall that the postsymbolist poet and critic Vladislav Khodasevich maintained that "the symbolists did not want to separate the writer from the person, the literary biography from the personal biography. Symbolism did not want to be just a literary movement. All of the time it attempted to be a life-creating method."[25] Though Blok's tendency to pit poetry against progeny and poetic creation against procreation would seem to go against the grain of this concept of authorship, it is worth noting that he did refer to his three volumes of verse as a "'trilogy of incarnation'" (*trilogiia vocheloveczheniia*) (*BBB*, 261). "Each poem," he wrote, "is essential to the structure of a chapter; several chapters make up a 'book'; each book is part of the trilogy; I could call the whole trilogy a 'novel in verse': it is devoted to a range of feelings and thoughts to which I was committed during the first twelve years of my conscious life" (*BBB*, 262). Not surprisingly, Blok's contemporaries tended to take his comments about the relationship between his art and life at face value. In his famous essay on Blok, composed after the poet's death, the formalist critic Yury Tynianov remarked that "when people speak about his poetry, they almost always subconsciously substitute a *human face* for it, and it is this *face* and not the *art* that everyone has come to love."[26]

Gippius differed significantly from Blok, though, in the way she created a myth of her self. In her case, we would have to amend Tynianov's statement to read that when people speak about her poetry, they almost always subconsciously substitute a body for it, and it is this body and not the art that has fascinated everyone. Although this fascination with the dead poet's body can be seen as akin to critical necrophilia, I would insist that this seemingly perverse interest in the female poet's body has been, in part, fueled by Gippius's own idiosyncratic form of symbolist mythmaking. She continually presented herself both in her writings and in her everyday behavior in a fashion that called attention to the nature of her body and sexuality, all the while eschewing the body and sex. In addition to evincing a certain antipathy toward the feminine and the female body in her writing, she admitted to feeling a profound ambivalence about her body and her sexuality. "I do not desire exclusive femininity," she wrote in her *Contes d'amour* (1893–1904), "just as I do not desire exclusive masculinity. Each time someone is insulted and dissatisfied within me; with women, my femininity is active, with men—my masculinity! In my thoughts, my desires, in my spirit—I am more a man; in my body—I am more a woman. Yet they are so fused together that I know nothing."[27] While I do not discount the fact that such confessional statements may reflect the poet's genuine confusion about her body and her sexuality, I maintain that they can also be read as an extension of her unique form of self-creation.

Time and time again, Gippius called attention to her troubled relationship with her own gender and body—not only in the salon where she assumed various gendered identities but also in her poetry where she frequently engaged in cross-voicing. Of all of Gippius's lyrics, her 1905 poem "You:" ("Ty:") probably goes the furthest in demonstrating this gender ambiguity. In this poem, not only does the gender of the addressee change from male to female, consonant with the grammatical gender of the nouns she evokes, but the gender of the speaker also shifts in relation to that of the addressee:

> Вешнего вечера трепет тревожный—
> С тонкого тополя веточка нежная.
> Вихря порыв, горячо-осторожный—
> Синей бездонности гладь безбережная.
>
> В облачном небе просвет просиянный—
> Свежих полей маргаритка росистая,
> Меч мой небесный, мой луч остогранный—
> Тайна прозрачная, ласково-чистая.
>
> Ты—на распутьи костер ярко-жадный—
> И над долиною дымка невестная.
> Ты—мой веселый и беспощадный,—
> Ты—моя близкая и неизвестная.

> Ждал я и жду я зари моей ясной,
> Неутомимо тебя полюбила я ...
> Встань же, мой месяц серебряно-красный,
> Выйди, двурогая,—Милый мой—Милая ...
> (*Stikh*, 159)

[An alarming trembling of a vernal evening, a tender little branch from a thin poplar, an ardently gentle gust of a whirlwind, limitless smoothness of blue bottomlessness. An outpouring of shining light through a break in a cloudy sky, a dewy daisy of fresh fields, my heavenly sword, my sharp-faceted ray, a transparent, caressingly clean secret. You are a brightly greedy bonfire at a crossroads and a bridal haze above a valley. You are my cheerful and merciless one. You are my near and unknown one. I waited and wait for my bright dawn. I have fallen in love with you untiringly ... Arise, my silvery-red crescent, come out, my double-horned one — My dear, my darling ...]

This entire poem is posited on gender indeterminacy and plays off, among other things, the fact that the moon, which is repeatedly addressed in this poem, has since ancient Greece been associated with androgyny. As Matich has perceptively observed, "Aristophanes' tale in *The Symposium* posits the moon as the source of the androgyne; the sun is the mythical ancestor of man and the earth of woman. In 'You:' the poet addresses the moon as his or her lover. Russian has two words for moon: the masculine *mesiats* and the feminine *luna*, both of which are alluded to in the poem, without being mentioned. The androgynous nature of the beloved is indicated indirectly, through allusion and grammatical gender. The 'lyrical I' of the persona also alternates between the masculine and feminine genders."[28] Because of the way the gender of the speaker changes in dialogical relationship to the gender of the addressee, this poem can be said to manifest that quality Osip Mandelstam would later refer to as "lyrical hermaphroditism" (liricheskii germafroditism) in his important essay "François Villon" ("Fransua Villon") (1910).[29] "The lyric poet" (liricheskii poet), Mandelstam maintains, "is a hermaphrodite by nature, capable of limitless fissions in the name of his inner dialogue" (po prirode svoei,—dvupoloe sushchestvo, sposobnoe k beschislennym rasshchepleniiam vo imia vnutrennego dialoga).[30] Though Mandelstam identifies the medieval French poet's "varied selection of enchanting duets: the aggrieved and the comforter, the mother and child, the judge and the judged, the proprietor and the beggar" (raznoobraznyi podbor ocharovatel'nykh duetov: ogorchennyi i uteshitel', mat' i ditia, sud'ia i podsudimyi, sobstvennik i nishchii) as representing the epitome of lyrical hermaphroditism, the gendered dialogue in Gippius's poem would seem to embody an even more literal type of poetic hermaphroditism in which the speaker and addressee undergo a series of changes in gender in complimentary relation to each other.[31]

Although Gippius presents lyrical hermaphroditism in this poem in a purely symbolic and discursive sense (the bodies that undergo a sex change are celestial not corporeal ones), her own proclivity for projecting various gendered identities encouraged her early critics and contemporaries to read the sex changes in such lyrics more literally. As we have already seen, during her lifetime, she posed for numerous photographs and portraits that positioned her in various gendered guises, thereby inviting speculation about her gendered identity. For instance, in the turn-of-the-century photograph taken at the studio of Otto Renar (figure 4), discussed in some detail in chapter 7, Gippius appears more like a shade or phantom than a woman of flesh and blood. She achieves this ethereal, disembodied effect by appearing in a long flowing white gown that covers her entire body with the exception of her hands and face. The whiteness of her diaphanous gown blends with the pallor of her skin, giving her a haunting appearance. But if in this photograph she emerges as distinctly asexual, like a Victorian angel in the house, then she appears in a very different light in the famous portrait by Bakst (figure 3), analyzed in chapter 6. Here she appears androgynously clad in a jabot and riding jacket and britches. Poised with her long legs languorously extended and her gaze disdainfully averted, she exudes the very type of androgynous allure for which the female film stars of the thirties and forties were to become famous.

The differences in these visual images can be attributed, in part, to the artist's and photographer's interpretations of the poet. However, Gippius's role in the production of these contradictory images of the self is not to be underestimated. Throughout her life, she relied heavily on the accouterments of feminine fashion and costume to create what might be termed a symbolist "theater of the body" in which the body, or rather bodies, she exhibited were actually the product of theatrical illusions. The poet not only wore her hair in a single braid as a sign or *znak* of her virginity—a fact about her marriage to Dmitry Merezhkovsky she proudly calls attention to in her memoirs—but she produced the opposite bodily sign when she appeared in the salon sporting a necklace that supposedly contained the wedding bands of her numerous married admirers.[32] While she took the idea for her virginal braid from Russian peasant customs, she probably received the notion for her necklace of conquests from an Eastern source, *The Thousand and One Nights*.³³ However, despite the fact that Gippius's girlish peasant braid would not have been appropriate to her aristocratic status and that her necklace of conquests derived from a markedly literary source, her contemporaries insisted in reading these symbols as true indications of her body and her sexuality rather than as authorial constructions. Whereas Sergei Makovsky was wont to interpret Gippius's single braid as a "most telling detail," the émigré writer Irina Odoevtseva feared that Gippius's necklace of little trophies represented a more accurate reflection of her body and sexuality.³⁴ In her memoirs *On the Banks of the Seine* (*Na beregakh Seny*) (1983), she reminisces: "Yes, she could snatch the wedding bands from the fingers of her admirers. I asked myself: Would she demand the wedding band from [my husband] Georgy Ivanov?"³⁵

Gippius probably relished the fact that critics and contemporaries such as Makovsky and Odoevtseva would read her bodily signs literally and would fill in for themselves the ellipses that she figuratively sketched on her own body with the aid of braids and necklaces. Her production of such opposing bodily signs was a self-conscious semiotic act designed to frustrate her critics' and contemporaries' attempts to read her body and to assign her any one stable identity. Like many of her fellow symbolists, Gippius was engaged in the creation of a text of the self known as *zhiznetvorchestvo* or life creation. But unlike some of the other Russian symbolists who, at least according to Khodasevich, seemed intent on blurring the boundaries between life and art and transforming their life into a narrative that could be read and interpreted much like a literary text, Gippius resisted this particular form of symbolist life creation.³⁶ Rather than constructing a coherent, linear narrative of her life, she fashioned a series of paradoxical images of the self that made her a virtually unreadable text. "There was," according to Georgy Adamovich, "a sharp disparity between [Gippius] and what she said and wrote, between her true self and her deliberate literary image. She wanted to seem to be that which she was not in reality. First and foremost, she wanted *to seem* [*kazat'sia*]."³⁷ This proclivity for creating illusion has also been noted by her personal secretary Vladimir Zlobin. In his words, "she generally loved to mystify people. [. . .] It was not for nothing that it was said of her that she was an Englishwoman named Miss Tification. [. . .] The aim of her mystification was to draw attention away from herself. She hid her true face under various disguises so that no one would guess or find out who she was or what she wanted."³⁸

One of the primary ways in which Gippius hid her identity or her "true face" was by engaging in the seemingly paradoxical process of making a spectacle of her body. For the most part, though, Gippius's early critics and contemporaries failed to make a distinction between her predilection for mystification—her love of putting on various masks—and her proclivity for producing various, often contradictory, texts of her body. In this regard, the theoretical sophistication of her contemporaries lagged behind her idiosyncratic method of self-creation. Rather than acknowledging the self-conscious, theatrical nature of Gippius's production of various bodily texts, they implicitly assumed that her bodily texts were symptoms of her abnormal physiology (i.e., hermaphroditism) or psychosexual development (i.e., aversion to sex or hysteria).[39] In reality, however, Gippius's proclivity for producing various bodily texts or signs was not the manifestation of a severe somatic or psychological abnormality but rather part of a larger gender performance that she readily engaged in for the benefit of her critics and contemporaries. Through this elaborate gender performance, she challenged her contemporaries' attempts to read and know her, as well as their implicit belief in the naturalness of the body and gender, and, in this respect, she was decades ahead of most of her contemporaries.

The notion of gender as a kind of performance has only recently gained wide currency in the writing of both Russian and Western theoreticians. In a chapter in his late work *Culture and Explosion* (*Kul'tura i vzryv*) (1992), Yury Lotman extends his earlier work on the theatricality of everyday life in Russia to a discussion of gender roles in eighteenth- and nineteenth-century European culture. Focusing on the "rupture" or, more precisely, "explosion" (vzryv) of cultural norms, Lotman discusses male cross-dressing in eighteenth-century Europe and female appropriation of an ultrafeminine pose in nineteenth-century salon society as disruptions of normative gender roles that are characteristic of "semiotic play" (semioticheskaia igra).[40] With its emphasis on disruption, play, and theatricality, Lotman's semiotic analysis of gender roles in eighteenth- and nineteenth-century society overlaps at points with American theorist Judith Butler's discussion of gender as performance. In her pioneering book *Gender Trouble: Feminism and the Subversion of Identity* (1990), Butler also employs a theatrical metaphor to discuss the phenomenon of gender. "As the effects of a subtle and politically enforced performativity," she notes, "gender is an 'act,' as it were, that is open to splittings, self-parody, self-criticism, and those hyperbolic exhibitions of 'the natural' that, in their very exaggeration, reveal its fundamentally phantasmic status."[41]

Despite their shared use of the theatrical metaphor, Lotman's and Butler's theories of gender as performance differ in one crucial aspect that has specific importance for Gippius: their treatment of the body. While Lotman's rhetoric would appear to suggest that he shares Butler's poststructuralist valorization of discontinuity and play (e.g. "disruption," "semiotic play"), his positioning of the body in the theater of gender differs radically from that of Butler. Lotman implies throughout his discussion of nonnormative gender roles that that these roles are disruptive because they are contrary to what is natural, which for him is synonymous with the body. While Lotman implicitly valorizes the natural and the natural body as the site of "truth," Butler states quite explicitly that the very notion of the natural and, by extension, the natural body is a fiction or illusion that is produced through the performativity of gender. She considers that the social compulsion to engage in so-called normative behavior produces a set of gender "acts" and "corporeal styles," as she also calls them, that masquerade as natural sex or the natural body. She urges us: "Consider that a sedimentation of gender norms produces the peculiar phenomenon of a 'natural sex' or a 'real woman' or any number of prevalent and compelling social fictions, and that this is a sedimentation that over time has produced a set of corporeal styles which, in reified form, appear as the natural configuration of bodies into sexes existing in binary relation to one another."[42] According to Butler, then, what we generally perceive to be the gendered body is, in actuality, a corporeal style that we unknowingly put on similar to the way that we would put on a costume prior to a masquerade or theatrical performance.[43]

Butler's distinction between the body and its performative or mimetic double, corporeal style, is especially useful for a discussion of Gippius and her construction of an elusive text of her body, for often what her critics and contemporaries construed as her body was, in reality, a corporeal style that she fashioned with the aid of the accouterments of fashion such as braids and necklaces. I would suggest that this is a phenomenon that the poet herself playfully revealed to an audience of her contemporaries when she appeared at the turn of the century at a meeting of the Religious Philosophical Society in a dress that created the illusion that she was nude. "For the first session of this society, which took place on 29 November 1901 in the hall of the Geographical Society on the Fontanka," Vladimir Zlobin recalls, "Gippius had a black, seemingly modest dress especially made. It was designed in such a way that, with the slightest movement, the pleats would part and a pale pink lining would show through. The impression was that she was naked underneath. She would often recall that dress with evident pleasure, even at an age, when, it would seem, it was time to forget such things. Either because of that dress or because of some of her other whimsies, the displeased church dignitaries who took part in the meetings nicknamed her the 'white she-devil.'"[44] According to this account, that which appears to be Gippius's body or flesh is, in actuality, a fabrication of the body — flesh-colored material. She plays here on clothing's function as a sort of second skin for the body by designing a seemingly modest dress with flesh-colored lining that resembles skin. In doing so, she engages in what would properly be termed decently indecent exposure. She produces shock effect not by exposing her body but by paradoxically concealing her body in clothing that is a double for her body or skin.[45]

The poet's fabrication of a faux nude body for an audience of her contemporaries (not to mention the church dignitaries!) does much more than simulate indecent exposure or exhibitionism. It reveals the extent to which what appeared to be her body was in actuality no more than an authorial construction. Judith Butler would argue that we are all unwitting players in such a performance of gender and that the body as we have come to understand it is constituted or "constructed" as a result of this performance. "'The body,'" Butler writes, "is itself a construction, as are the myriad 'bodies' that constitute the domain of gendered subjects."[46] If the body is a construction, then Gippius pushes this notion of the body as construction to an extreme. She parodies the very constructedness of her own body by quite literally fabricating a faux body that shows through the pleats of her modest little black dress.[47] And this would by no means be the only place where Gippius would "lay bare the device" of her idiosyncratic form of symbolist mythmaking, which might be aptly termed not *zhiznetvorchestvo* or life creation but *telotvorchestvo* or bodybuilding.

In fact, Gippius seemed acutely aware of the fact that her elaborate gender performances instigated critical speculation about her body and understood that they would continue to do so even after her death. And she took great pains to ensure authorial control over this ambiguous text of the self even after her death. If during her own lifetime she cultivated an enigmatic image of the self and the body through a complex interplay of her writings and salon behavior, in death she relied on the performative qualities of narrative poetry to guarantee that the mystery of her identity would remain intact. After the death of her husband Dmitry Merezhkovsky in 1941, Gippius began working on a long narrative poem based on Dante's *Divine Comedy* entitled *The Last Circle (and the Modern Dante in Hell)* (*Poslednii krug [i novyi Dant v adu]*) in which, among other things, she anticipates her future reader-critics' fascination with her body.[48] Illness and the artistic compulsion to rework *The Last Circle* prevented Gippius from completing it, just as they had prevented Blok from completing *Retribution* (*Vozmezdie*). During her lifetime, she managed to publish only the introduction to the poem. Two, more complete, versions of the poem, an early version composed in iambic pentameter with verse paragraphs of varying length and a later less complete version written in terza rima to better approximate Dante's *Divine Comedy*, were published posthumously by Temira Pachmuss in the émigré journal, *La Renaissance* (*Vozrozhdenie*).[49] Despite its incompleteness, this poem deserves special attention, since it occupies an important place in her personal myth.[50]

Pachmuss has referred to the poem as a kind of "poetic resumé." As she states in her introduction to the poem in *La Renaissance:* "As an artistic exposition of the metaphysical understandings of the author and as a poetic resumé of her religious thought, this work has great literary-historical significance. It reveals [ono vskryvaet] the complex personality of the poetess and sheds light on her major philosophical concepts—Love, Faithfulness, Time, and Death."[51] Pachmuss's characterization of *The Last Circle* as an "artistic exposition" and a "revelation" of the complex personality of the poetess clearly evokes Lipking's identification of the "modern 'epic'" as a genre that modern lyric poets frequently turn to in an effort to come to terms with those issues that had been central to their poetics. In many ways, this poem can be seen as occupying a place in her poetic mythology analogous to that of *Retribution* in Blok's. If Blok employed the genre of the long narrative poem to work out his vexed attitude toward generational succession, Gippius attempts in her *Last Circle* to come to terms with her problematic relationship with the body, and she does so through reference to a text that not only had served as one of the subtexts for Blok's *Retribution* but that also put an emphasis on the very figure of the body—Dante's *Inferno*. In *The Inferno*, after all, Dante is portrayed as continually traversing over dead souls that are represented as live bodies. As Dante writes, "We walked across the shades on whom there thuds / that heavy rain, and set our soles upon / their empty images that seem like persons" (Noi passavam su per l'ombre che adona / la greve pioggia, e ponavam la piante / sovra lor vanità che par persona).[52] And in its focus on the body, Gippius's Dante poem functions not only as a revelation or *vskrytie* of the poet's personality but also as dissection or *vskrytie* of the poet's body.[53]

In *The Last Circle*, Gippius reaches from beyond the grave, as it were, enacting a kind of "anatomy of criticism." The body that she offers up for scrutiny in the poem does not, however, lend itself to ready analysis; she self-consciously resists identifying the self with any one easily identifiable body or gendered role from *The Divine Comedy*. In this poem, Gippius, who had recently lost her own husband, represents herself as the shade of a dead poet who wanders through Hell and Purgatory in search of her deceased beloved. While this shade, referred to in the poem as the "white Shade" (belaia Ten'), displays many characteristics of the Solovievian figure of Sophia who graced much of symbolist poetry and who had become the subject of some of Gippius's own poems, she does not identify her poetic alter ego solely with the traditionally feminine role of Beatrice or muse. By representing her shade in search of a male beloved, Gippius identifies with Dante in a parallel, yet inverted fashion. At the same time, she identifies with Virgil, who is confined to the first two realms of Hell and Purgatory in Dante's *Divine Comedy*.[54] In character with the figure of Virgil, Gippius's shade meets the Modern Dante, a descendent of Dante Alighieri as well as one of Benito Mussolini's fighter pilots, and offers to serve as his guide on an inverted Dantean journey through Hell back to Earth.[55] In enacting this role of guide, Gippius serves as poetic predecessor and subject of critical interpretation for the Modern Dante. Throughout the third section of *The Last Circle*, which is the focus of my analysis here, the Modern Dante, who is as much a reader or critic as he is a poet, struggles with how to read and interpret the elusive figure of Gippius's shade. At the center of the Modern Dante's critical inquiries about Gippius's poetic alter ego is the seemingly impossible question raised by Gippius's own critics: How to read the body of the poet?

It bears mentioning that even in *The Divine Comedy* Dante Alighieri enacts the role of reader-critic of the bodies not only of dead souls but also of dead poets. In fact, before he can forge the literary affiliation with Virgil that will enable him to make the journey through Hell and Purgatory and eventually into Paradise, he must first determine how to read and interpret his poetic predecessor. This act of interpretation is by no means self-evident, for Dante is faced with the daunting task of reading the soul of a deceased poet that is paradoxically represented as a live body. It would seem that upon the appearance of Virgil's shade in the forest, Dante is so alarmed that he is unable to form a critical judgment about Virgil's identity. As lines 65 and 66 of canto 1 of the *Inferno* read: "'Have pity on me,' were the words I cried, / 'whatever you may be—a shade, a man'" ("*Miserere* di me," gridai a lui, / "qual che tu sii, od ombra od omo certo!"). As these lines suggest, Dante is unable to decide between the two possible readings of Virgil—man or shade, body or soul. However, in the following line, the poet Virgil offers the following response to his reader, "'Not man; I once was man'" ("Non omo, omo già fui"), making it possible for Dante to recognize Virgil as a shade.[56]

In *The Last Circle*, a similar act of "reading" focusing on how to interpret the representation of embodiment of the dead poet occurs in the initial interchange between the Modern Dante and Gippius's shade. Yet in Gippius's work this act of reading is framed in a highly parodic manner. Whereas in *The Inferno* Dante is frightened by the appearance of a being that he *perceives* to be either a man or a shade, in *The Last Circle* the Modern Dante is simply annoyed when he accidentally steps on a being who he *feels* to be either a frog or a baby:

> Вдруг что-то запищало у него
> Под правою ногою. "На кого
> Я наступил?—И Данте рассердился.—
> Вот не было напасти! Лягушонка
> Я раздавил, а то еще ребенка?"
> (*Stikh*, 394)

[Suddenly something let out a squeak beneath his right foot. "On whom have I stepped?" And Dante grew angry. "As if I needed more misfortune! Have I crushed a frog or else a baby?"]

The Modern Dante's "misstep" on what he feels to be a frog or a baby may be read as a misreading of the ironic representation of souls as live bodies in *The Inferno*. While Dante himself is initially unable to determine Virgil's true identity, he does reveal an understanding of the irony of representation in Hell when he presents the two possible interpretations of Virgil—man or shade. Gippius's Modern Dante, however, does not appear to understand, at least in this instance, that the soul of the dead poet is paradoxically represented as a body. Therefore, he takes the body as sign for the body itself, believing he has mistakenly stepped on a corporeal being, a frog or a baby.[57] Several lines later, however, the shade intercedes and attempts to correct the Modern Dante's critical false step. The shade reveals to the Modern Dante: "'My dear, don't search. You have not crushed anybody. I am a being to whom you can do no harm'" ("Moi milyi, ne ishchite. Nikogo / Ne razdavili Vy. Ia—sushchestvo, / Kotoromu ne sdelaesh' vreda") (*Stikh*, 394).

The Modern Dante's critical faux pas is especially ironic when we consider its context in *The Last Circle*. We might rationalize Dante Alighieri's initial hesitation in determining whether Virgil is man or shade, body or soul, in light of the fact that Virgil is the first of the inhabitants of the underworld whom Dante meets and must interpret. However, the Modern Dante's clumsiness upon confronting Gippius's shade cannot be explained by his critical inexperience. Prior to meeting up with Gippius's shade, the Modern Dante meets two other souls who do not present any problem of interpretation for him, despite their self-confessed problems with their own bodies on earth. The first soul the Modern Dante encounters is consigned to Hell for the sins of the flesh. As he tells Dante: "'I am here—and this is the main thing—for perversion of Love and the body'" ("Ia zdes'—a v etom glavnoe i delo,— / Za iskazhenie Liubvi i tela") (*Stikh*, 378). And it is this perversion of the body that has transformed him into a kind of symbolist Bertran de Born, whose soul, rather than body, has been split in two for refusing to adhere to the tenets of courtly love. For this reason the split soul might be read as a double for Blok, with whom Gippius had broken.[58] Similar to the split lyrical persona in Blok's poetry, the soul recounts: "'And it appeared anew: sometimes in a dream and sometimes in reality, my soul split in two, and even all of myself, so it seemed to me'" ("I vnov' iavlialos': izredka vo sne, / A to i naiavu: dusha dvoilas' / I dazhe ves' ia,—tak kazalos' mne") (*Stikh*, 379).[59] While the first soul "'sacrificed everything [. . .] to his own body'" ("vsem zhertvoval [. . .] sobstvennomu telu") (*Stikh*, 381), producing a split in his very self, the second soul, who may have been modeled on the longtime object of Gippius's unrequited affections, Dmitry Filosofov, is presented as denying his body, a sin that the poet sees as no less severe than that of the first soul. "He began to live," Gippius notes, "preserving his very body" (Stal zhit', svoe oberegaia telo) (*Stikh*, 402), and this prevented him from experiencing any true form of love.[60]

Ironically, in spite of their professed gender trouble, the bodies of these two souls do not interest the Modern Dante in any manner or form. During his encounters with them, he does not feel compelled to become a literal reader of their bodies. In contrast, upon meeting Gippius's shade, the Modern Dante insists on reading the soul of Gippius's poetic alter ego over or through her dead body. Not only does the Modern Dante initially presume that he has *fallen over* the shade's body, but even after the shade, designated by the feminine noun *ten'* in Russian, informs Dante that she is a disembodied being who is incapable of being harmed, he insists on reading her as a gendered body. Dante follows the movement of the poet's body through Hell and imagines it as a corporealized female being consonant with the grammatically feminine Russian noun for soul, *dusha*:

> "Нет, нет! Иду!"—воскликнул Дант, спеша
> За белой Тенью, что теперь, из вод
> Поднявшись, двигалась легко вперед.
> "Должно быть, это чья-нибудь душа,—
> Подумал Данте.—Как она стройна,
> Как движется, по черноте скользя!
> Хотел бы знать, однако, кто она?"
> (*Stikh*, 395)

["No, no! I'm coming!" exclaimed Dante, hurrying after the white Shade that having raised itself out of the waters, moved lightly ahead. "It must be that she is somebody's soul," thought Dante. "How shapely she is! How she moves, gliding through the darkness! I would like to know, however, who is she?"]

In Dante's description, the poet's soul or *dusha* gradually takes on the secondary meaning of *dusha*—that is to say, his dear or darling. The soul metamorphoses into a graceful woman whose shapely figure—whose body—becomes the object of Dante's male gaze. And in his obsession with the shade's body, he reveals a fascination with the female body not unlike that of many of Gippius's male contemporaries who persisted in reading the woman's body as a sign.[61]

The shade actively resists Dante's attempts here to objectify her, to see her as a female body or, for that matter, as a muse. Endowed, like Virgil in *The Divine Comedy*, with the ability to read Dante's thoughts, the shade chastises him for his speculations about her body. Dante, however, persists in attempting to read and recuperate the body of this soul. Though the shade or *ten'* appears to Dante in a feminine form—both visually and grammatically speaking since *ten'* is a feminine noun in Russian—he asks her the very question posed by Gippius's own readers: What is her "'true' sex"? He inquires: "'Just answer one thing if you can: Are you a woman? Are you a "he"—or a "she"?'" ("Lish' na odno otvet'te, esli mozhno: / Vy—zhenshchina? Vy 'on'—ili 'ona' ?") (*Stikh*, 395). The shade initially refuses to answer this question, claiming that she has taken a vow of silence on the matter. But in a suggestive play on words, the shade concedes to transgress her vow:

> "Но имя предка вашего я чту
> И для него молчания черту
> *Переступлю*, на ваш вопрос ответив.
> Ответ мой прост: не знаю".
> (*Stikh*, 395; my emphasis)

["But I cherish the name of your ancestor, and for him I will *cross over* the line of silence by answering your question. My answer is simple: I don't know."]

The Modern Dante is so shaken here by the possibility of a state of sexual indeterminacy—of sexual Limbo, so to speak—that he falls into the river of Hell and almost drowns. Once the Modern Dante recovers from this second critical stumbling, he urges the shade to mentally return from this state of Limbo to Earth to help him find the necessary answers to his critical inquiries about her body. Dante implores the shade: "You said: 'I don't know.' What kind of a word is that! You were also on Earth, and there . . ." ("Skazali vy: 'Ne znaiu.' Chto za slovo! / Vy byli zhe i na zemle, a tam . . .") (*Stikh*, 396). The shade, however, once again playfully eludes Dante's attempts to analyze her. She tells him simply:

> —"Там, на земле, я женщиной считался.
> Но только что заговорю стихами,
> Вот как сейчас, сию минуту, с вами,
> Немедленно в мужчину превращался.
> И то же в случаях других . . . Как знать
> Могу, кто я? И было так до смерти".
> (*Stikh*, 396)

["There on Earth I was considered a woman. But as soon as I would speak in verse, just like now this very moment with you, I quickly metamorphosed into a man. And also on other occasions . . . How can I know who I am? It was like this until death."]

In this passage, Gippius's poetic alter ego resists defining herself in terms of natural, earthly categories. She never alludes to her sex. Instead, she refers to the gender or *rod* that she would adopt depending on the genre or *literaturnyi rod* in which she spoke. The shade notes that though she was "considered" (schitalsia)—or read—as a woman on earth, she metamorphosed into a man upon speaking in verse. And in such a fashion, she divorces her gender from the physiological and biological categories that the modern Dante, the modern reader-critic, attempts to impose on her. The shade offers the modern Dante an explanation or theory of gender that is based not on biological sex but on performance, and she alludes to the fact that this performance can encompass many roles and acts.

The shade assumes a masculine role upon speaking in verse. However, later in the poem, the shade appears about to appropriate a feminine role or "persona" (litso) upon speaking in prose or daily discourse:

> И даже что-то изменилось в ней:
> Весь облик стал и легче, и нежней,
> И был теперь уже не бел, а розов,
> Вот-вот заговорит, казалось, прозой
> И станет женщиной. Однако нет.
> (*Stikh*, 404)

[And even something changed in her: her entire countenance became both lighter and gentler, and was already not white but rose. Suddenly she would speak, it seemed, in prose and become a woman. But no.]

In some key ways, this shade, who playfully shifts genders and genres, enacts a theory of gender as performance similar to that discussed by Judith Butler. By representing her poetic alter ego as a shade—or phantom—who can assume various genders, genres, and even gendered roles from *The Divine Comedy*, Gippius playfully calls attention to the phantasmic status of her own gender and to her critics' tendency to misread this phantom of gender as a body with a "'true' sex." In the poem, she misleads her Modern Dante, her reader-critic, into a series of critical faux pas, stumblings, and near drownings that ultimately result in a critical impasse.

When the shade brings the Modern Dante to the border of Earth—to the seam between embodiment and disembodiment—the Modern Dante finds himself unable to read the shade's contours and to determine her identity. What the Modern Dante expects to be the moment of "revelation," the return to the light (svet), is, in fact, shrouded in a fog that is produced on the shade:

> Черта на камне темном всё белела . . .
> Скользнула Тень в нее—и тотчас вслед
> Дант кинулся, уж не жалея тела,
> Не думая о том, пройдет—иль нет.
> Но щелка раздалась, как будто . . . Свет!
>
> Хоть оказался он не очень ярок—
> Для Данте и белесый, как подарок.
> А Тень? Ах, вот. И на свету, светла,

> Чуть контуры другие приняла,
> Но на лице туман какой-то лег,
> И Данте рассмотреть его не мог.
> <div align="right">(<i>Stikh</i>, 396)</div>

[A line on the dark rock continued to grow white . . . The Shade slipped into it, and now in turn Dante threw himself on it, no longer sparing his body, not thinking about whether or not he would make it through. But the chink widened, it seemed . . . Light! Although it turned out that it was not very bright, for Dante it was whitish, like a gift. And the Shade? Oh, here she is. In the light, she was light, and took on slightly different contours, but on her face lay a fog of some kind, and Dante could not make it out.]

By veiling her poetic alter ego at this crucial moment, Gippius refuses Dante's attempt to penetrate the chink and to comprehend the nature of her body and of her identity and, thus, she effectively remains true to her nickname of "Miss Tification." Throughout *The Last Circle*, Gippius flirts with her Modern Dante, her imagined future reader-critic, simultaneously inviting and frustrating his attempts to read her and to know her. By resisting the attempts of her Modern Dante to penetrate the core of her identity, Gippius "lays bare" the device of her own idiosyncratic form of symbolist mythmaking or *telotvorchestvo* and stages the difficulty of interpretation that her reader-critics encounter in attempting to analyze her. Through the performative nature of her posthumously published poem, Gippius warns the Modern Dante and, by extension, all of her future readers that they can read her only over her dead body or *cherez ee trup*, which is to say, with great difficulty. In this regard, Gippius might be said to disprove the Barthesian claims that the "death of the author" paves the way for the "birth of the reader."[62] Gippius shows that the shade of the dead poet continues to haunt not only her Modern Dante but all of her future reader-critics, leading them into critical traps of her own devising and tantalizing them with the enigmatic nature of her own identity.

For this reason, it is fitting that Gippius's *Last Circle* was not published in its entirety during her lifetime but appeared only posthumously in, of all places, a journal called *La Renaissance* (*Vozrozhdenie*). The resurrected rough drafts of the poem function as a sort of will and testament, since they instruct her surviving contemporaries, as well as her future readers and critics, in how to read her. Rather than providing them with definitive answers about the true nature of her body and self, Gippius leaves them with more questions than answers. The body she leaves them to ponder is a phantasmic textual body that defies the very "anatomy of criticism" or *vskrytie* in which they would like to engage. As such, the poem predicts the difficulties of interpretation that Gippius would continue to pose to her readers and critics; it also exposes the depths of her own troubled relationship with her body and her sexuality, one that was not atypical for the Russian symbolist context. If Gippius had been less anxious about issues of gender and sexuality, she might have been able to complete her poem. But it can also be argued that it was this same discomfort that had served as the impetus for the poem in the first place.[63]

Afterword
The Return of the Repressed: Illegitimate Babies and an Unwieldy Body

> To endow the writer publicly with a good fleshly body [...] is to make even more miraculous for me, and of a more divine essence, the products of his art. Far from the details of his daily life bringing nearer to me the nature of his inspiration and making it clearer, it is the whole mythical singularity of his condition which the writer emphasizes by such confidences.
>
> Roland Barthes, *Mythologies* (1957)

Alexander Blok and Zinaida Gippius suffered very different fates as individuals and as writers: Blok died in Petrograd in August 1921 and was consecrated by Soviet and émigré writers and critics as the poet of his generation and as successor to Alexander Pushkin, while Gippius emigrated from Russia in December 1919 and was denigrated by the Soviet literary establishment for her decadent behavior and counterrevolutionary activities.[1] Yet, despite the radically different positions they came to occupy within the Russian literary canon, Blok and Gippius are united by their reliance on the practice of the symbolist sublimation of sex. They each in their own way organized their poetic careers around the denial of sexuality and the body, a denial that manifested itself in a tendency to implicitly identify at times with the gender of the other: Blok with the feminine and the maternal and Gippius with the masculine and the dandified. And for both writers, this suppression of matters of the flesh resulted paradoxically in the production not of a sexless poetics but of a gendered poetics that put the body at the center of artistic praxis. In Blok's case, this preoccupation with the denial of procreation culminated in his attempt in his late, unfinished narrative poem *Retribution* (*Vozmezdie*) to compensate for his lack of a legitimate heir by imagining his alter ego fathering a love child with a Polish woman amid political strife. Thus, for all his resistance to procreation and a smooth line of generational continuity in his own life, kinship becomes the dominant concern of one of his last major poetic works. In a similar fashion, Gippius may have been implicitly concerned with repressing the feminine and the female body in her writings, but this practice transformed the body into one of the most important figures in her poetry, and it is the body of the poet that occupies center stage in her late, incomplete work *The Last Circle (and the Modern Dante in Hell)* (*Poslednii krug [i novyi Dant v adu]*).

Once the figure of the child or the body entered into the artistic discourse of these writers, there was a tendency not just among poets themselves but also their contemporaries and immediate successors to see these figures as coming to life. "Following romanticism," Irina Paperno contends, "the symbolists aspired to merge the antitheses of art and life into a unity. Art was proclaimed to be a force capable of, and destined for, the 'creation of life' (*tvorchestvo zhizni*), while 'life' was viewed as an object of artistic creation or as a creative act. In this sense, art turned into 'real life' and 'life' turned into art; they became one."[2] This blurring of the boundaries between art and life was something that was practiced and discussed by the symbolists in their philosophical writings, but it can be argued that it was the following generation of writers and critics who were largely responsible for codifying this artistic practice and endowing it with a literary term. Khodasevich, as I mentioned earlier, helped to introduce the concept of *zhiznetvorchestvo* or life creation into Russian literary criticism in his famous essay "The End of Renata." Other postsymbolist writers such as Marina Tsvetaeva subsequently took up this notion. In her memoirs, *A Captive Spirit* (*Plennyi dukh*) (1934), which she dedicated to Khodasevich, she echoes Khodasevich in this regard, indicating: "Symbolism is least of all a *literary* movement" (Simvolizm men'she vsego *literaturnoe* techenie).[3]

This understanding of Russian symbolism was, in part, instrumental to the legend that Blok had fathered a child out of wedlock just as his hero was destined to in *Retribution*. The Soviet writer Nadezhda Pavlovich recalls in her memoirs that in October 1920 Blok expressed despondency over the fact that he did not have a child. In response to the question of whether there ever was a child, she reports that he replied: "There was in Poland. She was a simple girl, she remained pregnant, but I lost contact with her. And I can no longer find her. Perhaps, there my son grows, but he doesn't know me, and I will never know him."[4] Although Pavlovich casts doubt on the idea that Blok fathered a child with a simple Polish woman following his father's funeral, just as his hero was supposed to do in *Retribution,* she does not question the idea that Blok did indeed father a love child in Poland at some point in his life.[5] And this would by no means be the only myth propagated about Blok having an illegitimate child. Rumors also circulated in Russian artistic circles that Blok had fathered a son with Nadezhda Nolle-Kogan, the wife of a famous Moscow critic with whom he had stayed during a trip to Moscow in the last year of his life. Here again Blok provided his contemporaries with grist for their literary rumor mill. In a letter he wrote to Nolle-Kogan on 8 January 1921, several months before the child's birth, he conveyed to her his best wishes for her unborn child. As if to suggest a possible kinship between himself and the child, he begins the letter with a frank assessment of his character and of those qualities he would like to pass on to the child:

> I have grown endlessly heavy from all of life, and you remember that and don't think about that 99 percent of me, about all that is weak, sinful, and worthless in me. But in me there is, true, 1 percent of that which should have been passed on to someone; that better part of me I would like to express in a wish for your child, a person of the near future. The wish is the following: Let him, if only it is possible, be a person of *peace,* not war; let him be calm and slowly build up that which was destroyed during the seven years of terror. If it is not possible, if the blood still seethes in him and rebels and destroys, like in all us sinners — then let his *conscience* first and foremost bother him always and relentlessly; let it at least neutralize the poisonous, terrible fits, with which our times are rich, and perhaps the immediate future will be rich.
>
> Understand how I say this. I speak with pain and despair in my soul; but I still cannot go to church, even though it beckons me. Spare and cherish your future child; if he will be good, what kind of a martyr he will be — he will pay for everything that we have done, for every minute of our days. (SS, 8:532)

Although nowhere in this letter does Blok actually speak of the child as his own, he does seem to see in this child the potential for rectifying the wrongs of his generation, and in this respect, his relationship with

Nolle-Kogan's child is not too different from that which he had with his wife's child Dmitry, a child many of his contemporaries wrongly believed to be his.[6] Perhaps because of Blok's strong psychic investment in the child, his contemporaries were inclined to view this child as the realization of the love child he had written about in the prologue to *Retribution*, even though this child was born not in Poland but Moscow. And here Marina Tsvetaeva, a firm believer in the mythmaking potential of symbolism, played a key role in fostering this legend. On 30 March 1924, while living in exile in Prague, Tsvetaeva wrote her friend Roman Gul: "It is strange that you are going to Russia. Where are you going to live? In Moscow? I want to make you a present of my friends, the Kogans, an entire family, all good. There Blok's child is growing—Sasha, already big, three years old [Khochu podarit' Vam svoikh druzei—Koganov, tseluiu sem'iu, vse khoroshie. Tam blokovskii mal'chik rastet—Sasha, uzhe bol'shoi, tri goda]. It is a very good home. You will be comfortable there."[7] And in another letter written to Gul on 11 April 1924, she returns to the subject of Blok's child:

> You asked about Blok's son. He exists. He was born in June 1921, two months before Blok's death. I saw him as a year-old baby: wonderful, severe with Blok's heavy eyes (heaviness in the upper lid) and a twisted mouth. Couldn't resemble him more. I read Blok's letter to his mother. I recall such an address: "If it is a son, I wish him only one thing—bravery." I saw Blok's gifts to the child: a mother-of-pearl family crest with entwined roses (doesn't *The Rose and the Cross* [*Roza i krest*] come from this), a dummy of Harlequin from *The Puppet Show* [*Balaganchik*], the offering of some female admirer. (Pierrot remained with his wife.) I saw the love of N. A. Kogan for Blok. Having learned of his death, she, nursing her son, grew internally uptight, and did not give into tears. But ten days later she walked around in a gauze mask—terrible nervous eczema from the "lingering affect."
>
> The child is growing beautiful and happy. In P. S. Kogan he has found the most adoring father. And that father has remained there—"in the picture."
>
> They will say it is "not Blok's"—don't believe it: that is what scoundrels say [Budut govorit' "ne blokovskii"—ne ver'te: eto negodiai govoriat].[8]

Tsvetaeva seems much more intent here on fostering the myth of the existence of Blok's child than in teasing out the truth about one of her beloved poets. For her, the existence of Blok's illegitimate son was absolutely essential to her attempts to construct a mediated relationship with the great poet Alexander Blok. Though Tsvetaeva chose not to meet Blok during his lifetime, she did at least in her own mind succeed in meeting his son.[9] And she imbued this meeting with mythical significance. In December 1921, the first Christmas season after Blok's death, Tsvetaeva not only dedicated a cycle of poems entitled *Girlfriend* (*Podruga*) to Nadezhda Nolle-Kogan, the woman she believed to have given birth to Blok's love child, but she dedicated two poems entitled "Bethlehem" ("Vifleem") "to the son of Blok—Sasha" (Synu Bloka,—Sashe). In the dedication, she indicates that these were "two poems accidentally not included in *The Verses to Blok*" (dva stikhotvoreniia, sluchaino ne voshedshie v "Stikhi k Bloku").[10] The fact that Blok's alleged son was born not in December but in June is no more problematic for Tsvetaeva than her own female gender is for her in these verses. In the first and most interesting of these Bethlehem poems, she envisions her feminine poetic alter ego not as a shepherdess but as a poor shepherd who successfully undertakes a pilgrimage to the Christ child:

> Не с серебром пришла,
> Не с янтарем пришла,—
> Я не царем пришла,
> Я пастухом пришла.
>
> Вот воздух гор моих,
> Вот острый взор моих
> Двух глаз—и красный пых
> Костров и зорь моих.
>
> Где ладан-воск—тот-мех?
> Не оберусь прорех!
> Хошь и нищее всех—
> Зато первее всех!
>
> За верблюдóм верблюд
> Гляди: на холм-твой-крут,
> Гляди: цари идут.
> Гляди: лари несут.
>
> О—поз—дали![11]

[Not with silver did I come, not with amber did I come, not as a tsar did I come, I came as a shepherd. Here is the air of my mountains, here is the sharp gaze of my two eyes, and the red blaze of my bonfires and dawns. Where is the incense-wax—that—fur? I have more tatters than I can count! Though poorer than all, but then I am first of all! Camel after camel; look: onto your steep hill; look: the kings are coming; look: they are bringing chests. They are too late!]

In a move typical for Tsvetaeva, she transforms her position as outsider into one of incredible strength. Though her female poetic speaker does not arrive in Bethlehem as one of the Three Kings bearing silver, amber, or any of the other precious gifts fit for the Christ child but as a lowly shepherd in torn clothing, she manages to bring with her other, even more precious, gifts: "Here is the air of my mountains, here is the sharp gaze of my two eyes, and the red blaze of my bonfires and dawns" (Vot vozdukh gor moikh, / Vot ostryi vzor moikh / Dvukh glaz—i krasnyi pykh / Kostrov i zor' moikh). Air and vision are important gifts, particularly for a poet. And it is these things that Tsvetaeva manages to pass on to the child—the child who is for her equivalent to the son of God, since he is supposedly the scion of Russia's leading modernist poet. She is the first to pay tribute to and recognize the existence of the child. As the first to arrive, she manages to transcend her own poverty: "Though poorer than all, but then I am first of all!" (Khosh' i nishchee vsekh— / Zato pervee vsekh!). Timing is crucial in this poem, as it was in the poet's own life. Tsvetaeva may have been too late for a meeting with Blok, but she was not too late for a meeting with the poet's son and namesake, Sasha. In paying homage to Blok's son, Tsvetaeva fosters a belated relationship with one of her beloved poets, and she also helps to create an heir for a poet who was to a large extent vexed by his own inability to have and raise a child of his own.

The fact that Blok's posthumous poetic myth is haunted by the legend of an illegitimate child is ironic given Blok's own resistance to the generative impulse throughout his poetic career. However, it is no less ironic than some of the poetic myths surrounding Gippius that sprang up in the West in the period following the poet's death in emigration in Paris in 1945. Whereas Blok's reputation was haunted by the presence of an illegitimate child, Gippius's was haunted by the rumor that her own death was spurred on by her female vanity, a fact that is particularly interesting given her own complicated relationship with the feminine in her works. And as with the legend of Blok's illegitimate child, the rumor about Gippius's death was fostered by one of her immediate contemporaries. In 1970, twenty-five years after Gippius's death, *A Difficult Soul* (*Tiazhelaia dusha*), the reminiscences of her personal secretary, Vladimir Zlobin, were published posthumously. Here Zlobin puts forth the specious theory that Gippius's death was brought on by her obsessive attention to her body and outward appearance. He alleges:

In the middle of March Gippius did something highly imprudent which accelerated the progress of her illness. She went to the hairdresser's to have her hair washed. But that was only a pretext. The secret reason for going was to get a permanent wave. Under no circumstances did she ever stop being concerned about her appearance.

In one of her old parodies, in which she spared no one, not even herself, she had a "Shady Lady," representing herself, utter a phrase that became a classic in the Merezhkovskys' circle: "On the day Pompeii was destroyed / I curled my hair with curling papers." In fact, she usually had her hair done on the anniversary of her mother's death and on that of Merezhkovsky's. She would have consented, it seems, even to having a permanent done in her grave. It was a lifesaving habit which helped her to endure and not lose her spirits in those moments when will power alone would not have been enough. Even when she no longer had any idea of what was going on around her, she still would massage her face every night with *lait de beauté* before going to bed and would try to do her hair without outside help. She imagined herself after death as still being alive. "When I die," she said a few weeks before her death, "please put a little makeup on my face." Her incredible, vital strength was the only kind she possessed, not only in her soul, but in her body as well, as she herself admitted. In spite of her fragility and delicacy, her hothouse airs, she was physically strong, much stronger and more hardy than Merezhkovsky had been. Her blood pressure was like a seventeen-year-old's and her heart and lungs were healthy. Anyone else in her place would not have survived even for a year.

She returned from the hairdresser in the best of spirits. But the results of her permanent soon became apparent. The dry heat of the electric current affected the blood vessels in her brain. In two days her condition became considerably worse. The thick volume of *Contemporary Annals* which she was reading on the couch after dinner fell from her hands. What was happening? Why? It was such a chore to move her arm. And her leg was dragging. She was perplexed. Everything was quite in order. What could be the matter? Doctor André, who was called the next day, found that the brain areas that coordinate movement had been affected. Gippius was reassured as if she were a child—it's nothing, it will pass. But the doctor was alarmed. The illness had taken a dangerous turn.[12]

Whether there is any scientific validity to Zlobin's account of Gippius's slow death by permanent wave is inconsequential.[13] What is important is that Gippius, who was vexed by her own femininity, was ultimately constructed as a victim of feminine fashion. The twentieth century had borne witness to actual fashion victims, the most famous of which was Isadora Duncan. But while there is no denying that Duncan was literally a victim of feminine style, of the fateful scarf that caught in the wheel of a tire in Nice in September 1927, I would suggest that Gippius's death at the hands of her hairdresser was the product of the twentieth-century Russian tendency not just to mythologize the poet's death but to do so in a fashion that had particular relevance to the poet's own personal myth.[14] Understanding all too well Gippius's own problematic relationship with her femininity and the female body, Zlobin views her as having been brought down by her femininity.[15] According to Zlobin's elaborate formulation, Gippius becomes not just a difficult soul but a burdened soul, one that is weighed down by the concerns of the body. And this heaviness would appear to be deeply at odds with Gippius's own unsuccessful attempt to present herself as an ethereal and disembodied soul in *The Last Circle* and elsewhere.

In the case of both Blok and Gippius, then, the very aspect they attempted to repress in their creative works ends up returning with a vengeance in their posthumous poetic myths. The childless male poet is revealed to have produced an heir, while the female poet who wrote predominantly in the masculine voice turns out to have been undone by her own femininity in one of the final conscious acts of her life. And the existence of these myths about the illegitimate child of Blok and the disastrously bad hair day of Gippius speaks of the difficulties inherent in their own attempts to engage in the symbolist sublimation of sex and of the persistence of their readers and critics in fleshing out the lives and even the bodies of these poets and in embodying the figures inherent in their poetry. This is a cultural phenomenon that has been perhaps most famously discussed by Roland Barthes in his *Mythologies* (1957) and by the contemporary British novelist A. S. Byatt in her Booker Prize–winning novel *Possession: A Romance* (1990). For the bourgeois reader in Barthes's *Mythologies,* as well as for the obsessed British scholars in Byatt's novel, to understand a writer is not simply to read his works, but to have intimate knowledge of his life and, in some cases, even of his ancestors. And a similar type of literary possession appears to have overtaken readers in contemporary Russia. With the dissolution of the Soviet Union, the infatuation not just with the life of the poet but with his body and his progeny does not seem to have waned.

This is particularly the case for Blok, among the most consecrated of the Russian modernists.

With the approach of the new millennium, there emerged renewed interest in Russia in the fate of Blok's supposed heirs. In May 1999, an article by Marx Tartakovsky entitled "Like Father, Like Son: The Wonderful Life of Alexander Blok's Son" ("Syn za otsa: Prekrasnaia zhizn' syna Aleksandra Bloka") appeared in the popular weekly magazine *Ogonek*. In this article, Tartakovsky revisits the myth, fostered in large part by Tsvetaeva, that Alexander Kogan, who was known in Soviet literary circles as Alexander Kuleshov, was the illegitimate son of Alexander Blok. But whereas Tsvetaeva was deeply invested in the idea that Sasha Kogan was Blok's child, Tartakovsky is much more skeptical and ironic. Toward the end of his essay, he makes reference to the parodic portrayals of Kuleshov in Yury Nagibin's "A Flight with the President" ("Polet s prezidentom") and Vladimir Voinovich's *The Ivankiad* (*Ivankiada*) (1976), noting: "Well there are still the letters of Tsvetaeva—but the description in them of the infant has so little in common with the man I recall . . ." (Nu i eshche pis'ma Tsvetaevoi—no opisannyi v nikh mladenets imeet tak malo obshchego s chelovekom, o kotorom ia vspominaiu . . .).[16] Though Tartakovsky does his part in deconstructing the myth of Blok's child that was so eloquently constructed by Tsvetaeva and others, by virtue of writing the article he acknowledges the importance of such mythologies for today's Russian readers. And Tartakovsky's article was by no means the only work in the Russian media dedicated to myth of Blok's child.

Some four months later, on 27 September 1999, an advertisement appeared in *Antenna* for the television program *Fate* (*Sud'ba*) that was to be dedicated to yet another of Blok's supposed illegitimate children: a long-lost daughter. "It is well known," the announcement states, "that the famous poet and lady-killer of the beginning of the 20th century Alexander Blok had no children. But . . . there lives in Russia a woman named Alexandra Pavlovna Liush. [. . .] Already as an adult, she learned that her father was Alexander Blok! There are no documents containing juridical proof or confirming the blood kinship of the poet with Alexandra Pavlovna. There is only the face, indistinguishable from the face of Blok."[17] In his memoir, "'Life is Incorrigible . . .': (Notes of a Theatrical Renegade)" ("'Eta zhizn' neispravima . . .' [Zapiski teatral'nogo otshchepentsa]"), which appeared in *The Star* (*Zvezda*) in 2004, the actor Vladimir Retsepter discusses how the rumor that Liush was Blok's illegitimate child gained widespread currency in theatrical circles in the 1930s, owing in part to the fact that Liush's adoptive mother, Maria Sakovich, was the doctor connected to the Bolshoi Dramatic Theater. Retsepter also reports here that the poet Anna Akhmatova took a special interest in the paternity of little Alexandra Liush, asking Sakovich outright in the final year of her life whether Blok was the father and receiving a positive answer. The emergence of this information lends nice symmetry to the myths of Blok's love children, with Tsvetaeva taking an interest in his alleged son and Akhmatova in his daughter.[18]

Rumors, however unsubstantiated, that Alexander Blok, the last of Russia's major aristocratic poets, fathered at least two children—a son Alexander and a daughter Alexandra—may very well be nothing more than wishful thinking on the part of members of the Russian intelligentsia obsessed with recovering their prerevolutionary heritage. If all members of the tsar's family perished in Ekaterinburg in July 1918, then at least the family line of Russia's last major aristocratic poet did not die with him, this in spite of his own insistence that he was a destroyer not a progenitor. This is dependent on a literal reading of Blok's poetry and on realizing the figures inherent within his poetry. It can be argued that similar readings continue to dog Gippius, particularly in the West where there have been numerous scholarly writings devoted to the poet's body—the present study included. For all of Gippius's resistance to the feminine and the corporeal, she has become somewhat of a *cause célèbre* for feminist scholars in the Slavic field. And this critical interest in the poets' lives and bodies testifies to the powerful afterlife of their particular mythmaking strategies. Although both of these writers may have attempted to move beyond the flesh in their lives and art, they wittingly or unwittingly moved the matters of the flesh from the margins to the center of artistic discourse. In so doing, they became responsible for the founding of a particular gendered tradition in Russian modernist poetry, providing the next generation of Russian readers not only with powerful metaphors but also with powerful mythmaking material. And a century later these legends continue to fascinate readers and critics alike.

Notes

Introduction

Book epigraph: D. S. Merezhkovskii, *Voskresshie bogi: Leonardo da-Vinchi*, ed. M. Bezrodnyi (Moscow: Khudozhestvennaia literatura, 1990), 486-87. Where not otherwise indicated, translations of epigraphs are mine.

Epigraph to introduction: Vladimir Solovyov, *The Meaning of Love*, trans. Thomas Beyer Jr. (Hudson, N.Y.: Lindisfarne, 1985), 19-20; Vladimir Solov'ev, *Smysl liubvi, Sochinenii v dvukh tomakh*, ed. A. F. Losev and A. V. Gulyga, 2 vols. (Moscow: Mysl', 1990), 2:493.

1. Recent monographs that treat the problem of gender and sexuality in Russian modernism include: Catherine Ciepiela, *The Same Solitude: Boris Pasternak and Marina Tsvetaeva* (Ithaca, N.Y.: Cornell University Press, 2006); Olga Matich, *Erotic Utopia: The Decadent Imagination in Russia's Fin de Siècle* (Madison: University of Wisconsin Press, 2005); Gregory Carleton, *Sexual Revolution in Bolshevik Russia* (Pittsburgh, Penn.: University of Pittsburgh Press, 2005); Alyssa W. Dinega, *A Russian Psyche: The Poetic Mind of Marina Tsvetaeva* (Madison: University of Wisconsin Press, 2001); Eliot Borenstein, *Men Without Women: Masculinity and Revolution in Soviet Literature* (Durham, N.C.: Duke University Press, 2000); Eric Naiman, *Sex in Public: The Incarnation of Early Soviet Ideology* (Princeton, N.J.: Princeton University Press, 1997); Aleksandr Etkind, *Sodom i Psikheia: Ocherki intellektual'noi istorii Serebrianogo veka* (Moscow: ITS-Garant, 1996); Olga Peters Hasty, *Tsvetaeva's Orphic Journeys in the Worlds of the Word* (Evanston, Ill.: Northwestern University Press, 1996); and Beth Holmgren, *Women's Work in Stalin's Time: On Lydia Chukovskaia and Nadezhda Mandelstam* (Bloomington: Indiana University Press, 1993). Edited collections that include discussions of gender and modernism are much more numerous. See, for example, M. M. Pavlova, ed., *Erotizm bez granits* (Moscow: Novoe literaturnoe obozrenie, 2004); Peter I. Barta, ed., *Gender and Sexuality in Russian Civilisation* (London: Routledge, 2001); Linda Edmonson, ed., *Gender in Russian History and Culture* (New York: Palgrave, 2001); Pamela Chester and Sibelan Forrester, eds., *Engendering Slavic Literatures*

(Bloomington: Indiana University Press, 1996); Rosalind Marsh, trans. and ed., *Gender and Russian Literature: New Perspectives* (Cambridge: Cambridge University Press, 1996); Helena Goscilo and Beth Holmgren, eds., *Russia / Women / Culture* (Bloomington: Indiana University Press, 1996); and Jane T. Costlow, Stephanie Sandler, and Judith Vowles, eds., *Sexuality and the Body in Russian Culture* (Stanford, Calif.: Stanford University Press, 1993).

2. For a more detailed discussion of the utopian orientation in Gippius's writings and in Russian symbolism generally, see Olga Matich's *Erotic Utopia* and her essays "The Merezhkovskys' Third Testament and the Russian Utopian Tradition," in *Christianity and the Eastern Slavs*, vol. 2, ed. Robert P. Hughes and Irina Paperno (Berkeley: University of California Press, 1994), 158–71; "The Symbolist Meaning of Love: Theory and Practice," in *Creating Life: The Aesthetic Utopia of Russian Modernism*, ed. Irina Paperno and Joan Delaney Grossman (Stanford, Calif.: Stanford University Press, 1994), 24–50; and "Dialectics of Cultural Return: Zinaida Gippius' Personal Myth," in *Cultural Mythologies of Russian Modernism: From the Golden Age to the Silver Age*, ed. Boris Gasparov, Robert P. Hughes, and Irina Paperno (Berkeley: University of California Press, 1992), 52–72.

3. For an appraisal of Freud's indebtedness to Merezhkovsky, see Richard Halpern, "Freud's Egyptian Renaissance: *Leonardo da Vinci and a Memory of His Childhood*," *Shakespeare's Perfume: Sodomy and Sublimity in the Sonnets, Wilde, Freud, and Lacan* (Philadelphia: University of Pennsylvania Press, 2002), 59–85, and Aleksandr Etkind, *Eros of the Impossible: The History of Psychoanalysis in Russia*, trans. Noah and Maria Rubins (Boulder, Colo.: Westview Press, 1997), 26.

4. Sigmund Freud, "Leonardo da Vinci and a Memory of His Childhood," *The Standard Edition of the Complete Psychological Works of Sigmund Freud*, trans. James Strachey, 24 vols. (London: Hogarth Press, 1953–74), 11:74–75.

5. Olga Matich offers the most extensive discussion of how the symbolists' ideas of love influenced the organization of their daily lives in "The Symbolist Meaning of Love." My approach to the Russian symbolists differs considerably from Matich's in that I am concerned here with the ways in which their notions of gender and sexuality influenced the creative process itself. While she draws a detailed picture of the erotic lives of the Russian symbolists, I am attempting to reconstruct the ways in which the symbolists' theories of gender and eros fueled their creativity.

6. On the symbolists' source of inspiration in ecstatic moments, see Joan Delaney Grossman, "Valery Briusov and Nina Petrovskaia: Clashing Models of Life in Art," in *Creating Life: The Aesthetic Utopia of Russian Modernism*, esp. 123.

7. Freud's first mention of the concept of sublimation within a published essay occurs in "Fragment of an Analysis of a Case of Hysteria" (1905 [1901]).

8. Etkind, *Eros of the Impossible*, 76. Certainly, the rationale that Etkind gives for the special kinship between symbolism and psychoanalysis could be broadly applied to any modernist movement. He indicates that "as intellectual trends, both movements were essentially semiotic. Both functioned in the linguistic sphere and both attempted to transcend language, moved by the belief that another, nonverbal reality had decisive significance in human affairs. Both movements prescribed refined methods of interpretation, correlation between

meanings and signs, emotional experiences and symbols, and dreams and words" (77). For Etkind there seems to be little difference between modernism and psychoanalysis, but I would insist that there is a difference and that it lies in the fact that psychoanalysis, unlike modernism, provided a system for analyzing the human psyche and behavior and had pretensions of being scientific.

9. See, in particular, Freud, "Leonardo da Vinci and a Memory of His Childhood," 11:63-137; Edward W. Said, *Beginnings: Intentions and Method* (New York: Columbia University Press, 1985), i-xxi; and Edward W. Said, *The World, the Text, and the Critic* (Cambridge, Mass.: Harvard University Press, 1983), esp. 16-25. And on the Victorian nature of modern society, see Michel Foucault, *The History of Sexuality*, vol. 1, trans. Robert Hurley (New York: Pantheon, 1978).

10. Vladislav Khodasevich, "Konets Renaty," *Sobranie sochinenii v chetyrekh tomakh*, ed. I. P. Andreeva and A. G. Bocharov, 4 vols. (Moscow: Soglasie, 1996-97), 4:7. The most extensive scholarly inquiry into the phenomenon of symbolist *zhiznetvorchestvo* or life creation can be found in Irina Paperno and Joan Delaney Grossman, eds., *Creating Life: The Aesthetic Utopia of Russian Modernism*. Although life creation is usually discussed in connection with Russian symbolism, the phenomenon has been detected in a variety of other literary movements including romanticism, realism, acmeism, and futurism. See, for example, Alexander Zholkovsky, "The Obverse of Stalinism: Akhmatova's Self-Serving Charisma of Selflessness," in *Self and Story in Russian History*, ed. Laura Engelstein and Stephanie Sandler (Ithaca, N.Y.: Cornell University Press, 2000), 46-68; David M. Bethea, *Realizing Metaphors: Alexander Pushkin and the Life of the Poet* (Madison: University of Wisconsin Press, 1998); Stephen C. Hutchings, *Russian Modernism and the Transfiguration of the Everyday* (Cambridge: Cambridge University Press, 1997); Svetlana Boym, *Death in Quotation Marks: Cultural Myths of the Modern Poet* (Cambridge, Mass.: Harvard University Press, 1991); Irina Paperno, *Chernyshevsky and the Age of Realism* (Stanford, Calif.: Stanford University Press, 1988); and Gregory Freidin, *A Coat of Many Colors: Osip Mandelstam and His Mythologies of Self-Presentation* (Berkeley: University of California Press, 1987).

11. In my contention that the early Russian modernists attempted to move beyond the flesh in the organization of their artistic practices, I offer a somewhat different approach to Russian modernism than Irene Masing-Delic, who sees the movement as driven by an attempt to overcome death (*Abolishing Death: A Salvation Myth of Russian Twentieth-Century Literature* [Stanford, Calif.: Stanford University Press, 1992]).

12. There are a number of books on Blok that originally appeared in English; however, all but one of these date back to the '60s, '70s, and '80s: Timothy C. Westphalen, *Lyric Incarnate: The Dramas of Aleksandr Blok* (Amsterdam: Harwood Academic Publishers, 1998); David A. Sloane, *Aleksandr Blok and the Dynamics of the Lyric Cycle* (Columbus, Ohio: Slavica, 1988); Gerald Pirog, *Aleksandr Blok's* Ital'ianskie stikhi: *Confrontation and Disillusionment* (Columbus, Ohio: Slavica, 1983); Avril Pyman, *The Life of Aleksandr Blok*, 2 vols. (Oxford: Oxford University Press, 1979-80); James Forsyth, *Listening to the Wind: An Introduction to Alexander Blok* (Oxford, England: W. A. Meeuws, 1977); Sergei Hackel, *The Poet and Revolution: Aleksandr Blok's* The Twelve (Oxford, England: Clarendon Press, 1975);

Lucy E. Vogel, *Aleksandr Blok: The Journey to Italy* (Ithaca, N.Y.: Cornell University Press, 1973); Irene Masing-Delic, *A. Blok's "The Snow Mask": An Interpretation* (Stockholm: Almqvist and Wiksell, 1970); Robin Kemball, *Alexander Blok: A Study in Rhythm and Meter* (The Hague: Mouton, 1965); F. D. Reeve, *Aleksandr Blok: Between Image and Idea* (New York: Columbia University Press, 1962); and C. H. Kisch, *Aleksandr Blok, Prophet of the Revolution* (New York: Roy Publishers, 1960). There are only two monographs on Gippius that were originally published in English, and they date back to the '70s: Olga Matich, *Paradox in the Religious Poetry of Zinaida Gippius* (Munich: Wilhelm Fink, 1972), and Temira Pachmuss, *Zinaida Hippius: An Intellectual Profile* (Carbondale: Southern Illinois University Press, 1971).

13. In the last decade, a number of excellent studies have appeared on Russian symbolism in English, but, for the most part, they shy away from Western critical theory. See, for example Victor Terras, *Poetry of the Silver Age: Various Voices of Russian Modernism* (Dresden: Dresden University Press, 1998); Avril Pyman, *A History of Russian Symbolism* (Cambridge: Cambridge University Press, 1994); Michael Wachtel, *Russian Symbolism and Literary Tradition: Goethe, Novalis, and the Poetics of Vyacheslav Ivanov* (Madison: University of Wisconsin Press, 1994); and *Creating Life: The Aesthetic Utopia of Russian Modernism*. A notable exception in this regard is Olga Matich's *Erotic Utopia*, which became available to me only after I completed the main writing of this book.

14. On the anxiety experienced by women writers in the face of maternity, see Barbara Johnson, "Apostrophe, Animation, and Abortion," *A World of Difference* (Baltimore, M.D.: The Johns Hopkins University Press, 1987), 184–99, and Susan Rubin Suleiman, "Writing and Motherhood," in *The (M)other Tongue: Essays in Feminist Psychoanalytic Interpretation*, ed. Shirley Nelson Garner, Claire Kahane, and Madelon Sprengnether (Ithaca, N.Y.: Cornell University Press, 1985), 352–77.

15. On Blok and Gippius's literary relationship, see A. V. Lavrov, "'Rozhdennye v gody glukhie . . .': Aleksandr Blok i Z. N. Gippius," *Etiudy o Bloke* (St. Petersburg: Izdatel'stvo Ivana Limbakha, 2000), 260–68; Z. G. Mints, "Blok v polemike s Merezhkovskimi," *Aleksandr Blok i russkie pisateli*, intro. A. V. Lavrov and ed. L. L. Pil'd (St. Petersburg: Iskusstvo-SPB, 2000), 537–620; and Avril Pyman, "Aleksandr Blok and the Merežkovskijs," in *Aleksandr Blok: Centennial Conference*, ed. Walter N. Vickery (Columbus, Ohio: Slavica, 1984), 237–70.

16. For the sake of consistency, I cite from the older eight-volume edition of Blok's works and the accompanying volume of notebooks rather than the newer twenty-volume edition-in-progress (*Polnoe sobranie sochinenii i pisem v dvadtsati tomakh*, ed. M. L. Gasparov et al., vols. 1–5 and 7 to date [Moscow: Nauka, 1997–]). However, I have consulted all available volumes of this new Russian edition.

17. While there have been a number of studies that discuss Blok's indebtedness to sublimated love, the work that best examines this phenomenon within the larger context of Vladimir Soloviev and Russian religious philosophy is Samuel D. Cioran's *Vladimir Solov'ev and the Knighthood of the Divine Sophia* (Waterloo, Canada: Wilfrid Laurier University Press, 1977).

18. On Gippius's ideas of love and marriage, see Matich, "The Symbolist

Meaning of Love," esp. 40-47; Olga Matich, "Zinaida Gippius: Theory and Practice of Love," in *Kul'tura russkogo modernizma: Stat'i, esse i publikatsii v prinoshenie Vladimiru Fedorovichu Markovu*, ed. Ronald Vroon and John E. Malmstad (Moscow: Nauka, 1993), 237-51, and Matich, "Dialectics of Cultural Return," esp. 60-66.

19. Quoted in Pachmuss, *Zinaida Hippius: An Intellectual Profile*, 17.
20. On Gippius and dandyism, see Matich, "Dialectics of Cultural Return," esp. 57-60.
21. *Tiazhelaia dusha* could also be translated as "burdened soul." However, I have opted to refer to this memoir in English as *A Difficult Soul*, since this is the term used by Simon Karlinsky in his translation of Vladimir Zlobin's memoir, *A Difficult Soul: Zinaida Gippius* (Berkeley: University of California Press, 1980).

Chapter 1. Unbearable Burdens

Epigraphs to part 1: Stéphane Mallarmé, "Gift of the Poem" ("Don du poème"), *Collected Poems*, trans. and commentary Henry Weinfield (Berkeley: University of California Press, 1994), 24; letter to Nora Barnacle Joyce, *Letters of James Joyce*, ed. Stuart Gilbert and Richard Ellman, 3 vols. (New York: Viking Press, 1957-66), 2:308; and Vladimir Nabokov, *Speak, Memory: An Autobiography Revisited* (New York: Vintage, 1989), 65.

Epigraph to chapter 1: Mallarmé, "Sea Breeze" ("Brise marine"), *Collected Poems*, 21.

1. Edward W. Said, *Beginnings: Intention and Method* (New York: Columbia University Press, 1985), xiii.
2. For an excellent discussion of the antiprocreative bent in Russian symbolism, see Olga Matich, "The Symbolist Meaning of Love: Theory and Practice," in *Creating Life: The Aesthetic Utopia of Russian Modernism*, ed. Irina Paperno and Joan Delaney Grossman (Stanford, Calif.: Stanford University Press, 1994), 24-50.
3. Cited in *Russian Futurism through Its Manifestoes, 1912-1928*, trans. and ed. Anna Lawton and Herbert Eagle (Ithaca, N.Y.: Cornell University Press, 1988), 51.
4. Since I am concerned here with Blok's immediate reaction to the appearance of the acmeists on the Russian cultural scene, I am limiting my comments to his notebook and diary entries from 1913. In chapter 4, I discuss his later essay on acmeism, "Without Divinity, without Inspiration" ("Bez bozhestva, bez vdokhnoveniia") (April 1921).
5. Harold Bloom primarily examines the way in which poets react to their precursors, thereby privileging that part of the Oedipal myth that deals with the violence inflicted by the son on the father (*The Anxiety of Influence: A Theory of Poetry* [Oxford: Oxford University Press, 1973]). In this sense, Bloom remains faithful to Sigmund Freud. However, as Lillian Corti has shown, the entire Oedipal narrative was set into motion by the violence inflicted by the father on the son, since Oedipus's parents abandoned him to die, making it possible for him to unknowingly kill his father (*The Myth of Medea and the Murder of Children* [Westport, Conn.: Greenwood Press, 1998]). More recently, Barbara Johnson has

incorporated this repressed aspect of the Oedipal myth into a revised Bloomian model of the anxiety of influence, examining Baudelaire's reactions to the younger Mallarmé (Johnson, "Les Fleurs du Mal Armé: Some Reflections on Intertextuality," *A World of Difference* [Baltimore, MD: Johns Hopkins University Press, 1987], 116–33).

6. Bloom is by no means unique in his tendency to envision literary history as a generational struggle. The formalists, Yury Tynianov and Viktor Shklovsky, had adopted this idea years earlier, but they had a much more expansive sense of the generational tensions among writers than Bloom. Yury Tynianov, for instance, insisted that in the struggle between poetic fathers and their offspring, the sons end up "resembling their grandfathers more than the fathers who fought with them" (*Arkhaisty i novatory* [Ann Arbor, Mich.: Ardis, 1985], 562), while Shklovsky insisted that "in the history of art, the legacy is transmitted not from father to son, but from uncle to nephew" (quoted in Katerina Clark and Michael Holquist, *Mikhail Bakhtin* [Cambridge, Mass.: Harvard University Press, 1984], 192). For an excellent discussion of Tynianov's and Shklovsky's theories of generational strife as they relate to Mandelstam's modernist self-creation, see Clare Cavanagh, *Osip Mandelstam and the Modernist Creation of Tradition* (Princeton, N.J.: Princeton University Press, 1995), 10–13.

7. Vladimir Maiakovskii, "Oblako v shtanakh," *Polnoe sobranie sochinenii v trinadtsati tomakh*, 13 vols. (Moscow: Gos. izd-vo khudozhestvennoi lit-ry, 1955–61), 1:175.

8. Among the better-known acmeists, there were few childbirths. Anna Akhmatova and Nikolai Gumilev had one child. Osip Mandelstam and his wife, Nadezhda Mandelstam, had none.

9. Edward W. Said, *The World, the Text, and the Critic* (Cambridge, Mass.: Harvard University Press, 1983), 17.

10. Anna Akhmatova, "On liubil . . . ," *Sobranie sochinenii v shesti tomakh*, ed. N. V. Koroleva and S. A. Kovalenko, 6 vols. (Moscow: Ellis Lak, 1998–2005), 1:36.

11. In the opening poem of *The Path of the Conquistadors* (*Put' konkvistadorov*) (1905), Nikolai Gumilev figures his poetic persona as a conquistador and conqueror of exotic realms. The image of the poet as conqueror of the exotic can also be found in the works of the Konstantin Balmont and Théophile Gautier.

12. This does not mean, however, that prosaic details did not find their way into the poems of the symbolists. In Blok's "The Stranger" ("Neznakomka") (24 April 1906), we encounter the following prosaic scene: "In the distance, above the dust of the alley, above the boredom of the suburban dachas, the bakery pretzel turns slightly golden, and the cry of a child resonates" (Vdali, nad pyl'iu pereulochnoi, / Nad skukoi zagorodnykh dach, / Chut' zolotitsia krendel' bulochnoi, / I razdaetsia detskii plach) (*SS*, 2:185). On Blok's use of prosaic expressions, see Lidiia Ginzburg, "O prozaizmakh Bloka," in *Blokovskii sbornik: Nauchnaia konferentsiia, posviashchennaia izuchenniiu zhizni i tvorchestva A. A. Bloka*, 2 vols. (Tartu: Tartuskii gosudarstvenni universitet, 1964–72), 1:157–71.

13. Cited in Cavanagh, *Osip Mandelstam and the Modernist Creation of Tradition*, 51.

14. Adam figures prominently in Mandelstam's poem "Notre Dame" and

Sergei Gorodetsky's "Adam," which both appeared in the March 1913 issue of *Apollo* (*Apollon*).

15. Osip Mandelstam, "Morning of Acmeism," *The Complete Critical Prose and Letters*, ed. Jane Gary Harris, trans. Jane Gary Harris and Constance Link (Ann Arbor, Mich.: Ardis, 1979), 63; O. E. Mandel'shtam, "Utro akmeizma," *Sobranie sochinenii v chetyrekh tomakh*, ed. G. P. Struve and B. A. Filippov, 4 vols. (Moscow: Terra, 1991), 2:322.

16. Vladimir Orlov, "Istoriia odnoi liubvi," in *Puti i sud'by: Literaturnye ocherki* (Leningrad: Sovetskii pisatel', 1971), 636.

17. Dmitrii Maksimov, "Ideia puti v poeticheskom soznanii Al. Bloka," in *Poeziia i proza Al. Bloka* (Leningrad: Sovetskii pisatel', 1975), 6-143. For more on the notion of the path in Blok, see Lidiia Ginzburg, "Nasledie i otkrytiia," *O lirike* (Moscow: Intrada, 1997), 229-91; David A. Sloane, *Aleksandr Blok and the Dynamics of the Lyric Cycle* (Columbus, Ohio: Slavica, 1988); Duffield White, "Blok's Nechaiannaia radost'," *Slavic Review* 50, no. 4 (1991): 779-91; and Viktor Zhirmunskii, "Poeziia A. Bloka," *Voprosy teorii literatury: Stat'i 1916-1926* (The Hague: Mouton, 1962), 190-268.

18. On the importance of Baudelaire in Russian modernism, see Adrian Wanner, *Baudelaire in Russia* (Gainesville: University of Florida Press, 1996). On the themes of home and homelessness in nineteenth- and twentieth-century Russian prose, see Amy C. Singleton, *No Place Like Home: The Literary Artist and Russia's Search for Cultural Identity* (Albany: State University of New York Press, 1997).

19. The city is a predominant image in Blok's cycle *The City* (*Gorod*) (1904-8) and Valery Briusov's earlier *Urbi et orbi* (1903) as well as in the poetry of Charles Baudelaire and Emile Verhaeren.

20. Blok had equally laudatory things to say about other futurists at this time. He referred to Igor Severianin as "a real, fresh, childish talent" and "suspect[ed] that Velimir Khlebnikov [was] significant" and that Elena Guro was "worthy of attention" (*SS*, 7:232).

21. On etymology, see Max Vasmer, *Etimologicheskii slovar' russkogo iazyka: V chetyrekh tomakh*, 4 vols. (Moscow: 1986-87), 1:155.

22. Mandelstam, "Morning of Acmeism," 63; Mandel'shtam, "Utro akmeizma," 2:323.

23. Quoted in Roger Shattuck, *The Banquet Years: The Origins of the Avant-Garde in France, 1885 to World War I; Alfred Jarry, Henri Rousseau, Erik Satie, Guillaume Apollinaire* (New York: Vintage, 1968), 322. While I am not suggesting that Blok was ready to defect to the futurist camp, he did express the utmost respect at this particular time even for the most irreverent of the futurists' interpretations of their literary ancestors. As regards the modern legacy of Pushkin, for instance, he poses the question: "And what if they learned to *love* Pushkin again *in a new way*—not Briusov, Shchegolev, Morozov, etc., but the futurists. They abuse [braniat] him in a new way, and he grows closer *in a new way*" (ZK, 198). In a later essay, "On the Calling of the Poet" ("O naznachenii poeta") (10 February 1921), he would take on the futurists. "Today they erect monuments [to Pushkin]," he notes, "tomorrow they will want to throw him overboard from the ship of modernity" (*SS*, 6:161).

24. Boris Tomashevsky, "Literature and Biography," in *Readings in Russian Poetics: Formalist and Structuralist Views,* ed. Ladislav Matejka and Krystyna Pomorska (Ann Arbor: University of Michigan Press, 1978), 47-55.

25. Kornei Chukovsky, *Alexander Blok: As Man and Poet,* trans. Diana Burgin and Katherine O'Connor (Ann Arbor, Mich.: Ardis, 1982), 1-4.

26. Blok's collected works contain numerous autobiographical documents and sketches dating from 1897 to 1915. See *SS,* 7:429-36.

27. Not surprisingly, the issue of intertextuality has been central to Blok studies. See, for example, Z. G. Mints, *Aleksandr Blok i russkie pisateli,* intro. A. V. Lavrov and ed. L. L. Pil'd (St. Petersburg: Iskusstvo-SPB, 2000); Z. G. Mints, "Funktsiia reministsentsii v poetike Al. Bloka," *Poetika Aleksandra Bloka,* intro. V. N. Toporov (St. Petersburg: Iskusstvo-SPB, 1999), 362-88; Iu. Iasenskii, "Poetika reministsentsii v rannei lirike A. Bloka," in *Aleksandr Blok: Issledovaniia i materialy,* ed. V. N. Bystrov, Iu. K. Gerasimov, N. Iu Griakalova, and A. V. Lavrov (St. Petersburg: Izdatel'stvo Dmitrii Bulanin, 1998), 40-54; Lidiia Ginzburg, *O lirike,* 240-92; A. P. Avramenko, *A. Blok i russkie poety XIX veka* (Moscow: Izdatel'stvo Moskovskogo universiteta, 1990); Pavel Gromov, *A. Blok: Ego predshestvenniki i sovremenniki* (Leningrad: Sovetskii pisatel', 1986); and Z. G. Mints, "Poeticheskii ideal molodogo Bloka," in *Blokovskii sbornik,* 1:175-225. For a recent reconsideration of the symbolists' indebtedness to literary tradition, see Michael Wachtel, *Russian Symbolism and Literary Tradition: Goethe, Novalis, and the Poetics of Vyacheslav Ivanov* (Madison: University of Wisconsin Press, 1994).

28. Quoted in Avril Pyman, *The Life of Aleksandr Blok,* 2 vols. (Oxford: Oxford University Press, 1979-80), 2:17.

29. The notion that the period before the Fall may be viewed as childlike has been noted by the Russian religious philosopher Nikolai Fedorov. For an excellent discussion of Fedorov's philosophy and its link to prelapsarian childishness, see Irene Masing-Delic, *Abolishing Death: A Salvation Myth of Russian Twentieth-Century Literature* (Stanford, Calif.; Stanford University Press, 1992), 76-104.

30. Matich, "The Symbolist Meaning of Love," 25-26.

31. Orlov has treated Blok's relationship with his wife rather extensively in "Istoriia odnoi liubvi." Barbara Heldt and Lucy Vogel have both offered feminist readings of the relationship that focus on the complicated position of Blok's wife (Heldt, *Terrible Perfection: Women and Russian Literature* [Bloomington: Indiana University Press, 1987], 94-98; Vogel, "The Poet's Wife: Ljubov' Dmitrievna Mendeleeva," in *Aleksandr Blok Centennial Conference,* ed. Walter N. Vickery and Bogdan B. Sagatov [Columbus, Ohio: Slavica, 1984], 379-403]), while Dmitry Maksimov has examined the different world views and philosophical outlooks that Blok and Mendeleeva brought with them into their relationship (K. M. Azadovskii and A. V. Lavrov, eds., "Nezakonchennyi ocherk D. E. Maksimova," *Novoe literaturnoe obozrenie,* no. 35 [1999]: 250-80).

32. Lyubov Mendeleeva-Blok, "Facts and Myths about Blok and Myself," in *Blok: An Anthology of Essays and Memoirs,* trans. Lucy Vogel (Ann Arbor, Mich.: Ardis, 1982), 39-40; L. D. Blok, *I byl', i nebylitsy o Bloke i o sebe,* ed. L. Fleishman and I. Paulmann (Bremen: Verlag-K Presse, 1979), 51-52.

33. As Phyllis Rose has shown, nineteenth-century British literary and artistic

marriages often failed to conform to typical bourgeois marriages (or to live up to arguably post-Freudian expectations of marriage), as did of course many of the marriages of those associated with the Bloomsbury group in the twentieth century (*Parallel Lives: Five Victorian Marriages* [New York: Knopf, 1983]).

34. For a discussion of the impact that the nineteenth-century Russian religious philosophers theories of love had on the subsequent development of Russian modernism, see Eliot Borenstein, *Men without Women: Masculinity and Revolution in Russian Fiction, 1917–1929* (Durham, N.C.: Duke University Press, 2000); Eric Naiman, *Sex in Public: The Incarnation of Early Soviet Ideology* (Princeton, N.J.: Princeton University Press, 1997), esp. 27–44; Matich, "The Symbolist Meaning of Love"; Olga Matich, "Remaking the Bed: Utopia in Daily Life," in *Laboratory of Dreams: The Russian Avant-Garde and Cultural Experiment*, ed. John E. Bowlt and Olga Matich (Stanford, Calif.: Stanford University Press, 1996), 59–78; Olga Matich, "The Merezhkovskys' Third Testament and the Russian Utopian Tradition," in *Christianity and the Eastern Slavs*, vol. 2, ed. Robert P. Hughes and Irina Paperno (Berkeley: University of California Press, 1994), 158–71; Eric Naiman, "Historectomies: On the Metaphysics of Reproduction in a Utopian Age," in *Sexuality and the Body in Russian Culture*, ed. Jane T. Costlow, Stephanie Sandler, and Judith Vowles (Stanford, Calif.: Stanford University Press, 1993), 255–76; and Irene Masing-Delic, *Abolishing Death*.

35. There exists some debate as to whether Blok suffered from syphilis at any point in his life. Several scholars have gone on record as saying that he died of the disease. On Blok and syphilis, see Olga Matich, *Erotic Utopia: The Decadent Imagination in Russia's Fin de Siècle* (Madison: University of Wisconsin Press, 2005), 106, 108–9, and 117; Aleksandr Etkind, *Sodom i Psikheia: Ocherki intellektual'noi istorii Serebrianogo veka* (Moscow, ITs-Garant, 1996), 71; Pyman, *The Life of Aleksandr Blok*, 2:147; and G. Nivat, "Alexandre Blok," in *Histoire de la littérature russe. Le XX siècle: L'Âge d' Argent* (Paris: Fayard, 1987), 135, 150. At any rate, like Henrik Ibsen and Joris-Karl Huysmans before him, Blok would employ syphilis as a metaphor for social anxieties, most notably in his essay "Neither Dreams nor Reality" ("Ni sny, ni iav'") (19 March 1921), which he opens with a strange description of how their entire family was having tea in the countryside twenty years earlier and the peasants began to sing. "The peasants, who were singing," he notes, "brought syphilis from Moscow and spread it throughout all of the villages" (*SS*, 6:169). This theme of the singing peasants appears already in a notebook entry of 23 July 1902. And as I discuss in chapter 2, Blok imagined himself among syphilitics in a sketch for an unfinished play that he began working on in 1908 while awaiting the birth of his wife's child. On the difficulties of retrospectively diagnosing the syphilitic, see Deborah Hayden, *Pox: Genius, Madness, and the Mysteries of Syphilis* (New York: Basic Books, 2003).

36. For a discussion of the ways in which Blok's literary debut was constructed to foster the idea that he was the heir to Soloviev, see Samuel Cioran, *Vladimir Solov'ev and the Knighthood of the Divine Sophia* (Waterloo, Canada: Wilfrid Laurier University Press, 1977), 139–40.

37. For a fascinating discussion of the various ways in which Zinaida Gippius mythologized her marriage to Dmitry Merezhkovsky, see Matich, "The

Symbolist Meaning of Love," esp. 44-47; Olga Matich, "Zinaida Gippius: Theory and Praxis of Love," in *Kul'tura russkogo moderna: Stat'i i publikatstii v prinoshenie Vladimuru Fedorovichu Markovu*, ed. Ronald Vroon and John Malmstad (Moscow: Nauka, 1993), 237-51; and Olga Matich, "Dialectics of Personal Return: Zinaida Gippius' Personal Myth," in *Cultural Mythologies of Western Modernism: From the Golden Age to the Silver Age*, ed. Boris Gasparov, Robert P. Hughes, and Irina Paperno (Berkeley: University of California Press, 1992), 52-72.

38. Gippius was not unique in her resistance to Blok's marriage. As Matich points out, Andrei Bely and Sergei Soloviev also had a problem with the marriage (*Erotic Utopia*, 96).

39. Interestingly enough, Gippius does not discuss her attempts to dissuade Blok from marrying in her memoirs; instead, she indicates, not without a bit of irony, that "for me it was so clear, as if another person had spoken to me that entire evening about the coming wedding" (ZL, 19).

40. In an 1864 letter to Henri Cazalis, Mallarmé laments the way in which family life has affected his creative output: "So no letters, no poetry. And do not imagine that these duties are replaced by charming domestic bliss. No. I suffer too much when I feel unable to write to be able to enjoy anything and in fact I am determined not to take any pleasure in things so as to avoid believing that such pleasures are the ones I prefer and the very source of my guilt and sterility" (quoted in Gordon Millan, *A Throw of the Dice: The Life of Stéphane Mallarmé* [New York: Farrar, Straus, and Giroux, 1994], 113).

41. Robert Greer Cohn, *Toward the Poems of Mallarmé* (Berkeley: University of California Press, 1980), 288.

42. Charles Baudelaire, "Exotic Perfume" ("Parfum exotique"), *Selected Poems from* Les Fleurs du mal: *A Bilingual Edition*, trans. Norman R. Shapiro (Chicago: University of Chicago Press, 1998), 46-47.

43. Mallarmé, "Sea Breeze" ("Brise marine"), *Collected Poems*, 21; Baudelaire, "Exotic Perfume" ("Parfum exotique"), 46-47.

44. Henry Weinfield, commentary to Mallarmé, *Collected Poems*, 164.

45. Maiakovskii, "Uzhe vtoroi. Dolzhno byt' ty legla," *Polnoe sobranie sochinenii v trinadtsati tomakh*, 13:138.

46. For a consideration of the importance of Mallarmé to the Russian modernists, see Georgette Donchin, *The Influence of French Symbolism on Russian Poetry* (The Hague: Mouton, 1958), and Roman Dubrovkin, *Stefan Mallarme i Rossiia* (Bern: Peter Lang, 1998).

47. Another place where Mallarmé treats the conflict between everyday life and poetry is in his "Gift of the Poem" ("Don du poème"), which, like "Sea Breeze," was also composed shortly after the birth of his first child but was not published until 1883. For a fuller consideration of the ways in which this poem highlights the tensions between poetry and progeny, see chapter 3.

48. John E. Bowlt has suggested to me that Blok's reluctance to procreate may have stemmed from his identification with the artist Mikhail Vrubel, who had contracted syphilis and was believed to have passed it on to his child. The child, who was born with a harelip, died of meningitis in May 1903.

49. It bears noting that while Liubov Mendeleeva did not express any actual infanticidal fantasies, she did admit to an aversion to motherhood and

apparently came to a prenuptial agreement with Blok that their marriage should be childless. For more on Liubov Mendeleeva's difficulty with maternity, see my discussion in chapter 2.

50. In a particularly telling passage, Sergei wonders: "Why was the body of this child so carefully placed upon the seaweed? From where came this suckling with its waxen face? The warmth of its mother's hand was almost still upon it as could be seen by this scarf, the carefully tied white cloth, and the tiny socks upon its chubby feet. Sergei looked at the dead child and could not tear himself away; it seemed to him that at any moment it would open its eyes and stare at him and smile. From where came this child, so inhumanly sacrificed, arousing in him such poignant pity? From a wrecked ship? Thrown into the sea by a frenzied mother?" (Fyodor Gladkov, *Cement*, trans. A. S. Arthur and C. Ashleigh [Evanston, Ill.: Northwestern University Press, 1994], 301–2; Fedor Gladkov, *Tsement, Sobranie sochinenii v piati tomakh*, 5 vols. [Moscow: Khudozhestvennaia literatura, 1983–85], 1:509). On the antiprocreative tendencies in Russian art, literature, and culture of the 1920s, see Matich, "Remaking the Bed"; Naiman, *Sex in Public;* and Borenstein, *Men without Women*.

51. Roman Jakobson, "On a Generation That Squandered Its Poets," in *Major Soviet Writers: Essays in Criticism*, ed. Edward J. Brown (Oxford: Oxford University Press, 1973), 21. In New York in 1925, Mayakovsky had an affair with the Russian émigré Ellie Jones (née Elizaveta Alekseeva) that resulted in the birth of a daughter, Patricia J. Thompson. Mayakovsky is known to have seen his daughter only once in 1928 in Nice. In the spring of 2000, Thompson's trip to Moscow to visit her father's grave and monument produced quite a stir in the Russian media. For more on this event, see "The Week in Review" in *Russian Life Online* (19 April 2000) at http://www.rispubs.com/online/041900.cfm (accessed 9 November 2003). Although there exists a rumor that the writer Francine du Plessix Gray was the product of her mother Tatiana Iakovleva's affair with Mayakovsky, du Plessix Gray disputes this rumor. She notes: "There was a widespread rumor in the nineteen seventies [...] that I was Mayakovsky's daughter, a myth in part traceable to a memoir of Mayakovsky written by the poet's oldest friend, David Burliuk, when he was approaching eighty and may have been in his dotage. 'In December [1929] or January, 1930,' Burliuk alleges, 'Tatiana [...] gave birth to a girl who was Mayakovsky's daughter' (I was born in September, 1930, more than sixteen months after my mother's last parting with the poet)" (du Plessix Gray, "Mayakovsky's Last Loves," *The New Yorker*, 7 January 2002, 38–55.)

52. Vladimir Maiakovskii, "Neskol'ko slov o sebe samom," *Polnoe sobranie sochinenii v trinadtsati tomakh*, 1:48.

53. Members of other Russian avant-garde movements also had similar feelings about children. The Oberiu writer Daniil Kharms, for example, apparently evinced a dislike of children. According to his wife, Marina Durnovo, "his entire life he could not stand children. For him they were, ugh, some type of rubbish. His antipathy toward children approached hatred. And that hatred received an outlet in that which he did for children. But here is a paradox: hating them, he enjoyed insane success with them. They simply died of laughter when he performed for them" (Durnovo, *Moi muzh Daniil Kharms*, ed. Vladimir Glotser

[Moscow: B. S. G. Press, 2000], 72). I am grateful to Jamilya Nazyrova for bringing this passage to my attention.

54. It bears noting, though, that children occur very rarely in Gippius's poetry, and when they do they are sometimes imagined as the devil's progeny. See, for example, "His Daughter" ("Ego dochka") (1911) and "The Little Gray Dress" ("Seroe platitse") (1913).

55. On Gippius's transgressive gender identifications, see Olga Matich, "Gender Trouble in the Amazonian Kingdom: Turn-of-the-Century Representations of Women in Russia," in *Amazons of the Avant-Garde: Alexandra Exeter, Natalia Goncharova, Liubov Popova, Olga Rozanova, Varvara Stepanova, and Nadezhda Udaltsova*, ed. John E. Bowlt and Matthew Drutt (New York: Guggenheim Museum Publications, 2000), especially 77–82, as well as chapters 5–8.

56. On maternity in Western religious culture, see Marina Warner, *Alone of All Her Sex: The Myth and Cult of the Virgin Mary* (New York: Knopf, 1976). On the importance of the semiotics of maternity in Western modernism, see Jane Silverman Van Buren, *The Modernist Madonna: Semiotics of the Maternal Metaphor* (Bloomington: Indiana University Press, 1989).

57. Julia Kristeva, "Stabat Mater," *The Kristeva Reader*, ed. Toril Moi (New York: Columbia University Press, 1986), 161.

58. Barbara Johnson, "Apostrophe, Animation, and Abortion," *A World of Difference* (Baltimore, M.D.: Johns Hopkins University Press, 1987], 197–98.

59. David M. Bethea, *Joseph Brodsky and the Creation of Exile* (Princeton, N.J.: Princeton University Press, 1994), 184. Recently, Alyssa W. Dinega has challenged this reading of Tsvetaeva's "On the Red Steed," arguing that "it is plausible that in Tsvetaeva's mind (perhaps subconsciously) there is a link between fact and fiction here; however, it seems to me unfair to suggest that poetic hindsight (which, in this case, may create a bearable narrative out of an unbearable fact) is at all the same thing as malice aforethought (apropos of Bethea's reference to Lady Macbeth)" (*A Russian Psyche: The Poetic Mind of Marina Tsvetaeva* [Madison: University of Wisconsin Press, 2001], 79).

60. It is also worth noting that the futurist Elena Guro apparently suffered from her own childlessness. She fostered the myth that she had a son who died and reportedly even wrote works for this child. This led to the belief among some of her contemporaries that her artistic output was fueled, in part, by her grief for a dead child. According to Viktor Kamensky, "Elena Guro did not believe in the death of her son and imagined and convinced herself that her son was still alive and that he continued to live around her. And Elena Guro counted the days, weeks, months of her child, saw him growing each minute; she bought him toys, and put poems for him on his little desk, wrote fairy tales for him, and told him stories. Furthermore, she painted his portrait, dressing him in clothes that were appropriate to his age" (quoted in Aleksandr Ocheretianskii, Gerald Janacek, and Vadim Kreid, eds., *Zabytyi avangard: Rossiia pervaia tret' XX stoletiia*, bk. 2 [St. Petersburg: n.p., 1993], 37).

61. Stephanie Sandler, "Embodied Words: Gender in Tsvetaeva's Reading of Pushkin," *Slavic and East European Journal* 34, no. 1 (1990): 150. More recently, Catherine Ciepiela has taken on the critical commonplace that Marina Tsvetaeva

was a good poet but a bad mother, focusing on the ways in which this misunderstanding derived, in part, from a misreading of Tsvetaeva's complicated use of apostrophe in her poetry ("The Demanding Woman Poet: On Resisting Marina Tsvetaeva," *PMLA* 111, no. 3 [1996]: 421-34).

62. Bloom's indebtedness to the romantics and Percy Bysshe Shelley in particular has been duly noted. David M. Bethea, for example, subtitles his critique of Bloom "the critic as romantic poet" and locates "the primary shortcoming in the Bloomian model ('revisionary ratios') as applied to Pushkin in the urge to place poets in a critical narrative in which they struggle with one another over the primacy, which is the same as authenticity, of their words [and to neglect] to imagine a time in which authorship was not romantic, oedipal, exclusively *word-worshiping*" (*Realizing Metaphors: Alexander Pushkin and the Life of the Poet* [Madison: University of Wisconsin Press, 1999], 78).

63. It is important to point out that European romanticism emerged in the wake of the French Revolution—a conflict that was imagined in distinctly domestic terms. For more on the ways in which the French Revolution was configured as family strife, see Lynn Hunt, *The Family Romance of the French Revolution* (Berkeley: University of California Press, 1992).

64. Caryl Emerson, *Boris Godunov: Transpositions of A Russian Theme* (Bloomington: Indiana University Press, 1986), 104. Stephanie Sandler has persuasively shown that "the death of the Tsarevich becomes the subject of four narratives in the course of *Boris Godunov*. Each of these stories [...] rejects dramatic conflict for an intensely remembered sequence of events. *Boris Godunov* takes refuge from its frustrations as drama in a tendency toward narrative; the play is singularly fascinated with the death of Dmitri the Tsarevich in Uglich" (*Distant Pleasures: Alexander Pushkin and the Writing of Exile* [Stanford, Calif.: Stanford University Press, 1989], 109-10).

65. Dmitry Merezhkovsky also took up the theme of filicide in his historical novel *The Antichrist: Peter and Alexis*.

66. I am grateful to Kirill Postoutenko for suggesting that I take a closer look at Pasternak's "Suboctave Story" in connection to the antiprocreative tendencies within Russian modernism.

67. Boris Pasternak, "Suboctave Story," *The Voice of Prose*, trans. Christopher Barnes (New York: Grove, 1986), 137; Boris Pasternak, "Istoriia odnoi kontroktavy," *Sobranie sochinenii v piati tomakh*, 5 vols. (Moscow: Khudozhestvennaia literatura, 1989-92), 4:449.

68. In his discussion of "Suboctave Story," Lazar Fleishman suggests that "a partial explanation of the parental theme [...] can be found in the fact that Leonid Pasternak had profound misgivings about Boris' decadent predilections in poetry and art; noticeable differences in taste begin to emerge around 1910, and the father disapproved of his son's creative tendencies" (*Boris Pasternak: The Poet and His Politics* [Cambridge, Mass.: Harvard University Press, 1990], 14).

69. Boris Pasternak, *Doctor Zhivago*, trans. Max Hayward and Manya Harari (New York: Pantheon, 1991), 284; Boris Pasternak, *Doktor Zhivago, Sobranie sochinenii v piati tomakh*, 3:282.

70. For a very fine discussion Pasternak's homage to Blok in *Doctor Zhivago*,

see Irene Masing-Delic, "Zhivago's 'Christmas Star' as Homage to Blok," in *Aleksandr Blok Centennial Conference*, ed. Walter N. Vickery and Bogdan B. Sagatov (Columbus, Ohio: Slavica, 1984), 207-24.

71. Blok dedicated numerous poems to his mother, including several poems entitled "To My Mother" ("Moei materi") (1898, 1899, 1901, 1904, 1905), "I am a human, hardly an equal to God" ("Ia—chelovek i malo Bogu raven'") (1899), "Son and Mother" ("Syn i mat'") (1906), "I planted my bright paradise" ("Ia nasadil moi svetlyi rai") (1907), "Having enjoyed myself at the wild feast" ("Poveselias' na buinom pire") (1912), "Dream" ("Son") (1910), and "The wind abated, and the sunset's fame" ("Veter stix, i slava zarevaia") (1914).

72. On the importance of death in Mayakovsky's poetic myth, see Roman Jakobson, "On a Generation That Squandered Its Poets," 7-32, and Svetlana Boym, *Death in Quotation Marks: Cultural Myths of the Modern Poet* (Cambridge, Mass.: Harvard University Press, 1991), 120-70.

73. Recently, Charles Nicholl has revealed Rimbaud to have been much more domestic than was previously thought, finding evidence that he cohabitated with a woman while in Africa (*Somebody Else: Arthur Rimbaud in Africa, 1880-91* [Chicago: University of Chicago Press, 1999]).

74. Pyman, *The Life of Aleksandr Blok*, 1:68-69.

75. Jakobson, "On a Generation That Squandered Its Poets," 21.

Chapter 2. Recurring Nightmares

Epigraphs to chapter 2: Leo Tolstoy, *Anna Karenina*, trans. Louise and Aylmer Maude, rev. George Gibian, 2nd ed. (New York: Norton, 1995), 577; L. N. Tolstoi, *Anna Karenina, Sobranie sochinenii v dvenadtsati tomakh*, 12 vols. (Moscow: Khudozhestvennaia literatura, 1958-59), 9:227; Valerii Briusov, "Medeia," *Sobranie sochinenii v semi tomakh*, ed. P. G. Antogol'skii et al., 7 vols. (Moscow: Khudozhestvennaia literatura, 1973-75), 3:387; and Aleksandr Blok, "Povest'," *SS*, 2:163.

1. On Bely and the myth of the Bronze Horseman, see E. G. Mel'nikova, M. V. Bezrodnyi, and V. M. Papernyi, "Mednyi vsadnik v kontekste skul'pturnoi simvoliki romana Andreia Belogo 'Peterburg,'" *Blokovskii sbornik* 6 (1985): 85-92.

2. By this time, Blok was already familiar with an early version of Dmitry Merezhkovsky's *The Antichrist: Peter and Alexis*. This text apparently had a negative impact on him. In a 1902 letter to his father, Blok writes: "Poor D. S. Merezhkovsky read to me a few days ago from a chapter of his new novel *Peter and Alexis*. Many have 'a cold white day' in their soul, and I often sense it—as well as the limitlessness of my own 'snakelike' cognition" (*SS*, 8:47-48).

3. For a recent consideration of Bely's own mother complex, see Monika Spivak, "Andrei Belyi, sem' ego vozliublennykh i odna mat'," in *Erotizm bez granits*, ed. M. M. Pavlova (Moscow: Novoe literaturnoe obozrenie, 1994), 208-41.

4. With this statement, Blok enacts a gender shift on the conventional Chronos myth, whereby, in Sigmund Freud's retelling, "Kronos devoured his children, just as the wild boar devours the sow's litter" (*The Interpretation of Dreams*,

The Standard Edition of the Complete Psychological Works of Sigmund Freud, trans. James Strachey, 24 vols. [London: Hogarth Press, 1953–74], 4:256).

5. For a more extensive discussion of Blok and Gogol, see: Z. G. Mints, "Blok i Gogol'," *Aleksandr Blok i russkie pisateli*, intro. A. V. Lavrov and ed. L. L. Pil'd (St. Petersburg: Iskusstvo-SPB, 2000), 22–85, and I. T. Kruk, "Blok i Gogol'," *Russkaia literatura*, no. 1 (1961): 85–101.

6. A fairy tale-like atmosphere, complete with dwarves, wizards, little devils, and little priests, permeates Blok's poetry during this period, particularly his cycles *Bubbles of the Earth* (*Puzyri zemli*) (1904–5) and *The City* (*Gorod*) (1904–8). See, for example, "Little Swamp Devils" ("Bolotnye cherteniatki") (January 1905), "The Little Swamp Priest" ("Bolotnyi popik") (17 April 1905), "On the spring path to the terem" ("Na vesennem puti v teremok") (24 April 1905), "The swamp is a deep hollow" ("Boloto—glubokaia vpadina") (3 June 1905), and "The Old Woman and the Little Devils" ("Starushka i cherteniata") (July 1905) in *Bubbles of the Earth* as well as the city poems "Illusion" ("Obman") (5 March 1904) and "In taverns, side streets, and bends of the road" ("V kabakakh, v pereulkakh, v izvivakh") (December 1904), and the individual poems "In shaggy and terrible paws" (V lapakh kosmatykh i strashnykh) (August 1905) and "I passed by the crimson sunset" ("Ia minoval zakat bagrianyi") (February 1908).

7. Kornei Chukovsky, *Alexander Blok: As Man and Poet*, trans. and ed. Diana Burgin and Katherine O'Connor (Ann Arbor, Mich.: Ardis, 1982), 54. It would appear that on revising the poem Blok did so in a fashion that reinforced the poem's vagueness and called into greater question the mother's complicity in the child's death. In the original fifth stanza of the poem, the mother appears as a more ominous figure capable of witchcraft and sorcery. The stanza reads: "And you stand, barely noticeable, guarding a dream or practicing sorcery? Above the child, dawnless quiet lowered itself" (I stoish', edva zametnaia, / Son bliudesh' il' vorozhish'? / Nad rebenkom, bezrassvetnaia, / Opustilas' nizko tish') (*SS*, 2:402).

8. Blok apparently also read the poem at Viacheslav Ivanov's Wednesday salon and Fedor Sologub's Sunday salon, as he lists it among poems "for reading at the Wednesdays and Sundays" in his notebook entry of 18 January 1906 (*ZK*, 74).

9. Nataliia Volokhova, "Zemlia v snegu," *Uchenye zapiski Tartuskogo gosudarstvennogo universiteta: Trudy po russkoi i slavianskoi filologii* 4 (1961): 372.

10. V. P. Verigina, "Vospominaniia ob Aleksandre Bloke," in *Aleksandr Blok v vospominaniiakh sovremennikov v dvukh tomakh*, 2 vols. (Moscow: Khudozhestvennaia literatura, 1980), 1:412–13. For an account of some of the other interactions Blok had with contemporaries about the meaning of this poem, see A. A. Blok, *Polnoe sobranie sochinenii i pisem v dvadtsati tomakh*, ed. M. L. Gasparov et al., vols. 1–5 and 7 to date (Moscow: Nauka, 1997–), 2:652–53.

11. While I do not want to suggest that Blok was not aware of the social reality of infanticide in Russia, it is my claim that he uses filicide primarily as a trope for revolution in his works of this period. For a historical account of infanticide in Russia, see Laura Engelstein, *The Keys to Happiness: Sex and the Search for Modernity in Fin-de-Siècle Russia* (Ithaca, N.Y.: Cornell University Press, 2000),

106–14, and David L. Ransel, *Mothers of Misery: Child Abandonment in Russia* (Princeton, N.J.: Princeton University Press, 1988), 8–31.

12. Sologub shared with Blok a tendency to depict children in a very disturbing way in both his poetry and prose. For more on this phenomenon, see Stanley Rabinowitz, *Sologub's Literary Children: Keys to a Symbolist's Prose* (Columbus, Ohio: Slavica, 1980).

13. For more on Dostoevsky's importance for Blok, see Z. G. Mints, "Blok i Dostoevskii," *Aleksandr Blok i russkie pisateli*, 86–112. On the *Poor Folk* subtext in "In October" and in other Blok texts from this same period, see Mints, "Blok i Dostoevskii," 101–2.

14. Roman Jakobson, "The Statue in Puškin's Poetic Mythology," *Puškin and His Sculptural Myth*, trans. and ed. John Burbank (The Hague: Mouton, 1975), 41. Recently, David M. Bethea has criticized Jakobson's insistence that in Pushkin the statue is always an ominous male figure associated with the act of vengeance, indicating that there is a "missing second element in Pushkin's intricately realized sculptural metaphor, what we have been referring to elsewhere as his 'Pygmalion myth': it is both what the stone will do to him (it will come to him as his death) and what it will do *for* him (it will bring him back to life even as he seems to be the one doing the touching and the creating)" (*Realizing Metaphors: Alexander Pushkin and the Life of the Poet* [Madison: University of Wisconsin Press, 1998], 107). Irene Masing-Delic has also touched on the importance of the Pygmalion myth for Pushkin and the Russian romantics in her discussion of the symbolist Pygmalion ("Creating the Living Work of Art: The Symbolist Pygmalion and His Antecedents," in *Creating Life: The Aesthetic Utopia of Russian Modernism*, ed. Irina Paperno and Joan Delaney Grossman [Stanford, Calif.: Stanford University Press, 1994], 51–82).

15. Adrian Wanner, "Aleksandr Blok's Sculptural Myth," *Slavic and East European Journal* 40, no. 2 (1996): 236–50. Wanner departs considerably from Jakobson in his discussion of Blok's sculptural myth in that he deals with both male and female statues that come to life or, in many cases, remain dead and lifeless, and, hence, he deals with the aspect of the female statue that Bethea sees as lacking in Jakobson's discussion of the Pushkinian sculptural myth. Wanner also discusses the largely androgynous or, more accurately, hybrid statue of the sphinx. More recently, Aleksandr Etkind has addressed the importance of the animated sphinx in the Russian modernist context generally ("Ozhivaiushchii sfinks: Mistika Zolotogo veka v mifologii Serebrianogo," *Sodom i Psikheia: Ocherki intellektual'noi istorii Serebrianogo veka* (Moscow: ITs-Garant, 1996), 140–213).

16. Jakobson insists that in Pushkin "the animated statue, in contrast to a spectre, is an instrument of evil magic, it bears destruction, and it is never the embodiment of woman" ("The Statue in Puškin's Poetic Mythology," 41). Though Jakobson seems to contradict himself here, since he does discuss at length the importance of the figure of the "bronze grandmother" (i.e., the Goncharovs' bronze statue of Catherine) to Pushkin's fate, I follow his logic in insisting that for Blok, at least, the ghost is markedly feminine, and this feminine figure, unlike the Pushkinian statue, is a much more fluid figure bearing responsibility for both creativity and destruction. In so doing, I do not mean to imply that this male/female and statue/shade distinction is universal. As

Tomas Venclova has perceptively shown, Fedor Sologub and Innokenty Annensky differ in their revisions of the myth of Protesilaus and Laodameia in their reliance on the male shade and statue, respectively ("Shade and Statue: A Comparative Analysis of Fedor Sologub and Innokentii Annenskii," *Russian Review* 53, no. 1 [1994]: 9-21).

17. Chukovsky, *Alexander Blok*, 3. I am by no means the only scholar to suggest that Blok's particularly close relationship with his mother was central to his poetic myth. Recently Alexis Eugene Emerson has suggested that Blok's complicated relationship with the feminine in his early poetry heralded from his close relationship to his mother and the absence of a strong paternal figure. For a more extensive discussion of Blok's psychic and creative investment in the mother figure, see Emerson, "Aleksandr Blok and the Mother-Figure" (Ph.D. diss., University of California, Berkeley, 1990).

18. Regina B. Thompson, "*Die Ahnfrau* by Franz Grillparzer and *Pramater'* by Aleksandr Blok," *Germano-Slavica* 1, no. 1 (1973): 45-64, and Edmund Hier, "Grillparzers *Ahnfrau* in Russland: A. Blok," *Comparative Literature* 23, no. 3 (1971): 193-208.

19. On the relationship of Grillparzer's text to Blok's notions of the aristocracy and of history, see Mints, *Aleksandr Blok i russkie pisateli*, 206, 208, 514, and 692.

20. As Blok mentions in his 1918 essay on the play, the 1830 production was based on a translation by Obodevsky entitled *Praroditel'nitsa* (*SS*, 4:293).

21. I have found no direct mention of Freud in the Soviet edition of Blok's collected works. However, Blok's wife does mention Freudian psychology in her memoirs (Lyubov Mendeleeva-Blok, "Facts and Myths about Blok and Myself," in *Blok: An Anthology of Essays and Memoirs*, trans. Lucy Vogel [Ann Arbor, Mich.: Ardis, 1982], 8-63; L. D. Blok, *I byl', i nebylitsy o Bloke i o sebe*, ed. L. Fleishman and I. Paulmann [Bremen: Verlag-K Presse, 1979]). In his study on psychoanalysis in Russia, Aleksandr Etkind makes the argument that, while they were not directly influenced by psychoanalysis, the Russian symbolists engaged in a discussion of the psyche and of sexuality that, in some ways, approximated that of psychoanalysis (*Eros of the Impossible: The History of Psychoanalysis in Russia*, trans. Noah Rubins and Maria Rubins [Boulder, Colo.: Westview Press, 1997]). For a more detailed account of the development of psychoanalysis in Russia during the first part of the twentieth century, see Etkind, *Eros of the Impossible*, 108-32, and Magnus Ljunggren, "The Psychoanalytic Breakthrough in Russia on the Eve of the First World War," in *Russian Literature and Psychoanalysis*, ed. Daniel Rancour-Laferriere (Philadelphia: John Benjamins, 1989), 173-92.

22. Chukovsky, *Alexander Blok*, 54.

23. Considerably later, Blok makes mention of Grillparzer's *Medea* in his "Zelinsky's Foreward and Notes to Grillparzer" ("Predislovie i primechaniia Zelinskogo k Gril'partseru"). At this time, Blok was, of course, familiar with Corneille's version of *Medea* via Briusov's poem "Medea." Blok comments on this poem briefly and rather negatively in his letter of 21 October 1904 to Sergei Soloviev (*SS*, 8:109-11).

24. Freud, *The Interpretation of Dreams*, 4:262.

25. Sarah Kofman, *The Enigma of Woman: Woman in Freud's Writings*, trans.

Catherine Porter (Ithaca, N.Y.: Cornell University Press, 1985), 28. In his letter to Fliess of 15 October 1897, Freud made very similar judgments on the play; however, in this letter, as opposed to in *The Interpretation of Dreams*, he embeds his comments on the play within a discussion of a dream about his mother, nanny, and sister Anna. Though this certainly has interesting implications for Freud's own personal mythology, an in-depth analysis of the role of this play in Freud's personal mythology does not fall within the purview of this study.

26. It bears noting that there has been a tendency among Blok's contemporaries to idealize his relationship with his mother. Chukovsky, for instance, notes: "Blok was on friendly terms with his remarkable mother, Alexandra Andreevna, up until his death, and he lived through most of the events of her inner life with her, as if the umbilical cord that joined mother and son had never been cut" (*Alexander Blok*, 4). Blok's aunt, M. A. Beketova, also reinforces this myth in her memoirs about Blok and his mother ("Aleksandr Blok i ego Mat'," *Vospominaniia ob Aleksandre Bloke* [Moscow: Pravda, 1990], 205–346). Though Blok did remain extremely close to his mother throughout his life, the relationship was apparently not always harmonious. In her memoirs, "Facts and Myths about Blok and Myself," Liubov Mendeleeva makes ample reference to the fact that Aleksandra Andreevna's bouts with what was diagnosed as neurasthenia often made life between them rather difficult.

27. C. G. Jung, *The Archetypes and the Collective Unconscious*, trans. R. F. C. Hull (Princeton, N.J.: Princeton University Press, 1959), 82. Erich Neumann also acknowledges the ambivalent nature of the mother in his discussion of ancient archetypes (*The Great Mother: An Analysis of the Archetype*, trans. Ralph Manheim [Princeton, N.J.: Princeton University Press, 1963]), as does Melanie Klein in her work on the child's fantasies in the pre-Oedipal period (*The Selected Melanie Klein*, ed. Juliet Mitchell [New York: Free Press, 1986]).

28. It is worth mentioning that in "The Soul of the Writer" ("Dusha pisatelia") (February 1909), an essay Blok wrote in this same period, he puts forth the notion that the task of the writer is to give voice to what he terms the "collective soul," thereby employing a term that sounds remarkably similar to Jung's idea of the collective unconscious. "It is not even the word, not even the voice," Blok writes, "but the light breath of the soul of the people [legkoe dunovenie dushi narodnoi], not of individual souls, but precisely of the collective soul [kollektivnaia dusha]" (*SS*, 5:367).

29. The figure of the Stranger is repeatedly associated with the veil in Blok's poetry. In "The Stranger," Blok writes: "And shackled by a strange nearness, I look beyond the dark veil" (I strannoi blizost'iu zakovannyi, / Smotriu za temnuiu vual') (*SS*, 2:186). And Blok once again associates the unknown lady with the veil in "There the women parade their fashions" ("Tam damy shchegoliaiut modami") (April 1906–April 1911), which directly follows "The Stranger" in his city cycle. Here we read: "Beyond the thick beer mugs, beyond the dream of the usual bustle, through a veil, covered in black specks, show eyes and fine features" (Za tolstymi pivnymi krushkami, / Za snom privychnoi suety / Skvozit vual', pokrytyi mushkami, / Glaza i melkie cherty) (*SS*, 2:187).

30. The connection between mimesis and social disorder is very much entrenched in Western culture and can be traced back to Plato. As Christopher

Prendergast observes, "the real worry [about mimesis] is initially (certainly the initial worry in the chronology of the *Republic*) less metaphysical than political; less an anxiety about duplicity than about duplication, or less a question of truth than of taxonomy. For what is at risk in the potentially uncontrollable proliferation of 'images,' the endless play of representations made possible by mimesis, is a proper sense of 'division' and classification. Through his doublings and multiplications, the mimetic artist introduces 'improprieties' (a 'poison') into a social system ordered according to the rule that everything and everyone should be in its/his/her 'proper' place" (*The Order of Mimesis: Balzac, Stendhal, Nerval, Flaubert* [Cambridge: Cambridge University Press, 1986], 10).

31. This act in the play would seem to anticipate Blok's poem "Dream" ("Son") (20 June 1910), which he dedicated to his mother. In this poem, the poet envisions himself in an ancient tomb alongside his mother. As the first stanza reads: "I had a dream: we are buried in an ancient crypt; but life goes on. Above it gets louder and more absurd, and the day of reckoning approaches" (Ia videl son: my v drevnem sklepe / Skhoroneny; a zhizn' idet / Vverkhu — vsë gromche, vsë nelepei; / I den' poslednii nastaet) (*SS*, 3:134).

32. In this regard, I concur with Samuel D. Cioran, who notes "the mood of ecstatic expectation and revelation is tempered by that skepticism of which Blok wrote Belyi in later years but which was ignored by many critics in his early poems" (*Vladimir Solov'ev and the Knighthood of the Divine Sophia* [Waterloo, Canada: Wilfred Laurier University Press, 1977], 141).

33. O. E. Mandel'shtam, "Bessonnitsa. Gomer. Tugie parusa," *Sobranie sochinenii v chetyrekh tomakh*, ed. G. P. Struve and B. A. Filippov, 4 vols. (Moscow: Terra, 1991), 1:49.

34. Andrei Bely, cited in *BBB*, 154. The figure of Pani Katerina would also be important for the next generation of Russian modernists. For consideration of the way in which it informed the poetics of Pasternak, see Irene Masing-Delic, "Gothic Historiography: The Pani Katerina Story in Pasternak's *Doctor Zhivago*," *Die Welt Der Slaven* 47, no. 2 (2002): 359–80.

35. On the figure of the sleeping beauty in Blok's creative mythology, see, for example, Rosamund Bartlett, "Wagner and the Russian Symbolists: Aleksandr Blok," *Wagner and Russia* (Cambridge: Cambridge University Press, 1995), 204–5; Avril Pyman, *The Life of Aleksandr Blok*, 2 vols. (Oxford: Oxford University Press, 1979–80) 1:212; and N. V. Kotrelev and Z. G. Mints, "Blok v neizdannoi perepiske i dnevnikakh sovremennikov," *Literaturnoe nasledstvo* 92, no. 5 (1982): 157. On the importance of the sleeping beauty motif within the larger twentieth-century cultural context, see Ellen Rutten, "Fighting for Princess Russia: The Politicization of Dragon-Slayer and Sleeping Beauty Motifs in Twentieth-Century Russian Literature," in *Perspectives on Slavic Literatures*, ed. Kris van Heuckelom and David Danaher, Oost-Europese Studies 6 (Amsterdam: Pegasus, 2007), 27–60.

36. Mendeleeva-Blok, "Facts and Myths about Blok and Myself," 48; L. D. Blok, *I byl', i nebilitsy o Bloke i o sebe*, 64. Apparently this abhorrence of motherhood was not uncommon among female modernists. Olga Matich notes that "Lilia Brik apparently had an aversion to childbirth. I was told by a male acquaintance of hers that she was repulsed by the appearance of his pregnant

wife, whom she liked otherwise" (Matich, "Remaking the Bed: Utopia in Daily Life," in *Laboratory of Dreams: The Russian Avant-Garde and Cultural Experiment*, ed. John E. Bowlt and Olga Matich [Stanford, Calif.: Stanford University Press, 1996], 68). Similarly, Nadya L. Peterson states that "the body can and should liberate one, in [Nina] Berberova's view, but it can also enslave. The only time in Berberova's life that she ever contemplated committing suicide was when she thought she was pregnant" ("The Private 'I' in the Works of Nina Berberova," *Slavic Review* 60, no. 3 [2001]: 500).

37. Mendeleeva-Blok, "Facts and Myths about Blok and Myself," 48; L. D. Blok, *I byl', i nebilitsy o Bloke i o sebe*, 64.

38. Mendeleeva-Blok, "Facts and Myths about Blok and Myself," 49; L. D. Blok, *I byl', i nebilitsy o Bloke i o sebe*, 66.

39. On 12 November 1908 Liuba wrote to Blok's mother imploring her to help them keep this secret: "Sasha still wishes that I should not tell even Mama of all the bitterness connected with him. It was one of the difficult questions for me—to find out the truth, to find a way to act with real simplicity, integrity, without defiance or anything forced. I think Sasha is right. Why should others know about something that they will never understand, and to humiliate and punish myself would be at least half a form of defiance and unnaturalness. I want everything to be as Sasha decides. Let those who know about my misfortune in connection with the child know, and as for the others—he will simply be *ours*. I beg of you, if you can without loss of your own integrity, speak of it as we do. . . . There is no point, now that he is to be ours, in keeping quiet about the nearness of the birth of the child, and for that matter no one who saw me could help noticing, but to let all the relations know—why should we? It is still painful for me to talk about it all, and if outsiders begin to speak of it, oh Lord! The more chance I am given to get used to it, the better and more simply shall I be able to cope, and you and Auntie do want to help me, don't you? I shan't be able to talk to Sasha's aunt, so please will you write? (quoted in Pyman, *The Life of Aleksandr Blok*, 2:17–18).

40. This is true, for instance, of the representation of Helen in W. B. Yeats's poetry.

41. This would not be the only place were Blok would give expression to syphilitic anxiety dreams. He would also do so "Neither Dreams nor Reality" ("Ni sni, ni iav'") (19 March 1921), an essay I discuss in some detail in chapter 3. Avril Pyman suggests, though, that it was not until January 1912 that Blok had a severe outbreak of syphilis and was treated for the disease (Pyman, *The Life of Aleksandr Blok*, 2:147).

42. On opening night, the following actors played the main roles: A. P. Nelidov (Count Borotin), E. L. Shilovskaia (Bertha), A. N. Feona (Jaromir), A. A. Mgebrov (Günther). Kommissarzhevskaia played the lead role of Bertha only once in September of 1909 for a performance in Moscow.

43. Viktor Zhirmunskii, "Poeziia A. Bloka," in *Voprosy teorii literatury: Stat'i 1916–1926* (The Hague: Mouton, 1962), 191. Boris Tomashevsky also comments that "it would be inaccurate to say that Blok put his life on display" ("Literature and Biography," in *Readings in Russian Poetics: Formalist and Structuralist*

Views, ed. Ladislav Matejka and Krystyna Pomorska [Ann Arbor: University of Michigan Press, 1978], 54).

44. According to the footnote appended to this entry in Blok's notebook, the phrase in brackets in this passage in Blok's notebook is crossed out and marked with the note, "'Rubbish!'" ("Vzdor!") (*ZK*, 130).

45. Pyman, *The Life of Aleksandr Blok*, 2:37. Although Pyman does not bring up this point, Blok had perhaps already implicitly identified with the historical figure of Dmitry Donskoi in the poems comprising *On the Field of Kulikova* (*Na Pole Kulikovom*), which he completed in June, July, and December 1908.

46. Tolstoy, *Anna Karenina*, 88; Tolstoi, *Anna Karenina*, 8:111.

47. I have found no references to Grillparzer in Lev Tolstoy's complete collected works, and I do not mean to imply that Tolstoy was somehow influenced by *Die Ahnfrau* in portraying Anna as an ambivalent mother to her second child. Tolstoy was, of course, most influenced by Gustave Flaubert's portrayal of Emma as a reluctant mother in *Madame Bovary*. And in a more general way, as Amy Mandelker has shown, the figures of the shadow and of Psyche are central to Tolstoy's characterization of Anna (*Framing* Anna Karenina: *Tolstoy, the Woman Question, and the Victorian Novel* [Columbus: Ohio State University Press, 1993], 141–62).

48. M.A. Beketova, *Vospominaniia ob Aleksandre Bloke*, ed. V. P. Enishlerov and S. S. Lesnevskii (Moscow: Pravda, 1990), 613.

49. While one should be careful about how much credence one gives to Gippius's memoirs, or for that matter those of any other of Blok's contemporaries, it bears noting that Blok's aunt gives a remarkably similar account of Blok's reaction. She notes that "he came to terms with the death. Perhaps it is good that the uninvited little one died" (Beketova, *Vospominaniia ob Aleksandre Bloke*, 613).

50. Konstantin Mochulsky, *Aleksandr Blok,* trans. Doris V. Johnson (Detroit, Mich.: Wayne State University Press, 1983), 239.

51. Vladimir Orlov observes that "in the draft [the poem] is dated 2 March 1909. The date shown in the text, 'February 1909,' signifies the time of the death of L. D. Blok's son, Dmitry, who lived all of eight days (2–10 February 1909)" (Orlov, notes, *SS*, 3:518).

52. On Gogol's disavowal of love and procreation, see Hugh McLean, "Gogol's Retreat from Love: Toward an Interpretation of *Mirgorod*," in *Russian Literature and Psychoanalysis*, ed. Daniel Rancour-Laferriere (Amsterdam: John Benjamins Publishing, 1989), 101–22. And for a consideration of Gogol's possible homosexuality, see Simon Karlinsky, *The Sexual Labyrinth of Nikolai Gogol* (Cambridge, Mass.: Harvard University Press, 1976).

53. The term "couvade" refers to male sympathetic pregnancy. As Felix J. Oinas notes in his discussion of cultural practices in Estonia, "couvade (from the French couver 'to hatch') designates a series of [. . .] customs connected with childbirth. The father, who occasionally reveals symptoms of childbearing (such as nausea, vomiting, lassitude) would take to bed at or before birth, pretending to be lying-in, and by groans and cries would simulate the pains of labor. In this way, he believes he lessens his wife's pains by sharing them. The husband's assistance may end with the birth of the child, or it may also continue some time

longer. While remaining in bed, he pretends to nurse the baby and is himself pampered and fed on dainties by his wife" ("Couvade in Estonia," *Slavic and East European Journal* 37, no. 3 [1993]: 340).

54. Fantasies about male childbirth abound in the avant-garde, particularly in the works of the futurists. In F. T. Marinetti's *Mafarka, the Futurist: An African Novel*, which appeared in French in 1909 and in Italian a year later, the hero, who for a large part of the novel eschews the company of women first to do battle and then to pay homage to his dead brother, dreams of giving birth to a male child named Gazourmah without the aid of woman. At the novel's end, after destroying his first love, he manages to create a mechanical child with wings that is in reality an airplane. Similarly, in his famous play *The Breasts of Tiresias* (*Les Mamelles de Tirésias*) (1915), the French futurist Guillaume Apollinaire endows man, not woman, with the ability to give birth, and, in so doing, he reflects a certain anxiety about the depopulation in France as a result of World War I. And the Russian poet David Burliuk reflects a similar type of futurist womb envy tinged with militarism when he writes: "I like a pregnant man . . . I like a pregnant tower; in it there are many living soldiers. And a pregnant spring field from which little green leaves protrude" (Mne nravitsia beremennyi muzhchina . . . / Mne nravitsia beremennaia bashnia, / V nei tak mnogo zhivykh soldat. / I veshniaia briukhataia pashnia, / Iz koei listiki zelenye torchat) (quoted in Aleksei Kruchenykh, *Nash vykhod: K istorii russkogo futurizma* [Moscow: Literaturno-khudozhestvennoe agenstvo RA, 1996], 80).

Chapter 3. Reproductive Fantasies

Epigraphs to chapter 3: I. S. Turgenev, "Neskol'ko slov o stikhotvoreniiakh F. I. Tiutcheva," *Sobranie sochinenii v desiati tomakh*, 10 vols. (Moscow: Khudozhestvennaia literatura, 1961–62), 10:240; Nikolai Gumilev, "The Life of Verse," *On Russian Poetry*, ed. and trans. David Lapeza (Ann Arbor, Mich.: Ardis, 1977), 13; and N. Gumilev, "Zhizn' stikha," *Sobranie sochinenii v chetyrekh tomakh*, ed. G. P. Struve and B. A. Filippov, 4 vols. (Washington, D.C.: Victor Kamkin, 1962–68), 4:160.

1. Based on Blok's dating of the poems in *Motherland*, it would appear that he completed no new poems for the cycle between 1 January 1909 and August 1909.

2. Julia Kristeva identifies hearing as the mode of perception most closely associated with the Virgin Mary. "We are entitled," she claims, "only to the ear of the virginal body, the tears and the breast. With the female sexual organ changed into an innocent shell, holder of sound, there arises a possible tendency to eroticize hearing, voice or even understanding" ("Stabat Mater," *The Kristeva Reader*, ed. Toril Moi [New York: Columbia University Press, 1986], 172–73).

3. Blok was refuted to be one of the most prolific writers of his generation. "There were miraculous days," Kornei Chukovsky contends, "when he could write up to three or four poems in a row. Once these lyric waves got started they carried him further and further along, seemingly without end" (*Alexander Blok: As Man and Poet*, trans. Diana Burgin and Katherine O'Connor [Ann Arbor, Mich.: Ardis, 1982], 64).

4. For a brief overview of Russian travel to Italy in the nineteenth and early twentieth century, see Lucy Vogel, *Aleksandr Blok: The Journey to Italy* (Ithaca, N.Y.: Cornell University Press, 1973), 1-15. On Russian emigration to Italy in the twentieth century, see N. P. Komolova, ed., *Rossiia i Italiia: Russkaia emigratsiia v Italii v XX veke* (Moscow: Nauka, 2003).

5. At the end of August and beginning of September 1908, on the occasion of Tolstoy's eightieth birthday, Blok devoted an essay to Tolstoy entitled "The Sun above Russia" ("Solntse nad Rossiei") in which he excoriated the authorities for their treatment of Tolstoy, comparing them to a vampire. On the importance of Tolstoy in Blok's oeuvre, see Z. G. Mints, "Blok and L. N. Tolstoi," *Aleksandr Blok i russkie pisateli*, intro. A. V. Lavrov and ed. L. L. Pil'd (St. Petersburg: Iskusstvo-SPB, 2000), 113-44.

6. Leo Tolstoy, *Anna Karenina*, trans. Louise and Aylmer Maude, rev. George Gibian, 2nd ed. (New York: W. W. Norton, 1995), 424; L. N. Tolstoi, *Anna Karenina, Sobranie sochinenii v dvenadtsati tomakh*, 12 vols. (Moscow: Khudozhestvennaia literatura, 1958-59), 9:39.

7. In *Anna Karenina* Tolstoy implicitly compares Vronsky to an unsuccessful Pygmalion when he observes that "[the artist Mikhailov] knew it was not possible to forbid Vronsky to trifle with art, knew that he and all the dilettanti had a perfect right to paint what they liked—but to him it was unpleasant. One cannot forbid a man's making a big wax doll and kissing it. But if the man came and sat down with his doll right in front of a lover, and began to caress it as the lover caresses his beloved, it would displease the lover. It was this kind of unpleasantness that Mikhaylov experienced when he saw Vronsky's pictures: he was amused, vexed, sorry, and hurt" (Tolstoy, *Anna Karenina*, 435; Tolstoi, *Anna Karenina*, 9:52). On the connection between the Pygmalion myth and *zhiznetvorchestvo*, see Irene Masing-Delic, "Creating the Living Work of Art: The Symbolist Pygmalion and His Antecedents," in *Creating Life: The Aesthetic Utopia of Russian Modernism*, ed. Irina Paperno and Joan Delaney Grossman (Stanford, Calif.: Stanford University Press, 1994), 51-82.

8. Blok discusses the importance of the earth and subterranean rumblings in his essays on the Messina-Reggio earthquake, "The Elements and Culture" ("Stikhiia i kul'tura") (December 1908) and "Gorky on Messina" ("Gor'kii o Messine") (October 1909), as well as in his unfinished impressions of his Italian journey *Lightning Flashes of Art* (*Molnii iskusstva*). He also refers to the Messina-Reggio earthquake in the first chapter of his unfinished narrative poem *Retribution* and in "The Scythians" ("Skify") (30 January 1918).

9. Rachel Polonsky, *English Literature and the Russian Aesthetic Renaissance* (Cambridge: Cambridge University Press, 1998), 125.

10. For a more comprehensive discussion of Blok's tastes in Italian art, see Polonsky, *English Literature and the Russian Aesthetic Renaissance*, 140-51; Gerald Pirog, *Aleksandr Blok's Ital'ianskie stikhi: Confrontation and Disillusionment* (Columbus, Ohio: Slavica, 1983); and V. Al'fonsov, *Slova i kraski: Ocherki iz istorii sviazei poetov i khudozhnikov* (Moscow: Sovetskii pisatel', 1966), 63-90. On the painterly aspect of Blok's poetics, see John E. Bowlt, "Here and There: The Question of Space in Blok's Poetry," in *Aleksandr Blok Centennial Conference*, ed. Walter N. Vickery and Bogdan B. Sagatov (Columbus, Ohio: Slavica, 1984), 61-72.

11. Walter Pater emphasizes the demonic quality of Leonardo's art in his famous description of *La Gioconda*'s beauty. "It is a beauty," he insists, "wrought out from within upon the flesh, the deposit, little cell by cell, of strange thoughts and fantastic reveries and exquisite passions. Set it for a moment beside one of those white Greek goddesses or beautiful women of antiquity, and how they would be troubled by this beauty, into which the soul with all its maladies has passed! All the thoughts and experience of the world have etched and moulded there, in that which they have of power to refine and make expressive the outward form, the animalism of Greece, the lust of Rome, the mysticism of the middle age with its spiritual ambition and imaginative loves, the return of the Pagan world, the sins of the Borgias. She is older than the rocks among which she sits; like the vampire, she has been dead many times, and learned the secrets of the grave; and has been a diver in deep seas, and keeps their fallen day about her; and trafficked for strange webs with Eastern merchants: and, as Leda, was the mother of Helen of Troy, and, as Saint Anne, the mother of Mary; and all this has been to her but as the sound of lyres and flutes, and lives only in the delicacy with which it has moulded the changing lineaments, and tinged the eyelids and the hands" ("The Renaissance: Studies in Art and Poetry," in *The English Literary Decadence: An Anthology*, ed. Christopher S. Nassaar [Lanham, M.D.: University Press of America, 1999], 66).

12. Quoted in Samuel Cioran, *Vladimir Solov'ev and the Knighthood of the Divine Sophia* (Waterloo, Canada: Wilfrid Laurier University Press, 1977), 140.

13. Blok's handwriting is apparently unclear here, as the word "black" is followed by a question mark in the published edition of his notebooks.

14. Blok's observation that the unearthed mosaic floor smelled like the insides of a railroad tunnel not only anticipates his pronouncement in the preface to *Lightning Flashes of Art* that "the nineteenth century is an iron age [zheleznyi vek]" (*SS*, 5:385) but also suggests that he may have associated the subterranean layers of Italy with the deathly realm of modern Russia and her railroads. The railroad theme also occurs in Blok's *Retribution*, as well as in his earlier essays "Henrik Ibsen" ("Genrikh Ibsen") (October–November 1908) and "Irony" ("Ironiia") (November 1908). For an assessment of the importance of the motif of the iron age in Russian modernism, see Boris Gasparov, "The Iron Age in the 1930s: The Centennial Return in Mandelstam," in *Rereading Russian Poetry*, ed. Stephanie Sandler (New Haven, Conn.: Yale University Press, 1999), 78–103.

15. During his Italian trip, Blok was apparently reading Lev Tolstoy's *War and Peace* (*Voina i mir*) (1865–69), as he mentions the novel twice in his notebooks. See ZK, 147 and 149.

16. A number of scholars have treated Blok's *Italian Verses*, and from various theoretical perspectives, too. Vogel (*Aleksandr Blok*) examines the poems within the context of Blok's journey to Italy, focusing on the facts of Blok's biography, while Pirog studies how the poems "operate together as a unified text, to discover the intrinsic properties which organize them as a group," paying particular attention to the ways in which the cycle transposes the Italian text into poetry (*Aleksandr Blok's Ital'ianskie stikhi*, xi). Polonsky discusses Blok's indebtedness to Ruskin and the Pre-Raphaelites (*English Literature and the Russian Aesthetic Renaissance*, 145–51), and Alfonsov focuses on Blok's

relationship to the art of the Renaissance (*Slova i kraski*). Anna Lisa Crone examines the intertextual connections between Blok's poems and travelogue and Mandelstam's Venice poem ("Blok's 'Venecija' and *Molnii iskusstva* as Inspiration to Mandelstam: Parallels in the Italian Materials," in *Aleksandr Blok Centennial Conference*, 73–88). Efim Etkind offers a detailed structural analysis of three of the poems ("Ten' Danta . . . [Tri stikhotvoreniia iz italianskogo tsikla Bloka]," *Voprosy literatury* 14, no. 11 [1970]: 86–96), and Pavel Gromov explores the way in which the poems comment on the situation in Russia following 1905 (*A. Blok: Ego predshestvennkiki i sovremenniki* [Leningrad: Sovetskii pisatel', 1986], 328–75). Most recently, Olga Matich treats the figure of the femme fatale that appears in the guise of Galla Placidia and Salome in "Ravenna" and "Venice 2" (*Erotic Utopia: The Decadent Imagination in Russia's Fin de Siècle* [Madison: University of Wisconsin Press, 2005], 126–211). While my own discussion has benefited from these studies, it focuses on the slightly different problem of the relationship of these poems to Blok's myth of maternity.

17. The poems, which were originally published in *Apollon* in 1910, included: "Ravenna" (May–June 1909), "Maria da Spoleto," which was later retitled "The Girl from Spoleto" ("Devushka iz Spoleto") (3 June 1909), the second and third Venice poems, "Cold wind from the lagoon" ("Kholodnyi veter ot laguny") (August 1909) and "The stubborn hum of life weakens" ("Slabeet zhisni gul upornyi") (26 August 1909), "Annunciation" ("Blagoveshchenie") (May–June 1909), and "Dormition" ("Uspenie") (4 June 1909).

18. On Pushkin and the childbirth metaphor, see Leighton Brett Cooke, "Pushkin and the Pleasure of the Text: Anal and Erotic Images of Creativity," in *Russian Literature and Psychoanalysis*, ed. Daniel Rancour-Laferriere (Philadelphia, Penn.: John Benjamins, 1989), 193–224, and Daniel Rancour-Laferriere, "The Couvade of Peter the Great: A Psychoanalytic Aspect of *The Bronze Horseman*," in *Puškin Today*, ed. David M. Bethea (Bloomington: Indiana University Press, 1993), 73–85. On Annensky's appropriation of the maternal metaphor and its origins in Mallarmé, see Leslie O'Bell, "Mallarmé and Annenskii: The Gift of a Poem," *Canadian Slavonic Papers* 23, no. 4 (1981), 371–83, and on Nabokov and the metaphor, see Ellen Pifer, "Her Monster, His Nymphet: Nabokov and Mary Shelley," in *Nabokov and His Fiction: New Perspectives*, ed. Julian Connolly (Cambridge: Cambridge University Press, 1999), 158–76.

19. Susan Stanford Friedman, "Creativity and the Childbirth Metaphor: Gender Difference in Literary Discourse," in *Speaking of Gender*, ed. Elaine Showalter (New York: Routledge, 1989), 74–75.

20. On the difficulty women writers experience in appropriating the maternal metaphor, see Barbara Johnson, "Apostrophe, Animation, and Abortion," *A World of Difference* (Baltimore, M.D.: Johns Hopkins University Press, 1987), 184–99, and Susan Rubin Suleiman, "Writing and Motherhood," in *The M(o)ther Tongue: Essays in Feminist Psychoanalytic Criticism*, ed. Shirley Nelson Garner (Ithaca, N.Y.: Cornell University Press, 1985), 352–77.

21. Marina Warner, *Alone of All Her Sex: The Myth and Cult of the Virgin Mary* (New York: Knopf, 1976), 4.

22. Boris Pasternak, *Doctor Zhivago*, trans. Max Hayward and Manya Harari (New York: Pantheon, 1991), 281; Boris Pasternak, *Doktor Zhivago, Sobranie*

sochinenii v piati tomakh, 5 vols. (Moscow: Khudozhestvennaia literatura, 1989-92), 3:278.

23. In "The Elements and Culture," Blok wrote: "we are experiencing a terrible crisis. We still don't know exactly what types of events await us, but *in our heart the arrow of the seismograph has already bent*. We see ourselves against the background of the sunset, on a light lacy airplane high above the earth; but beneath us there is a thundering and smoldering mountain" (*SS*, 5:359).

24. In her reading of a different poem by Blok, *The Twelve* (*Dvenadtsat'*) (January 1918), Irene Masing-Delic identifies the theme of abolishing death as central to an understanding of the work. She observes that at one point, "Christ descends into a 'snow coffin' (*su-grob kholodnyi* . . .). In other words, the Christ hidden in the snow pillar and carrying the blood-red banner, like the Gospel's, is killed and descends to the subterranean realm of death, depriving his apostles of their salvatory symbols for a while. Again like the Gospel Christ, he dies in order to demonstrate that death has no hold on mankind. But whereas the biblical Christ is resurrected by his heavenly Father, or by himself (he and his Father 'being one'), this Christ is resurrected by his own comrades (or 'friends' in Fyodorov's terminology)" (*Abolishing Death: A Salvation Myth of Russian Twentieth-Century Literature* [Stanford, Calif.: Stanford University Press, 1992], 210).

25. Lawrence Lipking, *The Life of the Poet: Beginning and Ending Poetic Careers* (Chicago: University of Chicago Press, 1981), 161.

26. For a more extensive consideration of the language used in this poem, see Pirog, *Aleksandr Blok's* Ital'ianskie stikhi, 72-86.

27. The conflation of maternity and death is not uncommon in Russian modernism. Jane T. Costlow, Stephanie Sandler, and Judith Vowles demonstrate that it figures prominently in Bunin's story "The Mordvinian Sarafan" ("Mordovskii sarafan") in their introduction to *Sexuality and the Body in Russian Culture* (Stanford, Calif.: Stanford University Press, 1993), 20-22.

28. Sergei Makovskii, *Na Parnase "Serebrianogo veka"* (Munich: Izdatel'stvo tsentral'nogo ob"edineniia politicheskikh emigrantov iz SSSR, 1962), 153,

29. Pirog, *Aleksandr Blok's* Ital'ianskie stikhi, 75.

30. Edgar Allan Poe, *The Portable Poe*, ed. Philip Van Doren Stern (New York: Penguin, 1973), 557. On the aesthetics of the dead woman in Western literature and culture, see Elisabeth Bronfen, *Over Her Dead Body: Death, Femininity and the Aesthetic* (New York: Routledge, 1992).

31. This recalls the image of Cleopatra in the second stanza of "Cleopatra" ("Kleopatra") (16 December 1907), which reads: "She lies in a glass coffin, neither dead nor alive, and people tirelessly whisper shameless words about her" (Ona lezhit v grobu stekliannom, / I ne mertva i ne zhiva, / A liudi shepchut neustanno / O nei besstydnye slova) (*SS*, 2:207).

32. The theme of listening to the sounds of the earth occurs frequently in Blok's oeuvre. See, for example, "I put my ear to the ground" ("Ia ukho prilozhil k zemle") (3 June 1907).

33. Vogel, *Aleksandr Blok*, 95.

34. Nine, a multiple of the Trinity, figures prominently in Dante's *Divine Comedy* as well as in *La Vita Nuova*.

35. Blok appears to have had Gippius in mind here. In her famous poem

"Song" ("Pesnia") (1893), she writes: "And I don't know whence the desire, whence it came, but the heart wants and demands a miracle, a miracle!" (I eto zhelanie ne znaiu otkuda, / Prishlo otkuda, / No serdtse khochet i prosit chuda, / Chuda!) (*Stikh*, 75).

36. Irene Masing-Delic has indicated that this image of the child "may well have been inspired by a personal trauma[,] . . . namely the loss of Liubov' Dmitrievna's child, recorded in the poem 'On an Infant's Death.' . . . There Blok speaks of the infant as blessed' ('*blazhennyi*'), quoting the funeral liturgy for infants. In the article Blok likewise and at greater length quoted the liturgy, emphasizing its promise that 'the blessed infants' will be in God's Kingdom 'forsooth'" ("The Symbolist Crisis Revisited: Blok's View," in *Issues in Russian Literature before 1917: Selected Papers of the Third World Congress for Soviet and East European Studies*, ed. J. Douglas Clayton [Columbus, Ohio: Slavica, 1989], 227 n 11).

37. Blok would by no means be the only Russian poet to enter into a love affair with Venice. For an overview of the theme of Venice in the Russian literary imagination, see A. Golovacheva, "'Plyvia v tainstvennoi gondole . . .': 'Sny' o Venetsii v russkoi literature zolotogo i serebrianogo vekov,'" *Voprosy literatury* 6 (November-December 2004): 157-78; A. A. Kara-Murza, *Znamenitye russkie o Venetsii* (Moscow: Izdatel'stvo Nezavisimaia gazeta, 2001); N. E. Mednis and T. I. Pecherskaia, *Venetsiia v russkoi literature* (Novosibirsk: Izdatel'stvo Novosibirskogo universiteta, 1999); and Jan Paul Hinrichs, *In Search of Another St. Petersburg: Venice in Russian Poetry, 1823-1997* (Munich: Otto Sagner, 1997).

38. On the origins of this stanza in Italian song, see Vogel, *Aleksandr Blok*, 58.

39. In her translation of the poem's third stanza, Vogel seems to suggest that there is an identity between the mourner and Christ. Her translation reads, "[He] comes from a somber Mass, / There is no more blood in his heart . . . / Christ, tired of bearing his cross . . ." (*Aleksandr Blok*, 57).

40. Vogel, *Aleksandr Blok*, 63.

41. Avril Pyman, *The Life of Aleksandr Blok*, 2 vols. (Oxford: Oxford University Press, 1979-80), 2:42.

42. Pirog notes that "there was a custom of performing public executions—hangings and beheadings—between the two columns, St. Mark's and St. Theodore's, at the edge of the Lagoon in the Piazza of San Marco" (*Aleksandr Blok's Ital'ianskie stikhi*, 23).

43. Matich is the first scholar to point out that Blok's representation of Salome in the Venice poem was probably influenced by his viewing of the mosaics representing Salome and John the Baptist in the baptistery of the Basilica of San Marco (*Erotic Utopia*, 144).

44. For an excellent discussion of the modernist Salome's connection to dancing, see Rhonda Garelick, *Rising Star: Dandyism, Gender, and Performance in the Fin de Siècle* (Princeton, N.J.: Princeton University Press, 1998).

45. It bears noting that Salome does appear in more distinctly erotic terms in the discarded stanzas of the poem (see *SS*, 3:530). These stanzas are crucial to Matich's reading of Salome as decadent femme fatale (*Erotic Utopia*, 142-54); however, they are less crucial to my analysis of the poem, which focuses on Salome's disembodied spectral quality.

46. The fact that Salome is a daughter, as opposed to a mother, is entirely consistent with Blok's spectral myth, since in Blok's *Pramater'* the shade of the Ancestress is a double for the daughter, Bertha, and, in some versions of the story, Salome is envisioned as fulfilling her mother's desire for the head of John the Baptist.

47. On the importance of the figure of Orpheus for the Russian symbolists, see Zoia Iureva, "Mif ob Orfee v tvorchestve Andreia Belogo, Aleksandra Bloka i Viacheslava Ivanova," in *American Contributions to the Eighth Congress of Slavists*, vol. 2, ed. Victor Terras (Columbus, Ohio: Slavica, 1978), 779–99. Though Blok did not evince the same fascination with Orpheus that Briusov did, he was often viewed as an Orphic poet. In her book on Tsvetaeva's appropriation of the myth of Orpheus, Olga Peters Hasty observes that "the first poet Tsvetaeva identified directly with Orpheus was Aleksandr Blok" and that "the recognition of Orpheus in Blok may well have been triggered specifically by the coincidence of her own poetic activity and her perusal of myths with her daughter, but the association has deeper roots. It emerges in the midst of Tsvetaeva's own distinctly Orphic process of confronting Blok's death. In the series of poems she wrote to Blok in 1916, while he was still alive, Tsvetaeva aligned Blok with Christ and emphasized the poet's sacrificial meekness, proximity to death, and unearthly qualities. Given her propensity for typological thinking, little effort was required to discern in Orpheus another suitable embodiment of these attributes of the poet" (*Tsvetaeva's Orphic Journeys in the Worlds of the Word* [Evanston, Ill.: Northwestern University Press, 1996], 14–15).

48. Cited in Garelick, *Rising Star*, 57.

49. This would not be the only time that Blok conflated Salome with Herodias. Matich points out that Blok would substitute Herodias for Salome in his discussion of Nikolai Minsky's poetry (*Erotic Utopia*, 149–50).

50. Another dance that is linked to illness in folk consciousness is the tarantella, which was thought to be a cure for a form of hysteria caused by the bite of a spider.

51. In his notebooks, Blok mentions seeing a portrait of Salome by Carlo Dolci in the Uffizi Gallery in Florence as well as a fresco by Giannicola Manni dealing with the "ill-starred history with Salome [zlopoluchnaia istoriia s Salomeei]" in the Collegio del Cambio in Perugia (*ZK*, 140–41).

52. Olga Matich, "Gender Trouble in the Amazonian Kingdom: Turn-of-the-Century Representations of Women in Russia," in *Amazons of the Avant-Garde: Alexandra Exeter, Natalia Goncharova, Liubov Popova, Olga Rozanova, Varvara Stepanova, and Nadezhda Udaltsova*, ed. John E. Bowlt and Matthew Drutt (New York: Guggenheim Museum Publications, 2000), 82–84. For a more extensive discussion of the Salome theme in the Russian context, see Olga Matich, "Pokrovy Salomei: Eros, smert' i istoriia," trans. O. V. Karpova, in *Erotizm bez granits*, ed. M. M. Pavlova (Moscow: Novoe literaturnoe obozrenie, 2004), 90–121.

53. The drafts of "Neither Dreams nor Reality" dating from this period suggest that thoughts of his wife's pregnancy and childbirth were very much on Blok's mind. In notes to the essay, dated 3 March 1909, Blok writes: "first we waited for something, not even calling it a child; then the child was born; right

away we unexpectedly fell in love with him; then again the child died; weeks went by, as before, without anything (*SS*, 6:488).

54. Stéphane Mallarmé, "Gift of the Poem" ("Don du poème"), *Collected Poems*, trans. Henry Weinfield (Berkeley: University of California Press, 1994), 24.

55. Harold Bloom, "Poetic Origins and Final Phases," in *Modern Criticism and Theory: A Reader*, ed. David Lodge (London: Longman, 1988), 245.

56. The subject matter of this stanza did not go unnoticed by Blok's contemporaries. Petr Pertsov observed: "Poets have asked about everything and have sung of everything. But to sing of your own conception—that, it seems, hasn't occurred to anyone. You have to hand it to Blok. In his own way, he broke the record for poetic brazenness [poeticheskaia bespardonnost']" (cited in A. A. Blok, *Polnoe sobranie sochinenii v dvadtsati tomakh*, ed. M. L. Gasparov et al., vols. 1-5 and 7 to date [Moscow: Nauka, 1997-], 3:738).

57. Blok's mother did marry army officer Frants Kublitsky-Piottukh when Blok was still a boy, but he apparently never felt particularly close to his stepfather.

58. Elsewhere, in a letter to his mother, written from Florence, Blok goes so far as to proclaim: "I curse Florence not only for the heat and mosquitoes, but for the fact that she has betrayed herself to European mold, has become a highfalutin city, and has disfigured all of her houses and streets. All that remains are a few palaces, churches, and museums, some distant outlying areas and Boboli. As for the rest, I am shaking the dust from my shoes and wish that it would undergo the fate of Messina [zhelaiu emu podvergnut'sia uchasti Messiny]" (*SS*, 8:286).

59. The word that Blok employs to refer to the Madonna's squinting or screwing up of her eyes—*shchurit'*—is the same word Lev Tolstoy uses to refer to Anna. In chapter 21 of part 6 of *Anna Karenina*, we encounter the following passage: "And she remembered that it was just when the intimate side of life was in question that Anna screwed up her eyes. 'As if she were blinking at her own life so as not to see it all,' thought Dolly" (I ei vspomnilas', chto Anna shchurilas', imenno kogda delo kasalos' zadushevnykh storon zhizn'. "Tochno ona na svoiu zhizn' shchuritsia, chtoby ne vsë videt'," podumala Dolli) (Tolstoy, *Anna Karenina*, 569; Tolstoi, *Anna Karenina*, 9:217).

60. Roland Barthes, *The Pleasure of the Text*, trans. Richard Miller (New York: Noonday Press, 1975), 37.

Chapter 4. A Time of Troubles

Epigraphs to chapter 4: Aleksandr Pushkin, *Boris Godunov*, *Polnoe sobranie sochinenii*, ed. V. D. Bonch-Bruevich, 17 vols. (Leningrad: Akademiia nauk, 1937-39), 7:22; Henrik Ibsen, *The Master Builder*, *The Complete Major Prose Plays*, trans. Rolf Fjelde (New York: Penguin, 1978), 830-31.

1. In a letter to his mother, Blok reveals his debt to *Eugene Onegin*. He writes: "Mama, just now, finally, my 'First Chapter' of the poem *Retribution* is finished. With the prologue, it consists of 1019 lines. [. . .] If in this manner, I succeed in

writing still the 2nd and 3rd chapters and the epilogue, which the plan of the poem requires, the poem can grow to the size of *Onegin*" (*PABR*, 2:289). Within the poem, Blok makes reference to a number of Pushkin texts besides *Eugene Onegin*, including *The Bronze Horseman* (*Mednyi vsadnik*), *Poltava*, and *Boris Godunov*, to name but a few. On Blok's indebtedness to Pushkin in *Retribution*, see, Z. G. Mints, "Blok i Pushkin," *Aleksandr Blok i russkie pisateli*, intro. A. V. Lavrov and ed. L. L. Pil'd (St. Petersburg: Iskusstvo-SPB, 2000), esp. 233-43; Carol Culley Ueland, "Autobiographical *Poemy* of the Russian Symbolists: Aleksandr Blok's *Retribution*, Viacheslav Ivanov's *Infancy*, and Andrei Bely's *The First Encounter*" (Ph.D. diss., Columbia University, 1995), 193-261; and L. K. Dolgopolov, *Poemy Bloka i russkaia poema kontsa XIX-nachala XX vekov* (Leningrad: Nauka, 1964). On some of the other literary sources of *Retribution*, see Z. G. Mints, "Blok i Gogol'," *Aleksandr Blok i russkie pisateli*, esp. 75-81; L. Allen, "Stolknovenie zhanrov v poeme Bloka 'Vozmezdie,'" in *Aleksandr Blok: Issledovaniia i materialy*, ed. Iu. K. Gerasimov et al. (Leningrad: Nauka, 1991), 189-97; and Dolgopolov, *Poemy Bloka i russkaia poema kontsa XIX-nachala XX vekov*.

2. Avril Pyman also discusses how *Retribution* is connected to the poet's quest for "stocktaking" (*The Life of Aleksandr Blok*, 2 vols. [Oxford: Oxford University Press, 1979-80], 2:69-144).

3. The turn to longer poetic forms such as the modern "epic" was by no means the only way in which male poets engaged in this process of "summing-up." As Lawrence Lipking notes, "many modern poets (Cavafy and Yeats are striking examples) seem to regard the ultimate fruit of all their work as a poetic autobiography in the shape of a single book" (*The Life of a Poet: Beginning and Ending Poetic Careers* [Chicago: University of Chicago Press, 1981]. 70). And Blok was a typical modernist in this regard. Around this same time, he undertook the reorganization of his poems into three volumes that would, in his words, form a "trilogy of incarnation" ("trilogiia vochelovecheniia") (*BBB*, 261). "Each poem," he noted in the preface to his 1911 collection of poems, "is essential to the structure of a chapter; several chapters make up 'a book'; each book is part of the trilogy; the whole trilogy could be called a 'novel in verse': it is devoted to a complex of thoughts and feelings to which I was committed during the first twelve years of my conscious life" (quoted in *BBB*, 262).

4. For a consideration of Blok's lyric cycles, see David A. Sloane, *Aleksandr Blok and the Dynamics of the Lyric Cycle* (Columbus, Ohio: Slavica, 1988).

5. Lipking, *The Life of a Poet*, 70.

6. In this same year, Blok devoted two memorial essays to Kommissarzhevskaia, with whom he had worked closely on *Die Ahnfrau* and other projects, and one to Vrubel. Earlier, on the occasion of Tolstoy's eightieth birthday, Blok devoted an essay to the prose writer.

7. The notion that the genesis of *Retribution* is to be found in the 1910 crisis in Russian symbolism has become somewhat of a critical commonplace in Blok scholarship. For a recent discussion of the problem, see Il'ia Serman, "Aleksandr Blok, krizis simvolizma i *Vozmezdie*," in *Res Slavica: Fetschrift für Hans Rothe zum 65. Geburtstag*, ed. Peter Thiergen and Ludger Udolph (Paderborn, Germany: Ferdinand Schöningh, 1994), 245-53.

8. I am not the first to liken the poem to a house. Kornei Chukovsky observes

that "the house itself—the whole house and not a separate person—is the real hero of the poem. Blok describes it as 'an hospitable, old house,' 'an hospitable good house'" (*Alexander Blok: As Man and Poet*, trans. and ed. Diana Burgin and Katherine O'Connor [Ann Arbor, Mich.: Ardis, 1982], 15).

9. During this period, Blok made repeated references to his inability to hear in a metaphorical sense. For example, the poet Nadezhda Pavlovich recounts that in the winter of 1920: "Blok spoke haltingly, almost brusquely. Then he began to tell about the indescribable noise and thunder he heard for three days straight, morning and night, as if the world collapsed, and then everything abruptly came to an end and grew quiet, and from that time forth he began to go deaf [stal glokhnut']. 'Have you read Kipling's *The Light That Failed*. There an artist goes blind. And I am growing deaf [glokhnu] . . . And, nonetheless, I heard that. Let it be that I can no longer write now'" ("Vospominaniia ob Aleksandre Bloke," ed. Z. G. Mints and I. A. Chernov, in *Blokovskii sbornik* 1 [Tartu: Tartuskii gosudarstvennyi institut, 1964], 487–88).

10. Konstantin Mochulsky, *Aleksandr Blok*, trans. Doris V. Johnson (Detroit, Mich,: Wayne State University Press, 1983), 272.

11. Sloane, *Aleksandr Blok and the Dynamics of the Lyric Cycle*, 323.

12. Cited in Pavlovich, "Vospominaniia ob Aleksandre Bloke," 489.

13. Cited in Sloane, *Aleksandr Blok and the Dynamics of the Lyric Cycle*, 327.

14. In growing up in isolation without knowledge of his parents, Blok's hero also recalls the figure of Siegfried from Richard Wagner's *Der Ring des Nibelungen*. For more on the importance of Wagner for Blok and for the implications of that importance in *Retribution*, see, for example, D. M. Magomedova, "Blok i Vagner," *Avtobiograficheskii mif v tvorchestve A. Bloka* (Moscow: Martin, 1997), 85–110, and Rosamund Bartlett, "Wagner and the Russian Symbolists: Aleksandr Blok," *Wagner and Russia* (Cambridge: Cambridge University Press, 1995), 195–217.

15. Blok's final, revised plan is outlined in the poem's preface, which he completed in July 1919. See *SS*, 3:295–300.

16. Boris Pasternak's indebtedness to Blok for this plot device is made quite clear. After learning of the existence of Tania, Gordon remarks: "'Blok says somewhere: we, the children of Russia's terrible years. Blok meant this in a metaphorical, figurative sense. The children were not children, but the sons, the heirs, the intelligentsia, and the terrors were not terrible, but were sent from above, apocalyptic; that's quite different. Now the metaphorical has become literal, children are children and the terrors are terrible, there you have the difference'" (Pasternak, *Doctor Zhivago*, trans. Max Hayward and Manya Harari [New York: Pantheon, 1991], 518; Pasternak, *Doktor Zhivago, Polnoe sobranie sochinenii v piati tomakh*, 5 vols. [Moscow: Khudozhestvennaia literatura, 1989–92], 3:510). Pasternak, however, is much more skeptical about this child of the revolution. For him, she does not represent the regeneration of the aristocratic line of the poet but rather degeneration. Referring to Tania, the love child of Zhivago and Lara, Gordon remarks toward the end of the novel, "'It has often happened in history that a lofty ideal has degenerated into cruel materialism. Thus Greece gave way to Rome, and the Russian Enlightenment has become the Russian Revolution'" (Pasternak, *Doctor Zhivago*, 518; Pasternak, *Doktor Zhivago*, 3:509–10).

17. Blok conceived the idea for poem in 1910 and worked on it extensively in 1911, returning to it in 1912, 1913, 1914, 1916, and in the last days of his life.

18. The editor Berlioz literally loses his head at the hands of the devil and his retinue, while the poet Bezdomny figuratively loses his head (he goes insane), as does the Master, though he is much more closely aligned with Christ than with John the Baptist.

19. In fact, Blok begins his autobiographical sketch with the statement: "The family of my mother was inclined toward literature and science" (Sem'ia moei materi prichastna k literature i k nauke) (SS, 7:7), and then he goes on to enumerate the various literary accomplishments of his mother's family, paying particular attention to those of his mother and her sisters. In contrast, he notes: "In the family of my father literature played a small role" [V sem'e otsa literatura igrala nebol'shuiu rol'] (SS, 7:11). Though it is not uncommon for male poets to identify literary fecundity with the maternal side of the family, in Blok's particular case, this would appear to be connected to his larger tendency within his poetic mythology to assign creative power to the feminine.

20. It bears noting, however, that Gumilev's essay did not appear until 1921; however, anatomical poetic discourse had already found firm footing in the works of the acmeists and particularly in the poems of Mandelstam. In his famous poem "Notre Dame" (1912), Mandelstam speaks about how "the basilica stands happy and first, like Adam once, spreading its nerves, the light cross-shaped dome playfully flexes its muscles" (Stoit bazilika, i radostnyi i pervyi, / Kak nekogda Adam, rasplastyvaia nervy, / Igraet myshtsami krestovyi legkii svod) (O. E. Mandel'shtam, "Notre Dame," *Sobranie sochinenii v chetyrekh tomakh*, ed. G. P. Struve and B. A. Filippov, 4 vols. [Moscow: Terra, 1991], 1:24).

21. Blok could, however, appreciate the talents of individual acmeist poets. In November 1911, he records in his diary that Akhmatova "read her poems, already moving me; the further [she reads] her poems, the better" (SS, 7:83).

22. Though a more accurate English translation for the word *muzhestvennoe* would be "courageous," I translate the word as "masculine," since it better approximates the meaning here.

23. In terms of his complicated relationship with masculinity, Blok shares certain characteristics with his younger contemporary, Vladimir Mayakovsky, who would proclaim in his most famous poem, "A Cloud in Trousers" ("Oblako v shtanakh") (1914–15), "if you wish, I will be irreproachably tender: not a man, but a cloud in trousers" (khotite— / budu bezukoriznenno nezhnyi, / ne muzhchina, a—oblako v shtanakh!) (Maiakovskii, "Oblako v shtanakh," *Polnoe sobranie sochinenii v trinadtsati tomakh*, 13 vols. [Moscow: Khudozhestvennaia literatura, 1955–61], 1:175). For an excellent discussion of the complicated construction of masculinity in Soviet literature, see Eliot Borenstein, *Men without Women: Masculinity and Revolution in Soviet Fiction, 1917–1929* (Durham, N.C.: Duke University Press, 2000).

24. Mandelstam would also represent the subject as drowning or suffocating in the final stanza of his lyric, "Sisters—heaviness and tenderness—your tokens are the same" ("Sestry—tiazhest' i nezhnost'—odinakovy vashi primety") (March 1920), which reads: "Like dark water, I drink turbid air. Time is turned by the plough, and the rose too was once earth. Heavy, tender

roses are in a slow whirlpool; roses heaviness and tenderness are entwined in a double wreath" (Slovno temnuiu vodu ia p'iu pomutivshiisia vozdukh. / Vremia vspakhano plugom, i roza zemleiu byla / V medlennom vodovorote tiazhelye nezhnye rozy, / Rozy tiazhest' i nezhnost' v dvoinye venki zaplela) (Mandel'shtam, "Sestry—tiazhest i nezhnost'," *Sobranie sochinenii v chetyrekh tomakh*, 1:77).

25. Aleksandr Etkind has argued that the image of castration figures prominently in Blok's essay "Catiline" ("Katilina") (22 April–17 May 1918), as well as in his other prose works dealing with the Bolshevik revolution ("Revoliutsiia kak kastratsiia: Mistika sekt i politika tela v pozdnei proze Bloka," *Sodom i Psikheia: Ocherki intellektual'noi istorii Serebrianogo veka* [Moscow: ITs-Garant, 1996], 59–139).

26. Andrei Belyi, *Masterstvo Gogolia: Issledovanie* (Ann Arbor, Mich.: Ardis, 1982), 296.

27. Chukovsky, *Alexander Blok*, 15.

28. Cited in Pyman, *The Life of Aleksandr Blok*, 2:112.

29. Blok turns repeatedly to Ibsen's idea of youth as retribution in his essays "Three Questions" ("Tri voprosa") (February 1908), "Henrik Ibsen" ("Genrikh Ibsen") (October–November 1908), and "From Ibsen to Strindberg" ("Ot Ibsena k Strindbergu") (April 1912).

30. While working on *Retribution*, Blok did enter into an epistolary relationship with a young girl, whom he mythologized in his private writings as Hilda from Ibsen's play. For more on this, see Pyman, *The Life of Aleksandr Blok*, 2:116, and Pavlovich, "Vospominaniia Aleksandra Bloka."

31. Ibsen, *The Master Builder*, 825.

32. Ibsen, *The Master Builder*, 830. For a sensitive discussion of Ibsen's paradoxical feelings about the death of children in *The Master Builder* and elsewhere, see Terry Otten, "Ibsen's Paradoxical Attitudes Toward Kindermord," *Mosaic* 22, no. 3 (1989): 117–31.

33. It is worth noting that on 3 April of 1918, several months prior to the execution of the tsar and his family, Blok completed a history of the end of the Romanov dynasty titled *The Last Days of Imperial Power* (*Poslednie dni imperatorskoi vlasti*), which appeared first in shortened form as "The Last Days of the Old Regime" ("Poslednie dni starogo rezhima") in the fifteenth issue of *Byloe* in 1919 and then as a separate book in 1921. Blok opens this history with an assessment of the withering body politic of the tsarist regime. "At the end of 1916," he writes, "all members of the government body of Russia were stricken with an illness, which no longer could pass on its own, or be cured by ordinary means, but required a difficult and dangerous operation" (*SS*, 6:188).

34. On the Beilis affair, see Albert S. Lindemann, *The Jew Accused: Three Anti-Semitic Affairs (Dreyfus, Beilis, Frank), 1894–1915* (Cambridge: Cambridge University Press, 1991), 174–93.

35. On Blok's treatment of the Beilis affair in *Retribution* and elsewhere, see Olga Matich, *Erotic Utopia: The Decadent Imagination in Russia's Fin de Siècle* (Madison: University of Wisconsin Press, 2005), 114–15.

36. Matich, *Erotic Utopia*, 114.

37. Though Soviet critics have often viewed Blok as a prophet of the

revolution, his identification of the civil war with the Time of Troubles would link him with what Richard Pipes has identified as a conservative strain of thought. Pipes observes that "conservative Russians, for their part, rejected as faulty the analogy with the French revolution or with historic events experienced by other societies. They viewed the Russian Revolution as an unmitigated disaster, a total collapse of organized life, brought about largely by the activities of foreign powers (notably the Germans) or disloyal ethnic minorities (Jews, Latvians, Ukrainians). For them the only meaningful analogy with what had happened in Russia in 1917 and in the years immediately following was Russia's own Time of Troubles" (*Struve: Liberal on the Right, 1905–1944* [Cambridge, Mass.: Harvard University Press, 1980], 299).

38. In her important essay on Blok and Pushkin, Mints indicates that the figure of Maryna Mniszek in the poem's foreword comes from Pushkin's *Boris Godunov*, but she does not elaborate on this point ("Blok i Pushkin," 241).

39. For an excellent discussion of the pleasures and dangers inherent in the representation of dance in nineteenth-century Russian literature, see Stephanie Sandler, "Pleasure, Danger, and the Dance: Nineteenth-Century Russian Variations," in *Russia / Women / Culture*, ed. Helena Goscilo and Beth Holmgren (Bloomington: Indiana University Press, 1996), 247–72.

40. The name Dmitry crops up in another important Russian text about vexed father-son relations, Turgenev's *Fathers and Sons* (*Otsy i deti*) (1862) as well as in Dostoevsky's *Brothers Karamazov* (*Brat'ia Karamazovy*) (1880). In *Fathers and Sons*, Dmitry is the name of the son that Nikolai Kirsanov fathers with the servant woman, Fenichka. As a product of both the aristocratic and lower classes, the figure of Dmitry in Turgenev's novel seems to represent the hope that some of the more negative aspects of the aristocracy could be overcome through the blurring of class lines. A similar type of dynamic would seem to be in operation in Blok's text where the child was to be the product of a Russian aristocrat and a simple Polish woman. However, the Polish theme in Blok's text would also appear to connect the unnamed figure of Dmitry more directly with the figure from Pushkin's and Mussorgsky's works.

41. While I have chosen to focus here on the way in which the impostor theme comments on Blok's creative process, one could also discuss the theme within the context of Russian culture generally. On the phenomenon of royal imposture in Russian culture, see B. A. Uspenskij, "Tsar and Pretender: *Samozvančestvo* or Royal Imposture in Russia as a Cultural-Historical Phenomenon," trans. David Budgen, in Ju. M. Lotman and B. A. Uspenskij, *The Semiotics of Russian Culture*, ed. Ann Shukman (Ann Arbor, Mich: Michigan Slavic Contributions, 1984), 259–92.

42. See Gregory Freidin, *A Coat of Many Colors: Osip Mandelstam and His Mythologies of Self-Presentation* (Berkeley: University of California Press, 1987), 100–124.

43. This is certainly in keeping with the False Dmitry theme that haunts the poem's preface. In spite of his inauthenticity, the False Dmitry would share the same fate as Dmitry — that of victim of history.

44. The passage reads: "Dostoevsky noticed him. 'Who is that handsome man?'—he asked not loudly, bending toward Vrevskaia:—'He looks like Byron'" (Ego zametil Dostoevskii. / "Kto sei krasavets?"—on sprosil / Negromko, naklonivshis' k Vrevskoi:— / "Pokhozh na Bairona") (*SS*, 3:321).

45. The image of the rapacious hawk that destroys the fledglings in this passage is reminiscent of the image of the kite that circles over the mother and child in Blok's famous poem "The Kite" ("Korshun") (22 March 1916), with which he concludes the *Motherland* [*Rodina*] cycle (1907–16). The first stanza of the poem reads: "Drawing smooth circle after circle above the sleepy meadow, the kite turns and looks at the deserted meadow; in the peasant hut the mother makes an effort over her son: 'Here's some bread, here, here take the breast, drink, grow, be obedient, carry the cross'" (Chertia za krugom plavnyi krug, / Nad sonnym lugom korshun kruzhit / I smotrit na pustynnyi lug.— / V izbushke mat' nad synom tuzhit: / "Ná khleba, ná, ná grud', sosi, / Rasti, pokorstvui, krest nesi") (*SS*, 3:281).

46. Dracula does not simply destroy adults but children as well. As Margot Gayle Backus points out in her discussion of *Dracula*, "it is within the frame narrative that the novel's most explicit sacrifice of a child accompanies its clearest expression of homosexual passion. At Castle Dracula, Dracula's unreserved expressions of desire for Jonathan Harker accompany the text's most horrific and explicit image of pedophagy, in which Dracula throws a moving, whimpering bag at the feet of his three wives in a transaction that explicitly exchanges a child's life for Harker's" (*The Gothic Family Romance: Heterosexuality, Child Sacrifice, and the Anglo-Irish Colonial Order* [Durham, N.C.: Duke University Press, 1999], 135).

47. On Blok's appropriation of the Pushkinian sculptural myth, see Adrian Wanner, "Aleksandr Blok's Sculptural Myth," *Slavic and East European Journal* 40, no. 2 (1996): 236–50.

48. Wanner observes that "'Vozmezdie' (1910) contains a description of 'Pan-Moroz' riding through Warsaw that is reminiscent of *Mednyi vsadnik* and Blok's own 'Statuia'" ("Aleksandr Blok's Sculptural Myth," 241). On the figure of the Bronze Horseman in this poem, also see Mints, "Blok i Pushkin," 240–42.

49. On the heroine's relationship to Maria in *Taras Bulba*, see Mints, "Blok i Pushkin," 241.

50. On her kinship with Maria in Pushkin's *Poltava*, see Vladimir Orlov, notes, *SS*, 3:619.

51. Pavlovich, "Vospominaniia ob Aleksandre Bloke," 476–77.

52. Pavlovich, "Vospominaniia ob Aleksandre Bloke, 463–64. In a more general way, Blok appears to have been drawn to the theme of the death of the tsarevich. Around this time, Blok dedicated a large portion of his essay "On Merezhkovsky" ("O Merezhkovskom") (March 1920) to a detailed discussion of the stage adaptation of Merezhkovsky's novel *The Antichrist: Peter and Alexis* (*Antikhrist: Petr i Aleksei*) (1905).

53. Pavlovich, cited in *SS*, 3:636.

Chapter 5. Style "Femme"

Epigraphs to part 2: O. E. Mandel'shtam, "Dano mne telo—chto mne delat' s nim?" *Sobranie sochinenii v chetyrekh tomakh*, ed. G. P. Struve and B. A. Filippov, 4 vols. (Moscow: Terra, 1991), 1:6; Andrei Belyi, "Tela," *Stikhotvoreniia i poemy*, ed. John Malmstad and A. V. Lavrov, 2 vols. (St. Petersburg: Akademicheskii proekt, 2006), 1:393-94; and Marina Tsvetaeva, "Sivilla," *Sobranie sochinenii v semi tomakh*, ed. A. A. Saakiants and L. A. Mnukhin, 7 vols. (Moscow: Ellis Lak, 1994-95), 2:137.

Epigraph to chapter 5: Mirra Lokhvitskaia, "Ia ne znaiu zachem uprekaiut menia," in *Sto odna poetessa Serebrianogo veka*, ed. M. L. Gasparov, O. B. Kushlina, and T. L. Nikol'skaia (St. Petersburg: DEAN, 2000), 130.

1. For an excellent discussion of Gippius's subversion of the traditional forms of bourgeois marriage, see Olga Matich, "The Symbolist Meaning of Love: Theory and Practice," in *Creating Life: The Aesthetic Utopia of Russian Modernism*, ed. Irina Paperno and Joan Delaney Grossman (Stanford, Calif.: Stanford University Press, 1994), esp. 40-47; Olga Matich, "Zinaida Gippius: Theory and Practice of Love," in *Kul'tura russkogo moderna: Stat'i, esse i publikatsii v prinoshenie Vladimiru Fedorovichu Markovu*, ed. Ronald Vroon and John Malmstad (Moscow: Nauka, 1993), 237-51; and Olga Matich, "Dialectics of Cultural Return: Zinaida Gippius' Personal Myth," in *Cultural Mythologies of Russian Modernism: From the Golden Age to the Silver Age*, ed. Boris Gasparov, Robert P. Hughes, and Irina Paperno (Berkeley: University of California Press, 1992), esp. 60-66.

2. One might claim that women played an indispensable role in Russian symbolist circles and that no salon was complete without the presence of a woman. The most famous literary salons in Russian symbolist circles were run by couples—Zinaida Gippius and Dmitry Merezhkovsky, Lydia Zinovieva-Annibal and Viacheslav Ivanov, and Anastasia Chebotarevskaia and Fedor Sologub. For a very fine discussion of women's roles in early twentieth-century Russian salon culture, see Beth Holmgren, "Stepping Out / Going Under: Women in Russia's Twentieth-Century Salons," in *Russia / Women / Culture*, ed. Helena Goscilo and Beth Holmgren (Bloomington: Indiana University Press, 1996), 225-46.

3. For a consideration of the ways in which women symbolists responded to this tendency to be positioned as muse rather than as writing subject, see Jenifer Presto, "Women in Russian Symbolism: Beyond the Algebra of Love," in *A History of Women's Writing in Russia*, ed. Adele Barker and Jehanne Gheith (Cambridge: Cambridge University Press, 2002), 134-52.

4. On Lokhvitskaia's influence on Akhmatova, see Christine D. Tomei, "Mirra Loxvickaja and Anna Axmatova: Influence in the Evolution of the Modern Female Lyric Voice," in *Critical Essays on the Prose and Poetry of Modern Slavic Women*, ed. Nina Efimov, Christine D. Tomei, and Richard Chapple (Lewiston, N.Y.: Edwin Mellen Press, 1998), 135-60.

5. While Gippius may have pursued a creative path that was distinct from that of Akhmatova, this does not mean that she did not have an effect on Akhmatova and her generation. N. V. Koroleva persuasively argues that Akhmatova was quite familiar with Gippius's poetry from the days of her youth and that there are some striking similarities in the themes and even language of the two women's poetry (Koroleva, "Z. N. Gippius i A. A. Akhmatova," in *Zinaida Nikolaevna Gippius: Novye materialy, issledovania*, ed. N. V. Koroleva [Moscow: IMLI RAN, 2002], 335-50).

6. Lokhvitskaia, "Ia ne znaiu zachem uprekaiut menia," 130. Gippius's case would seem to support Catriona Kelly's claim that "the Russian Symbolists

[...] evolved no inspiring notion, in poetics or practice, of *écriture féminine* as a *linguistic* alternative to the restrictive expressive powers of logic" ("Reluctant Sibyls: Gender and Intertextuality in the Work of Adelaida Gertsyk and Vera Merkureva," in *Rereading Russian Poetry*, ed. Stephanie Sandler [New Haven, Conn.: Yale University Press, 1999], 134).

7. In his brief, yet perceptive, discussion of the poet, Victor Terras discusses Gippius's connections to both Baudelaire and the Russian metaphysical tradition ("Hippius," *Poetry of the Silver Age: The Various Voices of Russian Modernism* [Dresden: Dresden University Press, 1998], 63-76). In her essay "The Necessary Thing about Verses" ("Neobkhodimoe o stikhakh"), Gippius not only identifies poetry in general with prayer but she draws her poetic genealogy from the metaphysical tradition in Russian poetry, citing, among others, Fedor Tiutchev as a formative influence. On Gippius's indebtedness to Tiutchev, see Sarah Pratt, "Two Dialogues with Chaos: Tiutchev and Gippius," in *Cultural Mythologies of Russian Modernism*, 315-26.

8. Quoted in Temira Pachmuss, *Zinaida Hippius: An Intellectual Profile* (Carbondale: Southern Illinois University Press, 1971), 17. Pachmuss observes that "according to Hippius, a woman can be, and must be, first of all a human being; she may be a woman only after having established herself as a human being. To avoid stressing her femininity, Hippius often used the masculine forms which are applicable to 'chelovek'" (17). Jane A. Taubman has seen Gippius's tendency to mask her sex as a reaction to symbolist poetics. "Symbolist poetics, which cast the poet in the role of priest, seer, or prophet," she suggests, "left little room for the distinctly female voice or experience. The women poets, associated with symbolism, still uncertain about their standing in this largely masculine club, generally avoided specifically feminine themes and sought a neutral voice" ("Women Poets of the Silver Age," in *Women Writers in Russian Literature*, ed. Toby W. Clyman and Diana Greene [Westport, Conn.: Greenwood Press, 1994], 172). More recently Laura Engelstein has discussed Gippius's lyrical androgyny within the context of blurred notions of gender in Russia in the fin de siècle (*The Keys to Happiness: Sex and the Search for Modernity in Fin-de-Siècle Russia* [Ithaca, N.Y.: Cornell University Press, 1992], 396-404).

9. Gippius did not use the masculine gender exclusively in her poetry, though she usually employed the unmarked signature Z. Gippius or Z. N. Gippius. However, she did use the male pseudonym Anton Kirsha for her *Marching Songs* (*Pokhodnye pesni*) (1920) and the pseudonym V. Vitovt for selected lyrics. Some of her artistic prose works do, however, bear the signature Z. N. Gippius-Merezhkovskaia. Whether this was a result of oversights by her editors or a matter of her own choosing remains unclear. In criticism, a genre that was even more male-dominated than poetry, she employed the male pseudonyms, Anton Krainy (Anton "the Extreme"), Tovarishch German (Comrade Herman), Lev Pushchin, Lev Denisov, and Roman Arensky, as well as sometimes the initials X. and M. G. On Gippius's use of gender in her poems, see Antonina Gove, "Gender as a Poetic Feature in the Verse of Zinaida Hippius," in *American Contributions to the Eighth International Congress of Slavists*, vol. 1, ed. Henrik Birnbaum (Columbus, Ohio: Slavica, 1978), 379-407, and on the

gender of her various literary and critical pseudonyms, see Mariangela Paolini, "Kriticheskaia proza Z. N. Gippius 1899-1918 gg.: Bibliograficheskoe vvedenie v temu," in *Zinaida Nikolaevna Gippius*, 357-80.

10. Given the paucity of Russian masculine first names that begin with the letter "z," it is highly likely that most readers would have been able to guess the author's sex.

11. For a very interesting discussion of the negative cultural associations of the term "poetess" in both the Western and Russian contexts, see Svetlana Boym, *Death in Quotation Marks: Cultural Myths of the Modern Poet* (Cambridge, Mass.: Harvard University Press, 1991), 192-200. I should note that not all critics perceived Gippius's writings in such negative or stereotypically feminine terms. Such luminaries of Russian modernism as Innokenty Annensky, Andrei Bely, and Valery Briusov regarded her poetry very highly.

12. Vladimir Novoselov, "Sovremennye russkie zhenshchiny-pisatel'nitsy," *Vestnik literatury*, no. 11 (1901): 114.

13. Sandra M. Gilbert, "Marianne Moore as Female Female Impersonator," in *Marianne Moore: The Art of a Modernist*, ed. Joseph Parisi (Ann Arbor: University of Michigan Research Press, 1990), 29-46.

14. Though this approach is most prevalent in early twentieth-century criticism, it also informs some post-Soviet criticism on Russian women writers. Iurii Bezelianskii, for one, entitles his book on nineteenth- and twentieth-century women *Faith, Hope, Love . . . Female Portraits (Vera, Nadezhda, Liubov . . . zhenskie portrety* [Moscow: Raduga, 1998]) and dedicates a fair amount of space to a rather uncritical discussion of the feminine qualities and stereotypes these women embodied. He titles his chapter on Gippius "The Green-Eyed Naida" ("Zelenoglazaia naida"), despite the fact that this was a term used derogatorily by Alexander Blok in his invective 1918 poem to Gippius, "Woman, mad hothead!" ("Zhenshchina, bezumnaia gordiachka!").

15. Kornei Chukovskii, *Litsa i maski* (St. Petersburg: Shipovnik, 1914), 168.

16. Nikolai Chernyshevsky was by no means the only Russian writer to associate the sewing machine with prostitutes. In "The Seizure" ("Pripadok") (1889), Anton Chekhov's hero generalizes that there are three ways in which men have attempted to save fallen women, two of which involve buying the women sewing machines.

17. Chukovsky's neologism *slovobludie* sounds very much like the Russian word *rukobludie* meaning "masturbation."

18. Chukovskii, *Litsa i maski*, 168.

19. Matich persuasively argues in her essay "Dialectics of Cultural Return" that Chernyshevsky's novel was an important cultural text for Gippius and her entire generation. She claims that in spite of the fact that Gippius ostensibly eschewed the values of the 1860s radicals, she fashioned her marriage to Merezhkovsky after the utopian marriage of Vera Pavlovna.

20. Elisabeth G. Gitter, "The Power of Women's Hair in the Victorian Imagination," *PMLA* 99, no. 5 (1984): 936-54.

21. Sigmund Freud, "Femininity," *The Standard Edition of the Complete Psychological Works of Sigmund Freud*, trans. James Strachey, 24 vols. (London: Hogarth Press, 1953-74), 22:132.

22. Freud, "Fetishism," *The Standard Edition of the Complete Psychological Works of Sigmund Freud*, 21:152-53.

23. Roland Barthes, "Erté, or à la lettre," *Responsibility of Forms: Critical Essays on Music, Art, and Representation*, trans. Richard Howard (New York: Hill and Wang, 1985), 109. There are many flaws with Freud's interpretation of plaiting and weaving. To begin with, he automatically assumes that plaiting and weaving are exclusively feminine activities. However, in ancient Egypt, for example, it was the men who did the weaving. In addition, he seems to assume that body hair is anatomically specific to women when he interprets the female arts of plaiting and weaving as unconsciously motivated by women's desire to replicate the natural plaiting or weaving of the pubic hair that supposedly conceals the absent (female) penis. And lastly, there is the problem of his insistence on viewing woman as nothing more than a castrated male, a concept that has been cogently critiqued by many feminist scholars and theorists. In spite of these problems, feminist critics have drawn on the Freudian concept of fetishism to discuss women writers. On female appropriation of the quintessentially male perversion of fetishism, see Marjorie Garber, "Fetish Envy," *Vested Interests: Cross-Dressing and Cultural Anxiety* (New York: Routledge, 1992), 118-27, and Naomi Schor, "Female Fetishism: The Case of George Sand," *Poetics Today* 6, no. 1-2 (1985): 301-10.

24. Such affinities may be explained by the fact that both thinkers were responding to notions of the feminine and female creativity that were not only in the air, so to speak, in Europe in the early twentieth century, but also had been an important part of Western thinking since early times. As Gitter has shown in "The Power of Women's Hair in the Victorian Imagination," the Victorian tendency to view the arts of plaiting and weaving as inherently sexual in nature can be traced as far back as ancient Greece and Rome. She demonstrates that a close examination of the etymologies of the Greek and Latin words associated with plaiting and weaving reveals that the arts of the distaff side were historically conceived as functions of the female sex. She notes that "*kteis* and *pectin*, the Greek and Latin words for 'comb,' mean the heckle for combing wool and the reed for weaving. Both meanings considered with the third meaning of *kteis* and *pectin*, the female pudenda, evoke the ultimately sexual and exclusively female power to weave the family web, to create the fabric of peaceful family existence" (936).

25. A. N. Sal'nikov's book, *Contemporary Russian Poetesses in Portraits, Biographies, and Models* (*Sovremennye russkie poetessy v portretakh, biografiiakh i obraztsakh*), was published by T-va. I. N. Kushnerev i Ko. in St. Petersburg in 1905.

26. Pavel Krasnov, "Nashi sovremennye poetessy," *Vestnik literatury*, no. 16 (1905): 356.

27. Krasnov, "Nashi sovremennye poetessy," 360.

28. For a very perceptive analysis of the ways in which women writers were marketed in the popular press in Russia at the turn of the century, see Beth Holmgren, "Gendering the Icon: Marketing Women Writers in *Fin-de-Siècle* Russia," in *Russia / Women / Culture*, ed. Helena Goscilo and Beth Holmgren (Bloomington: Indiana University Press, 1996), 321-46.

29. Irina Odoevtseva, *Na beregakh Seny* (Paris: La Presse Libre, 1983), 414.

Pachmuss is also apparently referring to this same incident when she notes that "Adamovich recalls a humorous incident told to him by Hippius. In St. Petersburg she was once requested by a poetess to recite her verses at a gathering of female writers. Hippius, Adamovich says, promptly answered: 'No, thank you. I don't form any unions according to sexual denominators!'" (*Zinaida Hippius*, 17).

30. For a very interesting discussion of the complex interplay between Gippius's male critical persona and her comments on femininity, see Mariangela Paolini, "Muzhskoe 'ia' i 'zhenskost' v zerkale kriticheskoi prozy Zinaidy Gippius," in *Zinaida Nikolaevna Gippius*, 274–89.

31. Lev Pushchin, "O zhenskom pole," *Zveno*, 7 May 1923, 3.

32. Lokhvitskaia, "Ia ne znaiu zachem uprekaiut menia," 130. A notable exception is the poem, "Theme for a Poem" ("Tema dlia stikhotvoreniia"), where Gippius, in a fashion similar to Lokhvitskaia or even Akhmatova, calls attention to her own female body and clothing. The poem reads: "I have on a long, long black dress; I am sitting down low with my face to the fireplace. In the fireplace, in one corner, there is black firewood; amongst it barely wanders a weak flame. In the background, beyond the window, it is twilight—vernal, snowy, pinkish-blue. From the edge of the heavens ascends the large moon; its initial glance turns my hair cold. A thin, poor, rare bell rings. An argument silently continues in my heart: silence argues with doubts, love with indifference" (U menia dlinnoe, dlinnoe chernoe plat'e, / ia sizhu nizko, litsom k kaminu. / V kamine, v odnom uglu, chernye drova, / mezh nimi chut' brodit vialoe plamia. / Pozadi, za oknom, sumerki, / vesennie, snezhnye, rozovo-sinie. / S kraia nebes podymaetsia bol'shaia luna, / ee pervyi vzor kholodit moi volosy. / Zvonit kolokol, tonkii, bednyi, redkii. / Spor idet neslyshno v moem serdtse: / Sporit tishina—s somnen'iami, / Liubov'—s ravnodushiem) (*Stikh*, 292). The distinctly feminine quality of this poem was remarked on by Petr Pertsov who commented that "in spite of its incompleteness and the very 'feminine' character [ochen' 'zhenskii' kharakter] of its theme and execution, this poetic embryo is not without interest, the least of which is that it realistically depicts the domestic existence of Zinaida Nikolaevna" (cited in *Stikh*, 528).

33. Akim Volynsky, "Sil'fida," in "A Fairy Tale of Love?: The Relationship of Zinaida Gippius and Akim Volynsky (Unpublished Materials)," ed. Stanley Rabinowitz, *Oxford Slavonic Papers* (Oxford, England: Clarendon Press, 1991), 135.

34. Nina Berberova, *The Italics Are Mine*, trans. Philippe Radley (New York: Harcourt, Brace, and World, 1969), 243; Nina Berberova, *Kursiv moi: Avtobiografiia* (Munich: Wilhelm Fink, 1972), 277.

35. In her memoirs, Odoevtseva continually makes reference to the fact that she was compared to Gippius, suggesting that Gippius embodied the image of the "poetess" against which subsequent generations of women writers were judged. She claims: "One time in Petersburg during my poetry reading I had to hear the excited outbursts of the elderly female representatives of literary Bohemia: 'Just like our Zina!' Although judging by her portrait, I did not resemble her in the least" (*Na beregakh Seny*, 386–87). And a little later she notes: "No, [Gippius] did not resemble Bakst's portrait or the

imaginary portrait I created based on stories about her. And she did not in the least resemble me. Absolutely not in the least. And thank God! (388).

36. Berberova, *The Italics Are Mine*, 243; Berberova, *Kursiv moi*, 277.

37. Sergei Makovskii, *Na Parnase "Serebrianogo veka"* (Munich: Izdatel'stvo tsentral'nogo ob"edineniia politicheskikh emigrantov iz SSSR, 1962), 90.

38. Vladimir Zlobin, *A Difficult Soul: Zinaida Gippius*, ed. and trans. Simon Karlinsky (Berkeley: University of California Press, 1980), 59; V. Zlobin, *Tiazhelaia dusha* (Washington, D.C.: Victor Kamkin, 1970), 278.

39. Berberova, *The Italics Are Mine*, 244; Berberova, *Kursiv moi*, 278.

40. Quoted in Luce Irigaray , *This Sex Which Is Not One*, trans. Catherine Porter and Carolyn Burke (Ithaca, N.Y.: Cornell University Press, 1985), 220.

41. For an excellent discussion of the trope of fashion in Russian modernism, see Elizabeth M. Durst, "Modern by Design: The 'New Woman' and the Evolution of the Trope of Fashion," in *A Cut Above: Fashion as Meta-Culture in Early-Twentieth-Century Russia* (Ph.D. diss., University of Southern California, 2003), 250-311.

42. Quoted in Georgii Adamovich, "Zinaida Gippius," *Mosty* 13-14 (1968), 207. I have translated *shpil'ki* rather literally as "pins," since Gippius herself seems to reinforce this meaning. Of course, *shpil'ki* could also be translated more figuratively as "caustic remarks" in the sense of the Russian expressions "zapuskat' shpil'ki" or "podpuskat' shpil'ki" (to get a dig at [someone]) (Vladimir Dal', *Tolkovyi slovar' zhivogo velikorusskogo iazyka v chetyrekh tomakh*, 4 vols. [Moscow: Progress, 1994], 4:1468).

43. In her criticism, Gippius frequently employed the metaphor of fashion to critique the style of her contemporaries. For instance, in *The Literary Diary* (*Literaturnyi dnevnik*) (1899-1907), which was published in 1908 under the pseudonym of Anton Krainy, she likens the bright spots in Anton Chekhov's *Cherry Orchard* (*Vishnevyi sad*) (1903) to individual beads that "are neither connected, nor strung together into a necklace, [since] they are too small for it [and] there is no thread which could pass through them" (*Dnev*, 1:275) and admonishes Leonid Andreev for his appropriation of a "fashionable theme" (*Dnev*, 1:296).

44. On the use of fashion tropes to refer to writing style, see M. H. Abrams, *The Mirror and the Lamp: Romantic Theory and the Critical Tradition* (Oxford: Oxford University Press), 229-35.

45. Although the Russian words *tekst* and *tkan'* would appear to have less of an etymological relationship than the English words "text" and "textile," it should be noted that, according to Max Vasmer, both *tekst* and *tkan'* are derived from the Latin word *textus* (*Etimologicheskii slovar' russkogo iazyka: V chetyrekh tomakh*, 4:36).

46. Vasmer, *Etimologicheskii slovar' russkogo iazyka*, 2:601.

47. Gippius picks up this thread again in her second collection of verse in the poems "Good News" ("Blagaia vest'") (March 1904) and "The Knot" ("Uzel") (1905) as well as in the poem, "Tie up" ("Zaviazhi"), which she did not include in a specific collection of poems.

48. In this regard, Gippius's tendency to disassociate the feminine from the speaking subject is symptomatic of the split feminine gaze that has been discussed by John Berger among others. According to Berger, "*men act* and *women*

appear. Men look at women. Women watch themselves being looked at. This determines not only most relations between men and women but also the relation of women to themselves. The surveyor of women in herself is male: the surveyed female. Thus she turns herself into an object—and most particularly an object of vision: a sight" (*Ways of Seeing* [London: British Broadcasting Corporation, 1972], 47).

49. There has been a tendency among some of Gippius's early commentators to assume that she always wrote using the masculine voice. Makovsky notes that her "'Classicism' answers to her masculine mood [muzhestvennoi ee nastroennosti]; Zinaida Nikolaevna's poems and her prose are always [written] with a masculine 'I'" (*Na Parnase "Serebrianogo veka,"* 95), and Zlobin compares a poem which Gippius purportedly wrote at age seven to one she wrote at the end of her life and asserts that it contains "the same theme, the same meter, with the invariable masculine gender, and the same attitude toward the world—offended and contemptuous, like Lermontov's Demon" (*A Difficult Soul*, 36; *Tiazhelaia dusha*, 14).

50. Gippius would not be unique in this regard. Alexander Blok also represents Mary as engaged in handiwork in his poem "Annunciation" ("Blagoveshchenie") (May–June 1909), composed five years later. In his discussion of Blok's poem, Gerald Pirog observes that "it is not surprising that Mary is creating something with her hands, weaving an object of great beauty and holiness, since she is viewed as a real participant in the creative process—both the aesthetic and the biological" (Pirog, *Aleksandr Blok's* Ital'ianskie stikhi: *Confrontation and Disillusionment* [Columbus, Ohio: Slavica, 1983], 98). Pirog's comments on Blok's poem have informed my discussion of Gippius's "Good News."

51. Olga Matich, *Paradox in the Religious Poetry of Zinaida Gippius* (Munich: Wilhelm Fink, 1972), 83.

52. D. S. Mirsky, *A History of Russian Literature* (New York: Knopf, 1960), 440–41.

53. Fyodor Dostoyevsky, *Crime and Punishment*, trans. Sidney Monas (New York: Signet Classic, 2006), 277; F. M. Dostoevskii, *Prestuplenie i nakazanie*, *Sobranie sochinenii v piatnadtsati tomakh*, ed. G. M. Friedlender and T. I. Ornatskaia, 15 vols. (Leningrad: Nauka, 1988–96), 5:272. Though the Dostoevsky subtext is the most obvious one, this poem also bears a striking similarity to some of the poetry of Charles Baudelaire and even Stéphane Mallarmé. For instance, in one of Baudelaire's *Spleen* poems in *Les Fleurs du mal* (1857), we encounter the lines: "And when a host of spiders, mute, set out / To weave their loathsome webs deep in our brain" (Et qu'un peuple muet d'infâmes araignées / Vient tendres ses filets au fond de nos cerveaux) (Baudelaire, *Selected Poems from* Les Fleurs du mal, trans. Norman R. Shapiro [Chicago: University of Chicago Press, 1998], 144–45). And in the prose poem, "Winter Shiver" ("Frisson d'Hiver") (1867), Mallarmé's speaker repeatedly makes reference to spider webs. On the motif of the spider in Russian modernism, see A. Hansen-Löve, *Russkii simvolizm: Sistema poeticheskikh motivov. Rannii simvolizm* (St. Petersburg: Akademicheskii proekt, 1999), especially 101–2; on the indebtedness of Gippius and the other Russian symbolists to French symbolism, see Georgette Donchin, *The Influence of French Symbolism on Russian Poetry* (The Hague: Mouton, 1958); Adrian Wanner,

Baudelaire in Russia (Gainesville: University of Florida Press, 1996); and Roman Dubrovkin, *Stefan Mallarme i Rossii* (Bern: Peter Lang, 1998).

54. On the importance of Ovid's *Metamorphoses*, as well as the more general theoretical problem of metamorphosis in Russian modernism, see Peter I. Barta, ed., *Metamorphoses in Russian Modernism* (Budapest: Central European University Press, 2000).

55. Some feminist critics have recuperated the figure of Arachne. Nancy K. Miller, for example, has coined the term "arachnology" to refer to "a critical positioning which reads *against* the weave of indifferentiation to discover the embodiment of writing in a gendered subjectivity; to recover within representation the emblems of its construction" ("Arachnologies: The Woman, the Text, and the Critic," in *The Poetics of Gender*, ed. Nancy K. Miller [New York: Columbia University Press, 1986], 272).

56. The connection between letter writing and spiders was acknowledged in the folk myths of various Slavic cultures long before the invention of the World Wide Web. A native speaker of Bulgarian has informed me that in Bulgaria it is believed that if you brush up against a spider web you will receive a letter in the near future, whereas a native Russian speaker told me that in Russia it is commonly held that if you see a spider you will receive a letter.

57. Gippius's neologism "svoestrunnyi" would seem to be related to the Russian word *svoeobrazhnyi* meaning "original," "peculiar," or "distinctive" but differs in its reliance on a root that has a clear musical (and by extension lyrical) resonance. *Strunnyi* refers to "stringed" as in "stringed instrument" or "string orchestra," whereas *obraznyi* refers to something that is either picturesque or figurative.

58. Vladimir Maiakovskii, "Prikaz no. 2 armii iskusstv," *Polnoe sobranie sochinenii v trinadtsati tomakh*, 13 vols. (Moscow: Gos. izd-vo khudozhestvennoi lit-ry, 1955–61), 2:86. In the poem "Tristia" (1918), Osip Mandelstam also implicitly compares the poetic process to weaving. He notes: "And I love the custom of weaving: The shuttle scurries, the spindle drones" (I ia liubliu obyknoven'e priazhi: / Snuet chelnok, vereteno zhuzhzhit) (Mandel'shtam, "Tristia," *Sobranie sochinenii v chetyrekh tomakh*, 1:73).

59. Roland Barthes, *The Pleasure of the Text*, trans. Richard Miller (New York: Hill and Wang, 1972), 64. Barthes's theory of the text as an hyphology may have been influenced by a letter of Stéphane Mallarmé to Théodor Aubanel where he notes that he "found the key to myself, the crown, or the center (if you prefer to call it that, so we won't get our metaphors mixed) — the center of myself where, like a sacred spider, I hang on the main threads which I have already spun from my mind" (Mallarmé, *Selected Poetry and Prose*, ed. Mary Ann Caws [New York: New Directions, 1982], 85).

60. "The Spiders" is by no means the only poem where Gippius expresses anxiety about the issue of female authorship or creativity. In the poem, "The Feminine 'It doesn't exist'" ("Zhenskoe 'Netu'") (1907), which she included in her second volume of poems, she presents the feminine as a child who is destined to create a wreath and to mourn because she doesn't exist and the masculine speaker as someone who simultaneously identifies and distances himself from her. This becomes clear in the poem's second stanza, which reads: "Girl,

who has offended you? Tell me: I too, like you, am alone. (Secretly I hated the girl and didn't understand why she would need a wreath)" (Devochka, kto tebia obidel? / skazhi mne: i ia, kak ty, odinok. / [Vtaine ia devochku nenavidel, / ne ponimal, zachem ei venok]) (*Stikh*, 179). For a brief yet perceptive account of the way in which this poem reflects Gippius's tendency to internalize symbolism's inhospitable views of feminine creativity, see Jane Taubman, "Tsvetaeva and the Feminine Tradition in Russian Poetry," in *Marina Tsvetaeva: One Hundred Years*, ed. Viktoria Schweitzer, Jane A. Taubman, Peter Scotto, and Tatyana Babyonyshev (Oakland, Calif.: Berkeley Slavic Specialties, 1994), esp. 78.

61. Dmitry Filosofov reportedly identified Gippius with the figure of the spider. Zlobin recalls that Filosofov expressed to him that "'the feeling doesn't leave me for a moment that she is practicing *sorcery* on me, that I have gotten entangled in the innumerable strands of Zina's *personal* spider web. I demand that Zina totally give up the relationship she wants from me. Perhaps temporarily, until our equilibrium is reestablished, perhaps even forever. But so long as I sense that things are muddled and confused, while I sense the use of *sorcery* here, she has no right to disregard my feelings, because this is a form of rape'" (*A Difficult Soul*, 99–100; *Tiazhelaia dusha*, 65–66). Based on Zlobin's account, it is possible to say that Filosofov apparently feared the "kiss of the spider woman."

62. In her discussion of Mitrich's caricature of Gippius, Olga Matich observes that "she is phallic, but not mannish—an image projected not only by the cigarette she holds in her mouth, but also from the profile view. According to philosopher and mathematician Pavel Florensky, the profile signifies power in contrast to the frontal view; it is a destabilizing facial angle that connotes forward movement. While Florensky does not address the question of gender, his interpretation explains why the profile might have had appeal for women like Gippius" ("Gender Trouble in the Amazonian Kingdom: Turn-of-the-Century Representations of Women in Russia," in *Amazons of the Avant-Garde: Alexandra Exeter, Natalia Goncharova, Liubov Popova, Olga Rozanova, Varvara Stepanova, and Nadezhda Udaltsova*, ed. John E. Bowlt and Matthew Drutt [New York: Guggenheim Museum Publications, 2000]. 79).

63. Pachmuss, *Zinaida Hippius*, 310.

64. See Catherine Schuler, "Zinaida Gippius: An Unwitting and Unwilling Feminist," in *Theatre and Feminist Aesthetics*, ed. Karen Laughlin and Catherine Schuler (Madison, N.J.: Fairleigh Dickinson University Press, 1995), 131–47.

65. Boym, *Death in Quotation Marks*, 262 n 55.

Chapter 6. The Dandy's Gaze

Epigraph to chapter 6: N. A. Teffi, "Demonicheskaia zhenshchina," *Antologiia satiry i iumora Rossii XX veka*, vol. 12 (Moscow: EKSMO-Press, 2001), 135.

1. Vladimir Zlobin suggests that the title of the "white she-devil" may have been conferred upon Gippius because of a particularly provocative dress she wore to a meeting of the Religious-Philosophical Society (*A Difficult Soul: Zinaida Gippius*, ed. and trans. Simon Karlinsky [Berkeley: University of California Press, 1980], 46–47, and *Tiazhelaia dusha* [Washington, D.C.: Victor Kamkin, 1970], 22; the specific passage where Zlobin describes the dress is cited in chapter 8).

And Georgy Adamovich recalls: "In the very beginning of the revolution Trotsky released a brochure on the struggle against religious prejudices. 'It's time, comrades, to understand that there is no God, there are no angels, there are no devils or witches,' and suddenly completely unexpectedly in parentheses: 'No, however, there is one witch, Zinaida Gippius.' I caught sight of that brochure already here in Paris, and brought it to Zinaida Nikolaevna. With her eternal lorgnette in her hands, she read through it, frowned, and grumbled: 'What is this? What is it that he has he imagined?,' and then she laughed gaily and admitted that at least it was witty" (Adamovich, "Zinaida Gippius," *Mosty* 13-14 [1968]: 207). Olga Matich also discusses the incident with Trotsky in her book (*Paradox in the Religious Poetry of Zinaida Gippius* [Munich: Wilhelm Fink, 1972], 9).

2. On Gippius's poems to the devil, see Olga Matich, "The Devil in the Poetry of Zinaida Gippius," *Slavic and East European Journal* 16, no. 1 (1972): 184-92; for a more subjective account of Gippius's encounters with the devil, see Zlobin, *A Difficult Soul,* 64-76 and 134-53; Zlobin, *Tiazhelaia dusha,* 37-46 and 94-110.

3. S. V. Golynets, *Lev Bakst: Zhivopis', grafika, teatral'noe dekoratsionnoe iskusstvo* (Moscow: Izobrazitel'noe iskusstvo, 1992), 16.

4. N. A. Teffi, "Zinaida Gippius," *Vozrozhdenie ("La Renaissance"),* notebook 43, July 1955, 88.

5. Nina Berberova compares Gippius rather negatively to Gertrude Stein. She observes: "I also see now that there was in Gippius much that was in Gertrude Stein (in whom there was also undoubtedly hermaphroditism, but who managed to liberate and realize herself to a much greater degree): the same inclination to quarrel with people and then somehow to make peace with them; and only *forgive* others their normal love, secretly scorning a little all that was normal and of course not understanding normal love at all. That same trait of closing one's eyes to reality in a man and placing under a microscope one's fantasies about him, or overlooking the bad books of anyone well disposed to her (and Merezhkovsky). As Stein ignored Joyce and did not invite to her place people who spoke of Joyce, so Gippius did not speak of Nabokov and did not listen when others spoke of him" (*The Italics Are Mine,* trans. Philippe Radley [New York: Harcourt, Brace, and World, 1969], 248; *Kursiv moi: Avtobiografiia* [Munich: Wilhelm Fink, 1972], 282).

6. Zlobin, *A Difficult Soul,* 59; Zlobin, *Tiazhelaia dusha,* 32.

7. Olga Matich has remarked on Gippius's connection to the figure of Cleopatra in the Pushkinian society tale as well as to the figure of the Pushkinian dandy ("Dialectics of Cultural Return: Zinaida Gippius' Personal Myth," in *Cultural Mythologies of Russian Modernism: From the Golden Age to the Silver Age,* ed. Boris Gasparov, Robert P. Hughes, and Irina Paperno [Berkeley: University of California Press, 1992], 53-60), and I build on her discussion of Gippius's dandyism in this chapter. Where my analysis of Gippius's dandyism differs from Matich's is in its focus on Gippius's assumption of a dandified gaze that is normally coded as masculine and that informs the way Gippius positions herself both in the salon and in her writings.

8. Iurii Lotman, "Russkii dendizm," *Besedy o russkoi kul'ture: Byt i traditsii russkogo dvorianstva (XVII-nachalo XIX veka)* (St. Petersburg: Iskusstvo-SPB, 1994), 129.

9. Lotman, "Russkii dendizm," 130. On Pushkin and dandyism, also see Monika Greenleaf, *Pushkin and Romantic Fashion: Fragment, Elegy, Orient, Irony* (Stanford, Calif.: Stanford University Press, 1994), 215–37; Sam Driver, "The Dandy in Pushkin," *Slavic and East European Journal* 29, no. 3 (1985): 243–57; and Leonid Grossman, "Pushkin i dendizm," *Etiudy o Pushkine* (Moscow: Izdatel'stvo L. D. Frenkel', 1923), 5–36; On dandyism in Russia in general, see Ol'ga Vainshtein, "Dendizm v Rossii," *Dendi: Moda, literatura, stil' zhizni* (Moscow: Novoe literaturnoe obozrenie, 2006), 485–539; Olga Vainshtein, "Russian Dandyism: Constructing a Man of Fashion," in *Russian Masculinities in History and Culture*, ed. Barbara Evans Clement, Rebecca Friedman, and Dan Healey (Houndmills, England: Palgrave, 2002), 51–75; Iuliia Demidenko, "Russkii dendi," *Rodina*, no. 8 (2000): 111–14; Mark Allen Svede, "Twiggy and Trotsky: Or, What the Soviet Dandy Will Be Wearing This Next Five-Year Plan," in *Dandies: Fashion and Finesse in Art and Culture*, ed. Susan Fillin-Yeh (New York: New York University Press, 2001), 243–69; and Helena Goscilo, "Keeping A-Breast of the Waist-land: Women's Fashion in Early-Nineteenth-Century Russia," in *Russia / Women / Culture*, ed. Helena Goscilo and Beth Holmgren (Bloomington: Indiana University Press, 1996), 33–34.

10. Sergei Makovskii, *Na Parnase "Serebrianogo veka"* (Munich: Izdatel'stvo tsentral'nogo ob"edineniia politicheskikh emigrantov iz SSSR, 1962), 90. Andrei Bely also makes reference to "the shine from a lorgnette" (blesk ot lorneta) in his portrait of Gippius (*Nachalo veka* [Moscow: Khudozhestvennaia literatura, 1990], 194).

11. Sergei Esenin, *Polnoe sobranie sochinenii v semi tomakh*, ed. Iu. L. Prokushev and L. D. Gromova, 7 vols. (Moscow: Nauka-Golos, 1995–2000) 5:230.

12. Irina Odoevtseva, *Na beregakh Seny* (Paris: La Presse Libre, 1983), 394.

13. Later in these same memoirs, Odoevtseva expresses outrage when she realizes that Alexander Kerensky and Gippius are standing in a room together with her and that Kerensky is sporting a lorgnette and Gippius a monocle. "He is extremely nearsighted," she remarks, "but owing to some incomprehensible coquetry he doesn't want to wear glasses or a pince-nez. Instead of glasses, he uses, as I was told, a lorgnette. A man with a lorgnette was for me as unthinkable and unbelievable as a woman with a monocle. But here they are—a woman with a monocle and a man with a lorgnette, it must be, the only ones in the world—standing right here in front of me" (*Na beregakh Seny*, 420).

14. Jessica Feldman, *Gender on the Divide: The Dandy in Modernist Literature* (Ithaca, N.Y.: Cornell University Press, 1993), 6. Other studies on dandyism that I have found particularly useful in formulating my discussion are Rhonda Garelick, *Rising Star: Dandyism, Gender, and Performance in the Fin de Siècle* (Princeton, N.J.: Princeton University Press, 1998); Bernard Howells, *Baudelaire: Individualism, Dandyism, and the Philosophy of History* (Oxford, England: Legenda, 1996); James Laver, *Dandies* (London: Weidenfeld and Nicolson, 1968); and Ellen Moers, *The Dandy: Brummell to Beerbohm* (New York: Viking Press, 1960).

15. Feldman, *Gender on the Divide*, 6. In *Rising Star*, Rhonda Garelick offers a somewhat different take on the dandy's investment in the feminine. She argues that the dandies of Charles Baudelaire, Joris-Karl Huysmans, Stéphane Mallarmé, and Oscar Wilde are all indebted to the figure of Salome and to her

dance of the seven veils for their self-images, and she connects this infatuation with the biblical figure to the rise in the predominance of the female performer in late nineteenth- and early twentieth-century Europe.

16. Oscar Wilde was an important cultural figure for the Russian modernists. On Wilde and Russian modernism, see Evgenii Bershtein, "The Russian Myth of Oscar Wilde," in *Self and Story in Russian History,* ed. Laura Engelstein and Stephanie Sandler (Ithaca, N.Y.: Cornell University Press, 2000), 168-88; Rachel Polonsky, "How Important It Is To Be Serious: Oscar Wilde's Popularity," *English Literature and the Russian Aesthetic Renaissance* (Cambridge: Cambridge University Press, 1998), 152-69; T. V. Pavlova, "Oskar Ual'd v russkoi literature (konets xix — nachalo xx v.)," in *Na rubezhe xix i xx vekov: Iz istorii mezhdunarodnykh sviazei russkoi literatury,* ed. Iu. D. Levin (Leningrad: Nauka, 1991), 77-128; and Betsy Moeller-Sally, "Oscar Wilde and the Culture of Russian Modernism," *Slavic and East European Journal* 34, no. 3 (1990): 459-72. Vainshtein remarks that "the dandy's style was particularly valued by the famous circle of avant-garde artists that called itself *Mir iskusstva* (World of Art). Theirs was, of course, not the military style of dandyism of the mid-nineteenth century, but one rather more in the aesthetic, decadent vein. Stylistically derivative, it was oriented toward the fin-de-siècle Western literature of Oscar Wilde, Charles Baudelaire, and Joris-Karl Huysmans. The fundamental originality here was not to be found in everyday clothing or the behavior of the *miriskusniki* (The World of Art-ites), but in their artistic innovations in painting and later in the design of scenery and costumes for the Ballets Russes, which had a real influence on European culture" ("Russian Dandyism," 68). On the aesthetic practices of the World of Art, see John E. Bowlt, *The Silver Age: Russian Art of the Early Twentieth Century and the "World of Art"* (Newtonville, Mass.: Oriental Research Partners, 1979).

17. Svetlana Boym, *Death in Quotation Marks: Cultural Myths of the Modern Poet* (Cambridge, Mass.: Harvard University Press, 1991), 262.

18. Cited in Alexander Von Gleichen-Russwurm, *Dandies and Don Juans: Concerning Fashion and Love Among the Great,* trans. Margaret M. Green (New York: Knopf, 1928), xxiii.

19. Bershtein has shown that there is a direct connection between Gippius and the phenomenon of Oscar Wilde. He remarks that "Zinaida Gippius's society tale 'Oxeye' (Zlatotsvet), published in *Severnyi vestnik* (Northern Herald) eight months after the [Wilde] trials, provides a lively satirical picture of the St. Petersburg artistic circles that had started discussing Wilde's writing and creating his reputation" ("The Russian Myth of Oscar Wilde," 175).

20. Lydia Ginzburg, *On Psychological Prose,* trans. Judson Rosengrant (Princeton, N.J.: Princeton University Press, 1991), 105 .

21. Olga Matich, "The Symbolist Meaning of Love: Theory and Practice," in *Creating Life: The Aesthetic Utopia of Russian Modernism,* ed. Irina Paperno and Joan Delaney Grossman (Stanford, Calif.: Stanford University Press, 1994), 39-40.

22. Gippius's choice of the surname "Martynov" is highly suggestive in this context, since it was Nikolai Martynov who was responsible for killing Mikhail Lermontov, one of the prototypical nineteenth-century Russian dandies. By naming her memoirist Martynov, she would seem to suggest that his memoirs

should be read within the context of the larger dandy tradition in Russian literature and culture. Kathryn Louise McCormack comments briefly on the Lermontovian connections in her discussion of the story, which focuses on its androgynous aspects ("Images of Women in the Poetry of Zinaida Gippius" [Ph.D. diss., Vanderbilt University, 1982], 185–90).

23. I am grateful to Hilde Hoogenboom for providing me with the information about Viktor Burenin's exotic society tale.

24. Gippius's Don Juanism has not gone unnoticed. Makovsky was the first to point out that "her desire for love carried the character of Don Juanism (not without aestheticism), but of course also Don Juanism striving toward 'a high ideal'" (*Na Parnase "Serebrianogo veka,"* 117). Matich has also discussed Gippius's Don Juanism ("Dialectics of Cultural Return," 57–60).

25. It was also in 1901 that Gippius composed her poem "The Notebook of Love (An Inscription on an Envelope)" ("Tetrad' liubvi [Nadpis' na konverte]") in which she articulates the unspeakable nature of the events contained within these memoirs. As the poem's second stanza reads: "And I want to break the seals ... But my will is bound with humility. Let the notebook lay forever closed. Let the story of my Love remain unfinished" (I khochetsia mne pechati slomat' ... / No volia moia smireniem sviazana. / Pust' vechno zakrytoi lezhit tetrad', / Pust' budet Liubov' moia — nedoskazana) (*Stikh*, 123). After sealing up her own diary of love affairs in 1901, Gippius eventually broke the seal in February 1904 so she could add two more entries.

26. Julia Kristeva, "Don Juan, or Loving to Be Able To," *Tales of Love*, trans. Leon D. Roudiez (New York: Columbia University Press, 1987), 191–92.

27. Gippius wrote this poem in response to Georgy Adamovich's "Don Juan, patron and protector" ("Don-Zhuan patron i pokrovitel'") (1926). With this work, Gippius joins a long line of Russian writers who wrote poems, dramas, and essays about the figure. For more on the theme of Don Juan in Russian literature and culture, see *Don Zhuan russkii*, ed. A. V. Parin (Moscow: Agraf, 2000).

28. François Roustang, *The Quadrille of Gender: Casanova's "Memoirs,"* trans. Anne C. Vila (Stanford, Calif.: Stanford University Press, 1988), 13.

29. René Girard, *Deceit, Desire, and the Novel: Self and Other in Literary Structure*, trans. Yvonne Freccero (Baltimore, M.D.: Johns Hopkins University Press, 1965).

30. Simon Karlinsky has pointed out that it was in Taormina that Gippius and her husband came into "close association with the male homosexual coterie of Baron Wilhelm von Gloeden, the pioneering photographer of male nudes" ("Introduction: Who Was Zinaida Gippius?" in Zlobin, *A Difficult Soul*, 8). And more recently, K. K. Rotikov has discussed the Merezhkovskys' connection with Taormina and homosexuality (*Drugoi Peterburg* [St. Petersburg: Liga plius, 2000], esp. 498–509). On the image of Taormina in Gippius's prose and its connection with homosexuality, see R. D. B. Tomson, "Vstrecha v Taormine: Tri redaktsii odnoi istorii," in *Zinaida Nikolaevna Gippius: Novye materialy, issledovaniia*. ed. N. V. Koroleva (Moscow: IMLI RAN, 2002), 262–73.

31. There is an inherently narcissistic element to Gippius's general understanding of romantic attraction. According to Gippius, all human beings are

essentially androgynous and are attracted to those who mirror their own androgynous attributes. In "The Arithmetic of Love" ("Arifmetika liubvi") (1931), a late essay inspired by the writings of Vladimir Soloviev and Otto Weininger, she claims that a "man-womanly" [muzhezhenskoe] being would be attracted to a "woman-manly" [zhenomuzhskoe] being whose degree of male-femaleness and female-maleness were in inverse proportion to each other ("Arifmetika liubvi," in *Russkii eros ili filosofiia liubvi v Rossii,* ed. V. P. Shestakov [Moscow: Progress, 1991], 211).

32. To be more precise, Alan Sinfield contends that after the Wilde trials the figure of the dandy not only became associated with the homosexual but also that homosexual men in fact modeled themselves on the dandified figure of Wilde. Thus, according to his Foucauldian reading of fin-de-siècle culture, the dandified or effete male homosexual was in effect produced by the juridical system (*The Wilde Century: Effeminacy, Oscar Wilde, and the Queer Movement* [New York: Columbia University Press], 1994).

33. Quoted in Feldman, *Gender on the Divide,* 7.

34. Vainshtein reports that "there was serious and more than intermittent interest during the Russian Silver Age in Barbey d'Aurevilly's work. He was eagerly translated (see his *Liki d'iavola* [St. Petersburg: 1908]; *D'iavol'skie maski* [Moscow: 1909, 1913], renderings of his *Les Diaboliques*) and quoted. Maximilian Voloshin devoted three articles to him for the Petersburg edition, which is highly indicative. D'Aurevilly's heroes became the sources and models for a number of characters in Russian prose fiction. Voloshin saw in him an 'underground classic' of French literature; 'of all the solitary minds he remained, perhaps, the most undervalued'" ("Russian Dandyism," 74-75 n 52).

35. Gippius did, after all, dedicate the beautiful poem "Orange Blossoms" ("Apel'sinnye tsvety") (1897) to Briquet and did have other dandified male muses, most notably Dmitry Filosofov, to whom she dedicated the highly suggestive poem "The Barrier" ("Predel") (1901) and with whom she had an epistolary relationship. For Gippius's letters to Filosofov, see *IIA,* 61-113.

36. Feldman, *Gender on the Divide,* 6.

37. Quoted in Feldman, *Gender on the Divide,* 6. The translation from the French is Feldman's.

38. The accusation of hysteria that Gippius levels against Madame Reif could well be turned against Gippius herself. If we were to read Gippius according to a strict psychoanalytic framework, we might proclaim that she demonstrates many of the classical characteristics of the hysteric. Though she does not demonstrate the somatic abnormalities classically associated with the hysteric, she was more than willing to transform her body into a text to be read by her contemporaries. On Gippius's creation of a text of her body, see chapter 8.

39. In terms not only of her bisexuality but also of her thriving on serial romances, Gippius could be compared to Marina Tsvetaeva. Tsvetaeva evinced a fascination with both the figure of Don Juan (she wrote a poem called "Don Juan" ["Don-Zhuan"]) as well as the related figure of Casanova, devoting her plays *An Adventure* (*Prikliuchenie*) and *The Phoenix* (*Feniks*), both completed in 1919, to the theme. On Tsvetaeva's identification with the figure of Casanova, see Peter Scotto, "Towards a Reading of Tsvetaeva's *Feniks,*" in *Marina Tsvetaeva:*

One Hundred Years, ed. Viktoria Schweitzer, Jane A. Taubman, Peter Scotto, and Tatyana Babyonyshev (Oakland, Calif.: Berkeley Slavic Specialties, 1994), 194-201.

40. In this regard, I concur with Catriona Kelly who observes that "Zinaida Gippius is a notable example of a poet whose 'androgyny' usually, though not invariably, takes the form of [. . .] conventional polarization: many of her love poems oppose a predatory masculine speaker to a shrinking feminine one, or vice versa. Some poems do, however, handle the issue of androgyny more ambiguously, representing internal conflicts whose oppositions are not resolved by a central governing conflict" (*A History of Russian Women's Writing, 1800-1992* [Oxford, England: Clarendon Press, 1994], 169). For a consideration of the philosophical underpinnings of Gippius's androgyny, see Olga Matich, "Zinaida Gippius and the Unisex of Heavenly Existence," *Die Welt der Slaven* 19-20 (1974-75): 98-104, and Olga Matich, "Androgyny and the Russian Religious Renaissance," in *Western Philosophical Systems in Russian Literature*, ed. Anthony Mlikotin (Los Angeles: University of Southern California Press, 1979), 165-75.

41. K. M. Azadovskii and A. V. Lavrov, commentary to *Soch*, 613-14.

42. In her earlier work on the poet, Matich reads some of these poems in a largely metaphysical context. She notes that "in the poem 'Progulka vdoem' (1900), the poet and her companion are climbing a mountain, which becomes increasingly steeper and therefore more difficult to climb. This motif of walking or moving in an upward direction in the quest for truth is not infrequent in Gippius's poetry (e.g. 'Lestnica,' 1897)" (*Paradox in the Religious Poetry of Zinaida Gippius*, 40).

43. This quality, it should be noted, is less apparent in some of the love lyrics she addressed to women in later years. For instance, the ethos of courtly love, not dandyism, seems to inform the poems she dedicated to the young Nina Berberova. Among the poems she dedicated to Berberova are: "The Eternal Feminine" ("Vechnozhenstvennoe"), the two poems comprising the short cycle *To Her in the Mountains* (*Ei v gorakh*), "To Her in Thorenc" ("Ei v Thorenc"), and "October" ("Oktiabr'") (1926). Gippius included the first three of these poems in her final collection *Radiances* (*Siianiia*) (1938) but without the dedication to Berberova.

44. It bears noting that in 1919 Gippius wrote a poem entitled "Disdain" ("Prezren'e"), which reads: "It seems: never again will I destroy the quiet of my soul. But a star flashed in my window, and again I am sorry for my soul. Everything died long ago in my soul. Hatred and indignation burned out. Oh, poor soul! One thing remains in it: squeamish disdain" (Kazalos': bol'she nikogda / Molchaniia dushi ia ne narushu. / No vspykhnula v okne zvezda,— / I ia opiat' moiu zhaleiu dushu. // Vsë umerlo v dushe davno. / Ugasli nenavist' i vozmushchen'e. / O bednaia dusha! Odno / Ostalos' v nei: brezglivoe prezren'e) (*Stikh*, 337).

45. Cited in *Soch*, 619.

46. In the first edition of Gippius's *Collected Poetry* (*Sobranie stikhov* [Moscow: Skorpion, 1904]), the first two lines of the fourth stanza appeared as: "Both bewilderment and closeness are the same—in both there is alarm" (I udivlenie, i tesnost' / Ravny,—v oboikh est' trevozhnost') (132).

47. Sibelan Forrester, "Wooing the Other Woman: Gender in Women's Love

Poetry in the Silver Age," in *Engendering Slavic Literatures,* ed. Pamela Chester and Sibelan Forrester (Bloomington: Indiana University Press, 1996), 111.

48. The reason that Arnolphe deprives his ward and future fiancée of an education is to ensure that he does not become cuckolded. His strategy, however, ends up backfiring. In Gippius's poem, the intricacies of the marriage plot of *The School for Wives* seems to be less important than the play's association of the name Agnès with ignorance and subservience.

49. Forrester, "Wooing the Other Woman," 112.

50. Max Vasmer, *Etimologicheskii slovar' russkogo iazyka: V chetyrekh tomakh,* 4 vols. (Moscow: Progress, 1986–87), 4:544–45.

51. Cathy Popkin approaches the story as a "meditation on kissing and telling, both as the sequence that produces Anton Chekhov's story 'The Kiss' ('Potselui'), and as a model for storytelling in general" ("Kiss and Tell: Narrative Desire and Discretion," in *Sexuality and the Body in Russian Culture,* ed. Jane T. Costlow, Stephanie Sandler, and Judith Vowles [Stanford, Calif.: Stanford University Press, 1993], 139).

52. In her reading of the poem, Forrester insists that Gippius does not "[set] out to degrade and objectify woman. Instead, her choice of masculine language, and hence the male role in a love poem addressed to a woman, leads in this case to manipulation and objectification of a female addressee, real or imagined. It is also the case that reading the poem in the word of a (butch) lesbian who speaks with masculine language changes its implication, undoing the assignment of untranscended sexuality to women though perhaps retaining its loaded presentation of femininity versus masculinity" ("Wooing the Other Woman," 113).

53. Luce Irigaray, *This Sex Which Is Not One,* trans. Catherine Porter and Carolyn Burke (Ithaca, N.Y.: Cornell University Press, 1985).

54. The situation was somewhat different in the case of homosexual lyrics. For an excellent discussion of homosexual identity and the Russian modernist lyric, see Luc Beaudoin, "Reflections in the Mirror: Iconographic Homoeroticism in Russian Silver Age Poetics," in *Rereading Russian Poetry,* ed. Stephanie Sandler (New Haven, Conn.: Yale University Press, 1999), 161–82.

55. Diana Burgin, "Laid Out in Lavender: Perceptions of Lesbian Love in Russian Literature and Criticism of the Silver Age," in *Sexuality and the Body in Russian Culture,* 179.

56. A narcissistic economy of desire would seem to inform her famous lyric "Dedication" ("Posviashchenie") (1894), where we find the lines: "But I love myself like God; love will save my soul" (No liubliu ia sebia, kak Boga,— / Liubov' moiu dushu spaset) (*Stikh,* 76). In her book on Gippius, Matich reads such seemingly narcissistic moments in Gippius's poetry within a spiritual context, remarking that "sometimes Gippius reveals the nature of this spiritual love in her love for herself or for her own soul. One cannot agree with S. Makovskij, who accuses Gippius of a Narcissus-like love for her own reflection, for this is not self-love but a love for the divine spark in man" (*Paradox in the Religious Poetry of Zinaida Gippius,* 65). And more recently, Stiliana Milkova has discussed the "intimately autoerotic aspect" of Gippius's articulation of faith ("Faith as Eros: The Modernist Rhetoric of Desire in the Poetry of Zinaida Gippius," *Berkeley Center for Slavic and East European Studies Newsletter* 19, no. 1 [2002]: 5–11).

57. Since "The Ballad" depicts the relations between man and mermaid, it also bears a resemblance to her early play *Sacred Blood* (*Sviataia krov'*) (1901), which deals with a Russian mermaid or a *rusalka* who parts company with her fellow mermaids and befriends the monk Panfuty in an effort to convince him to baptize her and, hence, allow her to possess a soul. But if in *Sacred Blood*, the mermaid is a figure that allows her to consider the relationship between the body and the sacred, in "The Ballad," the mermaid allows her to address relationships between women, and hence the mermaid plays a very different role in these two works. Melissa T. Smith has discussed *Sacred Blood's* reliance on an active female protagonist ("Waiting in the Wings: Russian Women Playwrights in the Twentieth Century," in *Women Writers in Russian Literature*, ed. Toby W. Clyman and Diana Greene [Westport, Conn.: Greenwood Press, 1994], 191–92.) More recently, Catherine Schuler has examined the play as an ambivalent feminist statement about the role of women in religion and society ("Zinaida Gippius: An Unwilling and Unwitting Feminist," in *Theatre and Feminist Aesthetics*, ed. Karen Louise Laughlin and Catherine Schuler [Madison, N.J.: Farleigh Dickinson University Press, 1995], 131–47), while Joanna Kot has read the play as an exemplar of modernist distance manipulation (*Distance Manipulation: The Russian Modernist Search for a New Drama* [Evanston, Ill.: Northwestern University Press, 1999], 49–62, and "Manipulating Distance in Zinaida Gippius' Drama *Holy Blood*: A Well-Balanced Experiment," *Slavic and East European Journal* 40, no. 4 [1996]: 649–66).

58. Of course, the Russian *rusalki* were somewhat different than their Western counterparts. As Linda J. Ivanits observes, "according to widespread belief," the *rusalki* "were the souls of unbaptized or stillborn babies and drowned maidens. In spite of their alluring beauty, peasants entertained no doubts that *rusalki* were connected with the unclean force" (*Russian Folk Belief* [Armonk, N.Y.: M. E. Sharpe, 1989], 75). In this poem, where there is an emphasis on the impossibility of uniting man and mermaid, the image of the *rusalka* would seem to merge with the Western mythological figure of the mermaid, who is half-woman and half-fish, rather than the Russian *rusalki* who were reported to be either "naked girls with long, flowing light-brown or green hair" or "pale-faced, ethereal beauties, sometimes in white shifts with garlands of flowers in their loose tresses" (75).

59. This fact was apparently not lost on Gippius's contemporaries. Alexander Blok imagined Gippius as a "green-eyed naiad" (zelenoglazaia naiada) (*SS*, 3:372) in the poem he dedicated to her in June of 1918 after their break, "Woman, mad hothead!" ("Zhenshchina, bezumnaia gordiachka!"). For more on the myth of Gippius as mermaid, see Olga Matich, "Dialectics of Cultural Return," 68 n 15.

Chapter 7. Eternal Feminine Problems

Epigraphs to chapter 7: Friedrich Nietzsche, *Thus Spoke Zarathustra*, *The Portable Nietzsche*, ed. and trans. Walter Kaufmann (New York: Penguin, 1982), 179; Vladimir Solov'ev, "Na Saime zimoi," *"Nepodvizhno lish' solntse liubvi . . .": Stikhotvoreniia, proza, pis'ma, vospominaniia sovremennikov*, ed. Aleksandr Nosov

(Moscow: Moskovskii rabochii, 1990), 96; and Aleksandr Blok, "Tebia skryvali tumani," *SS*, 1:195.

1. The notion that Gippius can profitably be discussed together with the second generation of Russian symbolists has been duly noted. Olga Matich contends that "if one must classify Gippius the poet, one should consider her together with the second generation of Symbolists, who in contrast with the decadents associate their art with religion rather than pure aestheticism" (*Paradox in the Religious Poetry of Zinaida Gippius* [Munich: Wilhelm Fink, 1972], 15). To date, the most extensive discussion of Gippius's treatment of the feminine has been offered by Kathryn L. McCormack in her fine dissertation, "Images of Women in the Poetry of Zinaida Gippius" (Vanderbilt University, 1982).

2. It is worth noting that toward the end of his life, Soloviev rebuffed the advances of the mystic Anna Schmidt, who considered herself to be the embodiment of his divine feminine principle. For a detailed account of this incident in Soloviev's life, see Samuel D. Cioran, *Vladimir Solov'ev and the Knighthood of the Divine Sophia* (Waterloo, Canada: Wilfrid Laurier University Press, 1977), 71–86.

3. Vladimir Solovyov, *The Meaning of Love*, trans. Thomas R. Beyer Jr. (Hudson, N.Y.: Lindisfarne Press, 1985), 93–94; Vladimir Solov'ev, *Smysl liubvi, Sochineniia v dvukh tomakh*, ed. A. F. Losev and A. V. Gulyga, 2 vols. (Moscow: Mysl', 1990), 2:535.

4. For consideration of the ways in which both these stories reflect Gippius's engagement with the concept of the new woman, see Peter Ulf Møller, *Prelude to the Kreutzer Sonata: Tolstoj and the Debate on Sexual Morality in Russian Literature in the 1890s*, trans. John Kendal (Leiden, Holland: E. J. Brill, 1988), 261–65.

5. A similar comparison of woman with a porcelain vessel occurs in Yury Olesha's novel *Envy*, which is deeply indebted to both romantic and symbolist aesthetics in terms of its views of woman and femininity. In the novel, the hero, Nikolai Kavalerov, envisions his feminine ideal, Valia, in vaguely similar terms. Her appearance in the text is preceded by an elaborate description of a porcelain vase on a balcony. And subsequently the narrator notes, "A tear, tiring itself out, ran down her cheek as down a vase" (*Envy*, trans. T. S. Berczynski [Ann Arbor, Mich.: Ardis, 1975], 23; *Zavist', Izbrannoe* [Moscow: Khudozhestvennaia literatura, 1974], 29).

6. Valery Bryusov, *The Diary of Valery Bryusov* (1893–1905), ed. and trans. Joan Delaney Grossman (Berkeley: University of California Press, 1980), 118; Valerii Briusov, *Dnevniki, avtobiograficheskaia proza, pis'ma*, ed. E. V. Ivanova (Moscow: OLMA-PRESS, 2002), 127.

7. In later years, this white dress gave her contemporaries fodder for envisioning her not as Aphrodite Uranus but as Aphrodite Pandemos, as they frequently associated her with the pagan statue of Aphrodite that is unearthed at the beginning of her husband's novel *The Resurrection of the Gods: Leonardo da Vinci*. In this novel the statue of Aphrodite is repeatedly referred to as the White She-Devil or *Belaia D'iavolitsa*, an epithet that was frequently applied to Gippius by her contemporaries. According to Olga Matich, "Gippius created her image based on the form and likeness of a Greek statue. And she in the end actually was transformed into a statue: her sister Natalia created a sculptural portrait of

three Gippius sisters in tunic-style garments; to this very day these statues stand in Petersburg in the Tavrichesky Gardens, next to the final apartment of the Merezhkovskys in Russia" ("'Rassechenie trupov' is 'sryvanie pokrovov' kak kul'turnye metafory," *Novoe literaturnoe obozrenie*, no. 6 [1993–94]: 139–50). Though the turn-of-the-century photograph of Gippius in the white gown can be seen as evoking a statue, it also recalls the seemingly opposite image of a shade. As I discuss in chapter 8, Gippius did identify with the figure of the "white Shade" or *belaia Ten'* in her final unfinished narrative poem, *The Last Circle (and the Modern Dante in Hell) (Poslednii krug [i novyi Dant v adu])*.

8. Despite the fact that she assisted Blok with his career, Gippius was not uniformly positive about his poems. On 19 September 1901, Olga Solovieva wrote Blok's mother a letter in which she informed him: "I sent Hippius Saša's poems for which I had no warrant whatsoever from him and don't know if he would have given permission. [. . .] Hippius tore the poems to pieces, wrote about them sharply, at length, even as if with passion" (quoted in Avril Pyman, "Aleksandr Blok and the Merežkovskijs," in *Aleksandr Blok Centennial Conference*, ed. Walter N. Vickery and Bogdan B. Sagatov [Columbus, Ohio: Slavica, 1984], 241).

9. Peter I. Barta, "Echo and Narcissus in Russian Symbolism," in *Metamorphoses in Russian Modernism*, ed. Peter I. Barta (Budapest: Central European University Press, 2000), 15–39.

10. This phonograph effect has its benefits. As the fictional Thomas Edison explains to Lord Ewald, "'Doesn't a man in love 'resay' to the woman he loves at every moment the three words so delectably sacred that he has already said them to her a thousand times? And what does he ask of her but the same three words, or a serious, joyous silence?'" (Villiers de L'Isle-Adam, *Eve of the Future Eden*, trans. Marilyn Gaddis Rose [Lawrence, Kans.: Coronado Press, 1981], 156).

11. Gippius would not be unique among the Russian symbolists in her skepticism about the cult of the Beautiful Lady. In his 1903 poem, "To the Younger Ones" ("Mladshim"), addressed to the younger second-generation of symbolists, Valery Briusov presents himself as un uninvited guest to a mystical wedding, ostensibly the wedding of Blok and his Lady. On Briusov's complicated relationship with the Beautiful Lady, see Joan Delaney Grossman, "Blok, Brjusov, and the *Prekrasnaja Dama*," in *Aleksandr Blok Centennial Conference*, 159–77.

12. It is worth noting that Gippius's personal secretary, Vladimir Zlobin, cites the passage from this poem where the madonna speaks about philosophy as if it came from the mouth of Gippius unmediated by a fictional persona. He writes: "From the very beginning of her days she lived as if outside time and space, concerned from the cradle with solving the 'eternal questions.' She herself ridiculed this in one of her parodies, a genre in which she was a master: I tried to solve—the problem is immense— / I followed logic to its very brink, / I tried to solve: In what especial sense / Are noumenon and phenomenon linked?" (*A Difficult Soul: Zinaida Gippius*, ed. and trans. Simon Karlinsky [Berkeley: University of California Press, 1980], 38; *Tiazhelaia dusha* [Washington, D.C.: Victor Kamkin, 1970], 15).

13. Not surprisingly, two of the existing monographs on Gippius focus on her status as thinker. See S. N. Savel'ev, *Zhanna d'Ark russkoi religioznoi mysli: Intellektual'nyi profil' Z. Gippius* (Moscow: Znanie, 1992) and Temira Pachmuss,

Zinaida Hippius: An Intellectual Profile (Carbondale: Southern Illinois University Press, 1971).

14. Zlobin, *A Difficult Soul*, 42–43; Zlobin, *Tiazhelaia dusha*, 19.

15. Pyman reads Blok's poem "The Tsaritsa looked at the illuminations" ("Tsaritsa smotrela zastavki"), dating from December 1902, as Blok's response to Gippius's attempts to meddle in his affairs. She notes that Gippius and her husband "did not approve of his early marriage, and Ljubov' Dmitrievna was rather jealous of the dazzling Zinaida. Blok composed for her the poem 'Carica smotrela zastavki' (I, 249) in which the 'Carica,' Hippius (who had in fact a predilection for poems about numbers) is pictured as seeking truth in occult calculation and study, while all that is needed for salvation is the innocence of the 'Carevna,' Ljubov'" ("Aleksandr Blok and the Merežkovskijs," 248).

16. M. A. Beketova, *Vospominaniia ob Aleksandre Bloke* (Moscow: Izdatel'stvo Pravda, 1990), 68. Liubov Mendeleeva-Blok would take on just this tendency to mythologize her role as the wife of the poet in her memoirs, "Facts and Myths about Blok and Myself" ("I byl', i nebilitsy o Bloke i o sebe"). In the beginning of these memoirs she proclaims, "I will not give the reader what he expects from 'Blok's wife.' It has been like that all of my life. 'The wife of Alexander Alexandrovich,' and suddenly people knew what I must be like, because they knew what the function of the term 'wife' was equal to in the mathematical expression 'the poet and his wife.' But I was not a 'function,' I was a person, and although I often did not know what I myself was equal to, I knew even less what 'the wife of the poet' should be equal to in the notorious expression. It often turned out to be equal to zero. And because I did not see myself as a function, I decided to plunge head first into my own 'private' life" ("Facts and Myths about Blok and Myself," in *Blok: An Anthology of Essays and Memoirs*, ed. and trans. Lucy Vogel [Ann Arbor, Mich.: Ardis, 1982], 8; L. D. Blok, *I byl', i nebylitsy o Bloke i o sebe*, ed. L. Fleishman and I. Paulmann [Bremen: Verlag-K Presse, 1979], 5–6).

17. Around this same time, Andrei Bely also took up the theme of Blok's marriage. On Bely's treatment of Blok's marriage, see Olga Matich, *Erotic Utopia: The Decadent Imagination in Russia's Fin de Siècle* (Madison: University of Wisconsin Press, 2005), 95–103.

18. Anton Krainii, "Stikhi o Prekrasnoi Dame," *Novyi put'*, no. 12 (1904): 274. Gippius, again writing as Anton Krainy, would revisit the theme of Blok's Beautiful Lady in 1908 ("Milaia devushka," *Rech'*, 19 October 1908, 2). Here she addresses the "sweet girl" of Blok's poetry directly, telling her that "in order to remain always beautiful, you must either grow or die" (chtoby ostavat'sia prekrasnoi vsegda—nuzhno ili rasti, ili umeret') (2). For a more detailed account of Gippius's critical responses to Blok's representation of the feminine, see Mariangela Paolini, "Muzhskoe 'ia' i 'zhenskost' v zerkale kriticheskoi prozy Zinaidy Gippius," in *Zinaida Nikolaevna Gippius: Novye materialy, issledovaniia*, ed. N. V. Koroleva (Moscow: IMLI RAN, 2002), 280–85.

19. I have translated *vodoskat* as "waterslide," since this seems to capture several of the definitions of *vodoskat* as outlined in Dal's dictionary. There *vodoskat* is defined as "a shoal, an inclined waterfall, a sloping place, a slope down which water rolls or runs" (perekat, skatnoi vodopad, otlogoe mesto, otlogost', po kotoroi voda skatyvaetsia, stekaet) as well as "an apparatus for the flow of water"

(ustroistvo dlia stoka vody) (Vladimir Dal', *Tolkovyi slovar' zhivogo velikorusskogo iazyka v chetyrekh tomakh*, 4 vols. [Moscow: Progress, 1994] 1:543).

20. Pyman mentions these three poems within the context of Blok and the Merezhkovskys' literary relationship ("Aleksandr Blok and the Merežkovskijs," 251), while Matich discusses the poems individually but in some detail in her book *Paradox in the Religious Poetry of Zinaida Gippius* (68, 79, and 88.)

21. Pyman, "Aleksandr Blok and the Merežkovskijs," 251.

22. J. Hillis Miller, "The Critic as Host," in *Modern Criticism and Theory: A Reader*, ed. David Lodge (London: Longman, 1988), 283.

23. Pachmuss observes that, "while the meter in 'She' is technically iambic, there is modulation on the sixth syllable in all lines except the second of the first stanza. [. . .] This metrical scheme, which is quite different from the rise and fall of iambic, is intended to suggest the undulations of a snake" (*Zinaida Hippius*, 33–34).

24. Gippius employed vaguely similar epithets to describe her own soul to her contemporaries. In a letter to Dmitry Filosofov, dated 13 September 1905, she remarks: "I am a petty, egotistical, lascivious, and cold soul. Even all that regarding 'burning coldness' is but posing. A cold soul is *usually* rather a dry and only slightly cool womanish soul" (Ia—melkovataia, samoliubivaia, pokhotlivaia i kholodnaia dusha. Dazhe i eto vse risovka, nashchet "zhguchego kholoda." Kholodnaia *obyknovenno*, skoree sukhaia i lish' kholodnovataia—bab'ia dusha) (*IAA*, 81).

25. For a more extensive discussion of Gippius's dialogue with Tiutchev on chaos, see Sarah Pratt, "Two Dialogues with Chaos: Tiutchev and Gippius," in *Cultural Mythologies of Russian Modernism: From the Golden Age to the Silver Age*, ed. Boris Gasparov, Robert P. Hughes, and Irina Paperno (Berkeley: University of California Press, 1992), 315–26.

26. Later, of course, Gippius entered into very heated political polemics with Blok and his friend Bely. After the revolution, she dedicated the poem "He walked" ("Along the iced-over edges") ("Shel" ["Po tortsam oledenelym"]) (1918) to Blok and Bely and the poems "All that was, it seems in the final" ("Vse eto bylo, kazhetsia, v poslednii") (April 1918) and "Christ did not walk in front of the 12" ("Vperedi 12-i ne shel Khristos") (April 1919) to Blok. For more on these polemics, see Z. G. Mints, "Blok v polemike s Merezhkovskimi," *Aleksandr Blok i russkie pisateli* (St. Petersburg: Iskusstov SPB, 2000), 537–620; A. V. Lavrov, "'Rozhdennye v goda glukhie . . .': Aleksandr Blok i Z. N. Gippius," *Etiudy o Bloke* (St. Petersburg: Izdatel'stvo Ivana Limbakha, 2000), 260–68; and Pyman, "Aleksandr Blok and the Merežkovskijs."

27. In the poem "Christ did not walk in front of the 12," which she dedicated to Blok after his composition of *The Twelve*, she appears to argue with the way in which he envisions the Beautiful Lady as the romantic partner of the soldier. The poem reads: "Christ did not walk in front of the 12: So the very louts told me. However, in Kronstadt a drunken sailor danced the polka with the Beautiful Lady. They say he died . . . But if not? Aren't you sorry for your Lady, poor poet?" (Vperedi 12-ti ne shel Khristos: / Tak skazali mne sami khamy. / Zato v Kronshtadte p'ianyi matros / Tantseval pol'ku s Prekrasnoi Damoi. //

Govoriat, on umer ... A esli b i net? / Vam ne zhal Vashei Damy, bednyi poet?) (*Stikh*, 335).

28. McCormack also foregrounds the antithetical views of femininity offered in the two poems ("Images of Women in the Poetry of Zinaida Gippius," 77-88). On the androgynous nature of her depiction of the eternal feminine, see Matich, *Paradox in the Religious Poetry of Zinaida Gippius*, 73.

29. Other places in *Radiances* where she presents the feminine in a positive light are in the two poems comprising *To Her in the Mountains* (*Ei v gorakh*), which she originally dedicated to Nina Berberova, and in the poems "She walked" ("Proshla") and "St. Thérèse de l'Enfant-Jésus" ("St. Thérèse of the Child Jesus"). For a consideration of the ways the figure of St. Thérèse informs *Radiances*, see Sarah Clovis Bishop, "St. Thérèse de l'Enfant-Jésus: The Radiant Inspiration behind Zinaida Gippius's *Siianiia*," *Slavic and East European Journal* 50, no. 2 (2006): 272-86.

Chapter 8. Body Trouble

Epigraphs to chapter 8: Ovid, *Metamorphoses*, trans. A. D. Melville (Oxford: Oxford University Press, 1986), 60-61; Fyodor Sologub, *The Petty Demon*, trans. S. D. Cioran (Ann Arbor, Mich.: Ardis, 1983), 134; Fedor Sologub, *Melkii bes* (Moscow: Khudozhestvennaia literatura, 1988), 133; Virginia Woolf, *Orlando: A Biography* (New York: Harcourt, Inc., 1928), 137.

1. Perhaps it was as a counterbalance to this tendency that the early generations of scholars on Gippius in the West tended to focus on her as a metaphysical or religious poet. See, for example, Olga Matich, *Paradox in the Religious Poetry of Zinaida Gippius* (Munich: Wilhelm Fink, 1972); Temira Pachmuss, *Zinaida Hippius: An Intellectual Profile* (Carbondale: Southern Illinois University Press, 1971); and Oleg A. Maslenikov, "Spectre of Nothingness: The Private Element the Poetry of Zinaida Hippius," *Slavic and East European Journal*, n.s., 4, no. 4 (1960): 299-311. Simon Karlinsky was the first scholar to address the myth of the supposed physiological basis of Gippius's gendered identity in detail ("Introduction: Who Was Zinaida Gippius?" in Vladimir Zlobin, *A Difficult Soul: Zinaida Gippius*, ed. and trans. Simon Karlinsky [Berkeley: University of California Press, 1980], 1-21), followed by Kathryn L. McCormack ("Images of Women in the Poetry of Zinaida Gippius?" [Ph.D. diss., Vanderbilt University, 1982], 168-200) and Olga Matich ("Dialectics of Cultural Return: Zinaida Gippius' Personal Myth," in *Cultural Mythologies of Russian Modernism: From the Golden Age to the Silver Age*, ed. Boris Gasparov, Robert P. Hughes, and Irina Paperno [Berkeley: University of California Press, 1992], 52-72).

2. I have borrowed Michel Foucault's term "'true' sex," with all its medico-juridical connotations, from his discussion of the nineteenth-century preoccupation with imposing one sex on the hermaphrodite (introduction to *Herculine Barbin: Being the Recently Discovered Memoirs of a Nineteenth-Century French Hermaphrodite*, trans. Richard McDougal [Brighton, England: The Harvester Press, 1980], vii-xvii).

3. Sergei Makovskii, *Na Parnase "Serebriango veka"* (Munich: Izdatel'stvo tsentral'nogo ob"edineniia politicheskikh emigrantov iz SSSR, 1962), 89.

4. Karlinsky, "Introduction: Who Was Zinaida Gippius?" in Zlobin, *A Difficult Soul*, 8.

5. Andrei Belyi, *Nachalo veka*, ed. A. V. Lavrov (Moscow: Khudozhestvennaia literatura, 1990), 194.

6. On spiritual androgyny in the Russian context, see Olga Matich, "Androgyny and the Russian Religious Renaissance," in *Western Philosophical Systems in Russian Literature*, ed. Anthony Mlikotin (Los Angeles: University of Southern California Press, 1979), 165-75. And on the tension between the mystical idea of the androgyne and the scientific figure of the hermaphrodite in Russian symbolism, see Evgenii Bershtein's abstract for "The Mystical Androgyne and the Scientific Hermaphrodite in Russian Symbolist Imagination," a paper he presented at the 2002 AATSEEL Conference in New York (http://www.aatseel.org/100111/pdf/program/2002/abstracts/Bershtein.html) (accessed 3 November 2003).

7. In so doing, Berdiaev would appear to read the feminine in the poem as a reference to Gippius herself rather than to the poet's soul. Similar misprisions were generated by Gippius's poem "Pain" ("Bol'") (1906), where pain is personified as a vampiric woman. For an overview of the way in which readers have identified the words of pain with those of a woman, finding the poem to be overly erotic or even in some cases pornographic, see the notes to *Stikh*, 487.

8. Nikolai Berdiaev, *Samopoznanie: Opyt filosofskoi avtobiografii* (Moscow: Kniga, 1991), 143.

9. It bears noting that snakes have been traditionally associated with the hermaphroditic poet Tiresias and, thus, when Berdiaev refers to Gippius's serpentine nature he may be drawing not only on her representation of the soul as snake in her earlier poem but also on the image of Tiresias.

10. Quoted in Eric Naiman, "Historectomies: On the Metaphysics of Reproduction in a Utopian Age," in *Sexuality and the Body in Russian Culture*, ed. Jane T. Costlow, Stephanie Sandler, and Judith Vowles (Stanford, Calif.: Stanford University Press, 1993), 265.

11. Based on a recent article by Nadya L. Peterson, it would appear that Berberova also shared with Gippius a certain antipathy toward the female self. As Peterson remarks, "the woman who emerges [in Berberova's writings] is one who views her success in the world of men as predicated on a 'balancing act' between the competing pulls of 'femininity,' characterized by calculated manipulation, and 'masculinity,' with its assertive and uncompromising agency. It is a woman who sees her own gender both as a source of her power and a burden" ("The Private 'I' in the Works of Nina Berberova," *Slavic Review* 60, no. 3 [2001]: 512).

12. Nina Berberova, *The Italics Are Mine*, trans. Philippe Bradley (New York: Harcourt, Brace, and World, 1969), 243; Nina Berberova, *Kursiv moi: Avtobiografiia* (Munich: Wilhem Fink, 1972), 277.

13. Berberova, *The Italics Are Mine*, 243-44; Berberova, *Kursiv moi*, 277-78. As Albert Sonnenfeld has pointed out to me, this particular passage, with its emphasis on the poet's jewels and veils, recalls the representation of Salome at the turn of the century. For a consideration of the importance of the figure of Salome for Gippius and her contemporary Ida Rubinstein, see Olga Matich, "Gender

Trouble in the Amazonian Kingdom: Turn-of-the-Century Representations of Women in Russia," in *Amazons of the Avant-Garde: Alexandra Exeter, Natalia Goncharova, Liubov Popova, Olga Rozanova, Varvara Stepanova, and Nadezhda Udaltsova,* ed. John E. Bowlt and Matthew Drutt (New York: Guggenheim Museum Publications, 2000), 82–85.

14. Berberova, *The Italics Are Mine*, 244; Berberova, *Kursiv moi*, 278.

15. S. N. Savel'ev, *Zhanna d'Ark russkoi religioznoi mysli: Intellektual'nyi profil' Z. Gippius* (Moscow: Znanie, 1992), 6.

16. Karlinsky maintains that Gippius was such a unique gendered being that it is difficult to classify her. "Even today," he notes, "when we have numerous terms to describe such things, it is hard to find the exact one that would fit her unique case. She was certainly not a bisexual, nor was she, despite an occasional infatuation with other women and a few love poems addressed to them, a lesbian. She was not a 'man trapped in a woman's body,' as some of today's transsexuals describe themselves. The closest term is one that existed in her day: she was an androgyne. Primarily, though apparently not totally, female physically, she felt herself to be a male intellectually and spiritually. Her ideal soul mate would have been a male androgyne, with a mirrorlike reversal of her traits. It was the tragic mistake of her life that she chose to settle for loving a male homosexual, whom she mistook for her true counterpart" ("Introduction: Who Was Zinaida Gippius?" in Zlobin, *A Difficult Soul*, 10).

17. Tatyana Mamonova also indicates that "physiologically, [Gippius] was a hermaphrodite, with an attractive, more feminine than masculine appearance" in an essay that was originally read at Harvard in 1985 ("Homosexuality in the Soviet Union," trans. Sarah Matilsky, *Russian Women's Studies: Essays on Sexism in Soviet Culture* [Oxford, England: Pergamon Press, 1989], 130). Commenting on Mamonova's statement, Diana Burgin observes that "in the context of the Silver Age medical theories and decadent stereotypes which identified the 'mannish' Lesbian as a hermaphrodite-like Third Sex, this gossip about Gippius could be read as an allusion to the poet's Lesbian orientation" ("Laid Out in Lavender: Perceptions of Lesbian Love in Russian Literature and Criticism of the Silver Age, 1983–1917," in *Sexuality and the Body in Russian Culture*, 327 n 21).

18. Olga Matich, *Erotic Utopia: The Decadent Imagination in Russia's Fin de Siècle* (Madison: University of Wisconsin Press, 2005), 210.

19. Svetlana Boym, introduction to *Death in Quotation Marks: Cultural Myths of the Modern Poet* (Cambridge, Mass.: Harvard University Press, 1991), 1–36.

20. Roland Barthes, "The Death of the Author," in *Modern Criticism and Theory: A Reader*, ed. David Lodge (New York: Longman, 1988), 168.

21. Roland Barthes, *The Pleasure of the Text*, trans. Richard Miller (New York: Hill and Wang, 1975), 27.

22. Not surprisingly, Barthes makes ample references to both Mallarmé and Valéry in his essay "The Death of the Author." "Mallarmé's entire poetics," he notes, "consists in suppressing the author in the interests of writing (which is, as will be seen, to restore the place to the reader). Valéry, encumbered by a psychology of the Ego, considerably diluted Mallarmé's theory but, his taste for classicism leading him to turn to the lessons of rhetoric, he never stopped calling into question and deriding the Author; he stressed the linguistic and, as it were,

'hazardous' nature of his activity, and throughout his prose works he militated in favour of the essentially verbal condition of literature, in the face of which all recourse to the writer's interiority seemed to him pure superstition" (168-69).

23. Quoted in Lawrence Lipking, *The Life of the Poet: Beginning and Ending Poetic Careers* (Chicago: University of Chicago Press, 1981), 167-68.

24. For some recent reconsiderations of the phenomenon of life creation, see Irina Paperno and Joan Delaney Grossman, eds., *Creating Life: The Aesthetic Utopia of Russian Modernism* (Stanford, Calif.: Stanford University Press, 1994).

25. Vladislav Khodasevich, *Sobranie sochinenii v chetyrekh tomakh*, ed. I. P. Andreeva and S. G. Bocharov, 4 vols. (Moscow: Soglasie, 1996-97), 4:7.

26. Yury Tynyanov, "Blok," in *Blok: An Anthology of Essays and Memoirs*, ed. and trans. Lucy Vogel (Ann Arbor, Mich.: Ardis, 1982), 121.

27. Gippius, *Contes d'amour, Between Paris and St. Petersburg: Selected Diaries of Zinaida Hippius*, trans. Temira Pachmuss (Urbana: University of Illinois Press, 1975), 77. This passage, which was deleted from the Russian version of Gippius's memoirs first edited by Temira Pachmuss, bears a striking resemblance to a passage from Marie Bashkirtseff's diary where she proclaims: "I have nothing of the woman about me but the envelope and that envelope is diabolically feminine. As for the rest it is quite another matter. It is not I who say this since it seems to be that all women are like myself" (*The Journal of Marie Bashkirtseff*, trans. Mathilde Blind [London: Virago, 1985], 290).

28. Matich, "Androgyny and the Russian Religious Renaissance," 169. Another place where Gippius plays off of the dual genders of the word "moon" in Russian is in the short cycle *Verses about the Moon* (*Stikhi o lune*).

29. On the importance of lyrical hermaphroditism in Mandelstam's poetics, see Svetlana Boym, "Dialogue as 'Lyrical Hermaphroditism': Mandel'shtam's Challenge to Bakhtin," *Slavic Review* 50, no. 1 (1991): 118-26.

30. Osip Mandelstam, "François Villon," *The Complete Critical Prose and Letters*, ed. Jane Gary Harris, trans. Jane Gary Harris and Constance Link (Ann Arbor, Mich.: Ardis, 1979), 56; O. E. Mandel'shtam, "Fransua Villon," *Sobranie sochinenii v chetyrekh tomakh*, ed. G. P. Struve and B. A. Filippov, 4 vols. (Moscow: Terra, 1991), 2:305.

31. Mandelstam, "François Villon," 56; Mandel'shtam, "Fransua Villon," 2:305. Gippius's poem can also be seen as an exposition of the theory of romantic attraction that she outlined in her essay "The Arithmetic of Love" ("Arifmetika liubvi") (1931). Drawing on Vladimir Soloviev's and Otto Weininger's notion that each male or female being is comprised of both male and female characteristics, she puts forth a theory of desire that is based on the attraction of people with mirroring androgynous attributes.

32. In *Dmitry Merezhkovsky* (1951), Gippius explicitly states: "I had the same thick reddish braid behind my back (I didn't change my hairstyle for the next five or six years)" (Z. N. Gippius-Merezhkovskaia, *Dmitrii Merezhkovskii*, in *14 dekabria. Dmitrii Merezhkovskii*, ed. O. N. Mikhailov [Moscow: Moskovskii rabochii, 1990], 308).

33. In the prologue to *The Thousand and One Nights*, a woman cuckolds the genie who holds her captive and records the number of her conquests with the rings of her lovers, which she keeps on a string.

34. Makovskii, *Na Parnase "Serebrianogo veka,"* 89.
35. Irina Odoevtseva, *Na beregakh Seny* [Paris: La Press Libre, 1983], 388.
36. In her *Literary Diary* (*Literaturnyi dnevnik*), Gippius, writing under the pseudonym of Anton Krainy, describes the process of *zhiznetvorchestvo* in terms that are far more kinetic than Blok. "Life," she writes, "is an event [sobytie], while daily existence [byt] is only eternal repetition, solidification, preservation of those events into a forged, immovable form. Daily existence is the crystallization of life. Therefore, life itself, that is to say movement forward, the growth of newer and newer events, only this alone is creation" (*Dnev*, 1:301).
37. Georgii Adamovich, "Zinaida Gippius," *Mosty* 13-14 (1968): 206.
38. Zlobin, *A Difficult Soul*, 56-60; V. Zlobin, *Tiazhelaia dusha* (Washington, D.C.: Victor Kamkin, 1970), 30-33.
39. The idea that her contemporaries might read her various bodily texts as the somatic symptoms of the hysteric was conditioned by the representation of woman in various symbolist texts. In his novel *The Fiery Angel* (*Ognennyi angel*) (1908), Valery Briusov, for example, focuses on the figure of a hysterical witch named Renata who is plagued by visitations from a fiery angel. Not only does Briusov's fictional narrator, Ruprecht, describe the convulsions in the witch's body during these visitations, but in the footnotes to this purportedly "found" manuscript Briusov compares the witch's convulsions to those of Charcot's hysterical patients: "These hysterical convulsions, which are currently being studied by the school of Charcot, were observed by the doctors of old and recorded by Johann Weyer in his book *Des illusions et impostures des diables*" (Briusov, *Ognennyi angel* [Moscow: Vysshaia shkola, 1993], 331). Igor P. Smirnov has touched on the symbolist movement's interest in hysteria ("Simvolizm, ili isteriia," *Russian Literature* 36, no. 4 [1994]: 403-26). And more recently Irina Zherebkina has identified the discourse of hysteria as central to the representation of women in late nineteenth- and early twentieth-century Russian literature and culture ("Izobretenie isteriki," *Strast': Zhenskoe telo i zhenskaia seksual'nost' v Rossii* [St. Petersburg: Aleteiia, 2001], 12-81).
40. Iurii Lotman, *Kul'tura i vzryv* (Moscow: Gnozis, 1992), 135.
41. Judith Butler, *Gender Trouble: Feminism and the Subversion of Identity* (New York: Routledge, 1990), 146-47.
42. Butler, *Gender Trouble*, 140.
43. In her insistence on the constructedness of the body and gender, Judith Butler, is of course, following in the footsteps of Michel Foucault. Not all scholars, though, have embraced this social constructionist approach to gender and the body. Richard D. Mohr, for one, takes on the Foucauldian notion of the body as socially constructed on the grounds that it cannot account for the very real and specific experiences of various bodies and of gay bodies in particular (*Gay Ideas: Outing and Other Controversies* [Boston: Beacon Press, 1992]). In her later book, *Bodies That Matter: On the Discursive Limits of "Sex"* (New York: Routledge, 1993), Butler addresses such criticisms concerning her notion of the constructedness and performativity of gender put forth in *Gender Trouble*.
44. Zlobin, *A Difficult Soul*, 46-47; Zlobin, *Tiazhelaia dusha*, 22.
45. In effect, by unveiling a faux nude body, Gippius produces the opposite final effect of the striptease, at least, according to Roland Barthes's reading of

it. As Barthes maintains, "the end of the striptease is [. . .] no longer to drag into light a hidden depth, but to signify, through the shedding of an incongruous and artificial clothing, nakedness as a *natural* vesture of woman, which amounts in the end to regaining a perfectly chaste state of the flesh" ("Striptease," *Mythologies*, trans. Annette Lavers [New York: Hill and Wang, 1972], 84-85).

46. Butler, *Gender Trouble*, 8.

47. If we are to believe Valery Briusov, Gippius did not just engage in a figurative type of exposure. In his diary he recalls a meeting with Gippius and her husband where "as previously agreed by letter, I arrived at twelve o'clock. I walked in, and the first thing I see is Zinaida Gippius undressed. Of course I had knocked, received a 'Come in,' but the mirror was so arranged in the corner that it reflected the whole bedroom" (*The Diary of Valery Bryusov [1893–1905]*, ed. and trans. Joan Delaney Grossman [Berkeley: University of California Press, 1980], 117; *Dnevniki, Avtobiograficheskaia proza, pis'ma*, ed. E. V. Ivanova [Moscow: OLMA-PRESS, 2002], 126).

48. In taking up the theme of Dante, Gippius is, no doubt, paying homage to her husband Merezhkovsky who wrote a historical novel about Dante and collaborated with her on a screenplay based on Dante's life. But while the Merezhkovsky connection is obvious, the Dante subtext may also have its origins in Blok's final narrative poem, *Retribution*, which Blok had conceived in Dante-like terms as being comprised of a series of concentric circles. For an excellent discussion of Dante in the symbolist context, particularly as it relates to the poetics of Viacheslav Ivanov, see Pamela Davidson, *The Poetic Imagination of Vyacheslav Ivanov: A Symbolist's Interpretation of Dante* (New York: Cambridge University Press, 1989).

49. For the purposes of this discussion, I will be focusing on the earlier, more complete version of *The Last Circle*.

50. Most scholars have focused on the way the poem comments on Gippius's philosophy. For consideration of the poem within the context of the poet's metaphysics, see Temira Pachmuss, *Zinaida Gippius: Hypatia dvadtsatogo veka* (Frankfurt am Main: Peter Lang, 2002), 221-46; Pachmuss, *Zinaida Hippius*, 287-304; and Temira Pachmuss, "Z. N. Gippius: *Poslednii krug*," reprinted in Z. N. Gippius, *Stikhotvoreniia i poemy*, ed. Temira Pachmuss, 2 vols. (Munich: Wilhelm Fink, 1972), 2:2-20. On the extent to which the poem reflects Gippius's view of death and time, see Matich, *Paradox in the Religious Poetry of Zinaida Gippius*, 108-11, and Olga Matich, "Lines on Circles: The Poetry of Zinaida Gippius," *Russian Literature Triquarterly*, no. 4 (1972): 292. In contradistinction to these two scholars, Kathryn L. McCormack's reads the poem as a commentary on Gippius's androgynous vision ("Images of Women in the Poetry of Zinaida Gippius," 190-200). Among other things, McCormack notes that "it is not accident or coincidence, as regards the depiction of androgyny, that Gippius chose Dante's model for her poem. *The Divine Comedy* of Dante holds a unique place in world literature for many reasons, but the significant one here is its own androgynous vision" (190).

51. Temira Pachmuss, "Z. N. Gippius: *Poslednii krug*," *Vozrozhdenie*, no. 198 (1968): 7.

52. Dante, *The Divine Comedy of Dante Alighieri: Inferno*, trans. Allen Mandelbaum (New York: Bantam Books, 1980), 52-53.

53. My interest here is in the figurative way in which this text is concerned with a revelation or dissection of the poet. On the more literal way in which realist and symbolist writers dealt with the subject of autopsy and the construction of knowledge in their prose, see Olga Matich, "'Rassechenie trupov' i 'sryvanie pokrovov' kak kul'turnye metafory," *Novoe literaturnoe obozrenie*, no. 6 (1993–94): 139–50.

54. Gippius's decision to identify her poetic alter ego with all of the major figures or bodies of *The Divine Comedy* simultaneously (Virgil, Dante, and Beatrice) can also be read as a parody of the Trinitarian structure of *The Divine Comedy* with Virgil as Father, Dante as Son, and Beatrice as the Holy Ghost. In keeping with this play on the Holy Trinity, Gippius's shade is the third to make its appearance in *The Last Circle*.

55. Through this reference to Mussolini's fighter pilots, Gippius exemplifies her own willingness to be a "fellow traveler" of fascism, if not an outright supporter. On the Merezhkovskys' complicated relationship with fascism and the reaction of their contemporaries, see A. N. Nikoliukin, "Zinaida Gippius i ee dnevniki (v Rossii i emigratsii)," in *Dnev*, 1:29–30.

56. Dante, *The Divine Comedy of Dante Alighieri: Inferno*, 4–5.

57. This playful reference to Gippius's shade as a frog may be an allusion to her parodic poem "The Frog" ("Liagushka"), the second of her *Southern Verses* (*Iuzhnye stikhi*), which she included in her final collection, *Radiances* (*Siianiia*) (1938). In this poem, Gippius presents her alter ego as a frog who espouses philosophical ideas. This is apparent already in the first stanza, which reads: "Some type of frog (it's all the same!) whistles beneath the damp black sky thoughtfully, insistently, for a long time . . . But what if [it whistles] about the most important thing?" (Kakaia-to liagushka [vsë ravno!] / Svistit pod nebom cherno-vlazhnym / Zabotlivo, nastoichivo, davno . . . / A vdrug ona — o samom vazhnom?) (*Stikh*, 267).

58. In taking on Blok, Gippius engages in a process not unlike that which Anna Akhmatova would undertake in the first part of her *Poem without a Hero* (*Poema bez geroia*) (1940–62), which she termed her "polemics with Blok." A comparison of the ways in which these two "survivors" of Russian modernism evaluated the wrongdoings of Blok in their respective long narrative poems is an interesting topic, but one that is not within the purview of this study.

59. This particular line would appear to point to Blok's late essay, "Neither Dreams nor Reality" ("Ni sny, ni iav'") (19 March 1921), where he recounts how peasant workers brought syphilis into the countryside. At one point in this essay, Blok implicitly identifies with John the Baptist, whose head appears on the charger of Salome. For more on this, see my discussion in chapter 3.

60. In her final monograph on Gippius, Pachmuss reads both the first and second souls that Gippius's shade encounters in Hell quite differently. She suggests that the first sinner is Vladimir Zlobin and the second Viktor Mamchenko (*Zinaida Gippius*, 225). I propose that the first soul can be read also as Blok and the second also as Filosofov since the amorous entanglements of Blok and Filosofov would seem to correspond to those of the two souls. In so doing, I am not ruling out that the souls may be composite figures that refer to other contemporaries of Gippius.

61. On the male symbolists' obsession with envisioning woman as a sign and/or body to be read, see Jenifer Presto, "Women in Russian Symbolism: Beyond the Algebra of Love," in *A History of Women's Writing in Russia*, ed. Adele Marie Barker and Jehanne M. Gheith (Cambridge: Cambridge University Press, 2002), esp. 134–37.

62. Barthes, "The Death of the Author," 172.

63. I read Gippius's inability to complete this poem as the natural extension of the poem's troubling and sensitive subject matter and not as a result of her status as woman poet. For a consideration of the anxieties that women modernists faced with the long poem, see Susan Stanford Friedman, "When a 'Long' Poem Is a 'Big' Poem: Self-Authorizing Strategies in Women's Twentieth-Century 'Long Poems,'" *Literature, Interpretation, Theory* 2, no. 2 (1990): 9–25, and Susan Stanford Friedman, "Gender and Genre Anxiety: Elizabeth Barrett Browning and H. D. as Epic Poets," *Tulsa Studies in Women's Literature* 5, no. 2 (1986): 203–28.

Afterword

Epigraph to afterword: Roland Barthes, *Mythologies*, trans. Annette Levers (New York: Hill and Wang, 1972), 31.

1. For an excellent discussion of the ways in which Blok was canonized by the Soviet literary establishment, see Galina Rylkova, "Literature and Revolution: The Case of Aleksandr Blok," *The Archaeology of Anxiety: The Russian Silver Age and Its Legacy* (Pittsburgh, Penn.: University of Pittsburgh Press, 2007), 23–44.

2. Irina Paperno, introduction to *Creating Life: The Aesthetic Utopia of Russian Modernism*, ed. Irina Paperno and Joan Delaney Grossman (Stanford, Calif.: Stanford University Press, 1994), 1.

3. Marina Tsvetaeva, *Captive Spirit: Selected Prose*, ed. and trans. J. Marin King (New York: Ardis, Inc., 1980), 144; Marina Tsvetaeva, *Plennyi dukh, Sobranie sochinenii v semi tomakh*, ed. A. A. Saakiants and L. A. Mnukhin, 7 vols. (Moscow Ellis Lak, 1994–95), 4:258.

4. Nadezhda Pavlovich, "Vospominaniia ob Al. Bloke," *Blokovskii sbornik*, ed. V. Adams, B. Egorov, Iu. Lotman, and D. Maksimov (Tartu: Tartuskii gosudarstvennyi universitet, 1964), 486.

5. Pavlovich writes: "I propose that the meeting with 'Maria' relates not to his stay in Warsaw after the death of his father, but to the period of his work in an engineering-construction detachment, to the years of the first imperial war. That stay in Warsaw was too brief" ("Vospominaniia ob Al. Bloke," 486).

6. Tsvetaeva and her generation apparently knew about the paternity of this child, whereas Gippius and many of her contemporaries did not. At one point in *A Captive Spirit* (*Plennyi dukh*), Tsvetaeva remarks: "And it was then I learned for the first time about Liubov Dmitrievna's son, her own son, not Blok's, and not Bely's—Mitka, about whom Blok was so troubled: 'How are we going to bring up Mitka?'—and whom he so sincerely lamented in the poem that ends with an apostrophe to God: 'No, over that child, over that blessed child / I will stand

without you! ['Net, nad mladentsem, nad blazhennym / Stoiat' [sic] ia budu bez tebia!']" (*A Captive Spirit*, 145; *Plennyi dukh*, 4:258).
7. Tsvetaeva, letter to Roman Gul', *Sobranie sochinenii v semi tomakh*, 6:532..
8. Tsvetaeva, letter to Roman Gul', 6: 536.
9. On Tsvetaeva's creative investment in a nonmeeting with Blok, see Alyssa W. Dinega, *A Russian Psyche: The Poetic Mind of Marina Tsvetaeva* (Madison: University of Wisconsin Press, 2001), 38–56.
10. Tsvetaeva, "Vifleem," *Sobranie sochinenii v semi tomakh*, 2:74.
11. Tsvetaeva, "Vifleem," 2:74.
12. Vladimir Zlobin, *A Difficult Soul: Zinaida Gippius*, ed. and trans. Simon Karlinsky (Berkeley: University of California Press, 1980), 185–87; V. Zlobin, *Tiazhelaia dusha* (Washington, D.C.: Victor Kamkin, 1970), 135–36.
13. Barbara Ann Brown has argued that the existing accounts of Gippius's death "suggest that [she] suffered a number of Transient Ischemic Attacks (small physically debilitating strokes that result in paralysis) before she most likely died of a Cerebral Vascular Accident (a major stroke that results in death)" ("'The Indissoluble Bond Between Her and Me': The Symbolist Poetics of Zinaida Nikolaevna Gippius and Colette Laure Lucienne Peignot" [Ph.D. diss., University of Oregon, 2002], 93 n 132).
14. On the different way in which the woman writer's death was mythologized in Russian modernism, see Svetlana Boym, *Death in Quotation Marks: Cultural Myths of the Modern Poet* (Cambridge, Mass.: Harvard University Press, 1991), 191–240.
15. In her last monograph on Gippius, Temira Pachmuss urges her readers to take Zlobin's memoirs with a grain of salt. "He wrote that book," she reports, "in the mid-60s, not long before his own death in a Paris psychiatric hospital in 1967. Gerell, Adamovich, Mamchenko, and Terepiano attempted (through me—T.P.) to stop the publication of this book that was clearly written in the affective condition which led Zlobin to the psychiatric hospital. But the publisher replied that he paid Zlobin when he was still alive an advance (which had already been spent), and the publication of the book *A Difficult Soul* could not be stopped. Unfortunately, many researchers into the life and activities of the Merezhkovskys have turned expressly to this distorted source of information about Zinaida Gippius" (*Zinaida Gippius: Hypatia dvadtsatogo veka* [Frankfurt am Main: Peter Lang, 2002], 249).
16. Marks Tartakovskii, "Syn za otsa: Prekrasnaia zhizn' Aleksandra Bloka," *Ogonek*, no. 17 (1999): 36.
17. Cited from private correspondence with Elena Glukhova.
18. Vladimir Retsepter maintains, however, that Blok scholar, Vladimir Orlov, apparently put little credence in the myth that Blok had fathered a love child. Upon being introduced to Blok's alleged daughter at an evening honoring Blok's hundredth anniversary at the Bolshoi Dramatic Theater, Orlov reportedly replied: "You understand, I'm familiar with this. But I wrote a book about Blok, and this doesn't fit into my conception . . ." (Retsepter, "'Eta zhizn' neispravima . . .' [Zapiski teatral'nogo otshchepentsa]," *Zvezda*, no. 10 [2004]: 98).

Index

Acmeism, 22-30, 33, 108, 111-12, 116-17, 118, 131, 156, 253n10, 255n4, 256n8, 282n20, 282n21
Adam and Eve, 26, 193
Adamism. *See* Acmeism
Adamovich, Georgy, 146-47, 227, 290n29, 291n42, 294-95n1, 298n27
Die Ahnfrau (Grillparzer). See *The Ancestress*
Akhmatova, Anna, 24-25, 137, 250, 256n8, 282n21, 286n5, 313n58
Alexander Blok: As Man and Poet (Chukovsky), 265n7, 267n17, 272n3, 281n8
Alexandra, Tsarina, 120, 130
Alexis, Tsarevich, 285n52
Alfonsov, V., 274n16
Allegro (Poliksena Solovieva), 136, 161, 162, 185
Amazon, as female image in Blok's works, 102
"Amorousness" (Gippius), 4, 183-84
The Ancestress (Blok's translation of Grillparzer's *Die Ahnfrau*), 11, 43, 49-60, 63-66, 93, 99, 112, 122, 278n46; as "intimate" tragedy, 50, 57, 59, 64
Andreev, Leonid, 22, 43-44
androgyny: dandyism and, 161, 163, 177; Gippius and gender fluidity or, 8, 165-69, 177-78, 214-16, 218-19, 224-26, 227, 235-37; Gippius and mirroring desire, 310n31; sexual indeterminacy as disorienting, 235-36; as spiritually ideal and physically monstrous, 219, 308n6
Anna Karenina (Tolstoy), 41, 65, 71-72, 75, 79, 103, 273n7, 279n59
Annensky, Innokenty, 266-67n17, 288
The Antichrist: Peter and Alexis (Merezhkovsky), 36, 42, 122, 285n52
antiprocreative stance: Blok and, 10-11, 22, 29-30; Futurists and, 10-11, 33; gender and, 34-35; modernism and, 10-11, 35-38, 169n36; poetry/progeny dichotomy and, 8-9, 12, 37-38, 131-32; Soloviev and, 3-4, 29-30. *See also* infanticide/filicide
anti-Semitism, 119-20
anxiety of influence, 27, 35-36, 108-9, 255-56n5
Aphrodite/Venus, 195, 197, 206-7, 218, 221, 303n7
Apollinaire, Guillaume, 28, 272n54
apple trees, 131-32, 192-94
"The Apple Trees Blossom" (Gippius), 192-94, 203
Arachne, 154
arachnology and gendered subjectivity, 293n55

Aristophanes, 225
"The Arithmetic of Love" (Gippius), 299n31, 310n31
autobiography, 167–68
"Autumn" (Gippius), 148
Azadovsky, Konstantin, 176

Backus, Margot Gayle, 285n46
Bakst, Léon: portrait of Gippius by, 161, *162*, 226
"The Ballad" (Gippius), 185–89, 302n57
Balmont, Konstantin, 5, 256n11
"The Barrier" (Gippius), 299n35
Barta, Peter, 200
Barthes, Roland, 78, 104, 141, 156, 222–23, 238, 241, 248, 289n23, 293n59, 309n22
Bashkirtseff, Marie, 310n27
Baudelaire, Charles, 27, 31–32, 137, 173, 255–56n5, 278n50, 292n53, 296n15, 297n16
the Beautiful Lady: Blok's concept of, 15, 30, 55–56, 197, 200, 204–5, 305n18, 306n27; Briusov and, 304n11; Gippius and autonomy of, 201–3; Gippius's self-identification with, 197, *198*, 199, 206, 226, 303n7; Mendeleeva as model for, 15, 30, 202–4
The Beginning of the Century (Bely), 219
Beilis, Mendel, 119
Beketova, Maria, 65–66, 203, 268n26, 271n49
Beketov family, 115, 123–24
Bely, Andrei (Boris Bugaev), 6, 26, 32, 42, 58, 72, 107, 118, 203–4, 288n11, 306n26; Blok's marriage and, 260n38, 305n17; description of Gippius by, 219
Benois, Alexander, 63, 64
Berberova, Nina, 34, 137, 144–46, 214, 219–21, 270n36, 295n5, 300n43, 307n29, 308n11
Berdiaev, Nikolai, 219–20, 308n7, 308n9
Berger, John, 291n48

Bershtein, Evgenii, 297n19
Bethea, David M., 35, 263n62, 266n14, 266n15
"Bethlehem" (Tsvetaeva), 245–46
Black, Max, 78
Blok, Alexander: Acmeism and, 22–27, 255n4, 282n21; antiprocreative stance, 22, 118; avoidance of infanticidal themes, 42, 44–47, 63; the Beautiful Lady and, 15, 30, 55–56, 197, 200, 202–5, 305n18, 306n27; biographical information (*See* Blok, biographical information); the child, self-identification with, 12, 40, 47, 55, 69, 73, 87–88, 107, 121–22; child death (infanticide or filicide) themes, 8–9, 11, 36, 39–40, 42–47, 51, 63, 67–68, 75–76, 119, 123–24, 130, 265n11 (See also *The Ancestress*); Christ, self-identification with, 91; Dante as influence, 81, 312n48; death linked to creativity in works of, 80–85; domesticity's lost golden age and, 22, 26–27, 43–44, 50, 66–67, 131; family romance as theme of, 7, 22, 42–47, 51–52, 57–58, 105, 120–21, 123, 131; and feminine passions as dangerous, 85–87; feminized spectral myth created by, 11, 48–60, 65, 69, 92–93, 95, 278n46; Futurists and, 22, 27, 257n23; generational succession as preoccupation of, 12; Gippius's relationship with, 30–31, 34, 197, 202–8, 302n59, 304n8, 313n60; history and, 22, 57–58, 85–87, 120; homelessness and, 22, 26–28, 38, 109, 118; impostor theme in works of, 121–22, 284n41, 284n43; infidelity as theme in works, 55–56, 62–63, 94, 105; John the Baptist, self-identification with, 91–92, 93, 94–95, 96–97; life creation, 9, 10, 11, 16–17, 47, 50, 56–57, 223, 282n19, 283n30; masculinity linked to creativity by, 116–17; maternal semiotic in works, 84–87;

Index

music or harmony in works of, 71, 78, 81, 86–87; narrative structure of works, 7; poetry/progeny tension and antiprocreative stance of, 8–9, 12, 33; as Pushkin's literary heir, 28, 122, 279n1; revolution and, 42–46, 58, 71, 120, 131, 265n11, 283n37; the subterranean in works of, 75, 81, 87–88, 273n8, 274n14, 276n24; syphilis and, 30, 63, 95, 120, 259n35, 260n48, 270n41, 313n59; vampirism as theme in works, 119–20, 126–28; visual arts and, 72–74; writer's block as problem for, 70–71, 76, 96, 115. *See also* Blok, biographical information; Blok, works of
Blok, Alexander Lvovich, 107
Blok, biographical information: aristocratic ancestry, 16, 22, 28, 110; biographical contexts of works, 40, 59–60, 62–65, 64, 66–67; children rumored to be fathered by, 16–17, 242–46, 249–50; death of infant Dmitry, 13, 40, 50, 65–67, 75–76, 111–12, 244, 271n49, 277n36; Ivanov and, 5; marriage to and relationship with Mendeleeva, 5, 10, 29–30, 59–60, 258n31; relationship with his father, 28, 50, 107, 109–10, 115–16; relationship with his mother, 28–29, 38, 49, 72, 74, 89, 115, 268n26, 282n19; travel to Italy, 12, 71, 72, 74, 94, 277n37
Blok, works of: *The Ancestress* (See *The Ancestress*); *Carmen*, 90; *City*, 47–48; "Colors and Words," 72–73; "Dream," 269n31; "Dreams," 58–59; "The fogs concealed You," 190; "Gogol's Child," 67–69, 70–71, 81, 104; "I have a premonition of You. The years pass by," 55; "In October," 47–48; "In the far away light-blue nursery," 44–47, 59, 265n7; *The Italian Verses*, 12, 76–77, 80, 88–89, 100, 104, 274n16; *Lightning Flashes of Art*, 76–77, 81, 85–86, 102, 103, 273n8, 274n14; *Motherland*, 70–71; "Neither Dreams nor Reality," 95, 259n35, 270n41, 278n53, 313n59; "Oh, I want madly to live," 39; "On a List of Russian Authors," 121; "On the Calling of the Poet," 86–87, 257n23; "On the Death of an Infant," 11–12, 67, 277n36; "On the Present State of Russian Symbolism," 88; "Peter," 42; "Poetry of Charms and Incantations," 93–94; *The Puppet Show*, 55, 64, 200; "Ravenna," 81–88, 98; *Retribution* (See *Retribution*); "Rus," 58, 59, 84–85; "Russia," 60, 62, 113; *The Scythians*, 110, 273n8; "Siena," 101–4; *The Song of Fate*, 62–63; "The Soul of a Writer," 109, 268n28; "Stagnation," 43, 44–45, 46, 47, 66–67, 81; "The Stranger," 52, 55, 56, 256n12, 268n29; "The Sugary Angel," 43–44; "The Sun above Russia," 72, 273n5; "A Tale," 48; "The Tsaritsa looked at the illuminations," 305n15; *The Twelve*, 27, 109–10, 205, 276n24; "Venice 1–3," 88–99, 104, 275n16, 277n43; *Verses about the Beautiful Lady*, 27, 204–5; *What the Wind Sings About*, 111; "Woman, mad hothead!," 288n14, 302n59
Blood libel, 119–20
Bloom, Harold: on birth of the poet, 98; Oedipal model of poetic history of anxiety of influence, 10–11, 23, 27–28, 35–36, 108–9, 255–56n5, 256n6, 263n62
Bloomsbury Group, 5, 108, 259n33
"Bodies" (Bely), 133
the body: androgyny as spiritual ideal, 219; of the author, 222; as authorial construction, 230; "autopsy" of the poet, 231–32, 313n53; Barthes on embodiment of the artist, 241, 248; Blok and Salome as disembodied specter,

the body (*continued*)
92–93; Blok's masculine and body-oriented description of the poetic process, 116; creativity linked to denial of, 5; critics and contemporaries as preoccupied with Gippius's, 218–24; female body conflated with sewing machine, 139–40, 288n16; gender and the body as socially constructed, 311n43; gender performance and, 228–29; Gippius and ambivalence or antipathy to female body, 13–16, 136, 146–47, 148, 152–53, 156–57, 159, 173, 184–89, 216, 218, 224, 231–32; Gippius's mythmaking as "bodybuilding" (*telovorchestvo*), 224, 226–31, 238; hermaphroditism, 8, 15–16, 219, 225–26, 228, 295n5, 308n6, 308n9, 309n17; modernism and the embodiment of creativity, 6; poetry as transcendence of physical, 10; Symbolist preoccupation with, 4–7; as text, 218; writing as disembodied act, 222
Boris Godunov (Mussorgsky), 121
Boris Godunov (Pushkin), 13, 36, 106, 120–21, 1263n64
Bowlt, John E., 260n48
"The Boy at Christ's Christmas Party" (Dostoevsky), 43, 48, 129
Boym, Svetlana, 222
Briquet, Henri, 171–76, 188, 299n35
Briusov, Valery, 5, 6, 27, 41, 75, 85–86, 89, 177, 197, 257n23, 267n23, 278n47, 304n11, 311n39
The Bronze Horseman (Pushkin), 42, 128–29, 280
Brown, Barbara Ann, 315n13
Bugaev, Boris (Boria). *See* Bely, Andrei (Boris Bugaev)
Bulgakov, Mikhail, 115
Bunin, Ivan, 145, 220
Burenin, Viktor, 168
Burgin, Diana, 184, 309n17
Burliuk, David, 27, 261n51, 272n54

Butler, Judith, 228–30, 237, 311n43
Byatt, A. S., 248

A Captive Spirit (Tsvetaeva), 242
Carmen (Blok), 90
castration, 115, 208–9, 283n25
Caucasus, 170, 171, 176
Cement (Gladkov), 33, 261n50
Chekhov, Anton, 182, 288n16
Chernyshevsky, Nikolai, 139–40, 288n19
the child: artists and childlike receptivity to the world, 73; symbolists and the childlike self, 88; as symbol of social change, 113–14. *See also* child death; infanticide/filicide
childbirth: in Blok's works, 87–89, 104–5; couvade and, 272n54; Mendeleeva and birth of Dmitry, 64, 65, 94, 278n53; as metaphor for male artistic creativity, 34–35, 68–69, 77–79, 104–5, 272n54, 275n18; as reenactment of Christ's birth, 79
child death: artistic identification with dead child, 37; Blok on child's sarcophagus, 75–77; conflated with the death of art, 104–5; female writers and themes of, 35; homosexuality linked to, 285n46; in Ibsen, 283n32; infant Dmitry's death as event in Blok's life, 13, 40, 50, 65–67, 75–76, 111–12, 271n49, 277n36; Madonna figures linked to inevitable, 77; as martyrdom or sacrifice, 36–37, 91, 119–20, 122, 285n46; the Romanov assassinations, 120, 130–31; *rusalki* as the souls of unbaptized children, 302n58
Christ and Antichrist (Merezhkovsky), 4–5
"Christ did not walk in front of the 12" (Gippius), 306n26, 306n27
Chronos myth, 264–65n4
Chukovsky, Kornei, 28, 42–43, 49, 51, 118, 138–40, 268n26, 272n3, 280n8

Ciepiela, Catherine, 262n61
Cioran, Samuel D., 254n17, 269n32
"Circles" (Gippius), 176
City (Blok), 47–48
class, social: Blok's aristocratic ancestry, 16, 22, 28, 110; clothing as signifier of, 164; lorgnette as signifier of, 164–65; peasants, 91, 95, 110–11, 113, 164, 226–27, 259n35, 285n45, 313n59; in Turgenev's works, 284n40
Cleopatra, 276n31, 295n7
clothing and costume: as aspect of Gippius's life-creation project, 144–45, 218–19, 226–27; clothing as double for the body, 229–30; eyewear as gendered aspect of, 161–65, 296n13; as fetishized, 145, 220; Gippius and nudity, 229–30, 311n45, 312n47; Gippius as female dandy, 161, 162; Gippius's "Beautiful Lady," 197, 198, 199, 226; Gippius's use of clothing as symbol in works, 193, 196; jewelry as sexual signifier, 207, 220–21, 226–27
"A Cloud in Trousers" (Mayakovsky), 38, 282n23
Cohn, Robert Greer, 31
"Colors and Words" (Blok), 72–73
Comrade Herman (Tovarishch German, pseud. Gippius), 166, 287n9
Contemporary Russian Poetesses in Portraits, Biographies and Models (Salnikov), 143, 144
"Contemporary Women Writers" (Novoselov), 137–38
Contes d'amour (Gippius), 14, 154, 167–71, 174–76, 188–89, 224
coquettishness, 142–43
Corti, Lillian, 255n5
Costlow, Jane T., 276n27
courtly love tradition, 10, 30, 191, 234, 300n43
creativity: Blok's concept of "world music" and the artist, 71, 78, 81; as childlike receptivity to world, 73; death linked to creativity in Blok's works, 80–85; fashion as trope for, 146–47; female creativity as debased or denigrated, 137–40, 152, 154; Freud's theory of feminine, 140–41; Gippius and ungendered nature of, 143–44, 146; reproductive metaphors for artistic, 8, 12, 69, 70, 77–79; as resurrection or rebirth, 69
"Creature" (Gippius), 212
"Crisis of Verse" (Mallarmé), 223
Crone, Anna Lisa, 275n16
Culture and Explosion (Lotman), 228

dance: illness linked to, 94, 95, 114–15, 278n50; as leitmotif in Blok's *Retribution*, 121, 122, 130; spiders linked to, 278n50
dandyism: ambivalence as characteristic of, 165–66, 180, 184, 188; Baudelaire on distinction between dandy and woman, 173–74, 189; Decadence and, 297n16; disdain (*prezrenie*) for the feminine, 161, 164, 176, 178–79, 181; distancing and the role of the Other in dandy identity, 14, 187–88; gender ambiguity and, 161, 163, 166; Gippius as self-identified with dandy, 8, 14, 159, 161–89, 162, 197, 214, 295n7; homosexuality linked to, 171–72, 299n32; intimacy avoidance and, 181–82; misogyny of, 14, 159, 165–66, 173–74; narcissism and, 163–64, 166; as object of gaze, 163, 165, 184–85; Russian literary traditions and, 297n16, 297n22; Salome linked to, 296n15
Dante Alighieri, 16, 81, 82–83, 87; as influence on Blok, 81, 312n48; as influence on Gippius, 16, 177, 231–39, 242, 248, 304n7, 312n48, 312n50, 313n13, 313n54
d'Aurevilly, Jules-Amédée Barbey, 172, 299n34
Dead Souls (Gogol), 81

deafness, 281n9
death: of the author, 222–23, 238, 309n22; Europe linked to decay and, 100–101; Italy as decadent space, 104–5; as mitigation or protection from passion, 85, 90–91; spectral feminine linked to loss of masculinity and, 93; suicide, 39–40, 194; tombs and catacombs, 54, 75, 80–81, 83–85, 87, 100–101, 269n31. *See also* child death
Death in Quotation Marks: Cultural Myths of the Modern Poet (Boym), 222
"The Death of the Author" (Barthes), 223, 238, 309n22
decadence, 5, 30, 44, 52, 118, 297n16, 303n1
"Dedication" (Gippius), 301n56
Delmas, Liubov, 10
De Man, Paul, 222
"The Demonic Woman" (Teffi), 160–61
Diaghilev, Sergei, 166
diaries: *zhiznetvorchestvo* (life creation) and, 167–68
Diary of a Writer (Dostoevsky), 47
A Difficult Soul (Zlobin), 16, 246–47, 315n15
Dinega, Alyssa W., 262n59
"Disdain" (Gippius), 300n44
disharmony, 71
Dmitry, Tsarevich, 13, 120–21, 122, 263n64, 285n52
Doctor Zhivago (Pasternak), 37–38, 79, 114, 281n16
domesticity: Acmeists and, 24–25; Blok and end of golden age of, 43–44, 66–67, 131; Blok as homeless, 22, 26–28, 38; French Revolution as family strife, 263n63; Futurists and rejection of, 33
Don Juanism, of Gippius, 168–71, 174–76, 298n24
"Don Juan's Answer" (Gippius), 169–70, 174, 175–76, 298n27

Dostoevsky, Fedor, 34, 38, 43–45, 47, 48, 111, 129, 153–55, 292n53
Dracula (Stoker), 111, 120, 125, 130, 285n46
"Dream" (Blok), 269n31
"Dreams" (Blok), 58–59
Duncan, Isadora, 248
Du Plessix Gray, Francine, 261n51
"Dust" (Gippius), 148

earthquakes, 72, 273n8
Echo and Narcissus, 200
écriture féminine, 8, 137, 183, 186n6
ecstasy, as artistic inspiration, 5
Eden and the fall from grace, 193–94
"Electricity" (Gippius), 211–12
Emerson, Alexis Eugene, 267n17
Emerson, Caryl, 36
"The End of Renata" (Khodasevich), 223, 242
Engelstein, Laura, 287n8
Envy (Olesha), 303n5
Eros of the Impossible: A History of Psychoanalysis in Russia (Etkind), 5–6
Esenin, Sergei, 164, 165
eternal feminine: Aphrodite/Venus and, 195, 197, 206–7, 218, 221, 303n7; Blok's "Beautiful Lady," 15, 30, 55–56, 197, 200, 202–5, 305n18, 306n27; Blok's interest in, 8; as Bride-Mother-Sister trinity, 214–15; as demonic or femme fatale, 209–10, 212; Echo myth and construction of, 200; embodiment of, 191–92; and fetishization of women writers, 138; Gippius as skeptical or resistant to embodiment of, 15, 191, 194, 201–3, 216; Gippius's self-identification with the Beautiful Lady, 197, 198, 199, 201–3, 206, 226, 303n7; in Gippius's works, 192–97, 199–202, 201–3, 205; Mendeleeva as physical incarnation of the, 15, 30, 202–4; as muse rather than artist, 136; nature linked to, 193, 205–6, 211–12, 213; Soloviev's

conception of divine Sophia and, 10, 15, 55, 136, 190, 191-92, 205, 232, 303n2; as soul, 15, 142, 205-14
"The Eternal Feminine" (Gippius), 214-16
Etkind, Alexander, 5, 252n8, 283n25
Etkind, Efim, 275n16
Eugene Onegin (Pushkin), 107, 121, 163, 279n1
Eve of the Future Eden (Villiers de l'Isle-Adam), 200-201
Evreinov, Nikolai, 94
"Exotic Perfume" (Baudelaire), 31

Faces and Masks (Chukovsky), 138-39
"Facts and Myths about Blok and Myself" (Mendeleeva), 59-60, 268n26, 305n16
family romance: Blok's thematic use of, 51-52, 105; the bloodline of kinship, 120; father/son dyad in, 105; French Revolution as family strife, 263n63; generational strife as theme in Blok's works, 55; generational succession as theme in Blok's works, 40, 107, 109, 112-14, 117, 118, 130, 242-43; generational succession of poets as, 21-28, 108, 112-14, 116-18, 257n23, 280n7; mother-son dyad, 104; primal scene in, 56, 98-99, 125, 279n56; revolution conflated with family drama, 43, 121, 131; Russian history as violent family drama, 42-43, 57-58, 120-21, 123, 131; the Time of Troubles as model of tragic, 120-21
fascism, 313n55
fatherhood: Adam as father and progenitor of human race, 26; Blok and, 13, 63, 66, 99; Blok rumored to have fathered illegitimate children, 16-17, 242-46, 249-50; father/son dyad in Blok's works, 105; filicidal themes in Russian literature, 42-43; linked to infanticide in Blok's works, 123-24; Oedipal model of poetic history of anxiety of influence, 10-11, 23, 27-28, 35-36, 108-9, 255-56n5, 256n6, 263n62; paternity as less obvious than maternity, 99; poetry/progeny tension as theme in Russian literature, 37-38
Fedorov, Nikolai, 30, 258n29
Feldman, Jessica, 165-66, 176-77, 178, 180, 188
Felzin, Yury, 221
female fetishism, 141, 289n23
"The Feminine 'It doesn't exist'" (Gippius), 212
"Femininity" (Freud), 140-41
"Femininity" (Gippius), 212-13
femme fatale: in Blok's works, 62, 85-86, 90, 93-94, 98-100; eternal feminine as demonic, 209-10, 212; Gippius depicted as, 157-59; Salome, 93-95, 275n16, 277n45; Teffi's "Demonic Woman," 160-61
fetishism: Freud and theory, 141, 289n23; hair and clothing as, 141-42, 148; women writers as fetishized, 138, 141-43, 145-46
The Fiery Angel (Briusov), 6, 311n39
Filosofov, Dmitry, 5, 136, 166, 234, 299n35, 313n60; on Gippius as spider, 294n61
fish, 178, 179, 182, 183, 185-89
Flaubert, Gustave, 31, 92-93, 96, 115, 271n47
Fleishman, Lazar, 263n68
"A Flight with the President" (Nagibin), 249
Florence, Italy: Blok and, 71, 74, 85-86, 100-101, 104, 279n58; Gippius and, 104
"The fogs concealed You" (Blok), 190
Forrester, Sibelan, 178, 301n52
Foucault, Michel, 218, 222, 307n2, 311n43
"François Villon" (Mandelstam), 225-26
Freidin, Gregory, 122

Freud, Sigmund, 4–6, 11, 36, 50–52, 140–42, 148, 255n5, 267–68n25, 267n21, 289n23
Friedman, Susan Stanford, 78–79
"The Frog" (Gippius), 313n57
Futurists, 9, 10–11, 22, 23, 27–28, 33–34, 36, 37, 108, 111, 116–17, 118, 156, 253n10, 257n20, 257n23, 262n60, 272n54

Galla Placidia, as figure in Blok's works, 83, 85–86, 100, 275n16
Garelick, Rhonda, 296n15
gaze: aesthetic distance and, 171; Blok's description of female, 85–86, 102–4; the dandy as object of, 163, 165; fetishization of women writers and male, 143; Gippius and appropriation of male, 149–50, 161–62, 163–64, 171, 176–77, 184–85, 295n7; profile views in portraits, 294n62; split feminine, 291n48
gender: arachnology and gendered subjectivity, 293n55; deployment of maternal metaphor and, 78; *mimétisme* (female mimicry), 146–47; pseudonyms as concealment of, 136, 143; soul as gendered, 142; Tiresias and gender fluidity or hermaphroditism, 217, 308n9; "true sex" and hermaphroditism, 218, 307n2. *See also* androgyny; dandyism; Gippius, gender performance of; hermaphroditism
Gender Trouble: Feminism and the Subversion of Identity (Butler), 228–29
generational succession: as contest or rivalry, 118–19, 126–27; modernism and crisis of filiation, 21–22; of poets, 21–28, 108, 112–14, 116–18, 257n23, 280n7; as revolution or upheaval, 121, 131; as theme in Blok's works, 40, 107, 109, 112–14, 117, 118, 130, 242–43
Gerell, Greta, 214, 315n15

"Gift of the Poem" (Mallarmé), 19, 96, 260n47
gifts, symbolic implications of, 207–8
Gilbert, Sandra M., 138, 143
Gippius, gender performance of, 159, 224, 228–29, 235–37; dandyism and, 8, 14, 159, 161–89, *162*, 197, 214, 295n7; Gippius's assertion of herself as "unsexed," 16; as phallic woman, 157–59, *158*, 175, 209, 221–22, 294n62; in salon culture, 13–14, 144–47, 159, 161, 164, 209, 216, 224, 226, 228, 230–31, 295n7; style *"femme,"* 14, 146–47, 148, 173; as subversive, 146–47, 166, 168–69, 209; as ultrafeminine, 13–14, 144–47, 159, 161, 197, 209, 226–27, 228. *See also* clothing and costume
Gippius, works of: "Amorousness," 4, 183–84; "The Apple Trees Blossom," 192–94, 203; "The Arithmetic of Love," 299n31, 310n31; "Autumn," 148; "The Ballad," 185–89; "The Barrier," 299n35; "Christ did not walk in front of the 12," 306n26, 306n27; "Circles," 176; *Contes d'amour*, 14, 154, 167–71, 174–76, 188–89, 224; "Creature," 212; "Dedication," 301n56; "Disdain," 300n44; "Don Juan's Answer," 169–70, 174, 175–76, 298n27; "Dust," 148; "The Eternal Feminine," 214–16; "The Feminine 'It doesn't exist,'" 212; "Femininity," 212–13; "The Frog," 313n57; "Good News," 150–53; "Grizelda," 148; "He to Her," 212; "He walked," 306n26; "He who has seen the Morning White One . . . ," 206–7; "In her dishonest and pathetic lowliness . . . ," 207–9; "The Kiss," 177–87, 189; *The Last Circle (and the Modern Dante in Hell)*, 16, 231–39, 242, 248, 304n7, 313n13, 313n54; *Living Faces*, 60, 204, 205; "Love for an Unworthy One," 197, 199–200; *The Memoirs*

of Martynov, 168–69, 175, 297n22; "Miss May," 194–97, 203; "The Necessary Thing about Verses," 155–56; "Nets," 148; "Orange Blossoms," 299n35; "Pain," 308n7; *Radiances*, 212–14; *Sacred Blood*, 302n57; "The Seamstress," 148, 149–50, 152, 159, 184–85; "She," 212, 219–20, 306n23; "Song," 86; "The Spiders," 148, 152–59, 184–85, 278n50, 293n60; "Stairs," 176; *Tales of Love* (See *Contes d'amour* under this heading); "Theme for a Poem," 290n32; "The Thread," 148; "A Thunderstorm," 205, 210–12; "A Walk Together," 176; *Waterslide*, 205, 305n19; "A Waterslide," 205, 209–10, 212, 305n19; "You," 224–25

Gippius, Zinaida: ambivalence or antipathy toward female body, 13–16, 136, 146–47, 148, 152–53, 156–57, 159, 173, 184–89, 216, 218, 224, 231–32, 246–48; as "Anton Krainy," 148, 166, 182, 291n43; Bely's description of, 219; on Blok, 60; Blok's relationship with, 30–31, 34, 197, 202–8, 302n59, 304n8, 313n60; "bodybuilding" (*telovorchestvo*) as life creation project of, 224, 226–31, 238; body/soul dichotomy and, 4, 7, 16; clothing as costume of (*See* clothing and costume); as critic, 148, 166, 182, 204–5, 291n43; critical reception of works, 15–16, 137–40, 221, 250, 288n11; Dante and, 16, 177, 231–39, 242, 248, 304n7, 312n48, 312n50, 313n13, 313n54; death of, 16–17, 230–31, 246–48, 315n13; as demon, witch, or sorcerer, 160–61, 222, 294n1, 294n61; distancing as literary and emotional strategy of, 148–49, 159, 171, 174–75, 176, 181, 184, 187–88, 293n60, 302n57; Don Juanism and, 168–71, 174–76, 298n24; and *écriture féminine*, 8, 137, 183, 186n6; emigration of, 15, 204, 212, 216, 241; fish as image in works of, 178, 179, 182, 183, 185–89; gender fluidity or androgyny of, 8, 165–69, 177–78, 214–16, 218–19, 224–26, 227, 235–37, 309n16 (*See also* Gippius, gender performance of); hermaphroditism and, 8, 15–16, 219–22, 225–26, 228, 295n5, 308n6, 308n9, 309n17; infanticidal and filicidal themes avoided by, 34; lesbian subtexts in works of, 14, 177, 182–86, 189; and life creation (*zhiznetvorchestvo*), 9, 10, 13, 15–16, 167–68, 224, 227, 230, 311n36; male muses and, 171–76, 188–89, 299n35; marriage to Merezhkovsky, 202; masculine pseudonyms used by, 143, 148, 166, 182, 287n9, 291n43, 305n18, 311n36; masculine voice deployed by, 8, 13, 137, 161, 166–67, 170–71, 176, 177–79, 185–87, 191, 209, 213–14, 218, 224–25, 237, 292n49; maternal feelings denied by, 34, 136; misogynist stereotypes deployed by, 146–47, 148–49, 159, 167, 212–14, 291n42, 301n52; narrative structure of works, 7; nudity and, 312n47; objectification of the feminine self in works of, 148–50; as phallic woman, 157–59, *158*, 175, 209, 221–22, 294n62; reaction to Blok's marriage, 30–31, 34, 202–4; relationship with Merezhkovsky, 4, 5, 166, 202, 221–22, 226; as religious poet, 153, 161, 231, 287n7, 301n56, 302n57, 303n1, 307n1; Renar's portrait of, *198*, 226; as representative of "demonic woman" social type, 160–61; signature of, 137, 143, 148; as spider, 294n61; as "unreadable text," 227, 238–39. *See also* Gippius, gender performance of; Gippius, works of

Girlfriend (Tsvetaeva), 245

Gitter, Elisabeth, 140, 289n24

Gladkov, Fedor, 33, 261n50
Goethe, Johann Wolfgang von, 55
Gogol, Nikolai, 12; *Dead Souls*, 81; *Taras Bulba*, 36, 129; "A Terrible Vengeance," 36, 44, 46–47, 55, 68, 84–85, 111, 123–25, 130
"Gogol's Child" (Blok) essay, 67–69, 70–71, 81, 104
"Good News" (Gippius), 150–53
"The Green Meadow" (Bely), 58
Grillparzer, Franz, 11, 43, 49–52, 57–58, 59, 60, 64, 93, 112, 267n23, 267n47
"Grizelda" (Gippius), 148
Gromov, Pavel, 275n16
Gumilev, Nikolai, 24–25, 26, 27, 33, 70, 116, 131, 256n8, 256n11, 282n20
Guro, Elena, 257n20, 262n60

hair: Freud's theory of fetishism and, 140–42; Gippius's single braid as symbol of virginity, 30, 218–19, 226–27, 310n32
Hasty, Olga Peters, 278n47
hearing, 272n2, 281n9
Heldt, Barbara, 258n31
"He loved . . ." (Akhmatova), 24–25
hermaphroditism, 8, 15–16, 219–22, 228, 295n5, 308n6, 308n9, 309n17; "lyrical hermaphroditism," 225–26
Herodias, 93–96, 114–15, 121, 278n49
Herodias (Mallarmé), 96, 114
A Hero of Our Time (Lermontov), 170–71
"He to Her" (Gippius), 212
"He walked" (Gippius), 306n26
Hier, Edmund, 50
history: female adultery linked to, 56; modernism and antagonistic model of, 39–40; as violent family romance, 42–43, 57–58, 120–21, 123, 131
homelessness and Blok, 26–28, 38, 118
homosexuality, 5, 8, 14, 171–72, 177, 285n46, 298n30, 299n32, 301n54
Huysmans, Joris-Karl, 93, 259n35, 296n15, 297n16

hysteria, 24–25, 174, 228, 278n50, 299n38, 311n39

"I am given a body—what should I do with it?" (Mandelstam), 133
Ibsen, Henrik, 52, 106, 118–19, 259n35, 283n29, 283n30
"I have a premonition of You. The years pass by" (Blok), 55
impostor theme, 121–22, 284n41, 284n43
impotence: Blok and, 79–80, 94–95, 114–15, 118, 283n25; Mallarmé's "Modern Muse of Impotence," 115
"In a sledge lined with straw" (Mandelstam), 122
infanticide / filicide: Abraham and child sacrifice, 33; Acmeists and avoidance of theme, 33; female writing as, 35; in Ibsen, 118–19; as male theme, 11; as modernist theme, 10–11; murder of Andrei Yushchinsky, 47, 119–20, 265n11; suicide linked as theme to, 39
infidelity: Blok and theme of, 55–56, 62–63, 94, 105
"In October" (Blok), 47–48
"Insominia. Homer. Taut sails" (Mandelstam), 56
Interpretation of Dreams (Freud), 50–51, 268n25
"In the far away light-blue nursery" (Blok), 44–47, 59, 265n7
"I put my ear to the ground" (Blok), 276n32
Irigaray, Luce, 146–47, 183
The Italian Verses (Blok), 12, 76–77, 80, 88–89, 100, 104, 274n16
The Italics Are Mine (Berberova), 220, 308n13
Italy: Blok's travels in, 12, 71, 72, 74, 94, 277n37; death and destruction linked to, 75–76, 104–5; Florence, 71, 74, 85–86, 100–101, 104, 279n58; Gippius and, 104; as "motherland," 12,

81–84, 101–2, 104–5; Siena, 80, 101–4; in Tolstoy's works, 71–72; Venice, 71, 88–99, 98, 104, 275n16, 277n43
Ivanits, Linda J., 302n58
The Ivankiad (Voinovich), 249
Ivanov, Evgeny, 76
Ivanov, Viacheslav, 5, 26, 88, 286n2, 312n48

Jakobson, Roman, 11, 33, 39, 42, 48–49, 261n51, 266n14, 266n15, 266n16
Jesus Christ: as figure in Blok's works, 90–91
Johnson, Barbara, 34–35, 78
John the Baptist, 91–93; Blok's self-identification with, 88, 94–96, 104, 278n46; Bulgakov and, 115, 282n18
Joyce, James, 19, 295n5
Jung, Carl, 52

Karlinsky, Simon, 219, 221, 298n30, 309n16
Kelly, Catriona, 286n9, 300n40
Kerensky, Alexander, 296n13
Kharms, Daniil, 261n53
Khitrova, Sophia, 191
Khlebnikov, Velimir, 257n20
Khodasevich, Vladislav, 6, 223, 227, 242
"The Kiss" (Chekov), 182
"The Kiss" (Gippius), 177–87, 189
Kniazhin, Vladimir, 118
Kommissarzhevskaia, Vera, 46, 50–51, 56, 63–64, 66, 108, 111, 270n42, 280n6
Kommissarzhevsky, Fedor, 64
Koroleva, N. V., 286n5
Kot, Joanna, 302n57
Krainy, Anton (pseud. Gippius), 148, 166, 182, 287n9, 291n43, 305n18, 311n36
Krasnov, Pavel, 142–43
The Kreutzer Sonata (Tolstoy), 37
Kristeva, Julia, 34, 154, 169, 272n2

Kuleshov, Alexander (Alexander Kogan), 243–44, 249
Kuzmin, Mikhail, 63

"Laid Out in Lavender" (Burgin), 184
The Last Circle (and the Modern Dante in Hell) (Gippius), 16, 231–39, 242, 248, 304n7, 313n13, 313n54
Lavrov, Alexander, 176
Leonardo da Vinci, 4–5, 73–74, 274n11
Lermontov, Mikhail, 47, 111, 170, 297n22
life creation (*zhiznetvorchestvo*): authorship and, 222–23; autobiography as, 167–68; Blok and, 9, 10, 11, 16–17, 47, 50, 56–57, 223, 282n19, 283n30; diaries and, 167–68; embodiment and preoccupation with the body linked to, 223; Gippius and, 15–17, 147; Gippius as involved in *telotvorchestvo* (body building) rather than, 224, 226–31, 238; Gippius as "unreadable text," 227, 238–39; Gippius (Krainy) on, 311n36; poet's oeuvre as cumulative autobiography, 280n3; Pygmalion myth and, 266n14, 273n7; as Symbolist project, 6–7, 9, 10, 223, 224, 230, 238, 242, 244, 250, 252n5, 253n10, 311n36; in Tolstoy's works, 72
The Life of the Poet: Beginning and Ending Poetic Careers (Lipking), 107–10
"The Life of Verse" (Gumilev), 70
Lightning Flashes of Art (Blok), 76–77, 81, 85–86, 102, 103, 273n8, 274n14
"Like Father Like Son" (Tartakovsky), 249
Lipking, Lawrence, 80, 107–8, 231, 280n3
"Little Angel" (Andreev), 43–44
Liush, Alexandra Pavlovna, 249–50
Living Faces (Gippius), 60, 204, 205
Lokhvitskaia, Mirra, 13, 135, 136–37, 142, 144, 160, 286n6, 290n32

lorgnettes, 14, 157–59, 163–65, 176, 181, 182, 219, 296n10, 296n13
Lotman, Yury, 163–64, 176–77, 228–29
"Love for an Unworthy One" (Gippius), 197, 199–200
love triangles, 6, 29, 55, 64, 171

Madonna figures: in Blok's works, 74–75, 77–78, 84, 102–3, 129, 279n59; in Gippius's works, 200–202, 304n12; and inevitable death of the child, 77–78
Makovsky, Sergei, 77, 84, 145, 164, 218–19, 227, 292n49, 298n24, 301n56
Maksimov, Dmitry, 27
male childbirth (couvade), 272n54
Mallarmé, Stéphane, 19, 21, 31–32, 80, 93, 94, 96, 114–15, 223, 256n5, 260n40, 260n47, 275n18, 278n50, 292n53, 293n59, 309n22
Mamanova, Tatyana, 309n17
Mamchenko, Viktor, 313n60, 315n15
Mandelker, Amy, 271n47
Mandelstam, Nadezhda, 256n8
Mandelstam, Osip, 26, 27, 29, 56, 122, 133, 225–26, 256–57n14, 256n8, 275n16, 282n20, 282n24, 293n58
Marfarka, the Futurist: An African Novel (Marinetti), 272n54
Marinetti, F. T., 272n54
marriage: adultery in Blok's works, 55–56; Blok/Bely/Mendeleeva love triangle, 55, 64; Blok's "white" marriage to Mendeleeva, 29–30; Gippius and "white," 10, 30, 226; Gippius's relationship with Merezhkovsky and Filosofov, 136, 166; in Gippius's works, 195–97; ménages-à-trois, 5, 136, 166; unconventional nature of nineteenth-century literary and artistic, 29–30, 258–59n33
Martynov, Nikolai, 297n22
Martynova, Sophia, 191
Mary Magdalene, 95

Masing-Delic, Irene, 253n11, 266n14, 276n24, 277n36
The Master and Margarita (Bulgakov), 115
The Master Builder (Ibsen), 106, 118–19, 283n32
maternal figures: Blok's feminized spectral myth, 11, 48–60, 65, 69, 92–93, 95, 278n46; childbirth as metaphor for literary creativity, 34–35, 68–69, 77–79, 104–5, 272n54, 275n18; churches as maternal spaces, 101–2; city as mother in Blok's works, 81–84, 99–101; earth as regenerative, 81; gender and deployment of maternal metaphor, 78; in Gippius's works, 193; as indifferent or unfaithful in Blok, 99–103; Madonna figures, 74–75, 77–78, 84, 102–3, 129, 200–202, 292n50, 304n12; as metaphor for artistic creativity, 12, 69, 77–79; monstrous mother figures, 35; mother-son dyad, 104; as neglectful or indifferent, 100; "reluctant" mothers in literature, 271n47; Russia as mother or motherland, 42–43, 62, 68, 81, 101–2; as suffocating, 47, 54, 83–84, 101; as violent or vengeful, 40, 42–43 (*See also* Blok's feminized spectral myth *under this heading*); Virgin Mary in Blok's works, 292n50; womb/tomb binary in Blok's works, 54, 80–81, 83–84, 88, 100–101
Matich, Olga, 29, 120, 153, 167, 221–22, 225, 252n5, 260n38, 269n36, 275n16, 277n43, 278n49, 288n19, 294n62, 295n7, 300n42, 301n56, 303n1
Mauss, Marcel, 207–8
Mayakovsky, Vladimir, 23, 33, 38, 156, 261n51, 282n23; infanticide as theme of, 9, 11, 33–34, 39–40, 42
McCormack, Kathryn Louise, 297n22, 303n1, 312n50
The Meaning of Love (Soloviev), 3, 37, 191–92

"Medea" (Briusov), 41, 267n23
Medea (Grillparzer), 50–51, 267n23
The Memoirs of Martynov (Gippius), 168–69, 175, 297n22
ménages-à-trois, 5, 6, 136, 166
Mendeleeva, Liubov: impact of birth and death of infant Dmitry, 11, 65–66, 270n39, 278n53; marriage to Blok, 29–30, 203–4, 260n49; relationship with Blok, 5, 10, 59–60, 258n31
Merezhkovsky, Dmitry, vii, 4, 122; reaction to Blok's marriage, 30–31; relationship with Gippius, 4, 5, 166, 202, 221–22, 226
Metamorphoses (Ovid), 154, 200, 217, 293n54
methodology, 7–8
Miliukov, Pavel, 147, 166
Miller, J. Hillis, 207
Miller, Nancy K., 293n55
mimétisme (female mimicry), 146–47
Mints, Zara, 50, 129, 284n38
"Miss May" (Gippius), 194–97, 203
Mitrich (Dmitry Togolsky): caricature of Gippius by, 157–59, *158*
Mochulsky, Konstantin, 67
modernism: antagonistic model of history and, 39–40; antiprocreative stance and, 10–11, 35–38, 169n36; child death as trope in, 10–11, 35–36, 39–40; child murder as trope in, 39–40; crisis of filiation and, 21–22; embodiment of creativity and, 6; motherhood and, 34, 269n36
"Modern Muse of Impotence" (Mallarmé), 115
Mohr, Richard D., 311n43
Molière (Jean-Baptiste Poquelin), 179
monocles, 161–62, 164–65, 296n13
the moon as androgynous, 224–25
Moreau, Gustave, 93
motherhood: Blok's ambivalence toward, 103–4; Gippius's denial of maternal feelings, 34; linked to femininity in modern society, 34; paternity as less obvious than maternity, 99. *See also* maternal figures
Motherland (Blok), 70–71
muse(s): Akhmatova and male, 24–25; the Beautiful Lady as, 202–3; eternal feminine as, 136; Gippius and male, 171–76, 188–89, 299n35; Mallarmé's "Modern Muse of Impotence," 115; Mendeleeva as Blok's, 136, 191; as voiceless or dependent upon the poet for expression, 202–3; women positioned as muses rather than writers, 136, 235, 286n3
music: Blok's concept of "world music" and artistic creativity, 71, 78, 81, 86–87. *See also* dance
Mussorgsky, Modest, 121, 130, 284n40
mythmaking. *See* life creation (*zhiznetvorchestvo*)
Mythologies (Barthes), 241, 248

Nabokov, Vladimir, 19, 78, 295n5
Nagibin, Yury, 249
names, significance of, 65, 121–23, 129, 179, 284n40, 297n22; pseudonyms as concealment of, 136
narcissism: dandyism and, 163–64, 166; Gippius and, 163–64, 166, 185, 298–99n31, 301n56; symbolists and, 298–99n31
"The Necessary Thing about Verses" (Gippius), 155–56
"Neither Dreams nor Reality" (Blok), 95, 259n35, 270n41, 278n53, 313n59
"Nets" (Gippius), 148
Nicholas II, Tsar, 120, 130
Nietzsche, Friedrich, 88, 190, 210
Nolle-Kogan, Nadezhda, 243–44, 245

Odoevtseva, Irina, 143, 145, 165, 227, 289n29, 290n35, 296n13
Oedipal drama, 10–11, 23
"Oh, I want madly to live" (Blok), 39
Olesha, Yury, 303n5

"On a List of Russian Authors" (Blok), 121
On Dandyism and George Brummell (d'Aurevilly), 172, 299n34
"On Lake Saima in Winter" (Soloviev), 190
On the Banks of the Seine (Odoevtseva), 165, 227
"On the Calling of the Poet" (Blok), 86-87, 257n23
"On the Death of an Infant" (Blok), 11-12, 67, 277n36
On the Parnassus of the "Silver Age" (Makovsky), 218-19
"On the Present State of Russian Symbolism" (Blok), 88
"On the Red Steed" (Tsvetaeva), 35, 262n59
"Orange Blossoms" (Gippius), 299n35
"Order No. 2 to the Army of the Arts" (Mayakovsky), 156
Orlando: A Biography (Woolf), 217-18, 221
Orlov, Vladimir, 26, 129
Orpheus, 93, 278n47
"Our Contemporary Poetesses" (Krasnov), 142-43
Ovid, 154, 200, 217, 293n54

Pachmuss, Temira, 159, 209, 231, 287n8, 306n23, 310n27, 313n13, 315n15
"Pain" (Gippius), 308n7
Paperno, Irina, 242
Paradox in the Religious Poetry of Zinaida Gippius (Matich), 153
passivity, 142-43
Pasternak, Boris, 36-38, 79, 113-14, 263n68, 281n16
Pater, Walter, 73, 274n11
paternity. *See* fatherhood
Pavlovich, Nadezhda, 131-32, 242-43, 281n9
peasants: in Blok's works, 91, 95, 110-11, 113, 259n35, 285n45, 313n59; Esenin as peasant poet, 164; Gippius and peasant style, 226-27
Pertsov, Petr, 74, 279n56, 290n32
perversion, 14, 234; feminine creativity as, 141
"Peter" (Blok), 42
Petersburg (Bely), 42
Peterson, Nadya L., 270n36, 308n9
Peter the Great, as figure in Russian literature, 42, 49
Petrarch, 177
Petrovskaia, Nina, 6
The Petty Demon (Sologub), 217
Pipes, Richard, 284n37
Pirog, Gerald, 84, 92, 103, 274n16, 277n42, 292n50
Pisarev, Dmitry, 142
The Pleasure of the Text (Barthes), 156, 222, 293n59
Poe, Edgar Allan, 52, 84-85
Poem without a Hero (Akhmatova), 313n58
"Poetry of Charms and Incantations" (Blok), 93-94
poetry/progeny dichotomy: and antiprocreative stance, 8-9, 12, 37-38, 131-32; Blok and creative "impotence," 115-16; gender and, 34-35; as theme in Russian literature, 37-38
Polonsky, Rachel, 72, 274n16
"Poltava" (Pushkin), 129
Poor Folk (Dostoevsky), 48
Popkin, Cathy, 301n51
Possession: A Romance (Byatt), 248
Prendergast, Christopher, 268n30
Pre-Raphaelites, 72-73
psychoanalysis and symbolism, 4-6, 252n8
The Puppet Show (Blok), 55, 64, 200
Pushchin, Lev (pseud. of Gippius), 143, 287n9
Pushkin, Alexander: child murder in works of, 36; as inspiration for Blok, 107, 129; "sculptural myth" of, 11, 42, 48-49, 266-67n16, 266n14, 266n15, 266n16

Pygmalion myth, 266n14, 273n7
Pyman, Avril, 39, 65, 91, 206, 270n41, 305n15

The Quadrille of Gender: Casanova's "Memoirs" (Roustang), 171

Radiances (Gippius), 212-14, 307n29
railroads, 75, 274n14
Ravenna, Blok's visit to, 71, 75-76, 80, 81-88
"Ravenna" (Blok), 81-88, 98
Raw Youth (Dostoevsky), 38
religion: antiprocreative theories linked to religious philosophy, 3-4, 29-30, 36-37; Gippius as religious poet, 153, 161, 231, 287n7, 301n56, 302n57, 303n1, 307n1; Religious Philosophical Society, 229-30. *See also* Madonna figures
Religious Philosophical Society, 229-30
Renar, Otto, 197, 226
The Resurrection of the Gods: Leonardo da Vinci (Merezhkovsky), vii, 4-5, 303n7
resurrection or rebirth: Blok and themes of, 74, 80-84; in Blok's works, 87-88, 97-99; reincarnation or Nietzschean self-begetting, 88
Retribution (long narrative poem, Blok), 12-13, 28, 49, 107, 109-12, 114, 116-21, 130, 231, 242-43, 274n14, 279-n1, 280n7, 283n30, 312n48; Dante as influence, 87, 312n48; death of child as theme in, 119, 130; generational succession as subject in, 107, 109, 112-14, 117, 118, 130, 242-43; Gogol as influence on (*See* "A Terrible Vengeance" [Gogol]); historical subjects, 109, 120-21; Ibsen as influence, 283n30; "Polish" theme in, 12-13, 113, 121, 128-29, 242, 243, 244, 284n40; Pushkin as influence on, 128-29, 279n1; Russia as subject in, 96; as unfinished work, 116, 242

Retribution (poem cycle, Blok), 67
Retsepter, Vladimir, 249-50, 315n18
Revolution of 1905, 11, 22, 40, 42, 43, 69, 71, 123
Revolution of 1917, as context for literature, 47, 58, 131
roads, 22, 26-27, 109
"A Romance in Kislovodsk" (Burenin), 168
Romanov executions, 120-21, 283n33
Rose, Phyllis, 258n33
Rosetti, Dante, 16
Roustang, François, 171
Rozanov, Vasily, 77
Rubinstein, Ida, 94, 308n13
rusalki, 185-86, 302n58
"Rus" (Blok), 58, 59, 84-85
Russia: as child, 68-69; as "motherland" or maternal figure, 42-43, 59, 62, 68, 81, 101-2; as "sleeping beauty," 58-59
"Russia" (Blok), 60, 62, 113

Sacred Blood (Gippius), 302n57
Sadovskaia, Ksenia, 10
Said, Edward W., 6, 21, 24
St. Mark's Square, 92, 277n42
Sakovich, Maria, 250
Salnikov, A. N., 143
Salome, 91-96, 114-15, 120, 121, 277n43, 277n45, 278n46, 278n49, 296n15, 308n13, 313n59
salon culture: women's role in, 136, 286n2
Sandler, Stephanie, 35, 263n64, 276n27
Saveliev, S. N., 221
Schmidt, Anna, 303n2
A School for Wives (Molière), 179
Schuler, Catherine, 302n57
sculptural myth: Blok's and, 128-29, 266n15, 266n16; Pushkin's and, 11, 42, 48-49, 127, 266-67n16, 266n14, 266n16
The Scythians (Blok), 110, 273n8
"Sea Breeze" (Mallarmé), 21, 31-32, 260n47

"The Seamstress" (Gippius), 148, 149–50, 152, 159, 184–85
Self-Knowledge: An Experiment in Philosophical Autobiography (Berdiaev), 219–20
Severianin, Igor, 257n20
sewing or weaving: female body conflated with sewing machine, 139–40, 288n16; Gippius's references to her own work as, 147–49, 155–56, 157; as metaphor for women's creativity, 138–40, 154; seamstresses as image in Gippius's works, 14, 149–52; as sexualized, 139–40, 140–41, 150–51, 156–57, 288n16; "text" as fabrication, 156; Virgin Mary and, 150–51
Shakhmatovo (Blok's family home), 109, 110, 204
"She" (Gippius), 212, 219–20, 306n23; "He who has seen the Morning White One . . . ," 206–7; "In her dishonest and pathetic lowliness . . . ," 207–9
Shkapskaia, Maria, 130–31
Shklovsky, Viktor, 256n6
"The Sibyl" (Tsvetaeva), 134
"Siena" (Blok), 101–4
Siena, Italy, 80, 101–4
Sinfield, Alan, 172, 299n32
sleep, 48; in Blok's works, 11, 45–48, 54, 58, 84–85; Russia as "sleeping beauty," 58–59
Sloane, David A., 111
Smith, Melissa T., 302n57
snakes or serpents, 208–9, 217, 219–20, 264n2, 306n23, 308n9
Sologub, Fedor, 22, 47, 217, 266–67n17, 266n12
Soloviev, Sergei (Serezha), 107, 110, 203–4, 260n38
Soloviev, Vladimir: antiprocreative theories of, 3–4, 29–30; Blok as literary heir of, 259n36; Blok's views of love linked to, 10, 30, 55; *The Meaning of Love*, 3, 37, 191–92; "On Lake Saima in Winter," 190; Sophia or eternal feminine as conceived by, 10, 15, 55, 136, 190, 191–92, 205, 232, 303n2
Solovieva, Olga, 304n8
Solovieva, Poliksena (Allegro), 136, 161, 162, 185
"Some Words about the Poems of F. I. Tiutchev" (Turgenev), 70
Somov, Konstantin, 50; portrait of Blok by, 60, *61*
"Song" (Gippius), 86
The Song of Fate (Blok), 62–63
Sonnenfeld, Albert, 308n13
sorcery, 44, 47, 48, 68, 123, 125–26, 265n7, 294; Gippius as demon, witch, or sorcerer, 160–61, 222, 294n1, 294n61
"The Soul of a Writer" (Blok), 109, 268n28
Speak, Memory (Nabokov), 19
spectral myth: Blok's feminized, 11, 48–60, 65, 69, 92–93, 95, 278n46; Blok's sculptural myth and, 128–29, 266n15, 266n16; Pushkin's sculptural myth and, 11, 42, 48–49, 127, 266–67n16, 266n14, 266n16
the sphinx, 266n15
spiders: Arachne, 293n55; Baudelaire's use of image, 278n50; Blok's works, 44, 66–67; dance linked to, 278n50; Gippius depicted as spider by Mitrich, 157–59, *158*; Gippius described as spider by Filosofov, 294n61; as images of female creativity in Gippius's works, 14, 148, 152–59, 184–85, 293n60; linked to dance in folk traditions, 278n50; Mallarmé's use of image, 278n50, 293n59; writing and letters linked to, 293n56
"The Spiders" (Gippius), 148, 152–59, 184–85, 293n60
"Stagnation" (Blok), 43, 44–45, 46, 47, 66–67, 81
"Stairs" (Gippius), 176
Stein, Gertrude, 161, 295n5
Stoker, Bram, 111, 120, 130

"The Stranger" (Blok), 52, 55, 56, 256n12, 268n29
strings, 148
style "femme," 14, 146–47, 148, 173
sublimation, symbolists and, 3–5, 7, 9–10, 30, 37–38, 139–40, 241
"Suboctave Story" (Pasternak), 36–37, 263n68
the subterranean in Blok's works, 75, 81, 87–88, 273n8, 274n14, 276n24
suffocation, 47, 54, 83–84, 101, 208–9, 282n24
"The Sugary Angel" (Blok), 43–44
suicide, 39–40, 194
"The Sun above Russia" (Blok), 72, 273n5, 280n6
"The Sybil" (Tsvetaeva), 35
"The Symbolist Meaning of Love: Theory and Practice" (Matich), 29
symbolists: antiprocreative stance and, 24; the body as preoccupation of, 4–9; child death as model of poetic creation, 36; cult of the feminine among, 14–15, 136, 191, 304n11, 314n61 (*See also* eternal feminine); domesticity rejected by, 32–33; French Symbolism as influence on Russian, 292n53; metaphysical inclinations of, 4; 1910 crisis, 22, 108, 280n7; role of women in Russian, 136, 286n3, 287n8; sublimation and, 3–5, 7, 9–10, 30, 37–38, 139–40, 241; sublimation of sex and, 4–5; travel and, 24; unconventional marriages and erotic relationships, 29. *See also* life creation (*zhiznetvorchestvo*); specific authors
syphilis, 30, 63, 95, 120, 259n35, 260n48, 270n41, 313n59

"A Tale" (Blok), 48
Tales of Love (Gippius). See *Contes d'amour*
Tales of Love (Kristeva), 169
Taras Bulba (Gogol), 36, 129
Tartakovsky, Marx, 249

Taubman, Jane A., 287n8
Teffi, Nadezhda, 144, 160–61
Terras, Victor, 287n7
"A Terrible Vengeance" (Gogol), 36, 44, 46–47, 55, 68, 84–85, 111, 123–25, 130
"Theme for a Poem" (Gippius), 290n32
Thompson, Regina B., 50
"The Thread" (Gippius), 148
"Three Meetings" (Soloviev), 192
"A Thunderstorm" (Gippius), 205, 210–12
Thus Spoke Zarathustra (Nietzsche), 190, 210
the Time of Troubles, 13, 120–21, 130, 283n37
Tiresias, 217, 308n9
Tiutchev, Fedor, 70, 211, 287n7
Tolstoy, Lev, 37, 41, 71–72, 76, 108, 271n47, 273n5, 280n6
Tomashevsky, Boris, 28, 270n43
tombs and catacombs, 54, 75, 80–81, 83–85, 87, 100–101, 269n31
"Transcending Gender: The Case of Zinaida Gippius" (Matich), 221
Trotsky, Leon, 161, 222
"The Tsaritsa looked at the illuminations" (Blok), 305n15
Tsvetaeva, Marina, 35, 122, 134, 242, 244–46, 249–50, 262–63n61, 262n59, 278n47, 299–300n39, 299n39, 314n6
Turgenev, Ivan, 70, 78, 108, 284n40
The Twelve (Blok), 27, 109–10, 205, 276n24
Tynianov, Yury, 223, 256n6

"Under the Shawl" (Tsvetaeva), 35
utopianism, 4, 29, 288n19

Vainshtein, Olga, 297n16, 299n34
Valéry, Paul, 223, 309n22
vampirism, 119–20, 125, 127, 274n11, 308n7
"Venice 1–3" (Blok), 88–99, 104, 275n16, 277n43

Venice, Italy, 71, 104, 277n37; as femme fatale, 90–96, 275n16; as St. Petersburg's double, 88–89, 98
Venus/Aphrodite, 195, 197, 206–7, 218, 221, 303n7
Verigina, Valentina, 47
Verses about the Beautiful Lady (Blok), 27, 204–5
Verses to Blok (Tsvetaeva), 245
Vertinsky, Alexander, 47
Villiers de l'Isle-Adam, Jean-Marie-Mathias-Phillippe-Auguste, Count, 200–201
Virgil, 16, 81, 232–35, 313n54
virginity: Gippius and signifiers of, 30, 218–19, 226–27. *See also* Virgin Mary
Virgin Mary, 56, 77, 78–79, 272n2, 292n50
Vogel, Lucy, 87, 91, 258n31, 274n16, 277n39
Voinovich, Vladimir, 249
Volokhova, Natalia, 10, 94
von Gloeden, Baron Wilhelm, 298n30
Vowles, Judith, 276n27
Vrubel, Mikhail, 108, 111, 260n48, 280n6

walking as motif in Gippius's works, 300n42
"A Walk Together" (Gippius), 176
Warner, Marina, 79
Waterslide (Gippius), 205, 305n19
"A Waterslide" (Gippius), 205, 209–10, 212, 305n19

weaving, 140–41, 148, 289n23, 293n58; in Blok's works, 292n50; in Gippius's works, 148, 152–57, 289n24; rhymed poetry as "woven" composition, 155–56
webs, 148
Weinfield, Henry, 32
Weininger, Otto, 299n31, 310n31
What Is to Be Done? (Chernyshevsky), 139–40
What the Wind Sings About (Blok), 111
Wilde, Oscar, 93, 160, 166–67, 296n15, 297n16, 297n19, 299n32
"Winter Shiver" (Mallarmé), 292n53
"Woman, mad hothead!" (Blok), 288n14, 302n59
woman question, 138
women writers: *écriture féminine* and, 8, 137, 183, 186n6; as fetishized, 138, 141–43, 145–46, 289n23; as verbally promiscuous, 140
Woolf, Virginia, 108, 217–18, 221
World of Art, 14, 166, 297n16

Yanovsky, Vasily, 221
"You:" (Gippius), 224–25
Yushchinsky, Andrei, 119–20

zhiznetvorchestvo. See life creation (*zhiznetvorchestvo*)
Zinovieva-Annibal, Lydia, 5, 286n2
Zlobin, Vladimir, 16–17, 145, 161–62, 202, 227, 229–30, 246–48, 292n49, 294n1, 294n61, 304n12, 313n60, 315n15

www.ingramcontent.com/pod-product-compliance
Lightning Source LLC
Chambersburg PA
CBHW070909100426
42814CB00003B/114